The Anthropology of Religion, Magic, and Witchcraft

Rebecca L. Stein

Los Angeles Valley College

Philip L. Stein

Los Angeles Pierce College

Boston • New York • San Francisco
Mexico City • Montreal • Toronto • London • Madrid • Munich • Paris
Hong Kong • Singapore • Tokyo • Cape Town • Sydney

For Elijah

Series Editor: *Jennifer Jacobson*
Series Editorial Assistant: *Emma Christensen*
Marketing Manager: *Kris Ellis-Levy*
Editorial-Production Service: *Omegatype Typography, Inc.*
Composition and Prepress Buyer: *Linda Cox*
Manufacturing Manager: *Megan Cochran*
Cover Administrator: *Kristina Mose-Libon*
Electronic Composition: *Omegatype Typography, Inc.*

For related titles and support materials, visit our online catalog at www.ablongman.com.

Between the time Website information is gathered and then published, it is not unusual for some sites to have closed. Also, the transcription of URLs can result in typographical errors. The publisher would appreciate notification where these errors occur so that they may be corrected in subsequent editions.

Library of Congress Cataloging-in-Publication Data

Stein, Rebecca L.
    The anthropology of religion, magic, and witchcraft / Rebecca L. Stein, Philip L. Stein.
      p. cm.
    Includes bibliographical references and index.
    ISBN 0-205-34421-6 (alk. paper)
    1. Religion. 2. Anthropology. 3. Religion and culture. I. Stein, Philip L. II. Title.

GN470.S73 2005
306.6—dc22

2004050570

Printed in the United States of America

10 9 8 7 6 5 4 3 2 1   09 08 07 06 05 04

Photo credits appear on page 292, which constitutes an extension of the copyright page.

4   *Ritual*   **83**

Contents

8   *Gods and Spirits*   **194**

Preface

Although courses in the anthropology of religion are usually upper-division courses taught at four-year institutions to anthropology majors, the course is increasingly being taught at the lower-division level, especially at community colleges. Here the emphasis is not on the training of majors, of whom there are few, but on meeting a general education requirement in the social sciences or humanities. Most significantly, this course is probably the only anthropology course that such students will take. Therefore the instructor has the obligation not only to discuss the topics of religion, but also to teach the student about the nature of anthropology and to present its basic principles.

We have had great difficulty in finding a textbook that is appropriate for this type of course. Three types of books currently exist. First is the reader, which often includes articles that are too advanced for the introductory student. A major problem is the inconsistency of terminology and concepts as the student moves from article to article. The second is the general textbook on the anthropology of religion; but these appear to be written for upper-division students who have already been introduced to the field and often heavily emphasize theory. Third, there are abundant books on the more familiar world religions but few that discuss religions in small-scale societies, where much of the anthropological studies have been conducted. Our goal in writing this text has been to introduce the beginning student to the basic concepts involved in the anthropological study of religion including an introduction to ethnographical information from a wide range of societies and a basic introduction to the field of anthropology.

One of the most difficult decisions we have had to make in writing this text is the organization and order of presentation of topics. The range of topics is large, and they overlap in myriad ways—everyone has his or her own approach. We have attempted to present the material beginning with basic concepts and proceeding to the more complex. For example, we begin with myth, symbolism, and ritual before moving on to magic and witchcraft later in the text.

We have attempted to include a number of ethnographic examples with a good geographical distribution. Of course, many topics are associated with classic ethnographic studies, which have been included. We have also attempted to balance the presentation of a wide variety of cultures with the inclusion of certain key societies that reappear as examples of several topics throughout the text, to give students some continuity and a deeper understanding of a small group of societies. These societies include the Navaho of North America, the Yanomamö of South

America, the Azande and Yoruba of Africa, the Murngin of Australia, and the Tro-briand Islanders off the coast of New Guinea.

To assist the student in learning the material, we have divided each chapter into several sections with different levels of headings. Terms that appear in the Glossary have been set in bold. Occasionally, a term is used that is not defined within the body of the text. However, it is given in bold so that the student is cued to find that term in the Glossary. Each chapter concludes with Summary, Suggested Readings, Suggested Web Sites, and Study Questions. Additional material and suggested exam questions are presented in the Instructor's Manual.

Acknowledgments

We want to take this opportunity to thank the many people who have aided us in the writing of this book. Many thanks to the reviewers: Nicola Denzey, Bowdon College; Charles O. Ellenbaum, College of DuPage; Karen Fjelstad, Cabrillo College; Wendy Fonarow, Glendale College; Arthur Gribben, Los Angeles Pierce College; Lilly M. Langer, Florida International University; Phillip Naftaly, Adirondack Community College; Lesley Northup, Florida International University; and Terry N. Simmons, Paradise Valley Community College. We would especially like to thank our editor, Jennifer Jacobson, for her help and for her patience through the many delays that this project saw, including those due to pregnancy and childbirth. Diana Neatrour and the team at Omegatype worked very hard to meet an accelerated schedule for which they also have our heartfelt thanks. In all, the staff on this project were nothing less than a joy to work with.

We also want to thank our students for their assistance in writing this book. After all, this book was written for them. The text was originally based on our lecture notes for an anthropology of religion course which developed over many years with student dialogue. The manuscript was then used as a textbook, which provided an opportunity for student feedback.

Finally, we wish to thank our respective spouses, Robert Frankle and Carol Stein, for their patience and support, assistance, and babysitting.

1

The Anthropological Study of Religion

Human beings pose questions about almost everything in the world, including themselves. The most fundamental of these questions are answered by a people's religious beliefs and practices, which is the subject of this book. We will examine the religious lives of a broad range of human communities from an anthropological perspective.

The term *anthropological perspective* means many things. It is a theoretical orientation that will be discussed later in the chapter. It is also an approach that compares human societies throughout the world—contemporary and historical, industrial and tribal. Many college courses and textbooks focus on the best-known religions, those that are practiced by millions upon millions of people and are often referred to as the "world's great religions"—Judaism, Christianity, Islam, Hinduism, and Buddhism, among others. This book will expand the subject matter to include and focus on lesser-known religious systems, especially those that are found in small-scale, traditional communities. As we do this, we want to look for commonalities as well as to celebrate diversity.

This book will not simply describe a series of religious systems. We will approach the study of religion by looking at particular topics that are usually included in the anthropological definition of religion and providing examples to illustrate these topics from the anthropological literature. We obviously are unable to present the thousands of religious systems that exist or have existed in the world, but we can provide a sample.

The Anthropological Perspective

The subject of this book is religion as seen from an anthropological perspective. What does this mean? The term *anthropology* refers to the study of humanity. However, anthropology shares this subject matter with many other disciplines—sociology,

1

psychology, history, and political science, to name a few. So how is anthropology different from these other disciplines?

One way in which anthropology differs from other subjects is that anthropology is an integrated study of humanity. Anthropologists study human societies as systematic sums of their parts, as integrated wholes. We call this approach **holism.** For example, many disciplines study marriage. The anthropologist believes that a true understanding of marriage requires an understanding of all aspects of the society. Marriage is profoundly influenced by politics and law, economics, ethics, and theology; in turn, marriage influences history, literature, art, and music. The same is true of religious practices and beliefs.

The holistic nature of anthropology is seen in the various divisions of the field. Traditional anthropologists speak of *four-fields anthropology*. These four fields are physical anthropology, archaeology, linguistics, and cultural anthropology. Today, with the rapid increase and complexity of anthropological studies, anthropologists are becoming more and more specialized and focused on particular topics. The often-simplistic concept of anthropology as being composed of the integrated study of these four fields is rapidly breaking down, but a review of these four fields will acquaint those who are studying anthropology for the first time with the essential nature of the discipline.

Physical anthropology is the study of human biology and evolution. Physical anthropologists are interested in genetics; evolutionary theory; the biology and behavior of the primates, the group of animals that includes monkeys, apes, and humans; and paleontology, the study of the fossil record. Anthropologists with a biological orientation discuss the evolutionary origins and the neurobiology of religious experience.

Archaeology is the study of people who are known only from their physical and cultural remains; it gives us insight into the lives of now extinct societies. Evidence of religious expression can be seen in the ruins of ancient temples and in the art and writings of people who lived in societies that have faded into history.

The field of **linguistics** is devoted to the study of language, which, according to many anthropologists, is a unique feature of humans. Much of religious practice is linguistic in nature, involving the recitation of words, and the religious beliefs of a people are expressed in their myths and literature.

Cultural anthropology is the study of contemporary human societies and makes up the largest area of anthropological study. Cultural anthropologists study a people's social organization, economics and technology, political organization, marriage and family life, child-rearing practices, and so forth. The study of religion is a subject within the general field of cultural anthropology. However, we will be drawing on all four subfields in our examination of religion.

The Holistic Approach

Studying a society holistically is a very daunting task. It is one that requires a great deal of time—time to observe human behavior and time to interview members of a society. Because of the necessity of having to limit the scope of a research project, anthropologists are noted for their long-term studies of small, remote communities.

However, with the breakdown of the isolation of small communities and their incorporation into larger political units, anthropologists are turning more and more to the study of larger, more complex societies. Yet even within a more complex society anthropologists maintain a limited focus. For example, within an urban setting anthropologists study specific companies, hospitals, neighborhoods, gangs, clubs, and churches. Anthropological studies take place over long periods of time and usually require the anthropologist to live within the community and to participate to a degree in the lives of the people under study while at the same time making objective observations. This technique of study is referred to as **participant observation.**

Students of anthropology are initially introduced to small communities such as **foraging bands,** small **horticultural** villages, and groups of **pastoral nomads.** They become familiar with the lives of the Trobriand Islanders off the coast of New Guinea, the Navaho of the American Southwest, the Yanomamö of northern South America, the Murngin of northern Australia, and the San of southern Africa. Some people refer to these societies as being "primitive," but *primitive* is a pejorative term, one laden with negative connotations such as inferior and "less than." Perhaps a better term is **small-scale.** When we say *small scale,* we refer to relatively small communities, villages, and bands that practice foraging, herding, or technologically simple horticulture.

We will also be examining aspects of what are often referred to as the "world's great religions." Like the term *primitive,* the term *great* involves a value judgment. These familiar religions include Judaism, Christianity, Islam, and Buddhism. They are similar in that the origins of these religions are based on the lives of a particular individual or founder, such as Moses, Christ, Mohammad, and the Buddha. These religions have spread into thousands of different societies, and their adherents number in the millions. The small-scale societies that are more traditionally studied by anthropologists, by contrast, are usually not based on the lives of particular prophets or founders. They tend to be limited to one or a few societies, and adherents might number only a few hundred or a few thousand.

If they involve only a very small number of people, then why study these smaller religions? Among the many questions that anthropologists ask about humanity are the following: Are there characteristics that are found in all human societies, what we might call **human universals**? And when we look at universals, or at least at very widespread features, what are the ranges of variation? Returning to the example of marriage, we could ask the following questions: Is marriage found in all human societies? And what are the various forms that marriage takes? We might ask similar questions about religion. To answer these questions, anthropologists go out into the field, study particular communities, and write reports describing these communities. Answers to questions of universality and variability can be answered on the basis of descriptions of hundreds of human societies.

In addition, the goal of anthropology is to study the broad range of human beliefs and behaviors, to discover what it means to be human. This is best accomplished by examining religious and other cultural phenomena in a wide variety of cultures of different sizes and structures, including our own. It is often said that the aim of anthropology is to make the strange familiar and the familiar strange. Only through cross-cultural comparisons is this possible.

The Study of Human Societies

Ethnography is the descriptive study of human societies. People who study human societies and write ethnographies about them are cultural anthropologists; they are sometimes referred to as **ethnographers.**

However, not all descriptions of human societies are written by ethnographers. For example, an archaeologist is someone who studies the physical and cultural remains of societies that existed in the past and are known today only from their ruins, burials, and garbage. Yet archaeologists can, to a limited degree, reconstruct the lives of people who lived in ancient societies. Sometimes the only descriptions we have of people's lives are those written in diaries and reports by explorers and colonial administrators. Although these descriptions are far from complete and objective, they do provide us with some information.

Although we will visit a few societies that are known solely from their archaeological remains, most of the examples in this book are from societies that exist today or have existed in the recent past. Many of the societies we will discuss were first visited and described by anthropologists in the early to mid-1900s. Although these societies have changed over time, as all groups do, and although many of these societies have passed out of existence, anthropologists speak of them in the **ethnographic present;** that is, we discuss these groups in the present tense as they were first described by ethnographers.

Throughout this book we will be presenting examples from the ethnographic literature. These communities are found throughout the world, including some very remote areas. To better understand their nature and distribution, we will organize these societies into **culture areas.** A culture area is a geographical area in which societies tend to share many cultural traits. This happens because these groups face similar challenges from the environment and often come up with similar solutions and because cultural traits that develop in one group will easily spread to other nearby groups.

Each human society—and even subgroups within the society—exhibits unique characteristics. The common traits that define a culture area tend to lie in the realm of subsistence activities and technology, a common response to the challenges from the environment, although some similarity in other facets of the society, including religion, may also be found. For example, the California culture area, whose boundaries are somewhat different from the present-day political unit, includes a group of communities that exploit acorns. Acorns require processing that involves many steps and much equipment, but acorns provide a food resource that is plentiful and nutritious and that can be stored. These features permit the development of permanent and semipermanent communities, unlike those developed by most hunting-and-gathering peoples.[1] Table 1.1 lists the major culture areas of the world along with the names of the groups that will be used as examples in this book.

Besides geographical distribution, there are other ways in which anthropologists organize societies. One commonly used scheme is to organize societies in terms of their subsistence strategy, focusing on how they make a living (Table 1.2). Commonly used categories are foragers, horticulturalists, pastoralists, and agriculturalists.

TABLE 1.1   *Culture Areas of the World*

North America

Arctic Coast (Inuit, Yup'ik)
Hunting of sea mammals and caribou, fishing; shelters made of snow blocks, semisubterranean sod houses, summer tents made of skins; dog-drawn sledges, tailored skin clothing; settlement in small family groups.

Northern Subarctic (Chipawyan, Winnebago)
Hunting caribou, fishing; conical skin tents, bark or skin canoes, snowshoes, toboggans; highly nomadic bands with chiefs.

Great Basin-Plateau (Paiute, Shoshoni)
Acorn collecting, fishing, hunting of small game; small brush windbreaks, elaborate basketry; band organization.

California (Cahuilla, Chumash, Pomo)
Acorn collecting, fishing, hunting of small game; simple brush dwellings, semisubterranean lodges; basketry; multiplicity of small contrasting tribes, semipermanent villages.

Northwest Coast (Haida, Kwakuitl, Tlingit)
Salmon and deep-sea fishing, hunting and collecting; large rectangular plank dwellings with gabled roofs, large canoes, lack pottery, elaborate development of decorative art; permanent villages, chiefs, elaborate system of rank.

Plains (Arapaho, Blackfeet, Cheyenne, Crow, Kiowa, Lakota, Ojibwa, Sioux)
Hunting of bison, some horticulture; tipi dwellings; transport by dog, later horse, absence of basketry and pottery, hide utensils; large bands, competitive military and social societies, warfare important.

Eastern Woodland (Iroquois, Seneca)
Horticulture, hunting; multiple-family dwellings of bark (longhouses); matrilineal clans, village chiefs.

Southeast (Cherokee, Natchez)
Similar to Eastern Woodland with Meso-American influence.

Southwest (Apache, Hopi, Navaho, Tewa, Zuni)
Intensive cultivation of beans, maize, and squash; pueblos consisting of great multifamily terraced apartments, single-family dwellings with more nomadic groups; highly developed pottery and loom weaving; village as largest political unit.

Meso-America (Aztec, Huichol, Maya)
Intensive agriculture; state societies with developed technology including monumental stone architecture, stone sculpture, system of writing, woven textiles, metallurgy; fully developed dynastic empires, social classes.

South America

Marginal (Siriono, Yahgan)
Hunting, fishing, and gathering; family as basic social unit.

Tropical Forest (Jivaro, Yanomamö)
Slash-and-burn horticulture; villages often consist of one communal dwelling located on rivers; bark canoes and dugouts, clubs and shields, bows and arrows, blow guns, bark cloth, hammock, tobacco; village settlements under chiefs, warfare strongly developed with cannibalism present.

Circum-Caribbean (Arawak, Carib)
Intensive farming, hunting and fishing; pole and thatch houses arranged in streets and around plazas surrounded by palisade; hammocks, poisoned arrows, loom weaving of domesticated cotton, highly developed ceramics, gold and copper worked; large villages, social classes, chiefs, extreme development of warfare.

Andean (Araucanian, Inca)
Intensive irrigation agriculture; paved roads, monumental architecture, highly developed ceramics, weaving, and metallurgy; large cities, divine ruler over large empires.

(continued)

TABLE 1.1 *Continued*

Africa

Mediterranean (Berbers)
Agriculture and sheep herding; marginal Near Eastern culture, towns and cities, Islam.

Desert (Tuareg)
Livestock herding (horse and camel) and tent shelters; intensive fruit and cereal cultivation, camels, sheep, goat herding, stone and plaster dwellings; Islam.

Egypt (Egyptians, Nubians)
Flood-irrigated agriculture (wheat and barley); early civilization.

Western Sudan (Fulani, Hausa)
Agriculture and cattle herding; urban centers, dynastic rule and empires; Islam and animism.

Eastern Sudan (Dinka, Nuer)
Cattle herders and scattered agriculturalists; Islam and animism.

East Horn (Abyssinians, Somali)
Agriculture and cattle herding; Coptic Christianity.

East African Cattle (Bunyoro, Maasai, Swazi, Zulu)
Cattle herding, dairying, hoe agriculture; iron work, age grades, warfare, ancestor worship.

Madagascar (Tanala)
Marginal Indonesian culture; wet rice irrigation agriculture.

Khoisan (Ju/'hoansi San)
Hunting and gathering; nomadic bands, brush shelters.

Guinea Coast (Ashanti, Beng, Bushongo, Dogon, Edo, Gwari, Nupe, Sefwi, Yoruba)
Hoe agriculture, root crops and maize; large dynastic kingdoms, city and towns, market centers, judicial systems, craft guilds, artistic development.

Congo (Azande, Kongo, Pygmies)
Yam and banana cultivation; double-court kingdoms, markets, native courts; iron and brass work; Pygmies: hunting and gathering, trade with agriculturalists.

Eurasia

Southwest Asia (Bedawin)
Cereal irrigation agriculture, plow, herding; Islam.

Central Asian Steppe (Mongols)
Horse domesticated for transportation, milk, hides; Islam.

Siberian (Tungus, Tuva)
Fishing, hunting, reindeer domestication; conical skin dwellings; tailored skin clothing.

East Asian Civilizations (Chinese, Japanese, Korean)
Intensive agriculture including wet rice and animal husbandry; ancient civilizations; urban centers and industrialization; several religious systems including Shinto and Buddhism.

Southeast Asia (Hmong, Javanese, Karen Padaung)
Wet and dry rice agriculture, water buffalo; bamboo houses; Hinduism, Buddhism, Islam.

India (Nayar, Toda)
Plow agriculture, wheat and barley; caste system.

European (Basques, Viking)
Mixed agriculture and animal husbandry; urbanization and industrialization; mainly Christian.

Oceania

Indonesia-Philippine (Berawan, Ifugao, Tana Toraja)
Irrigation and terracing, wet rice agriculture, water buffalo; large multifamily dwellings on piles, betel chewing, elaborate textiles, blow guns, Hinduism, Buddhism, Islam, animism.

TABLE 1.1 *Continued*

Australia (Murngin, Yir Yoront)
Hunting and gathering economy; simple windbreaks, spears and spear-throwers, bark containers; independent bands, highly elaborate kin organization; totemism.

Melanesia (Asmat, Buka, Dani, Fore, Gururumba, Trobriand Islanders, Wogeo)
Yams and taro horticulture, fishing; elaborate ceremonial houses, high development of wood carving, canoes, bows and arrows, isolated hamlets under local chief, regional specialization in economic production, trading voyages; chronic petty warfare.

Micronesia (Palau, Truk)
Yams and taro horticulture, fishing, collection of breadfruit and coconut; expert navigation in sailing canoes; intertribal warfare.

Polynesia (Maori, Samoan)
Taro, yams, coconut, breadfruit cultivation, fishing; large thatched dwellings, tapa cloth, kava, tattooing, sculpture in wood and stone, outrigger canoes with sails; hereditary social classes and divine chiefs; mana, tabu.

TABLE 1.2 *Food-Getting Strategies*

	Foragers	*Pastoralists*	*Horticulturalists*	*Intensive Agriculturalists*
Examples	San, Murngin, Shoshoni	Nuer, Massai	Gururumba, Yanomamö, Azande	Aztec, Korea, Amish
Food getting	Food collectors: gathering, hunting, fishing	Animal husbandry	Farming with simple hand tools	Farming with advanced technology (e.g. irrigation, fertilization, plows)
Community variables	Low population density, small community size	Low population density, small to medium community size	Moderate population density, medium community size	High population density, large community size
Settlement patterns	Nomadic or seminomadic	Nomadic or seminomadic	Basically sedentary, may move after several years	Permanent settlements
Specialization	No full-time specialists, some part-time	Few full-time specialists, some part-time	Few full-time specialists, some part-time	Many full-time specialists
Social stratification	Generally none	Some	Some	Significant

Of course, these are not precisely delineated categories but divisions of a continuum. Foragers are peoples without any form of plant or animal domestication. They tend to live in small, isolated groups that are found today primarily in areas that are difficult to farm. Horticulturalists are peoples who garden in the absence of fertilization, irrigation, and other advanced technologies. Pastoralists are peoples whose primary livelihood comes from the herding of domesticated animals. Peoples who plow, fertilize, and irrigate their crops are termed agriculturalists. The latter develop relatively large communities with more complex technologies. Societies that have the same subsistence strategy generally have other features in common, such as settlement patterns, population density, and the presence of specialists.

The Fore of New Guinea: An Ethnographic Example

In the preceding sections of this chapter we learned about some basic concepts of anthropology, such as holism, and we were introduced to the concept of ethnography. Now let us turn our attention to a particular example to illustrate these ideas.

The holistic approach sees human behavior as a complex set of interacting behaviors and ideas. In examining a society, we might begin with a particular problem that interests us, but we soon realize that to truly understand this problem, we have to look at many other aspects of the society.

An example of this was a study of the Fore, a group of about 14,000 horticulturalists living in the eastern highlands of New Guinea (Melanesia culture area). The problem that brought the Fore to the attention of the Western world was a medical one. The solution to the problem brought the Nobel Prize in Medicine to one of the investigators.

When the Australian government first contacted the Fore in the 1950s, a significant number of individuals were found to be suffering from a particular illness. The illness was having a major impact on the population, since about 200 people were dying of the illness each year, the victims being primarily women and children.

This illness is characterized by a variety of symptoms, but the most obvious ones are jerking movements and shaking, which make planned motor activity difficult. The course of the illness is about nine months. At the end the victim can no longer stand or sit up and can no longer eat or drink water and soon dies. The Fore call this illness *kuru,* which means "to tremble with fear" in the Fore language.

The medical team that was sent in to deal with the disease sought the cause. Because it appeared to be largely confined to the Fore, the team thought it might be genetic or due to a toxin in the environment. However, *kuru* was finally determined to be the result of an infectious agent. The major question was how the *kuru* infectious agent was passed from one person to another. Was it passed on through contaminated water, or through the air, or through sexual activity? The answer to the puzzle was proposed by anthropologists: cannibalism.

It was the custom of the Fore to eat the body as part of the funeral rituals—one aspect of their religious practices. The body of the deceased was carried down to an abandoned field, where kin dismembered and cooked it. Close relatives then consumed the pieces. Because cooking does not destroy the infectious particles, some of them entered the bloodstream through cuts and open sores and eventually entered the brain, where, many years later, the person began to show symptoms of the disease. Because women and children, who have lower social status, were more likely to eat the brain, they were the most likely to develop the disease.

The modern medical community now had an explanation for what caused the disease and knew how it was transmitted from one individual to another. The government had a "cure" to the epidemic: eliminate the practice of cannibalism. As a result, cannibalism stopped, and *kuru* eventually disappeared, although this took some time, since the disease has a long incubation period. However, the Fore themselves did not understand this explanation and stopped eating the bodies of their dead only because not to do so would mean spending time in jail. The Fore failed to understand the scientific explanation of the disease. Think about how difficult it would be for the doctors to convince the Fore that *kuru* was caused by tiny infectious particles that no one could see (at least without a very powerful microscope). One might as well be talking about tiny evil spirits that also cannot be seen.

The Fore knew the cause of *kuru*, at least in their world. It was the result of sorcery. The sorcerer would steal something that was once a part of or in contact with the victim, such as a piece of clothing or a lock of hair. The material was then made into a bundle along with some leaves, bark, and stones and was bound up into a package. After reciting a spell, the sorcerer would place the bundle into muddy ground, and as the bundle rotted, the victim would develop the symptoms of the disease. This belief influenced everyday behavior, as individuals were careful to hide things that could be retrieved and used by a sorcerer.

In spite of this caution, people still developed *kuru*. In this case a divination technique was used to reveal the identity of the sorcerer causing the illness. As we will see in a future chapter, many people use such techniques to reveal things that are difficult or impossible to discover by other means. Once the sorcerer was identified, the Fore had many options to counter the activity of the evildoer. A person with *kuru* might also have consulted a healer.

The fact that *kuru* struck primarily women had significant social consequences. Many men lost wives through *kuru*, and the shortage of women meant that many men were unable to find wives. In addition, men with children who had lost their wives had to perform many domestic chores normally reserved for women, including farming.

The ethnography of the Fore and the description of *kuru* illustrate the concept of holism (Figure 1.1). From the Western point of view, we begin with a medical problem, a disease. Then we see how this fatal disease affects various aspects of the society because of the death of women of childbearing age. This includes marriage, the family, the raising of children, farming, and so forth. Also, we see how the society attempts to explain and deal with the disease through religion. A description of *kuru* among the Fore as only a medical problem fails to provide us with a complete understanding of that disease.

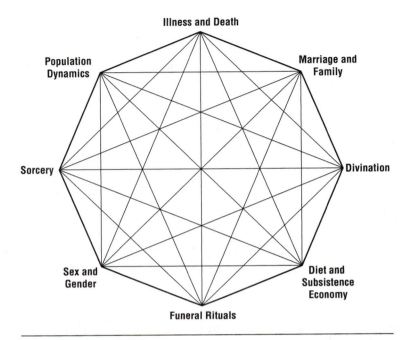

FIGURE 1.1   *Holism.* A complete understanding of the disease *kuru* among the Fore of New Guinea requires an understanding of the relationship of *kuru* to other aspects of Fore culture, some of which are shown in this diagram.

Two Ways of Viewing Culture

We can ask the question: What causes *kuru* among the Fore? From our viewpoint a complete answer to that question includes both biological factors (the disease-causing organism) and cultural factors (the practice of cannibalism). However, the Fore themselves would give another answer to this question: *Kuru* is caused by sorcery. Another aspect to the holistic approach is to consider both insider and outsider perspectives.

An anthropologist—or any scholar, for that matter—cannot be completely neutral and objective when describing a culture. Observation, recording, and analysis involve processing data in one's mind. One's own cultural background, education, training, and other factors will act as a filter or lens that colors what are thought of as objective observations. Physicians, using a medical model, searched for the cause of *kuru* through techniques learned in medical school that are based on a set of postulates developed through the scientific method. Although the physicians were able to discover the biological cause of *kuru*, the disease-causing organism, they were unable to discover the mode of transmission. Medical science identifies a series of transmission pathways, and none of them offered a valid explanation. It took anthropologists, viewing the situation from a holistic, anthropological viewpoint, to make the connection between *kuru* and cannibalism, although this had to be confirmed through a set of procedures mandated by the scientific method.

The physician and the anthropologist are outsiders looking in. They see Fore culture in terms of Western philosophy and theory. They speak of the Fore using words that categorize experience in a particular way. This is referred to as an **etic analysis.** There are advantages to an etic analysis. Just as a friend or therapist might see patterns to a person's life that the person might overlook, an outside analyst might see patterns of behaviors or beliefs in a culture that the members of that group might be unaware of. Another advantage is that the anthropologist can apply a consistent form of analysis to many different societies that are being studied. This permits anthropologists to make comparisons between societies and perhaps to discover some universal principles about human behavior.

Yet the Fore see their world from an altogether different perspective, using linguistic categories and basic assumptions about their world that differ profoundly from ours. To the Fore, sorcery is *the* ultimate cause of *kuru,* and this makes sense in their culture. An **emic analysis** is one that attempts to see the world through the eyes of the people being studied. Of course, the big question is: How successful can we really be at this?

Cultural Relativism

How do you feel about the Fore practice of cannibalism? In the course of looking at different societies, anthropologists often observe behaviors that seem strange and sometimes disturbing. We have grown up in a particular society, and the behaviors and ideas of our own society seem to us to be natural and correct. It is also natural to use our own society as the basis for interpreting and judging other societies. This tendency is called **ethnocentrism.**

Anthropologists realize, however, that a true understanding of other peoples cannot develop through ethnocentric interpretations. Thinking of other people as primitive, superstitious, and immoral only colors our observations and prevents us from reaching any kind of true understanding about human behavior and thought. Anthropologists attempt to remain neutral and to accept the ways of life of other communities as appropriate for those who live in these communities. Anthropologists attempt to describe and understand people's customs and ideas but do not judge them. This approach is known as **cultural relativism.** The goal is to study what people believe, not whether or not what they believe is true.

For example, funeral rituals differ from other rituals in one major respect: There is a dead body. All societies have ways of disposing of the corpse in one way or another. Burial is quite common, but there are a number of variables such as where the grave is located, what the body is buried in, what objects are buried with the body, and so on. Bodies can also be placed in trees to decay, and later the bones may be cleaned and buried. Bodies can be cremated, and the remains kept in a container, buried, or scattered at sea. Among the Yanomamö of Venezuela and Brazil, the cremated remains are ground into a powder. At various times after a person's death, the family gathers together and prepares a banana stew into which some of the cremated ashes are mixed. Then they drink the mixture. And, of course, as we saw with the Fore, there is the custom of eating the body.

The practice of drinking cremated remains or eating human flesh would probably horrify most Americans, and its practice in U.S. society would probably lead to some type of reaction on the part of the society—most likely psychiatric confinement. On the other hand, the Yanomamö are horrified by the U.S. practice of burial because it leads to the decay of the body in the ground. They believe that the finest expression of love is for close relatives to provide a final resting place for their loved ones within their own bodies. Is this practice wrong, immoral, or dangerous? The answer to this question, of course, lies within the cultural practices of the group and how that group defines correct and appropriate behaviors.

Postmodernism.   In recent years the field of anthropology has been influenced by the **postmodern** movement, which greatly extends the concept of cultural relativism. Beginning mainly in the 1980s, postmodernism has had a broad academic impact across many disciplines. Postmodernism was partly a reaction to the philosophical movement called **modernity,** which came into being during the Renaissance. Modernity highlighted science and the scientific method. Rationality, objectivity, and reason were stressed as was the discovery of knowledge and truth. Progress and the creation of order were a main area of focus. In contrast, postmodernism denies the existence of absolute, true knowledge of the world. All knowledge is seen as being a human "construction" that we must try to "deconstruct." Postmodernism points out the limitations of science and stresses that there are always multiple viewpoints and truths. Reflexivity and being aware of our own viewpoint and biases are seen as key. In contrast to modernity's emphasis on order, postmodernism sees contradictions and instabilities as being a natural part of any social group or practice.

The value of postmodernism for anthropology has been to reinforce the idea of multiple valid ways of seeing the world—that there is no one right way to think or to do things. For ethnographers, postmodernism served as a reminder of how the ethnographer himself or herself can influence the fieldwork situation. As a result, ethnographers are more self-conscious and more aware of their own positions and biases (Box 1.1). Every person sees the world through the lens of his or her own culture. We cannot remove the lens, but we can become more aware of it.

Critics of the postmodernism movement point out that taken to its logical extreme, a postmodern approach really says that it is impossible for a person from one culture to understand someone from another culture. Perhaps it is even impossible for any one person to truly understand any other person. Postmodernism also rejects the scientific method and the search for scientific truths. Given all this, could anthropology as a discipline even exist? Most anthropologists have taken a middle ground approach—appreciating the lessons of postmodernism while attempting to avoid the extremes.

BOX 1.1 • *Karen McCarthy Brown and Vodou*

Karen McCarthy Brown first met Mama Lola in 1978. On the basis of a dozen years of research and writing, Brown would write the classic ethnography *Mama Lola: A Vodou Priestess in Brooklyn*. This book was at the forefront of many important trends in anthropology. It was centered on the experiences of a single individual and was influenced by feminist and postmodern ideologies. In the book Brown speaks candidly of her own experiences doing participant observation research and how she became involved in the religion of Vodou to a degree that perhaps even goes beyond that standard—becoming a Vodou priestess herself. (The Vodou religion will be discussed in Chapter 10.)

The book focuses on the life and practices of Mama Lola, a Haitian immigrant living in New York City. Among the themes of the book is the persecution experienced by Haitians in the United States and the difficulties they face in trying to practice their religion. Brown continues to focus on religious practices that take place outside of standard religious institutions. This kind of activity has become a major part of religious life in modern urban cultures. This is especially true in the United States, where religious pluralism is on the rise, partly owing to recent immigration patterns.

Brown is currently a professor at Drew University, where she has been leading the university's Newark Project since 1993. This field-based program seeks to link ethnographic research, curriculum development, advocacy, and community organizing. Of particular concern is trying to understand how people practice their religion when they are ignored or condemned by traditional religious institutions and teachings.

Universal Human Rights.   Some anthropologists, however, question the approach of complete neutrality represented by cultural relativism and the approach of complete subjectivity of postmodernism and ask: Are there any basic human rights and universal standards of behavior? This is an area of debate, one that often focuses on the religious practices of other peoples that may include such customs as physical alterations of the genitalia or cannibalism.

Cultural relativism is one of the basic concepts necessary to anthropology, and it should not be put aside lightly. Our first approach to any cultural practice should be to try to understand it in context—to understand the meaning it has for people in that culture. After doing so, however, is it possible to say, "I understand this practice and why this culture does it, but it is still wrong"? The difficulty in this is knowing where to draw the line, and strict criteria must be used. One such set of criteria was proposed by Robert Edgerton:[2]

> I shall first define [maladaptation] as the failure of a population or its culture to survive because of the inadequacy or harmfulness of one or more of its beliefs or institutions. Second, maladaptation will be said to exist when enough members of a population are sufficiently dissatisfied with one or more of their social institutions or cultural beliefs that the viability of their society is threatened. Finally, it will be considered to be maladaptive when a population maintains beliefs or practices that so seriously impair the physical or mental health of its members that they cannot adequately meet their own needs or maintain their social and cultural system.

It is important to note that the criteria are based on the survival of the society and its ability to function—not on an outsider's perception of morality. Edgerton includes as an example the high levels of stress and fear related to witchcraft beliefs in some cultures, a topic to which we will return to in Chapter 9.

The Aztec practice of cannibalism is another example. The Aztecs were an agricultural society located in the Meso-America culture area. In Aztec society a small elite used religious and military power to conquer neighboring groups. They took tribute in the form of gold and other valuables from the people they conquered. Both slaves and captured prisoners of war were sacrificed and eaten. The benefits of the conquest went almost exclusively to the elite. One analytical approach to the practice of cannibalism by the Aztecs argues that it was an adaptation to a protein-poor environment. A culturally relativistic approach would also point out that the sacrifices were done to please the Aztec gods. Edgerton argues against both of these interpretations.

Edgerton points out that sacrifice and cannibalism were conducted with very little ritual preparation—bodies were rolled down steeply sloped temple steps to be butchered below. The bodies were dealt with in much the same way as a side of beef might be. Human flesh was considered a delicacy and greatly desired, to such an extent that wars were fought with the primary goal of gaining human captives for sacrifice.

The negative impacts were not only on the neighboring groups. The Aztec elite did not share the wealth with the commoners. Even commoners who served in the army did not do so as equals. While the nobles wore helmets, armor, and shields, the commoners had none of this equipment. As Edgerton writes, "The splendors of Aztec culture cannot be denied, but they were achieved at great cost by the many largely for the benefit of the ruling few."[3]

Despite this questioning, cultural relativism remains of utmost importance to anthropologists. Our first approach should always be to try to understand a culture's beliefs and behaviors in context, to learn what meaning the world has through their eyes.

The Concept of Culture

In the earlier examples of the Aztec and Fore we observed a number of specific behaviors and beliefs. For example, an anthropologist living among the Fore for a period of time would, of course, record descriptions of Fore life in much more detail and cover many other aspects of their lives—marriage and family, child rearing, hunting and farming, trade, technology, political organization, folklore, and so on. It is obvious that the body of behaviors and beliefs of the Fore are quite different from ours. These behaviors and beliefs make up Fore **culture.**

In anthropology the term *culture* is used as a technical term. It does not refer to the arts or the "finer things of life." Although the term is widely used and discussed, finding a definition that is acceptable to all anthropologists is a difficult task.

The British anthropologist Edward B. Tylor first used the term *culture* in its anthropological sense. In 1871 Tylor wrote, "Culture . . . is that complex whole, which includes knowledge, belief, art, morals, law, customs, and any other capabilities and habits acquired by man as a member of society."[4] In this definition Tylor recognized that culture is a "complex whole," which is a reference to the holistic concept. And he noted that culture includes customs that people acquire by growing up in a particular society; that is, culture is learned.

When we look at a group of social insects, such as ants, we see a society in which individuals behave in certain stereotypic ways. When we look at a group of humans, we also see certain behaviors that appear to be stereotyped, repetitive, or customary. Yet besides the much greater complexity of human behavior, there is a major difference between ant and human behavior. Ant behavior is innate, that is, it is coded in the genes—it is a part of the ant's biological heredity. Although some aspects of human behavior are likely to be innate, the preponderance of human behavior is learned, handed down from one generation to the next, and is shared by a group of people. Culture is seen in the way people dress, how they greet one another, how they go about their chores, and how they worship their gods. For example, the actions that are performed in a ritual are actions that are learned from someone else, perhaps a parent or a priest, and thus they are passed down from one generation to the next.

One of the consequences of the social transmission of culture is that human behavior is complex and variable. Unlike biological inheritance, in which change occurs slowly through the mechanisms of biological evolution, learned behavioral patterns can change very rapidly in response to changing conditions. Also, the human species, which is very homogenous biologically, possesses a great many different cultures.

Another important feature of culture is that it is based on the use of **symbols.** Symbols are shared understandings about the meaning of certain words, attributes, or objects, such as the color red symbolizing "stop" in traffic signals. The connection between the two is arbitrary; there is no obvious, natural, or necessary connection. For example, in U.S. culture, black is the color associated with mourning. However in other cultures, the color associated with mourning is white, red, or even green.

Culture is learned primarily through symbols. Language can be thought of as a string of symbols, and we learn, communicate, and even think through the use of these symbols. Symbols are obviously an important area of discussion for the study of religion. The Christian cross, for example, symbolizes not just the religion itself, but a particular philosophy and history. Chapter 3 discusses the nature of symbols and their role in religious practice.

Viewing the World

The idea of culture involves much more than describing human activity. People also have different belief systems and different perceptions and understandings of their world and their lives.

Culture gives meaning to reality. We live in a real, physical world, yet this world is translated through the human mind onto a different plane. We look out a window and see a mountain rising above us. To the geologist the mountain is a structure made of rock formed through natural processes. To the hydrologist concerned with bringing water to a desert town the mountain is the place where snowfields are found. To the biologist it is the home of a great many plants and animals, many of them perhaps endangered.

To many people, however, a mountain is much more than a physical thing. The mountain might be the home of the gods or the place where the souls of the dead congregate after death. Mountains figure prominently in many Biblical stories; for example, Mount Sinai was where Moses received the Ten Commandments, and Mount Ararat was where Noah's ark came to rest. Psalm 121 reads: "I will lift up mine eyes unto the hills, from whence cometh my help."[5] Other sacred mountains include Mount Olympus, where the gods of ancient Greece lived, and the four sacred mountains of the Navaho world. We may label these images as being part of the imagination of a people, yet to the people the sacredness of a mountaintop may be as real as the presence of rocks, snow, or plants.

The stars are a dramatic feature of the night sky. In an area away from city lights a person can see thousands of stars seemingly scattered randomly across the sky. Yet the human mind has a propensity for seeing patterns, even if none are inherent in what is being observed. One grouping of stars appears to be recognized in a great number of cultures because it contains some of the brightest stars in the sky, stars that can be seen even in the city. These are the stars that make up the constellation of Orion, observable during the winter months in the northern hemisphere.

An astronomer looking at Orion sees stars of various types, distances, and brightness. The very bright star Betelgeuse, which forms the upper left corner of the constellation, is a variable red giant, and Rigel, the bright star found in the lower left corner, is a blue-white giant. In ancient Greek mythology, Orion was the son of Poseidon, the God of the Sea, and was half mortal. The goddess Artemis fell in love with Orion. Her brother, Apollo, was determined to prevent his sister from marrying a half-mortal and so sent a scorpion to kill Orion. After Orion's death Artemis and Apollo placed Orion's body in the sky so that Artemis could always remember him. Apollo also placed the scorpion halfway around the sky as the constellation Scorpio so that it would be chasing Orion across the sky for eternity. As Scorpio rises in the east, Orion sets, symbolizing the victory of the Scorpion over Orion.

The same stars that make up the constellation of Orion are seen differently in other cultures. In Japan, for example, there are many different interpretations of these stars. In contrast to Greek astronomy, in which the stars most often represent deities, Japanese constellations frequently represent objects that are important in Japanese culture. A common term for this constellation is *Tsuzumi Boshi*. A *tsuzumi* is a Japanese drum that has heads at both ends and is shaped like an hourglass (Figure 1.2). The three stars that make up Orion's belt in Greek astronomy are the cord that tie the strings together in the center of the drum. However, these three stars are given other interpretations in the several regions of Japan: Kimono sleeves, ruler stars to measure land, joints of the bamboo pole, or the three prongs of a fishing spear.[6]

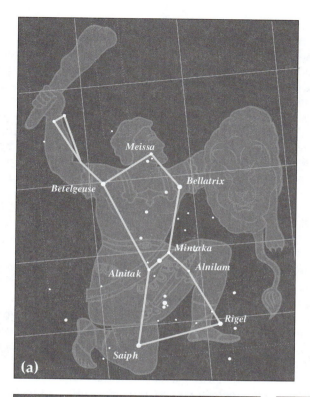

(a)

FIGURE 1.2 *Greek and Japanese Constellations.* People in different societies interpret the same group of stars in different ways. (a) This group of stars is known in the Western world as Orion, from the Greeks. The same group of stars is seen in many different ways in Japan including (b) *tsuzumi,* a type of drum and (c) a kimono sleeve.

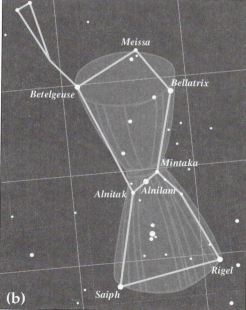

(b)

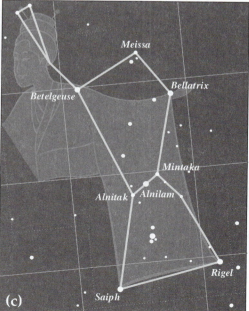

(c)

In terms of anatomy and physiology the brains of all people throughout the world are essentially the same. The process whereby the lens of the eye focuses light on the retina and generates electric impulses that reach the brain is identical in all human beings. Yet the brain takes these impulses and "creates" a reality sensed by the individual, and this reality is influenced by that individual's culture. People belonging to different cultures "see" the world differently, having different interpretations and perceptions of what surrounds them. It is as if there is a cultural lens through which people view and interpret the world about them. It is how culture gives meaning to the world above and beyond the physical reality of that world. And religion is a part of that cultural world. It is through religious narrative and religious ritual that meaning is given to the existence and life of a people.

The Definition of Religion

The beginning point of any discourse is to define the object of study—in this instance, **religion.** Yet the task of defining this term is a challenging one indeed. We must avoid using a definition that is too narrow or one that is too vague. Many definitions that have been proposed have been very narrow in that they apply only to some cultures and only to some of the phenomena that anthropologists traditionally place within the category of religion. Such definitions often are ethnocentric, including only those ideas that are considered "religious" for that culture. In such definitions many topics, such as magic and witchcraft, are often excluded. On the other hand, a definition that is too inclusive and vague loses much of its meaning and usefulness.

Attempts at Defining Religion

In spite of the difficulties of defining religion, anthropology is a social science, and the methodology of science requires that we define our terms. We need to use an **operant definition.** This is one in which we define our terms so that they are observable and measurable and therefore can be studied. So what would a good operant definition of religion be? We can start by looking at the various ways in which scholars have attempted to define the term.

Many definitions of religion share many of the elements that we included in our definition of culture. Perhaps we can define a religion as a system of beliefs and behaviors, based on a system of symbols. But how can we distinguish religious beliefs and behaviors from other aspects of culture? After all, we can recognize, for example, particular beliefs, behaviors, and symbols that define political or economic processes.

Different approaches to defining religion have been labeled analytic, functional, and essentialist. **Analytic definitions** focus on the way religion manifests itself or is expressed in a culture. An example would be defining religions by stating that religious practices generally include rituals.

Ninian Smart, for example, stated what he felt were the six dimensions of religion.[7] These include the following:

1. The institutional dimension (the organization and leadership)
2. The narrative dimension (myths, creation stories, worldview)
3. The ritual dimension (rites of passage and other important activities)
4. The social dimension (religion being a group activity that binds people together)
5. The ethical dimension (customs, moral rules)
6. The experiential dimension (religion involving experiences of a sacred reality that is beyond ordinary experience)

Other theorists have defined religion according to what they thought to be the core religious beliefs of any religious system. Two examples of this include Edward Burnett Tylor's definition of religion as **animism,** or a belief in spirit beings (gods, souls, ghosts, demons, etc.), and Melford Spiro's definition of religion as "An institution consisting of culturally patterned interactions with culturally postulated superhuman beings."[8] Both of these anthropologists and their approaches will be discussed in further detail later.

Functional definitions are concerned with the role that religion plays in a society. For example, a religion might enforce social cohesion by bringing members together for rituals and providing a foundation of shared beliefs. Religion might also function on the individual level to relieve individual anxiety by providing explanations and meaning.

Explanations for the universality of religion have usually been based on the cognitive, emotional, and social needs that religion is thought to fulfill. For example, religion provides explanations. Humans are faced with many difficult questions. How did the world come into being? How were humans created? Why is there evil and suffering in the world? How can we explain phenomena such as thunder, lightning, earthquakes, and volcanoes? What happens when we die? Religion provides answers to these questions.

Religion provides more than simple explanation. Religion provides comfort in that it helps people to face death and other misfortune by providing meaning and hope. Religion also acts on a social level. Both rituals and belief bring people together. Furthermore, religion provides a moral code, including supernatural punishments for those who break the rules.

An **essentialist definition** of religion looks at what is the essential nature of religion. It emphasizes the fact that religion is the domain of the extraordinary—things beyond the commonplace and the natural. On the basis of this idea we would say that a religion is a system of beliefs and behaviors that deals with the relationship between humans and the sacred supernatural.

The term *supernatural* refers to things that are "above the natural." Supernatural entities and actions transcend the normal world of cause and effect as we know it. In the supernatural world wondrous things occur. Supernatural beings defy the basic laws of nature. In the supernatural world objects move faster than light, heavy objects fly, and creatures become invisible.

However, not all supernatural phenomena are thought to be religious. Consider the folktale in which the handsome prince is turned into a frog. This is surely a supernatural occurrence—handsome princes do not turn into frogs in the natural world—but this occurrence is hardly a religious one. To address this problem, we add the term *sacred* to the definition of religion. **Sacred** denotes an attitude wherein the subject is entitled to reverence and respect.

A true understanding of the breadth of religious practices among the world's societies will become clear as you progress through this text. We encourage you to keep an open mind and settle on your own definition as you gain more knowledge and understanding. However, as was discussed above, as an endeavor in the social sciences this text needs an operant definition in order to proceed. Therefore we will generally be using an essentialist definition of religion while also using elements from other approaches, such as the functionalist. In other words, we consider religion to be the domain of human interaction with the sacred supernatural and recognize the important functional role of religion in society.

The Domain of Religion

The discussion of definitions highlights the contrasting concepts of etic and emic, which we discussed above. The very concept of religion as a separate cultural category is a Western one. Western cultures are divided into very distinct cultural domains, such as economics, politics, technology, and, of course, religion. As we move through our day, we move from one domain to another, yet the domains do not overlap, or they overlap to a small degree. For example, when we go to work, we might punch a clock or sign in, for "work" is a distinct segment of our life, which we can define in terms of location, activity, relationships to coworkers, and so forth. Religion as a domain may be restricted to very specific activities held in special places during specific times—a Sunday morning church service, for example. When we use the term *religion,* we might immediately picture such things as special buildings dedicated to religious activities (churches, temples, and mosques) and full-time specialists who perform religious rituals (priests, rabbis, and imams).

Our analysis of religion becomes more difficult when we turn our attention to more traditional societies. If we analyzed small-scale religious systems by applying the definitions and concepts that have been developed in Western cultures, we would likely find that certain elements that we consider to be vital parts of our religious systems simply do not exist—*in our terms.* For some people it follows from this that other religious systems are "defective," "incomplete," "primitive," "false," or "full of superstitions." Clearly, this leads us into highly ethnocentric conclusions that cloud our ability to understand the religious systems of other peoples.

When we study traditional societies using an emic (insider) approach, there might be no equivalent term to our concept of religion. Religion is not separated out from other dimensions of life but is fully integrated into fabric of beliefs and behavior. As Wilfred Cantwell Smith wrote, "To the believer, they are parts of the universe; to the observer, they are parts of a religion."[9]

Theoretical Approaches to the Study of Religion

Just as there are many definitions of religion, there are also many approaches to the study of religious phenomena. Here we will focus on three main approaches that anthropologists have used to study religion: evolutionary, functional, and psychosocial.

The Evolutionary Approach. The **evolutionary approach** was focused on the questions of when and how religion began. This viewpoint developed in the late 1800s when the focus was on the concepts of science, logic, and monotheism as the pinnacles of human achievement. For example, this was a time when **positivism** was popular. This philosophy emphasized empiricism, or observing and measuring, saying that the only real knowledge is scientific knowledge; any knowledge beyond that is impossible.

The latter half of the nineteenth century saw the rise of the concept of a general evolution of culture. It was thought that religion naturally evolved from the simple to the complex and that this evolution was a natural consequence of human nature. An interest in the religion of "primitive" peoples arose from the supposition that "primitive" peoples represented an early stage of cultural evolution and that one could learn about and understand the historical roots of the religion of "civilized" societies by studying living "primitive" peoples.

Edward B. Tylor, who first used the term *culture* in its modern sense, used this approach in his book *Primitive Culture* (1871).[10] He concluded that all religions had a belief in spiritual beings. Whereas the religions of "civilized" peoples included beliefs in gods and souls, those of "primitive" peoples focused on the belief in spirits and ghosts. He termed this early belief system *animism*.

Tylor thought that the belief in spirit beings was the natural and universal conclusion reached by all peoples through the observation of sleep and dreams, possession, and death, during which the soul is thought to leave the body, temporarily or permanently. Because other animals are also living, they must also have souls that leave the body when the animal is killed by a hunter, for example. All living things are animated by souls, as are nonliving things such as waterfalls and rocks.

In attempting to find a common thread in all religious systems, Tylor failed to discover the great variability among the world's religious systems. This was in part because Tylor did not go into the field to become immersed in the complexity of a particular culture. Instead, he relied on reports of explorers, missionaries, and colonial administrators who described, often in simplistic and biased ways, the peoples they encountered in their travels.

Robert R. Marett developed the concept of a simpler, more basic, and more ancient supernatural force that he labeled **animatism.** Marett thought that the idea of animatism simply grew out of human emotional reaction to the power of nature. This belief in an impersonal supernatural power is well articulated in the religions of Polynesia and Melanesia, where it is referred to as *mana*. In Chapter 6 we will discuss the ideas of another scholar from the evolutionary school, James

Frazer, who wrote extensively about magic, a category that he considered to be separate from religion. Frazer saw a natural progression in cultures from magic to religion to science.

The evolutionary approach has many critics. Many of the ideas found in this school of thought are ethnocentric—for example, Tylor's idea that the religion of "primitive" peoples focused on spirits and ghosts while more "civilized" peoples focused on gods. In addition, any ideas about the origin of a cultural practice are, of course, highly speculative. Although the idea of cultural progression, with Western societies being more "evolved" than smaller-scale traditional ones, is no longer used in anthropology, the general question of the origins of religion has remained a concern.

The Functional Approach.   In contrast to the evolutionary school, the **functional approach** asks the question: What does religion do? Émile Durkheim, for example, saw society as problematic. Although sanctions exist to keep people in line, Durkheim thought that these were not enough. He believed that the key lies in the **collective conscious,** a system of beliefs that act to contain natural selfishness of individuals and to promote social cooperation. Collective representations, or symbols, are a reflection of the collective conscious. During rituals, these collective representations are displayed, resulting in a reattachment to the value system of the group.

Both Durkheim and Alfred R. Radcliffe-Brown saw society as being like an organism in which the parts act to maintain the whole. Radcliffe-Brown also thought that for society to survive, certain feelings need to be encouraged in people's minds. He thought that anything of great social value is seen as possessing supernatural power; the greater the value, the more powerful it is. Rituals, then, function to express the basic sentiments of a society and to pass these ideas down from generation to generation. Religion, in general, is seen as an integrative force in society.

Radcliffe-Brown's approach to function was in terms of a part contributing to the maintenance of the whole society. Another important theorist in the functional school, Bronislaw Malinowski, had a different approach (Box 1.2). Malinowski looked at religion and other features of a society in terms of their purpose in meeting basic human needs. For example, in his analysis of magic Malinowski stressed that magic is a logical system that people turn to in times of uncertainty or emotional stress. Magic functions to provide control and certainty in an otherwise uncertain world.

The functional approach is still used today and will be referred to in future chapters. Researchers have recognized many phenomena that we will address as contributing to the health and maintenance of the society or the individuals in that group. In general, religious phenomena function to provide answers and explanations and to provide a course of action.

However, the functional school is not without its critics. Historians of religion, for example, argue that analyzing religion in terms of functionality implies that religion is purely illusory, existing only to fulfill those functions. For instance,

BOX 1.2 • *Malinowski and the Trobriand Islands*

Bronislaw Malinowski was born into the no-bility in Krakow, Poland, in 1884. He studied mathematics and physical sciences and received his Ph.D. from the University of Krakow in 1908. However, illness prevented him from continuing his research, and while recovering, he read the *The Golden Bough* by James Frazer, a classic anthropological work that describes magical beliefs in cultures around the world. Malinowski later wrote in 1926, "no sooner had I begun to read this great work than I became immersed in it and enslaved by it."[a] Reading this book changed his life. From then on, Malinowski devoted himself to the study of anthropology, and he traveled to England to study at the London School of Economics.

In 1914 Malinowski joined an expedition to the Pacific. He would not return to Europe until 1920 because, being an Austrian subject, he was considered to be an enemy alien by the British during World War I. However, during the war he was allowed to continue his research in the Pacific and to spend the time between expeditions in Australia. Because of these circumstances, Malinowski spent a greater amount of time conducting field research than had ever been done before. This included a total of twenty-six months spent in the Trobriand Islands, located off the coast of New Guinea.

During his stay in the Trobriand Islands, Malinowski completed the most detailed study that had been done at that time, and the Trobriand Islands remains one of the most fully described of any small-scale society. Unlike other anthropologists of his day, Malinowski participated in the life of the society he was studying. He pitched his tent in the middle of the village and learned the language. Malinowski was a pioneer of the participant observation method that became a hallmark of the field of anthropology.

Malinowski became a major figure in the development of British anthropology and influenced nearly everyone who trained in the field during the 1920s and 1930s. Among his pioneering contributions was the concept of functionalism. He thought that culture does something—that social institutions exist to fulfill the needs of, and serve the interests of, members of a society.

[a] B. Malinowski, *Magic, Science and Religion and Other Essays* (Garden City, NY: Anchor Books, 1948), p. 94.

some functionalists see religion as just a crutch for the masses or a power play by the ruling class. Instead, historians of religion emphasize a powerful and lived experience of a sacred reality.

Others argue that while the functional approach is useful, more care needs to be taken in terms of which possible functions are logically valid. For example, Melford Spiro states that when arguing that a certain function is the cause of a religious behavior, it is necessary for individuals to both recognize and seek to satisfy that functional requirement. He argues that an unintended functional consequence (recognized only by outsiders) could not possibly be its cause.

The Psychosocial Approach.   The **psychosocial approach** to the study of religion is concerned with the relationship between culture and personality and the connection between the society and the individual. One example is the work of

BOX 1.3 • *Evans-Pritchard and the Azande*

E. E. Evans-Pritchard was born in Sussex, England, in 1902. After receiving his master's degree in anthropology from Oxford University, he went on to study at the University of London, where he became one of Malinowski's first students. He conducted several field expeditions to Central, East, and North Africa from 1926 until the beginning of World War II. During the war he left teaching and research to join the military. After the war he returned to academia and ultimately held the position of Chair of Social Anthropology at Oxford University.

Evans-Pritchard is best known for his work with the Azande of southern Sudan, which was then the British colony of Anglo-Egyptian Sudan. Between 1926 and 1930 he made three different visits and spent a total of twenty months among the Azande. Following his work with the Azande, he went on to study the Nuer. He had found the Azande to be friendly, but his work with the Nuer was much more difficult. In the early days of his research in particular, they were hostile and uncommunicative, and he was frequently ill.

The Azande are known today as the classic anthropological example of witchcraft in a small-scale society. Evans-Pritchard's early articles on the subject were greatly influenced by the functional perspective of his teacher, Malinowski. For example, Evans-Pritchard believed that witchcraft beliefs provided explanations for events and helped to uphold moral standards (see Chapter 9). Ultimately, however, he was not satisfied with this type of explanation alone. He emphasized the importance of looking at beliefs and behaviors from an insider perspective and wanted to show how even seemingly irrational beliefs were in fact logical and coherent from the insider perspective.

Sigmund Freud. Freud's model of the mind and his concept of defense mechanisms have been used both by Freud himself and by his followers to explain religious phenomena. For example, defense mechanisms are psychological maneuvers by which we distort reality in ways that help us to avoid conflict and reduce anxiety. The most important of these for our discussion is projection, in which the subject is transposed and the emotion is projected. So "I hate X" becomes "You hate X." Psychosocial anthropologists believe that individual emotions also get projected at the cultural level.

The best example of this is studies that look cross-culturally for correlations between various beliefs and behaviors. One example of this approach uses this methodology to hypothesize a connection between the characteristics of parents and the characteristics of supernatural beings. Childhood experiences are dominated by powerful figures—parents. Children build up parental images that stay with them throughout life. In adult life these parental images are projected onto spirit beings. For example, if parents are generally nurturing, the expectation is that the gods would be considered to be nurturing as well. However, correlation does not equal causation, and this and several other issues challenge the correlational approach.

More recent work using the psychosocial approach has addressed the issue of how the individual uses cultural materials to express his or her own experiences. For example, Gananath Obeyesekere, in his book *Medusa's Hair,* looks at how female ascetics in Sri Lanka choose and manipulate the symbol of matted hair.[11] Obeyesekere feels that although the symbol conveys a public message, it also becomes a personal symbol, created anew by each individual. The public meaning of the symbol, while not unrelated, may be different from the personal meaning the symbol has for the person expressing it. For example, Obeyesekere found that most people reacted to the matted hair with fear and revulsion, but this was certainly not true for the women themselves. To understand the meaning the symbol had for the ascetics, he examined their life histories and found common elements that were related to the origin of their matted locks. These elements involved the emotional and sexual relationship the woman had with her husband, later replaced by a relationship with a god, symbolized by the gift of the matted locks.

Combining the Psychosocial and Functional Approaches. The work of Melford Spiro is a good example of how these theoretical approaches can be combined. Spiro's work is both psychosocial and functional. Spiro says that religion satisfies both psychological and sociological functions. From a psychological perspective three kinds of desires are satisfied by religious beliefs and behavior: cognitive, substantive, and expressive. Cognitive desires include the desire to find meaning in life, to know and to understand the world around us. Religion functions to answer questions and provide meaning.

Substantive desires involve the attempt to overcome difficult life situations, be they economic, political, physical, or other. Examples would include the desire for rainfall during drought, for victory over an enemy during warfare, for health during an illness, or to go to heaven after death. An example that Spiro uses is Hopi rain rituals. One analysis of these rituals is that they serve the function of social integration (and do not actually *cause* rain to fall). Spiro points out that this is a real but only latent function. For the Hopi the function of these rituals is to make it rain, a manifest but apparent function.

The last category, expressive desires, is the one that is most based on psychoanalytic theory. Spiro describes these as "painful drives which seek reduction and painful motives which seek satisfaction."[12] The "painful drives" refers to those described by classic psychoanalytic theory—such as fear of destruction and castration anxiety. Spiro describes these as "infantile and primitive fears which threaten to overpower the weak and defenseless ego of the young child."[13] The "painful motives" refers to the conflict between personal desires and cultural rules, for example, when the individual desires to act in aggressive, sexual, or dependent ways that are forbidden by society. Religion can function to handle or express these issues.

Spiro thinks that two motives may be universal in this context: satisfying forbidden dependency needs and expressing repressed aggression. The dependency needs are satisfied in religion by a dependency on "superhuman beings." The aggression can be expressed in rituals surrounding malevolent beings.

The Universality of Religion

Religion endures, and according to our definition, religion is universal. Explaining the universality of religion has been a major area of inquiry in anthropology and other disciplines.

Some theorists have focused on the workings of the human brain for an explanation of religious beliefs and experiences, especially in the study of human cognition. **Cognition** is a general term for processes of the human brain, including perception, attention, learning, memory, concept formation, and problem solving. It is the way in which humans recognize, interpret, reason, and know. For example, humans seek patterns even in randomness. Consider random stucco ceilings or cloud formations in which we see faces and other figures. People often see causes in what are in actuality coincidences and random events. Also researchers note the tendency of the human brain to see the world in terms of binary opposites—such as black and white—even in the stories we tell, a phenomenon we will return to in Chapter 2.

More recent research on the universality of religion has expanded this interest in the effects of human cognition into the realm of neurobiology. The suggestion has been made that the universality of spiritual experiences may be grounded in a shared human biology. Research in this area has included doing CAT scans of Buddhist monks in deep meditation and Catholic nuns in prayer.

On the basis of these studies of the brain of individuals in the midst of a religious experience, researchers have designated a part of the temporal lobe of the brain as the **God module.** The investigators hypothesize that this module affects how intensely a person responds to religious stimuli. The location of the module was first suggested during a study of people with temporal lobe epilepsy. People suffering from this type of seizure reported that their attacks were associated with an intense spiritual experience. They also tended to be preoccupied with religious thoughts between seizures. The idea is that all human brains have the God module but that in those people with this form of temporal lobe epilepsy the region is overstimulated. The neurobiology of religion is an interesting new field of inquiry and fits well with anthropology's emphasis on holism. We will return to this research in Chapter 5, in which we discuss altered states of consciousness.

These various explanations for the universality of religion have often been used to explain its origin. With the emerging interest in biology and religion, new explanations for the origin of religion have been proposed that look at the question from the perspective of biological evolution. If humans have a biological mechanism for religion, why did it evolve?

Evolutionary explanations are actually not all that different from the functional, needs-fulfillment explanations we discussed earlier. For example, evolutionary scientists have suggested that religion evolved as a way to fulfill social needs such as encouraging cooperation between individuals, reinforcing kinship ties, and imposing order and stability on society. Others have focused on emotional needs and have argued that as humans became more intelligent and self-aware, anxiety would have been a natural response. Once we are aware that we exist, we become aware that we will die and therefore begin to worry about dying. The argument is that the evolution of greater awareness and consciousness would create a dys-functional, anxiety-ridden species if religion had not evolved as an adaptation to cope with this by providing explanations of and meanings for both life and death.

Others have argued that religion is based on the way in which human cognition has evolved. These theorists view the brain as a machine that operates according to rules that have developed through evolutionary processes. An example of this approach is the work of Pascal Boyer. He points out that although religious concepts do violate some expectations about the world, they preserve other expectations. He focuses in particular on the social nature of human beings and the inferences that the human brain draws that regulate social interaction.

For example, Boyer points out that gods and other supernatural agents are seen as being very humanlike in cultures around the world. However, there are crucial differences. Boyer defines gods as "full-access strategic agents" in that they, unlike humans, have access to all the possible "strategic information." He defines *strategic information* as information that is relevant to the issue at hand in a social interaction.

He points out that gods are rarely omniscient cross-culturally. For example, the idea that "God knows you are lying" seems more natural than "God knows the content of every refrigerator in the world"—unless in your refrigerator is something that you stole. The main point of Boyer's discussion is that supernatural concepts are just extensions of everyday cognitive categories and the way in which the human brain processes information. As he writes, "People do not invent gods and spirits; they receive information that leads them to build such concepts."[14]

Conclusion

As we have seen in our discussion of the definition of religion and different approaches to the study of religion, ethnocentrism can be and has been a major impediment to developing a true understanding of religious beliefs and practices in other societies. The goal of anthropology is to move past ethnocentrism toward an approach of cultural relativism. This is especially true in the study of religion. The anthropological approach—and the central way of looking at the religious world in this book—is to study what people believe and do in regards to a sacred supernatural, not to judge whether these beliefs and actions are based in an objective truth or not. The anthropological study of religion calls for a methodological agnosticism.

Although **agnosticism** has taken on the connotation of not having made up one's mind, the original meaning of the word is different. Agnostics say that the nature of the supernatural is unknowable, that it is as impossible to prove the nonexistence of the supernatural as it is to prove its existence. In this book we will be seeking neither to prove nor to disprove but merely to observe. In the words of the philosopher Baruch Spinoza, who wrote in the seventeenth century, "I have made a ceaseless effort not to ridicule, not to bewail, not to scorn human actions, but to understand them."

Summary

Anthropology is the study of humanity. Anthropologists study human societies as integrated wholes, an approach that is termed holism. This approach is seen in the broad scope of anthropology, which is often divided into the fields of physical anthropology, archaeology, linguistics, and cultural anthropology. This approach requires that societies be studied over long periods of time, during which the investigator lives within the community and participates in the lives of the people under study, a technique known as participant observation. The final product is an ethnography, a descriptive study of a human society.

An outside observer of a community usually imposes his or her system of analysis on the group under study (etic analysis). It is natural to use one's own society as the basis for interpreting and judging other societies, a tendency called ethnocentrism. Many anthropologists attempt to see the world through the eyes of the people being studied (emic analysis) and describe and understand people's customs and ideas but do not judge them, an approach called cultural relativism. The goal is to study what people believe, not whether or not what they believe is true.

A central concept in anthropology is culture. In 1871 Tylor wrote, "Culture . . . is that complex whole, which includes knowledge, belief, art, morals, law, customs, and any other capabilities and habits acquired by man as a member of society." Culture includes all aspects of the human experience that are passed down from generation to generation. Culture gives meaning to reality; we live in a real, physical world, but our minds interpret this world through a cultural lens and even create new realities.

Religion is a difficult concept to define when we try to be inclusive of all human societies. We can list some approaches to a definition. An operant definition is one in which we define our terms so that they are observable and measurable and therefore can be studied. An analytic definition focuses on the way in which religion manifests itself or is expressed in a culture. A functional definition is concerned with the role that religion plays in a society. Finally, an essentialist definition looks at what the essential nature of religion is and emphasizes the fact that religion is the domain of the extraordinary.

There have been many theoretical approaches to the study of religion. The evolutionary approach, developed in the late 1800s, focused on the questions of when and how religions began and how they evolved from the simple to the complex. This evolution was seen as a natural consequence of human nature, and the religions of "primitive" peoples were remnants of an earlier, simpler evolutionary stage. Early religions included animism, the belief in spirits and ghosts, and animatism, the belief in a generalized supernatural force.

The functional approach asks the question: What does religion do? For example, Malinowski concluded that magic functions to provide control and certainty in an otherwise uncertain situation. The psychosocial approach is concerned with the relationship between culture and personality and the connection between the society and the individual.

Suggested Readings

Pascal Boyer, *Religion Explained: The Evolutionary Origins of Religious Thought* (New York: Basic Books, 2001).

William Paden, *Interpreting the Sacred: Ways of Viewing Religion* (Boston: Beacon Press, 1992). [An overview of theoretical approaches to religion.]

Carl Sagan, *The Demon Haunted World: Science as a Candle in the Dark* (New York: Ballantine Books, 1996). [A skeptical look at supernatural beliefs and phenomena.]

Suggested Web Sites

www.aaanet.org/
Web site of the American Anthropological Association.

www.uwgb.edu/sar/index.htm
The Society for the Anthropology of Religion of the American Anthropological Association.

www.religioustolerance.org/
Ontario Consultants on Religious Tolerance.

www.wamware.com/world-religions/map.htm
Map of religions in the world.

www.religioustolerance.org/rel_basic.htm
Links to various sources of religious data.

Study Questions

1. How does one go about conducting a holistic study of a society? How would this be different from a study on a specific topic?

2. We can examine human societies from an etic or an emic viewpoint. Do you think it is possible to really understand a society other than your own from an emic viewpoint?

3. How would you balance cultural relativism and universal human rights? Do you think that you could remain neutral in your judgment of all of the behaviors you might see in a small-scale society?

4. What is the basic difference between a society and a culture? Can these two terms be used interchangeably?

5. Think back to a ritual that you have attended—a wedding ceremony, for example. Write three brief descriptions from each of the following viewpoints: analytic, functional, and essentialist.

6. One of the major debates in studies of human behavior is that between nature (biology) and nurture (culture). Do you think that there is any biological basis for the development of religion in human societies? Do you think that someday someone might discover a society that has no religious practices?

7. Some scholars have argued that religion is not definable in any real sense. Ludwig Wittgenstein wrote: "We sometimes demand definitions for the sake not of their content, but of their form. Our requirement is an architectural one; the definition a kind of ornamental coping that supports nothing."[15] Discuss.

Endnotes

1. Note that we are using the ethnographic present in describing these cultures. Members of the California tribes no longer gather and process acorns, and their way of life is very similar to non–Native American peoples among whom they live.

2. *Sick Societies: Challenging the Myth of Primitive Harmony* by Robert B. Edgerton. Copyright © 1992 by Robert B. Edgerton. Reprinted with permission of The Free Press, a Division of Simon & Schuster Trade Publishing Group, p. 45.

3. Ibid., p. 93.

4. E. B. Tylor, *Primitive Culture: Researches into the Development of Mythology, Philosophy, Religion, Language, Art and Custom* (London: J. Murray, 1871), p. 1.

5. All Bible quotations in this text are taken from *The King James Bible.*

6. S. Renshaw and S. Ihara, "*Yowatashi Boshi;* Stars That Pass in the Night: Japan's Cultural Heritage Reflected in the Star Lore of Orion," *Griffith Observer,* 63 (October, 1999), pp. 2–17.

7. N. Smart, *Worldviews: Crosscultural Explorations of Human Beliefs,* Third Edition (Upper Saddle River, NJ: Prentice Hall, 1999), pp. 8–10.

8. M. E. Spiro, "Religion: Problems of Definitions and Explanations," in M. Banton (ed.), *Anthropological Approaches to the Study of Religion* (London: Tavistock Publications, 1966), p. 96.

9. W. C. Smith et al., *The Meaning and End of Religion* (San Francisco: Harper, 1978).

10. E. B. Taylor, op. cit.

11. G. Obeyesekere, *Medusa's Hair: An Essay on Personal Symbols and Religious Experience* (Chicago: University of Chicago Press, 1981).

12. M. E. Spiro, op. cit., pp. 114–115.

13. Ibid.

14. P. Boyer, *Religion Explained: The Evolutionary Origins of Religious Thought* (New York: Basic Books, 2001), p. 161.

15. L. Wittgenstein, *Philosophical Investigations,* trans. G. E. M. Anscombe (Oxford, England: Blackwell, 1953), #217.

2

Mythology

A good place to begin our study of religion is by looking at **myths.** Myths are religious narratives or stories that provide the basis for religious beliefs and practices. Myths tell of the origins and history of the world and the creation of the first human beings. They also prescribe the rules of proper conduct and articulate the ethical and moral principles of society. Some myths exist as written texts, while in nonliterate societies they exist as oral narratives. Religious stories also can be told in art, music, and dance. In this chapter we will discuss the nature of myths and provide several examples of myths from various religious systems.

The Nature of Myths

As we learned in Chapter 1, the lives and experiences of a people are seen through a cultural lens that imposes meaning on their world. Within this world all people have a body of knowledge within which many things are understood and controlled. However, all people also experience things that they cannot understand and cannot control. They ponder the origin of their world. They seek to understand the interconnectedness between humanity and the world around them, including the physical landscape, the plants and animals that dwell in this landscape, and other human beings and other societies. And they question the existence and meaning of disaster, illness, and death.

Worldview

The way in which societies perceive and interpret their reality is known as their **worldview.** Their worldview provides them with an understanding of how their world works; it forms the template for thought and behavior; and it provides them with a basic understanding of the origin and nature of humankind and their relationship to the world about them.

To better understand the concept of worldview, we can compare the worldview of two cultures, Navaho and Euro-American. The Navaho today is the largest Native American group in the United States. They occupy a large reservation in Arizona and New Mexico, although today many Navaho have left the reservation and live elsewhere.

The Navaho see their world in terms of the relationships and connections that bind the various elements that make up the world. All of these elements—the land, the plants, the animals, people, and the gods—are bound together into a system wherein all elements affect all other elements. Nature exists. Humans are a part of nature. For the universe to function, people must behave properly as defined by Navaho culture. Failure to behave properly brings about disharmony in the universe, and this disharmony can lead to natural disaster, illness, and even death. The goal of a Navaho is to remain in harmony with the universe or, as they like to put it, to "walk in beauty."

Tony Hillerman is a Euro-American author who writes murder mysteries that are set on the Navaho reservation and are solved by members of the Navaho Tribal Police. Although not a Navaho, Hillerman has a deep understanding and appreciation of the Navaho worldview. The following is an excerpt from his book *Dance Hall of the Dead:*[1]

> It had been Nashibitti who had taught Leaphorn the words and legends of the Blessing Way, taught him what the Holy People had told the Earth Surface People about how to live, taught him the lessons of the Changing Woman—that the only goal for man was beauty, and that beauty was found only in harmony, and that this harmony of nature was a matter of dazzling complexity.
>
> "When the dung beetle moves," Hosteen Nashibitti had told him, "know that something has moved it. And know that its movement affects the flight of the sparrow, and that the raven deflects the eagle from the sky, and that the eagle's still wing bends the will of the Wind People, and know that all of this affects you and me, and the flea on the prairie dog and the leaf on the cottonwood." That had always been the point of the lesson. Interdependency of nature. Every cause has its effect. Every action its reaction. A reason for everything. In all things a pattern, and in this pattern, the beauty of harmony. Thus one learned to live with evil, by understanding it, by reading its cause. And thus one learned, gradually and methodically, if one was lucky, to always "go in beauty," to always look for the pattern, and to find it.

Whereas Navaho culture sees humans as one cog in the natural world, Euro-Americans see their world quite differently. Here humans occupy a very special place in the universe. After all, were not humans made in the image of God? The following is from the Eighth Psalm:

> What is man, that thou art mindful of him? and the son of man, that thou visitest him?
>
> For thou hast made him a little lower than the angels, and hast crowned him with glory and honor.
>
> Thou makest him to have dominion of the works of thy hands; thou hast put all things under his feet;
>
> All sheep and oxen, yea, and the beasts of the field;
>
> The fowls of the air and the fishes of the sea, and whatsoever passeth through the paths of the seas.

It is clear here that the world was created for the benefit of humankind and that humankind has the authority, the right, to exploit the natural world. This active relationship with nature is seen in attempts to control nature—through dams and irrigation projects, for example. Whereas the Navaho sees illness as a manifestation of disharmony and attempts to bring resolution of the illness through ritual designed to reestablish harmony, the Euro-American seeks the empirical cause and then, through medical technology, proceeds to "fix it."

Stories of the Supernatural

People describe their world and express their worldview in stories and other creative expresssions. This includes modes as diverse as art, drama, jokes, writing on the walls of public bathrooms, folk music, and festivals. Here we will focus on stories that are told about the supernatural world.

The following is a story that is European in origin and was first published in 1823, written down from oral presentations. It has been told and retold countless times and is probably familiar to the reader in some form. It is the story of *Snow White*.

> The story of *Snow White* involves an evil queen who flies into a jealous rage whenever she learns that someone in the kingdom is more beautiful than she. She keeps tabs on her status in the beauty arena by using a talking mirror. This is a type of divination instrument (see Chapter 6) that can be used to gather information about things and events in ways that are supernatural. (Certainly, one would have to agree that talking mirrors do not exist in our empirical, rational world.)
>
> Snow White is the evil queen's stepdaughter. As Snow White matures she eventually becomes more beautiful than the queen, who sees Snow White as a threat that must be eliminated. The queen orders Snow White killed, but the huntsman who is ordered to do the killing takes pity on Snow White and lets her escape into the forest. The huntsman then kills a wild boar and presents its lungs and heart to the queen as being Snow White's. The evil queen then cooks and eats the lungs and heart, thinking them to be those of her dead stepdaughter. This is an example of ritual cannibalism. Perhaps the queen believes that by eating the remains of her rival, the elements of beauty in Snow White will pass to her.[2]
>
> Thus Snow White escapes and moves in with seven dwarfs. The evil queen, learning through her magic mirror that Snow White is still alive, finally kills her with a poison apple. After many years Snow White is discovered by a prince who, on kissing her, brings her back to life.

When we read the story of Snow White, it is clear that this is a story that is told for entertainment, primarily for children. However, like many such stories, it also provides a moral lesson. In this case we are told of the evils of envy and jealousy and what can happen to someone who exhibits these attributes. (In one early version of the story the evil queen is invited to the wedding celebration of Snow White and the Prince. Her evil deeds are revealed and she is made to put on a pair of red-hot iron slippers. She dances until she dies.)

Yet although this story talks about moral issues and contains many supernatural elements (the magic mirror, for example), no one would classify it as a religious story. The dwarfs are not sacred, the mirror is not holy, and the awakening of the beautiful maiden does not elevate her to the status of deity. The story does not tell of the actions of any gods; it is not the basis for religious rituals; there are no churches or temples dedicated to Snow White.

Myths

In contrast, myths are sacred stories. They tell of the origin of the world and humankind, the existence and activities of gods and spirits, the origin of human traditions, and the nature of illness and death. They tell how to behave and how to distinguish good from evil. Myths are thought by the people who tell them to recount real, historical events that took place in the remote past.

Although anthropologists and folklorists use the term *myth* to refer to a religious story, the term is frequently used in a negative sense. People think of myths as false stories, stories told by primitive peoples, or untrue reports or beliefs. A statement might be dismissed as "only a myth." As religious stories, however, myths are thought to be an accounting of real people, supernatural beings, places, and events that took place in the past. Therefore in this sense the stories of the Bible are myths, as are the writings in the Qur'an.

Myths can be both written and oral. In literate societies written texts may form the basis of scholarly discourse and analysis as well as ritual. Although written, a religious text may be a platform to support its recitation or to serve as an aid to memorization. Although many texts are written, they are often meant to be recited orally.

The Nature of Oral Texts

In nonliterate societies, and in many literate societies as well, texts are recited. Recitation is much more than a simple rote presentation of the text—recitation is performance. In reciting the text, a person might speak in a manner that is not found in everyday speech. Costumes, facial expressions, body postures, changes in the quality of the voice—all serve to create an experience. In some societies we find specialists—actors and storytellers—who memorize and recite texts.

Oral narratives are frequently very long and complex. They are not always recited as a single, complete narrative and might not even be seen as a single entity. Particular segments might be recited at certain times in particular circumstances. One of the consequences of the oral transmission of stories is that they are frequently unconsciously altered with each generation. As a result of this learning process, different versions of the same myth can exist in different families or groups within a society. For example, there are several versions of the Navaho creation story. Each was collected by a different anthropologist working with a different elder. Although they have much in common, there are major differences.

Folklorist Alan Dundes points out that written texts that are derived from oral narratives frequently incorporate more than one version of a particular story.[3] For example, the Old Testament opens with two creation stories (Box 2.1).

BOX 2.1 • *Genesis*

Genesis (1:1–2:3)

In the beginning God created the heavens and the earth.

And the earth was without form and void; darkness was upon the face of the deep. And the Spirit of God moved upon the face of the waters.

And God said, Let there be light; and there was light.

And God saw that the light, that it was good: and God divided the light from the darkness.

And God called the light Day, and the darkness he called Night. And the evening and the morning were the first day.

And God said, Let there be a firmament in the midst of the waters, and let it divide the waters from the waters.

And God made the firmament, and divided the waters which were under the firmament from the waters which were above the firmament: and it was so.

And God called the firmament Heaven. And the evening and the morning were the second day.

And God said, Let the waters under the heaven be gathered together unto one place, and let the dry land appear: and it was so.

And God called the dry land Earth; and the gathering together of the waters called he Seas: and God saw that it was good.

And God said, Let the earth bring forth grass, the herb yielding seed, and the fruit tree yielding fruit after his kind, whose seed is in itself, upon the earth: and it was so.

And the earth brought forth grass, and herb, yielding seed after his kind, and the tree yielding fruit, whose seed was in itself, after his kind: and God saw that it was good.

And the evening and the morning were the third day.

And God said, Let there be lights in the firmament of the heaven to divide the day from the night; and let them be for signs, and for seasons, and for days, and years:

And let them be for lights in the firmament of the heaven to give light upon the earth: and it was so.

And God made two great lights; the greater light to rule the day, and lesser light to rule the night: he made the stars also.

And God set them in the firmament of the heaven to give light upon the earth.

And to rule over the day and over the night, and to divide the light from the darkness: and God saw that it was good.

And the evening and the morning were the fourth day.

And God said, Let the waters bring forth abundantly the moving creature that hath life, and fowl that may fly above the earth in the open firmament of heaven.

And God created great whales, and every living creature that moveth, which the waters brought forth abundantly, after their kind, and every winged fowl after his kind: and God saw that it was good.

And God blessed them, saying, Be fruitful and multiply, and fill the waters in the seas, and let fowl multiply in the earth.

And the evening and the morning were the fifth day.

And God said, Let the earth bring forth the living creature after his kind, cattle, and creeping things, and beasts of the earth after his kind: and it was so.

And God made the beast of the earth after his kind, and cattle after their kind, and every thing that creepeth upon the earth after his kind: and God saw that it was good.

And God said, Let us make man in our image, after our likeness: and let them have dominion over the fish of the sea, and over the fowl of the air, and over the cattle, and over all the earth, and over every creeping thing that creepeth upon the earth.

So God created man in his own image, in the image of God created he him; male and female created he them.

(continued)

BOX 2.1 • *Continued*

And God blessed them, and God said unto them, Be fruitful, and multiply, and replenish the earth, and subdue it: and have dominion over the fish of the sea, and over the fowl of the air, and over every living thing that moveth upon the earth.

And God said, Behold, I have given you every herb bearing seed, which is upon the face of all the earth, and every tree, in the which is the fruit of a tree yielding seed; to you it shall be for meat.

And to every beast of the earth, and to every fowl of the air, and to every thing that creepeth upon the earth, wherein there is life, I have given every green herb for meat: and it was so.

And God saw every thing that he had made, and, behold, it was very good. And the evening and the morning were the sixth day.

Thus the heavens and the earth were finished, and all the host of them.

And on the seventh day God ended his work which he had made; and he rested on the seventh day from all his work which he had made.

And God blessed the seventh day, and sanctified it: because that in it he had rested from all his work which God created and made.

Genesis (2:4–2:10, 2:15–2:23)

These are the generations of the heavens and of the earth when they were created, in the day that the Lord God made the earth and heavens.

And every plant of the field before it was in the earth, and every herb of the field before it grew: for the Lord God had not caused it to rain upon the earth, and there was not a man to till the ground.

But there went up a mist from the earth, and watered the whole face of the ground.

And the Lord God formed man of the dust of the ground, and breathed into nostrils the breath of life; and man became a living soul.

And the Lord God planted a garden eastward in Eden; and there he put the man whom he had formed.

And out of the ground made the Lord God to grow every tree that is pleasant to the sight, and good for food; the tree of life also in the midst of the garden, and the tree of knowledge of good and evil.

And a river went out of Eden to water the garden; and from thence it was parted, and became into four heads.

And the Lord God took the man, and put him into the garden of Eden to dress it and to keep it.

And the Lord God commanded the man, saying, Of every tree of the garden thou mayest freely eat:

But of the tree of the knowledge of good and evil, thou shalt not eat of it: for in the day that thou eatest thereof thou shalt surely die.

And the Lord God said, It is not good that the man should be alone; I will make him a helpmate for him.

And out of the ground the Lord God formed every beast of the field, and every fowl of the air, and brought them unto Adam to see what he would call them: and whatsoever Adam called every living creature, that was the name thereof.

And Adam gave names to all cattle, and to the fowl of the air, and to every beast of the field; but for Adam there was not found a helpmate for him.

And the Lord God caused a deep sleep to fall upon Adam, and he slept: and he took one of his ribs, and closed up the flesh instead thereof;

And the rib, which the Lord God had taken from man, made he a woman, and brought her unto the man.

And Adam said, This is now bone of my bones, and flesh of my flesh: she shall be called Woman, because she was taken out of Man.

The earlier text, Genesis 2:4 to 3:23, dates from the period of the Two Kingdoms, Israel and Judah. It might have first been written between 960 and 915 B.C.E. and contains the story of the Garden of Eden and Man's Fall. This story sets forth the order of creation as man first, then a garden for him to cultivate, next the animals for his entertainment, and finally woman from his rib.

The later text, Genesis 1:1 to 2:3, might have been written after the fall of Jerusalem in 586 B.C.E. during the Exile, but it might have been written earlier. This is the story of the seven days of creation in which the plants and animals were created before man and man and woman were created together on the sixth day.

The stories of Genesis are reflections of the Judeo-Christian worldview. They are very patriarchal in many ways. For example, woman (Eve) is derived from man (Adam). In many Western societies men dominate woman, and many positions of authority, such as the priesthood, are restricted to men. Here the religious text is acting as a **social charter** that explains the proper organization of human relationships.

Genesis also expresses the Judeo-Christian worldview with respect to nature. This worldview appears to be based on two assumptions. The first is that the universe is mechanistic and humans are its master. The second is that humans are a categorically different form of creature than all other forms of life.

How Myths Change through Time.   Written narratives that are transmitted from generation to generation tend to be very stable through time, especially if they are not translated into other languages. An example of a written text is the Qur'an, which forms the foundation of Islam. Muslims believe that the Qur'an represents the word of God as revealed to Mohammad by the archangel Gabriel in the early seventh century. It was spoken to Mohammad and was initially handed down orally but was soon set down in written form. As the spoken word of God, verses from the Qur'an are recited and memorized by devout Muslims. Because the Qur'an was revealed to Mohammad in Arabic, it is learned and memorized in Arabic throughout the Islamic world. (Of course, translations of the Qur'an do exist, but they are not used in ritual. Commentaries on the Qur'an are made in the local language.) Because printing presses produce millions of copies of this text, all identical in content, the exact text not only is found throughout the world, but also is transmitted unchanged generation after generation. For Muslims this lack of change is particularly important. Muslims believe that the true text exists in heaven and was given to Mohammad through revelations, which he memorized perfectly word for word. Thus the Qur'an (the word actually means "recitation") represents a perfect transcription of God's vision and should not change.

Of course, language does change, and written religious texts that do not change will, over time, appear to use words and phrases that are no longer a part of the spoken language. Written texts are often written in a "religious" form of a language, using words and phrases that are not used in everyday speech. Some societies even have distinctive dialects or languages that are reserved for recitation of religious narratives. These dialects are frequently derived from archaic forms of the language as it was spoken in the past. For example, consider the following excerpt from the Eighth Psalm: "When I consider thy heavens, the work of thy fingers, the moon and the stars, which thou hast ordained; what is man, that thou art mindful of him?" Forms such as *thy, hast,* and *thou,* were once commonly used words in English, but no longer. Today their presence in a narrative often labels that narrative as being religious.

Changes do occur in written texts, but they are usually deliberate changes that are the consequences of translation or scholarly discourse over the meaning of particular words and passages. In some religious traditions, such as Christianity, the text—in this case, the Bible—is usually found in a translated form to be read by any literate member of the community. This was not always true. It was in the Middle Ages (roughly 500 to 1500 C.E.) that Catholicism as we know it today truly emerged. In the absence of a strong central government that followed the collapse of the Roman Empire, the Church became both a religious and a secular power. During this time the Church was seen as the intermediary between humankind and God—God's message for people came to them through the Church. The official Church language was Latin, which was not the spoken vernacular language of the people. As a result most people did not understand church services. Very few people were literate, and the Bible was available only in Latin. This was not seen as a problem, because the Church existed to interpret God's word. Later, the Protestant Reformation would emphasize the Bible, and not the Church, as the source for true Christianity. Among the central beliefs of Martin Luther, who began the Reformation, was that laypeople should read the Bible for themselves. This meant not only that everyone needed to learn to read, but also that the Bible had to be translated into the local languages.

Perhaps one of the most famous translations of the Bible was that ordered by King James I of England and published in 1611. The King James Bible is still widely used today. Many Bible scholars, however, note what they consider to be inaccurate translations of certain words and passages, resulting from the knowledge and political atmosphere of the seventeenth century. Also, the King James Version is written in what is now an older form of English.

Many modern versions of the Bible exist today. These are attempts to create what are considered to be more accurate translations of the earliest extant versions of the Bible, written in modern language that is easier to read and understand by people today. Yet many people are uncomfortable with modern translations and retain the King James Version because it sounds more "religious." This resembles the special religious language forms reserved for religious narrative that are found in many societies. Interestingly, there are versions of the King James Bible that attempt to modernize the language yet retain the use of religious linguistic forms. (See Box 2.2 for a discussion of gender-neutral translations of the Bible.)

Wogeo Narratives

As an example of narratives in a nonliterate society, we can look at the Wogeo, who inhabit a small island off the north coast of New Guinea (Melanesia culture area).

BOX 2.2 • *The Gender-Neutral Christian Bible*

In the late 1990s Zondervan, the world's largest publisher of Bibles, announced that it was going to publish a translation of the New Testament that used gender-neutral language (*Today's New International Version*). Although this was not the first translation of the Bible to attempt to use gender-neutral language, it was notable because the company's original *New International Version* is second in sales only to the *King James Version*, which is very similar to its original 1611 version. The *New International Version* is also a translation that is popular with evangelical Christians. The reaction to the proposed new version was immediate. Many Christians, including James Dobson and Pat Robertson, spoke out about the changes, some of which they thought changed the meaning of the scriptures.

The impetus behind gender-neutral translations is the idea that language is not inconsequential but in fact both reflects and shapes the way we think about the world. According to this view, for example, use of the masculine generic in the Bible (e.g., saying "man" to mean all people) unnecessarily excludes women. Changing such language is seen as a step toward changing people's beliefs and behaviors and achieving gender equality.

The changes made in today's *New International Version* were made only in regard to human beings. Some critics thought that the changes did not go far enough because God is still referred to as masculine (e.g., Father) and neutral terms (e.g., parent) were not used.

Examples of language that was changed in other translations includes replacing references to "he," "man," and "son" with more neutral terms such as "they," "humankind," and "children." Other gender-neutral versions include changes such as calling Eve the "partner" of Adam instead of his "helper."

Proponents of this approach say that the Bible reflects outdated gender roles and ideology and the patriarchal roots of Christianity. Gender-neutral translations are seen as updating the message of the Bible for a different time. However, critics of the gender-neutral translations argue that these changes often also change the original meaning of the text and in some cases are unnecessary and go too far. For example, when comparing the *Revised Standard Version* (RSV) and *New Revised Standard Version* (NRSV), we see the following translations of John 14:23:

> Jesus answered him, "If a man loves me, he will keep my word, and my Father will love him, and we will come to him and make our home with him." (RSV)

> Those who love me will keep my word, and my Father will love them and we will come to them and make our home with them. (NRSV)

Critics argue that the new translation obscures the original meaning that Jesus and his Father would come dwell with individual believers.

Another example comes from Acts, when Cornelius fell down and began to worship Peter. In the *Revised Standard Version* Peter lifted him up and said, "Stand up; I too am a man" (Acts 10:26, RSV). In the *New Revised Standard Version* Peter says, "Stand up; I am only a mortal." Again, it is argued that this is an important shift in meaning from an emphasis on one's humanity ("I too am a man") to an emphasis on one's mortality ("I too am mortal").

In other cases critics argue that the changes are unnecessary and do not make sense—for example, making the army of Israel gender-neutral (using the term "warriors" instead of "men of war") when it is historically accurate that the army was composed only of males. Similarly, they see changing Paul's statement in Corinthians (1 Corinthians 13:11) from "When I became a man, I gave up childish ways" to "When I

(continued)

BOX 2.2 • *Continued*

became an adult" as unnecessary because Paul is in fact a man.

Obviously, there are many issues involved that shape this controversy. They include the degree to which language shapes thought and society, whether the masculine emphasis of the Bible was intended and should be preserved, and how true translations must stay to the original text. The debate is not merely about language, but also about the Christian worldview as it regards gender issues in general.

The Wogeo myths are called *nanasa*. These are religious stories that took place before recorded time. They are accepted by the Wogeo as being historical in that they are thought to recount actual events. The *nanasa* are stories of the ancestral gods, or *nanarang*. The *nanarang* created the world and the landscape, invented important material objects, and set forth customary forms of behavior. The Wogeo explain contemporary customs by referring to the stories of the *nanarang*. The *nanarang* looked and behaved as people do. They married, had children, and died. After a time they disappeared and were replaced by the Wogeo, the ancestors of the people living on the island today.

The following is an example of a Wogeo *nanasa*. This story explains the origin of places other than the island of Wogeo, which is considered to be the center of the universe. Note the reason why the *nanarang*, named Tidlap, was dismembered to create these lands. He behaved in a socially inappropriate way and suffered the consequences.[4]

> On reaching manhood, Tidlap took a girl from a village nearby as his wife. In the beginning everything went well, but he was by nature suspicious and soon accused her of infidelity. Although she protested innocence, he not only refused to listen but beat her so unmercifully that the blood flowed from the wounds. His relatives, fearing her kinsmen might take vengeance on them for failing to prevent such cruelty, decided to launch their canoes and sail away. Tidlap, now alone, became terrified and followed. But his brothers, in the interests of their own safety, killed him and dismembered the body. The trunk turned into the island of Mushu, which is low and flat, the head into the hilly island of Kairiru, the fingers into various coral reefs, and the legs into the Torricelli Mountains of the New Guinea mainland.

The Navaho Creation Story

Many scholars have studied the Navaho, and the Navaho creation story, *Diné hahanè*, is well known. *Diné hahanè* is a very complex story. It is never recited in its entirety; various sections are recited as a part of particular rituals. Several versions exist, as is typical of oral narratives.

Diné hahanè is the history of the Navaho people from the very beginnings during the time of creation. Earlier we defined the supernatural as things that are "above the natural," that are not subject to the laws of nature. In this narrative we encounter the Holy People, who are immortal, who travel on the rainbow, swiftly following the path of the sun ray, and who can control the winds and thunder.

The events in Genesis take place in a location that is remote from the reader; in fact, the locations of Eden and other landmarks are matters of debate. In many tribal myths, by contrast, the stories tell of the world that is directly around them. People can relate to their landscape, the very same landscape that exists in the narrative. In fact, the items within their landscape were created or played an important role in the stories contained within the narrative. This, of course, makes it more difficult for an outsider who is unfamiliar with the land to understand.

The Navaho landscape can be described in terms of the four points of the compass. Each point is associated with one of the four Holy People. Each has certain attributes, such as the color white, blue, yellow, or black. The Navaho can walk through the landscape referring to different parts of the narrative. However, many of the early parts of the narrative take place in layers underneath the ground; these are thought to be as real as geographical features on the surface of the earth.

Box 2.3 presents an early portion of the story that describes the creation of the first real humans by the Holy People. In this passage we see how First Man and First Woman were made from ears of corn. (Corn, cornmeal, and corn pollen play important roles in Navaho rituals.) The life force comes from the wind, which is likened to a person's breath.

BOX 2.3 • *The Navaho Creation Story: Diné Hahanè*

As for the gods, they repeated their visit four days in a row. But on the fourth day, *Bits'íís łizhin* the Black Body remained after the other three departed. And when he was alone with the onlookers, he spoke to them in their own language. This is what he said:

"You do not seem to understand the Holy People," he said.

"So I will explain what they want you to know.

"They want more people to be created in this world. But they want intelligent people, created in their likeness, not in yours.

"You have bodies like theirs, true enough.

"But you have the teeth of beasts! You have the mouths of beasts! You have the feet of beasts! You have the claws of beasts!

"The new creatures are to have hands like ours. They are to have feet like ours. They are to have mouths like ours and teeth like ours. They must learn to think ahead, as we do.

"What is more, you are unclean!

"You smell bad.

"So you are instructed to cleanse yourselves before we return twelve days from now."

That is what *Bits'íís łizhin* the Black Body said to the insect people who had

(continued)

BOX 2.3 • *Continued*

emerged from the first world to the second, from the second world to the third, and from the third world to the fourth world where they now lived.

Accordingly, on the morning of the twelfth day the people bathed carefully. The women dried themselves with yellow corn meal. The men dried themselves with white corn meal.

Soon after they had bathed, they heard the distant voice coming from far in the east.

They listened and waited as before, listened and waited. Until soon they heard the voice as before, nearer and louder this time. They continued to listen and wait, listen and wait, until they heard the voice a third time as before, all the nearer and all the louder.

Continuing to listen as before, they heard the voice again, even louder than the last time, and so close now that it seemed directly upon them, exactly as it had seemed before. And as before they found themselves standing among the same four *Haashch'ééh dine'é*, or Holy People as *Bilagáana* the White Man might wish to call them.

Bits'íís doot l'izh the Blue Body and *Bits'íís l'izhin* the Black Body each carried a sacred buckskin. *Bits'íís l'igaii* the White Body carried two ears of corn.

One ear of corn was yellow. The other ear was white. Each ear was completely covered at the end with grains, just as sacred ears of corn are covered in our own world now.

Proceeding silently, the gods laid one buckskin on the ground, careful that its head faced the west. Upon this skin they placed the two ears of corn, being just as careful that the tips of each pointed east. Over the corn they spread the other buckskin, making sure that its head faced east.

Under the white ear they put the feather of a white eagle.

And under the yellow ear they put the feather of a yellow eagle.

Then they told the onlooking people to stand at a distance.

So that the wind could enter.

Then from the east *Ni l'ch'i l'igai* the White Wind blew between the buckskins. And while the wind thus blew, each of the Holy People came and walked four times around the objects they had placed so carefully on the ground.

As they walked, the eagle feathers, whose tips protruded slightly from between the two buckskins, moved slightly.

Just slightly.

So that only those who watched carefully were able to notice.

And when the Holy People had finished walking, they lifted the topmost buckskin.

And lo! the ears of corn had disappeared.

In their place there lay a man and there lay a woman.

The white ear of corn had been transformed into our most ancient male ancestor. And the yellow ear of corn had been transformed into our most ancient female ancestor.

It was the wind that had given them life: the very wind that gives us our breath as we go about our daily affairs here in the world we ourselves live in.

When this wind ceases to blow inside of us, we become speechless. Then we die.

In the skin at the tips of our fingers we can see the trail of that life-giving wind.

Look carefully at your own fingertips. There you will see where the wind blew when it created your most ancient ancestors out of two ears of corn, it is said.

Source: P. G. Zolbrod, *Diné behané* (Albuquerque: University of New Mexico Press, 1984), pp. 49–51. Courtesy of the University of New Mexico Press.

Understanding Myths

In this section we will look at various ways of studying and understanding myths. Many different theoretical approaches to the study of myths have been used over the years, and each has something to offer in the way of increasing our understanding of the importance of religious narratives.

Approaches to Analysis of Myths

Of the different ways of analyzing religious narratives, many are based on the different theoretical approaches to the study of religion that we discussed in Chapter 1. Here we will examine the functional, structural, and psychoanalytic approaches to the study of myths.

Functional Analysis.   As we saw earlier, the functional school analyzes cultural traits in terms of the function they serve for the society. In this view myths are seen as a force to help maintain the society. Émile Durkheim, for example, focused on the impact of myth on social structure. He emphasized the role of myth as the basis for rituals and saw rituals as the means by which individuals come together and bond with one another.

Another functionalist was Bronislaw Malinowski, who wrote:[5]

> Myth fulfills in primitive cultures an indispensable function; it expresses, enhances, and codifies belief; it safeguards and enforces morality; it vouches for the efficacy of ritual and contains practical rules for the guidance of man. Myth is thus a vital ingredient of human civilization; it is not an idle tale, but a hard-worked active force; it is not an intellectual explanation or an artistic imagery, but a pragmatic charter of primitive faith and wisdom.

However, critics of this approach point out that myth is always selective in the features that it chooses to emphasize. Myths also can often be divisive, such as when there are different, competing versions of a story.

Structural Analysis.   A second approach is structural analysis, which, as it sounds, focuses on the underlying structure of the myth. This approach is based on the work of Claude Lévi-Strauss, who pointed out that humans tend to think and categorize the world in terms of binary opposites, such as black and white. This same division of the world into binary opposites can be seen cross-culturally in myths. One example of this approach is the analysis done by Edmund Leach of the structure of the story of Genesis.[6] Examples of the binary opposites contained in Genesis are light/dark, day/night, heaven/earth, man/animal, and man/woman. Leach also points out that these opposites are frequently mediated by a third, anomalous category, such as life and death being mediated by the third category of eternal life as found in Paradise.

In the following portion of Genesis, the binary oppositions of light and dark and heaven and earth are established (Genesis 1:4–8):

And God saw that the light, that it was good: and God divided the light from the darkness.

And God called the light Day, and the darkness he called Night. And the evening and the morning were the first day.

And God said, Let there be a firmament in the midst of the waters, and let it divide the waters from the waters.

And God made the firmament, and divided the waters which were under the firmament from the waters which were above the firmament: and it was so.

And God called the firmament Heaven. And the evening and the morning were the second day.

Structural analysis focuses on the structure, not the content, of religious narratives. It demonstrates that stories that seem very different on the surface may have a similar underlying structure. We can also apply structural analysis to a story from the Gururumba of New Guinea (Melanesia culture area). The primary binary opposition in Gururumba culture is that of nature and culture. We can see this opposition being expressed in several ways in the Gururumba myth of the origin of women, told in Box 2.4.

From this story we can see that the nature versus culture dichotomy is related to the differences between the sexes. Women are seen as being nature, and men are seen as being associated with culture. That women are clearly associated with nature can be seen in the origin of the first woman from an egg and that she reverts to various animal forms when she is being pursued. The wild female is culturally transformed only through human (male) agency. The sugarcane is a symbolically male plant and is used to change the biologically unuseful woman into a culturally useful wife. Her son is the first male born of female and thus is not fully cultural, as can be seen when he turns into a fish. He is not a complete adult, both biologically and socially, until his final transformation in the men's house. The boy himself then becomes a transformer, changing his sisters into wives and other men into social allies.

Critics of structuralism argue that it is a very sterile approach to the study of religious narrative and that is ultimately dehumanizing. Structural analysis can also be very complicated, leaving mythical analysis only to those who are well versed in this approach.

Psychoanalytic Analysis. A third approach is psychoanalytic in nature. Freud saw individual dreams as symbolically expressing unconscious wishes and a similar process occurring with myths for groups. Myths are therefore a type of shared dream. Much of his analysis is sexual in nature. For example, the story of Little Red Riding Hood is seen as the story of a girl who has become sexually mature, the red cape representing menses, but is still a virgin, symbolized by her carrying an unbroken wine bottle. She meets a wolf/man in the forest, the trees being seen as phallic symbols, and later the wolf eats her, representing aggressive intercourse.

BOX 2.4 • *The Gururumba Creation Story*

The story begins in the distant past when things were not as they are today. There were no villages, no pigs, and no women. One day two brothers go into the forest to look for food. They come upon an eagle's nest in which they find eggs and food that the eagle parents have left. The brothers take the food for themselves. They return several times to do this until one time when one of the eggs hatches and the first woman emerges. The boys take the woman back to their home and feed her and she grows up.

Then one day the younger brother decides to try to have sex with the woman. However, he is unable to do so because she does not have a vagina. He asks his older brother what to do. His older brother takes a sugarcane (a symbolically male plant for the Gururumba) and hurls it at the woman to make an opening, but she runs away. The younger brother chases her, but every time he catches on to her arm or leg she turns into an animal and slips away. Finally he is able to

catch hold of her thumb and have sex with her.

The woman gives birth to a son and several daughters. Later when the son is grown he asks his father if he can accompany him into the forest, but the father says no. The boy becomes very upset and jumps into the river and becomes a fish. The father does not know what to do but the brothers see smoke coming from the forest (which means a wise old man lives there). This man comes and uses magic to change the fish back into a boy. The father is so happy that he builds the first men's house and puts his son inside to make him a man. When the son emerges from the men's house, pigs spring from the ground. The boy later notices smoke coming from the grasslands and realizes that there are other men out there who have no women and no pigs. So he gives each of his sisters a pig and sends them to the other men, beginning an exchange relationship.

Source: As told by Philip Newman, lecture in the Anthropology of Religion at the University of California at Los Angeles, 1990.

The narrative that the psychoanalytic approach is most associated with is the story of Oedipus, the Greek tragic hero who unknowingly kills his father and marries his mother. Freud argued that this story represented a deep psychological conflict experienced by all boys. Because Freud believed that these were universal developmental issues, he would have expected a similar story to be found cross-culturally. In fact, Allen Johnson and Douglas Price-Williams in their research have found Oedipus-type stories from cultures around the world.[7]

Similar to Freud in its emphasis on human psychological processes is the approach of Carl Jung. In contrast to Freud, Jung thought that myths stemmed from something beyond the individual unconscious. Just as individuals have an unconscious mind, Jung believed that humans as a group share a **collective unconscious,** or inborn elements of the unconscious that are manifested in dreams and myths. The main characters of the collective unconscious are termed **archetypes.** The Oedipus story is just one example of an archetype. Examples of archetypal characters that have been suggested include the figures of the Trickster, the Hero, the Orphan, the Seeker, the Destroyer, the Creator, the Sage, and the Fool. Another example is the Phoenix. The name of the phoenix archetype is taken from the Greek story of the bird that rises from its own ashes. The phoenix is a story of rebirth. A familiar telling of the phoenix archetype is the Christian story of the death and rebirth of Jesus Christ.

Common Themes in Myths

As we can see from the preceding discussion, underlying the diversity of narratives found cross-culturally are some common elements and themes. These similarities have been explained in various ways. Diffusion, or the spread of cultural traits from one group to another, is always a possible explanation. Others focus on the shared nature of human cognition and psychology. The ideas of Freud and Jung are good examples of this approach, although Freud saw the similarities stemming from shared individual experiences, while Jung focused on a universally shared collective unconscious. In this section we will explore some of the common stories that are found in religious narratives around the world.

Origin Myths.   Origin myths answer some of the most basic questions that humans have: Who are we? Why are we here? What is our relationship to the world? As we saw in our discussion of the Judeo-Christian and Navaho origin stories, these stories play an important role in laying out the culture's worldview. Origin stories address the most basic questions of identity, both personal and communal. Creation myths are generally the most sacred of the religious narratives. All other narratives ultimately build on the groundwork laid down in origin myths.

A common element in origin stories is the birth metaphor. When the supernatural power doing the creating is female, this is generally a spontaneous and independent birth. When the supernatural power is male, the birth is more symbolic: The god vomits or excretes the world or perhaps sacrifices part of his own body to make the world. In the following origin story from the Bushongo, a Bantu people from Zaire (Guinea Coast culture area), the male deity vomits the world.[8]

> In the beginning, in the dark, there was nothing but water. And Bumba was alone. One day Bumba was in terrible pain. He retched and strained and vomited up the sun. After that light spread over everything. The heat of the sun dried up the water until the black edges of the world began to show. Black sandbanks and reefs could be seen. But there were no living things. Bumba vomited up the moon and then the stars, and after that the night had its own light also. Still Bumba was in pain. He strained again and nine living creatures came forth [a leopard, crested eagle, crocodile, fish, tortoise, lightning, white heron, beetle, and a goat]. Last of all came forth men.

Many origin myths begin with creation out of chaos, darkness or the void. The following story is from the Yoruba, a society in West Africa (Guinea Coast culture area).[9]

> In the beginning the world was a watery, formless Chaos that was neither sea nor land, but a marshy waste. Above it, in the sky, lived the Supreme Being, Olorun,

attended to by other gods, including Orisha Nla, called the Great God. Olorun called Orisha Nla into his presence and ordered him to make a world. It was time to make a solid land and Orisha Nla was given a snail full of magic earth, a pigeon, and a five-toed hen to accomplish the assignment. Orisha Nla came down to the Chaos and set to work organizing it. He threw magic earth into a small patch. The pigeon and the hen began to scratch in the magic earth, and they scratched until land and sea were entirely separated. . . . Orisha Nla was sent back to earth to plant trees, including the first oil palm. Olorun made the rain fall from heaven to water the seeds, which grew into a great forest. In heaven, Olorun began to make the first people. They were fashioned from earth by Orisha Nla, but only Olorun, the Supreme Being, could give them life. Orisha Nla hid in Olorun's workshop to watch. However, Olorun knew that Orisha Nla was hiding there and put him into a deep sleep, and so only Olorun knows the secret of how to bring a body to life. To this day Orisha Nla, through the agency of parents, makes the body, but only the Supreme Being can give it life.

Because of the process of diffusion, certain culture areas share narrative elements in common. One example of this is the primordial egg as an element of creation stories in Asia. One Chinese origin story says:[10]

At first there was nothing. Time passed and nothing became something. Time passed and something split into two: the two were male and female. These two produced two more, and these two produced P'an Ku, the first being, the Great Man, the Creator. First there was the great cosmic egg. Inside the egg was Chaos, and floating in Chaos was P'an Ku, the Undeveloped, the divine Embryo. And P'an Ku burst out of the egg, four times larger than any man today, with an adze (or a hammer and chisel) with which he fashioned the world.

Flood Myths. Stories of a flood are also widespread. A disciple of Freud's once explained this as being related to dreams that happen when the person has a full bladder. An alternative explanation lies in the fact that floods are likely to be frequently experienced, as people need to live near a water source. The Judeo-Christian flood myth is the story of Noah's ark in which God sends the flood to rid the earth of the wickedness of man. Parallels can be seen in the following story from the ancient Aztecs of Mexico.[11]

During the era of the fourth sun, the Sun of Water, the people grew very wicked and ignored the worship of the gods. The gods became angry and Tlaloc, the god of rains, announced that he was going to destroy the world with a flood. However, Tlaloc was fond of a devout couple, Tata and Nena, and he warned them of the flood. He instructed them to hollow out a great log and take two ears of corn—one for each of them—and eat nothing more.

So Tata and Nena entered the tree trunk with the two ears of corn, and it began to rain. When the rains subsided and Tata and Nena's log landed on dry land, they were so happy that they caught a fish and ate it, contrary to the orders of Tlaloc. It was only after their stomachs were full that they remembered Tlaloc's command.

Tlaloc then appeared to them and said, "This is how I am repaid for saving your lives?" They were then changed into dogs. It was at this point, where even the most righteous people were disobedient, that the gods destroyed the world, ushering in the present era of the Fifth Sun.

The Aztec flood story is also a story of **apocalypse,** or the end of the world, another common theme in religious narratives.

Trickster Myths.   Some myths tell of serious matters—the origins of the world—while others tell of smaller things, usually to provide explanations of why things are the way they are or how people should and should not behave. In this latter category are a series of stories known as **trickster stories.**

The **trickster** is found in stories from all over the world. He is part human, part animal and is often able to change form. Perhaps the best-known tricksters are Raven from the Northwest Coast of North America, Coyote from the American Plains, and Spider from West Africa. These tricksters are adventurers, gluttons, searchers of sexual pleasures, lazy and easily bored, dishonest and impulsive. At the same time the trickster is responsible for creating or bringing into the world many elements, such as fire or the sun, yet often these things happen inadvertently as a by-product of some other activity. Box 2.5 is the story of Ananse, the spider trickster of the Sefwi peoples of the Guinea Coast culture area.

Box 2.6 tells the Haida story of Raven, the trickster found in the Northwest Coast culture area. Notice that in this story the reason Raven wants to steal the light is purely selfish: He is tired of stumbling around in the dark. And his method of obtaining his goal is deceitful, yet the outcome is a benefit to the world.

Hero Myths.   Joseph Campbell described the hero story in his book *The Hero with a Thousand Faces.* The title refers to the fact that although there are thousands of different heroes, they all follow the same basic hero story, or what Campbell calls the **monomyth.** Campbell describes the monomyth as follows: "A hero ventures forth from the world of common day into a region of supernatural wonder: fabulous forces are there encountered and a decisive victory is won: the hero comes back from this mysterious adventure with the power to bestow boons on his fellow man."[12]

The monomyth is a common theme encountered in many myths. Sometimes the hero is based on a real person whose story has been idealized. Other times the hero has no basis in real life. The pattern of the monomyth follows the three stages of the rite of passage, which will be discussed in Chapter 4. Generally, the first stage is the separation. The hero, frequently an orphaned youth, is thrust out of his community for one of several reasons. A common reason is the destruction of his home by some supernatural force. The second phase includes the hero's training, as he learns to utilize supernatural tools, such as a sacred sword, under the direction of a master, who frequently possesses supernatural power. In the third phase the hero returns and accomplishes the task. The monomyth is frequently found in origin stories, where the hero often is responsible for bringing some knowledge to humans. We will have an example of this in Chapter 3 when we examine the Navaho story of the Whirling Log.

Entire religious systems may be based on a hero story, as is the case with Buddhism, which is based on the story of the Prince Siddhartha Gautama. Gautama led a very sheltered life in his father's palace until he becomes aware of sickness, suffering, and death and the fact that he too is subject to them. He

BOX 2.5 • *The Return of Ananse*

Many seasons ago Ananse and his wife, Aso Yaa, made a bean farm. It looked good and promised a big harvest. Both Aso and Ananse had worked hard. In rain and sun they had worked until their backs ached.

Now the crops were growing. The farm was a bean farm, but they had planted other crops, too. The plantains were tall. The yam vines were bushy and green, and you could tell there were some big tubers under the mounds. There were also tomatoes, okra, peppers, and eggplant. Ananse was very pleased with himself.

The weeks went by. The crops grew and ripened. The smell of sweet things was in the air. Ananse stood in the middle of his farm and studied the crops. They were fine specimens, especially the beans, which were Ananse's favorite vegetable. Now they were there, ripe and ready to be eaten. Ananse stood in the middle of his farm and watched the beans swaying on their stalks. He was making plans—plans to have all the beans for himself.

He said, "These beans will be good almost any way they can be cooked." He congratulated himself for having married Aso Yaa, who had worked so hard to get such a fine crop. Before he returned home he had completed his plan for having all those wonderful beans for himself.

A few days later he called his family together, and he said in a sad voice, "My wife and children, I can see now that I haven't long to live. I shall soon die. When I am dead, bury me on the farm so that my spirit won't wander. Put something to cook with in my grave so that my spirit may feed."

The family were all saddened by what they had heard, but they did not expect their father to die too soon. In two or three days, however, Ananse lay down on his bed looking seriously ill. Within a few days he was dead. According to custom, a man's last wishes should be fulfilled. So Ananse was buried in the bean farm. Plenty of pots and pans were put in the grave to please Ananse's spirit. For forty days, while the customary rites were being performed, no one visited the bean farm.

As soon as the funeral procession had left the graveside, Ananse worked his way out, for he was not really dead. He built himself a little hut on the edge of the farm and cooked himself a bean feast. By day he slept in his grave, but every night he got out and had a meal. By the end of the forty days there was very little left on the farm, for Ananse was a greedy man.

At the end of the forty days, after Aso had been purified, she went to the farm to collect some food. But what did she find? The farm had been stripped almost bare. She stood there and lifted her voice, "May he die whoever stole my beans! May he die alone in pain!"

A voice answered from far away: "Peace, Aso! Peace! She who has lost her husband should not complain over lost beans."

Aso cursed the thief again. Again the voice answered: "Peace, Aso! Peace! She who has lost her husband should not complain over lost beans."

Aso now understood, so she returned home. Early the next morning she went with her eldest son, Endekuma, to the farm. She had Endekuma cut down a tall tree that stood on the farm. When he had cut nearly through the tree, he asked Aso, "Mother, where is the tree likely to fall?"

She said, "Quick, run! The tree is going to fall on our father's grave."

When Ananse heard that the tree was going to fall on his grave, he rushed out, shouting, "Aso, Aso, here I am. I have come up from the Ghost Land. You understand? From Ghost Land?"

He was very, very ashamed and rushed into a nearby bush and hid under some dry leaves. That is why Ananse is always found among dry leaves.

Source: "The Return of Ananse," in *West African Folk Tales,* collected and translated by J. Berry (Evanston, IL: Northwestern University Press, 1991), pp. 90–91. © 1991 by Northwestern University Press. Used with permission.

BOX 2.6 • *The Raven Steals the Light*

Before there was anything, before the great flood had covered the earth and receded, before the animals walked the earth or the trees covered the land or the birds flew between the trees, even before the fish and the whales and seals swam in the sea, an old man lived in a house on the bank of a river with his only child, a daughter. Whether she was as beautiful as hemlock fronds against the spring sky at sunrise or as ugly as a sea slug doesn't really matter very much to this story, which takes place mainly in the dark.

Because at that time the whole world was dark. Inky, pitchy, all-consuming dark, blacker than a thousand stormy winter midnights, blacker than anywhere has been since.

The reason for all this blackness has to do with the old man in the house by the river, who had a box which contained an infinite number of boxes each nestled in a box slightly larger than itself until finally there was a box so small all it could contain was all the light in the universe.

The Raven, who of course existed at that time, because he had always existed and always would, was somewhat less than satisfied with this state of affairs, since it led to an awful lot of blundering around and bumping into things. It slowed him down a good deal in his pursuit of food and other fleshly pleasures, and in his constant effort to interfere and to change things.

Eventually, his bumbling around in the dark took him close to the home of the old man. He first heard a little singsong voice muttering away. When he followed the voice, he soon came to the wall of the house, and there, placing his ear against the planking, he could just make out the words, "I have a box and inside the box is another box and inside it are many more boxes, and in the smallest box of all is all the light in the world, and it is all mine and I'll never give any of it to anyone, not even to my daughter, because, who

knows, she may be as homely as a sea slug, and neither she nor I would like to know that."

It took only an instant for the Raven to decide to steal the light for himself, but it took a lot longer for him to invent a way to do so.

First he had to find a door into the house. No matter how many times he circled it or how carefully he felt the planking, it remained a smooth, unbroken barrier. Sometimes he heard either the old man or his daughter leave the house to get water or for some other reason, but they always departed from the side of the house opposite to him, and when he ran around to the other side the wall seemed as unbroken as ever.

Finally, the Raven retired a little way upstream and thought and thought about how he could enter the house. As he did so, he began to think more and more of the young girl who lived there, and thinking of her began to stir more than just the Raven's imagination.

"It's probable that she's as homely as a sea slug," he said to himself, "but on the other hand, she may be as beautiful as the fronds of the hemlock would be against a bright spring sunrise, if only there were light enough to make one." And in that idle speculation, he found the solution to his problem.

He waited until the young woman, whose footsteps he could distinguish by now from those of her father, came to the river to gather water. Then he changed himself into a single hemlock needle, dropped himself into the river and floated down just in time to be caught in the basket which the girl was dipping in the river.

Even in his much diminished form, the Raven was able to make at least a very small magic—enough to make the girl so thirsty she took a deep drink from the basket, and in doing so, swallowed the needle.

The Raven slithered down deep into her warm insides and found a soft, comfortable spot, where he transformed himself once more, this time into a very small human being, and went to sleep for a long while. And as he slept he grew.

The young girl didn't have any idea what was happening to her, and of course she didn't tell her father, who noticed nothing unusual because it was so dark—until suddenly he became very aware indeed of a new presence in the house, as the Raven at last emerged triumphantly in the shape of a human boychild.

He was—or would have been, if anyone could have seen him—a strange-looking boy, with a long, beaklike nose and a few feathers here and there. In addition, he had the shining eyes of the Raven, which would have given his face a bright, inquisitive appearance—if anyone could have seen these features then.

And he was noisy. He had a cry that contained all the noises of a spoiled child and an angry raven—yet he could sometimes speak as softly as the wind in the hemlock boughs, with an echo of that beautiful other sound, like an organic bell, which is also part of every raven's speech.

At times like that his grandfather grew to love this strange new member of his household and spent many hours playing with him, making him toys and inventing games for him.

As he gained more and more of the affection and confidence of the old man, the Raven felt more intently around the house, trying to find where the light was hidden. After much exploration, he was convinced it was kept in the big box which stood in the corner of the house. One day he cautiously lifted the lid, but of course could see nothing, and all he could feel was another box. His grandfather, however, heard his precious treasure chest being disturbed, and dealt very harshly with the would-be thief, threatening dire punishment if the Raven-child ever touched the box again.

This triggered a tidal wave of noisy protests, followed by tender importuning, in which the Raven never mentioned the light, but only pleaded for the largest box. That box, said the Ravenchild, was the one thing he needed to make him completely happy.

As most if not all grandfathers have done since the beginning, the old man finally yielded and gave his grandchild the outermost box. This contented the boy for a short time—but as most if not all grandchildren have done since the beginning, the Raven soon demanded the next box.

It took many days and much cajoling, carefully balanced with well-planned tantrums, but one by one the boxes were removed. When only a few were left, a strange radiance, never before seen, began to infuse the darkness of the house, disclosing vague shapes and their shadows, still too dim to have definite form. The Ravenchild then begged in his most pitiful voice to be allowed to hold the light for a just a moment.

His request was instantly refused, but of course in time his grandfather yielded. The old man lifted the light, in the form of a beautiful, incandescent ball, from the final box and tossed it to his grandson.

He had only a glimpse of the child on whom he had lavished such love and affection, for even as the light was traveling toward him, the child changed from his human form to a huge, shining black shadow, wings spread and beak open, waiting. The raven snapped up the light in his jaws, thrust his great wings downward and shot through the smokehole of the house into the huge darkness of the world.

That world was at once transformed. Mountains and valleys were starkly silhouetted, the river sparkled with broken reflections, and everywhere life began to stir. And from far away, another great winged shape launched itself into the air, as light struck the eyes of the Eagle for the first time and showed him his target.

(continued)

BOX 2.6 • *Continued*

The Raven flew on, rejoicing in his wonderful new possession, admiring the effect it had on the world below, reveling in the experience of being able to see where he was going, instead of flying blind and hoping for the best. He was having such a good time that he never saw the Eagle until the Eagle was almost upon him. In a panic he swerved to escape the savage outstretched claws, and in doing so he dropped a good half of the light he was carrying. It fell to the rocky ground below and there broke into pieces—one large piece and too many small ones to count. They bounded back into the sky and remain there even today as the moon and the stars that glorify the night.

The Eagle pursued the Raven beyond the rim of the world, and there, exhausted by the long chase, the Raven finally let go of his last piece of light. Out beyond the rim of the world, it floated gently on the clouds and started up over the mountains lying to the east.

Its first rays caught the smokehole of the house by the river, where the old man sat weeping bitterly over the loss of his precious light and the treachery of his grandchild. But as the light reached in, he looked up and for the first time saw his daughter, who had been quietly sitting during all this time, completely bewildered by the rush of events.

The old man saw that she was as beautiful as the fronds of a hemlock against a spring sky at sunrise, and he began to feel a little better.

Source: Bill Reid and Robert Bringhurst, *The Raven Steals the Light* (Vancouver: Douglas & McIntyre, 1996), pp. 19–24. Copyright © 1984, 1996 by Bill Reid and Robert Bringhurst. Published in Canada by Douglas & McIntyre Ltd. Reprinted by permission of the publisher. U.S. rights courtesy of the University of Washington Press.

leaves behind his worldly possessions and spends years wandering, fasting, and meditating. He learns all he can from various teachers, but nothing seems to appease his sorrow and emptiness. In desperation he resolves to sit under a Bodhi tree until he finds the answers he has been looking for. He is attacked by Kama-Mara, the god of love and death, but is victorious. During his time under the tree Gautama gains knowledge and enlightenment and is thereafter referred to as the Buddha, or the "Enlightened One."

The same monomyth structure is also frequently used in American films, such as *Star Wars, The Wizard of Oz, The Matrix, The Lord of the Rings,* and *Harry Potter and the Sorcerer's Stone.* Table 2.1 compares some elements that are common to some of these movies.

Conclusion

The most fundamental questions asked by human beings—about the nature of life, existence, and death—are answered in the religious narratives we tell. These stories both explain and structure the world of a particular group of people. By ex-

TABLE 2.1 *The Monomyth in American Cinema: A Sampling of Common Features*

	The Wizard of Oz (1939)	*Star Wars* (1977)	*Harry Potter* (2001)
Hero	Dorothy Gale	Luke Skywalker	Harry Potter
Remote childhood	Lives with aunt and uncle in arid Kansas	Lives with aunt and uncle on arid Tatooine	Lives with aunt and uncle; is unaware that his parents had magical powers
Call to adventure	Follows Toto fleeing witch	Follows R2D2 fleeing Empire	Invited to attend Hogwarts
Introduction of the helper	Good Witch	Ben Kenobi	Dumbledorf
Given amulet	Red shoes	Light saber	Wizard's wand
Physical transportation out of previous life	Tornado	Mos Eisely Spaceport on Millennium Falcon	Train to Hogwarts
Enters Land of Enchantment	Oz and witch's castle	Death Star	Hogwarts Academy
Companions	Scarecrow, Tin Woodman, Cowardly Lion	Han Solo, C3PO, Chewbacca	Hermione Granger, Ron Weasley
Faces challenges	Wizard makes impossible demands	Freeing Princess Leia	Three-headed dog, Devil's snare plant, winged keys, etc.
Uses magic to accomplish goal	Dorothy uses red shoes to return to Kansas	Luke uses the Force to destroy Death Star	Harry uses magic to defeat Voldemort

amining religious narratives, we learn much about a specific group's worldview, including rules for moral behavior. Myths are stories to live by. They create networks of meaning that affect the life of people in that culture far beyond the domain of religion.

As we explore other topics in the study of religion, we will frequently return to the issue of religious narratives, because these stories often form the foundation of religious practices. This will be particularly important in the next two chapters on symbols and rituals.

Summary

The ways in which a society perceives and interprets its reality is known as their worldview. The worldview provides them with an understanding of how their world works; it forms the template for thought and behavior; and it provides a basic understanding of the origin and nature of humankind and its relationship to the world. People express their worldview in stories.

Myths are sacred stories that tell of the origin of the world and humankind, the existence and activities of gods and spirits, the origin of human traditions, and the nature of illness and death. They tell how to behave and how to distinguish good from evil. Myths are thought to recount real, historical events that took place in the remote past. They provide the basis for religious beliefs and practices.

Myths can be both written and oral. Written forms tend to be very stable through time, and changes that do occur are usually deliberate changes that are the consequences of translation or scholarly discourse about the meaning of particular words and passage. Oral texts are recited, and this recitation often has the characteristics of performance. One of the consequences of the oral transmission of stories is that they are frequently unconsciously altered with each generation, which explains the existence of different versions of the same myth within a society.

There are many ways of interpreting myths. Functional analysis sees myths as forces that help to maintain the society. Structural analysis focuses on the underlying structure of myths. The psychoanalytic approach sees myths as symbolically expressing unconscious wishes.

Certain basic themes are common through the world. Origin myths provide answers to the questions: Who are we? Why are we here? What is our relationship to the world? These stories play an important role in laying out the culture's worldview. One common element is the birth metaphor, in which the world is born from a god or goddess or by creation out of chaos, darkness, or the void.

Tricksters are part human, part animal. They are adventurers, seekers of sexual pleasures, lazy, dishonest, and impulsive. Yet tricksters are responsible for creating or bringing into the world many elements, often as a by-product of some other activity. Hero myths are stories about culture heroes who, through knowledge and mastery of certain skills, are able to bring about marvelous results.

Suggested Readings

Joseph Campbell, *The Hero with a Thousand Faces* (New York: Pantheon Books, 1949).
[A description of the hero myth in societies around the world.]

Ian Hogbin, *The Island of Menstruating Men: Religion in Wogeo, New Guinea* (Prospect Heights, IL: Waveland Press, 1970).
[The study of the Wogeo, including myths and religious practices.]

Scott Leonard and Michael McClure, *Myth and Knowing: An Introduction to World Mythology* (New York: McGraw-Hill, 2002).

Fiction:

Rudolfo Anaya, *Bless Me Ultima* (New York: Warner Books, 1999).
[In a story filled with symbolism, a young boy grows up in New Mexico in the 1940s.]

Dan Brown, *The Da Vinci Code* (New York: Doubleday, 2003).
[A symbologist and cryptographer interpret symbols and other clues in a search for the secret protected by an ancient secret society.]

Peter Blue Cloud, *Elderberry Flute Songs: Contemporary Coyote Tales* (Buffalo, NY: White Pine Press, 2002).
[A series of contemporary stories involving the trickster Coyote written by a Mohawk.]

Neil Gaiman, *American Gods* (New York, Harper Collins, 2001).
[The old gods of mythology battle the new gods of technology for control in America.]

Suggested Web Sites

www.wam.umd.edu/~stwright/index.htm
  A comprehensive collection of religious writings from many religious systems.

http://pantheon.org/mythica.html
  Encyclopedia Mythica is an encyclopedia of mythology, folklore, and legend.

www.pitt.edu/~dash/folktexts.html
  An extensive collection of folk and mythology texts.

Study Questions

1. A society's worldview includes how that society sees the environment and its relationship to the environment. Do you think that two societies with two radically different worldviews could ever come to an agreement on how to deal with issues of environmental exploitation such as lumbering and mining?

2. In our society a religious organization might set up a table on a college campus and distribute copies of the Bible. In a small-scale society a storyteller might set up a "stage" at a local market and offer to tell stories. How are these two activities similar and how are they different? How does the transmission of religious stories differ in these two societies?

3. Using the Navaho creation story and Genesis, show how a religious narrative can be a social charter for a society.

4. Why do we label the movies *Star Wars, The Wizard of Oz, The Matrix, The Lord of the Rings,* and *Harry Potter and the Sorcerer's Stone* monomyths? What are some other movies or television shows that are monomyths?

5. Why do you think that commonalities exist in myths found in different cultures?

Endnotes

1. Pages 76–77 from *Dance Hall of the Dead* by Tony Hillerman. Copyright © 1973 by Anthony G. Hillerman. Reprinted by permission of Harper-Collins Publisher Inc.

2. We realize that most readers are familiar with the *Snow White* story. The story has been retold and changed over the decades. Unfortunately, some of the most fascinating elements of the story have been eliminated from recent versions. We encourage you to read the early versions, which are much more interesting than the sanitized versions that are most frequently found today.

3. A. Dundes, *Holy Writ as Oral Lit* (Lanham, MD: Rowman & Littlefield, 1999).

4. Reprinted by permission of Waveland Press, Inc., from I. Hogbin, *The Island of Menstruating Men,* 1996. All rights reserved.

5. B. Malinowski, *Myth in Primitive Psychology* (Westport, CT: Greenwood Publishing Group, 1954), p. 101.

6. E. Leach, "Genesis as Myth," *Discover* (May 1982), pp. 30–35.

7. A. Johnson and D. Price-Williams, *Oedipus Ubiquitous* (Palo Alto, CA: Stanford University Press, 1991), p. 44.

8. Page 44 from *Primal Myths* by Barbara C. Sproul. Copyright © 1979 by Barbara C. Sproul. Reprinted by permission of HarperCollins Publisher Inc.

9. From *Parallel Myths* by J. F. Bierlein, copyright © 1994 by J. F. Bierlein. Used by permission of Ballantine Books, a division of Random House, Inc.

10. B. Sproul, *op. cit.,* p. 201.

11. From *Parallel Myths* by J. F. Bierlein, copyright © 1994 by J. F. Bierlein. Used by permission of Ballantine Books, a division of Random House, Inc.

12. J. Campbell, *The Hero with a Thousand Faces,* Second edition (Princeton, NJ: Princeton University Press, 1968), p. 30.

3

Religious Symbols

All animals communicate with one another. Most often, this communication is simple and very specific to the situation. A stimulus—such as the sight of a stranger, predator, or food—may bring about a response of some kind: threat, flight, or eating. However, the situation exists in the here and now. The reaction is an immediate response to the specific circumstances.

Humans also encounter strangers, predators, and food. However, the human response is more complex than that of other living creatures. Humans react to the presence of a stranger entering their midst, but the stranger may be seen as an enemy warrior, a merchant, or a monk and will be dealt with appropriately. The reaction to a predator might be to prepare a spear for defense or to perform magical rites to ward off the danger. Humans feel hunger and respond to the presence of food, but many edible and nutritious foods are shunned because of cultural or religious prohibitions. All of these behaviors involve communication, be it storytelling, ritual, or the articulation of food prohibitions.

The complexity of human communication is made possible through the ability of humans to create and use symbols. Symbols permit people to discuss abstract topics and to talk about things in the past, in an envisioned future, or even in a supernatural world. The world of religion is a symbolic world.

What Is a Symbol?

Let us begin by picking up an apple in our hand. We know that this is an apple by its shape, color, and smell, and we know what to do with it. Many nonhuman animals will react to an apple in very much the same way. Show an apple to a horse, and the horse will know by its shape, color, and smell exactly what it is and might take the apple from your hand and eat it. In this way humans and other animals are very similar.

As humans, however, we can do something that horses cannot do. For example, we can draw a blue triangle on a piece of paper and declare that this blue triangle represents an apple. It certainly does not look like an apple or smell or taste like an apple, but as long as everyone in our community accepts the idea that a blue triangle stands for an apple, we can use it in place of a real apple in communication. If we have a fruit stand at an outdoor market, we can fly a banner with a blue triangle above our booth so that people will know that we have apples for sale. Newcomers might not know that a blue triangle stands for apples, but we can tell them, and once they become regular customers, members of our small community, they will participate in our system of communication. (Of course, a nonhuman animal can be trained to respond to a blue triangle, but a human creates the symbol and a human does the training.) This ability to use symbols to refer to things and activities that are remote from the user is termed **displacement.**

In our community the blue triangle is acting as a symbol. It is something that stands for something else. Most symbols have no direct connection with the thing they refer to. The association of a blue triangle with an apple is arbitrary; it could as easily be a yellow circle or a green square. As long as there is agreement within our community as to the meaning of the symbol, we can communicate with one another using symbols rather than real objects.

Being able to create and use symbols is extremely useful. We can use symbols to refer to things that are not directly in front of us—a faraway place, for example, or something we would like to do in the future. We might talk about going to the grocery store to buy apples, yet there might not be an apple in sight. We also can talk about fruits that we have never seen or tasted, perhaps a durian fruit from Southeast Asia. And if we discover a new fruit that no one has ever seen before, we can create a new symbol, such as a name, to refer to it. These are examples of displacement.

We can also use symbols to stand for things that are more complex than simple objects. Symbols can stand for emotions and complex philosophical concepts that exist only in our minds. Symbols can create a supernatural world or create myths about the past. Joseph Church, discussing language, writes:[1]

> we can use symbols in ways impossible with the things they stand for, and so arrive at novel and even creative versions of reality. . . . We can verbally rearrange situations which in themselves would resist rearrangement . . . we can isolate features which in fact cannot be isolated . . . we can juxtapose objects and events far separated in time and space . . . we can, if we will, turn the universe symbolically inside out.

In our initial example we used a geometric shape, a blue triangle, as a symbol. Many symbols are physical objects or artistic representations. Symbols do not have to be physical, however. Language is a system of symbols, but here the symbols are sounds. The only reason that the word *apple* means a particular type of fruit is because when we learned our language, in this case English, we learned that the combination of sounds that make up the word *apple* stands for that particular fruit. There is nothing inherently "applish" about the sound of the word *apple,* just as there is nothing "applish" about a blue triangle. In fact, this fruit is known by many other names in other languages—*manzana* in Spanish and *elma* in Turkish, for example.

Religious Symbols

Symbols are important elements in religious practice, and religious rituals center on symbols and the manipulation of symbols. In Hinduism we might approach a statue that represents the god Brahma. In ritual the statue may be bathed with milk, and strings of flowers may be hung around its neck. People in many different culture areas use masks to impersonate gods, such as the masks of the Hopi of the American Southwest and the Dogon of western Africa. The sand painting of the Navaho, created as a part of ritual, becomes a portal into the supernatural world.

Of course, not all symbols are physical things or artistic representations. Words, both written and spoken, are critical elements in religious behavior. In Jewish ritual the Torah is taken from the ark with great ceremony to be read. In Tantric Buddhism, found in Tibet, words or formulas have great spiritual power, which builds as they are chanted over and over. Elements of music and dance and of space and time can also serve as symbols. We will begin our discussion of symbols by looking at basic artistic representations.

The Swastika

One form of the **swastika** is illustrated in Figure 3.1a. It is basically a pattern of lines set at right angles to one another and, as such, carries no inherent meaning. A person seeing this symbol for the very first time will have no idea what it represents.

A symbol such as the swastika can stand for very complex ideas and can carry great emotional resonance. Most Americans and Europeans looking at the swastika experience anger or dread. In 1919, the German Nazi Party adopted the swastika as its symbol. Because of this the swastika has been associated with the terrible events perpetrated by the Nazis in World War II. A swastika spray-painted on a wall is often defined in law as a hate crime.

The Japanese-American Museum in Los Angeles occupied what was once a Buddhist temple. In the main hall there was a staircase with a metal bannister. Running along the top of the bannister, just beneath the handrail, was a row of swastikas. The swastika is a symbol that is found in many religious systems that predate its Nazi usage. (In fact, the Nazi Party borrowed the swastika from Nordic mythology.) In Japanese Buddhism the swastika represents abundance, prosperity, and long life, and it is frequently found in decorations and carvings in Buddhist temples. The reverse swastika is called the sauvastika and stands for darkness, misfortune, and suffering.

The swastika is also found in Navaho art, where it represents the Whirling Log, an element of a story found in the creation myth (see Figure 4.1 on p. 90). The Whirling Log was a type of dugout canoe built by the gods. The symbol represents the log with a support pole attached beneath. Attached to each end is a feather, which, as the log is whirling, stands out straight. The culture hero Self Teacher traveled in this canoe on an epic journey. This design element is used in many rituals, including the Night and Feather chants.

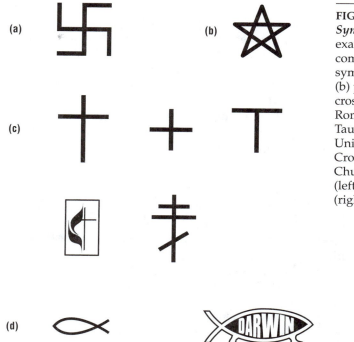

FIGURE 3.1 *Religious Symbols.* These are examples of some commonly seen religious symbols: (a) swastika, (b) pentagram, (c) Christian crosses (from left to right: Roman cross, Greek cross, Tau cross, Cross of the United Methodist Church, Cross of the Orthodox Church); (d) Christian fish (left) and Darwin fish (right).

The Pentagram

The term **pentagram** comes from the Greek *pente,* meaning "five," and *gamma,* which is a letter in the Greek alphabet. The term *pentagram* can refer to any five-sided figure but is generally used to refer to a five-pointed star, also called a **pentacle** (Figure 3.1b). Pentagrams are among the most widely used religious symbols, both historically and cross-culturally.

Some researchers believe that the pentagram originated as the symbol of a pagan goddess. The pentagram became associated with this goddess because her sacred fruit was the apple. If an apple is cut in half through its equator, the seeds of the apple form a pentagram in each half. The pentagram is also used by the Masonic order, which traces it origins back to Pythagoras and ancient Greece.

The pentagram was associated with the Hebrew Scriptures as a symbol of the five books of the Pentateuch (the Torah). Early Christians used the symbol with a variety of meanings, including the representation of the five wounds of Christ and the star that prophesied the birth of Jesus. It was only during the Witchcraze (see Chapter 9) that the pentagram began to take on a connotation of evil. During this time the symbol was actually referred to as the "witch's foot." This association with evil became stronger for many when twentieth century Satanists adopted the pentagram as their symbol. The Satanist symbol is an inverted pentagram, most commonly shown with a goat's head in the center.

As we saw with the swastika, there are many misunderstandings about the meaning of the pentagram owing to its various associations. Most recently, the symbol has been adopted by Wiccans, members of a Neo-Pagan religion that is reviving pre-Christian religious practices. (We will discuss the Wiccan religion in more detail in Chapter 9.) Wicca is a nature-based, polytheistic religion that emphasizes the use of good magic and not doing harm. For some Wiccans the pentagram represents earth, air, fire, water, and spirit; for others it refers to the four directions and spirit. However, many Americans still associate the pentagram with evil when they see a person wearing it.

Christian Symbols

The **cross** is the symbol that is most clearly associated with Christianity. Yet the cross did not gain general acceptance for many centuries after the founding of the Christian religion. Of course, there are many versions of the cross, and the depiction of the cross used centuries ago was not necessarily the Roman cross that is most widely seen today (Figure 3.1c). A Vatican sarcophagus from the fifth century shows one of the first depictions of a cross in Christian art. It is a Greek cross (with arms of equal length); Jesus' body is not shown. Some early Christians even argued against the use of the cross as a symbol of Christianity because it had earlier pagan associations, most specifically the Tau cross (in the shape of the letter T).

The cross that is widely used today is a Roman cross, but there is still considerable variation in the exact look of the cross symbol. For example, Roman Catholic crosses are crucifixion scenes, complete with the body of Christ. The Protestant cross does not show the body of Christ because Protestants emphasize that Jesus has risen from the cross and is no longer on it. A cross with a dual flame behind it is the symbol of the United Methodist Church. The cross represents Christ, and the flame represents the Holy Spirit. The cross of the Orthodox Church has three cross bars: one for the inscription, one for the arms, and one for a footrest.

If the cross was not the most important early Christian symbol, what was? It was the simple fish symbol (Figure 3.1d). There are several reasons why the fish is used. One that is often given is that Jesus referred to the apostles as "fishers of men." The most commonly given reason, though, is that the letters of the Greek word for fish, *icthus*, form an **acrostic.** An acrostic is a word that is derived from the first letter of a series of words. So *icthus* is derived from *Iesous Christos Theou Uiou Soter* ("Jesus Christ of God the Son the Savior"). In the early days, when Christians were a small, persecuted group, the symbol served as a type of password. One person would draw the first arc in the sand, and if the second person was also Christian, he or she would draw the second arc to complete the fish.

More recently, we have seen the creation of the Darwin fish symbol. The Darwin fish is a reversed Christian fish, with feet and the word "DARWIN" written inside. Although the creator of this symbol says that it was meant solely to be humorous, it has sparked many responses. Even more new fish have been created, such as the truth fish eating the Darwin fish.

Sacred Art

Although the swastika, pentagram, cross, and other simple symbols are important representations in their respective religious systems, they are usually elements found in more complex settings or works of art. Imagine, for example, walking into a great European cathedral with its massive stained glass windows, statuary, and paintings, all containing a myriad of symbols, or walking through a Buddhist temple in Thailand, with its many representations of the figure of Buddha, each with its own complex meaning and referents.

The Sarcophagus of Lord Pakal

Artistic representations are often used to illustrate and supplement religious texts. The following is an archaeological example from the ancient Maya of southern Mexico in the Meso-America culture area. Although contemporary Mayan religion has many parallels with the ancient Mayan religion, contemporary studies can provide only a limited understanding of ancient Mayan art. The fact that we can know as much as we do about the ancient Maya is because they built monumental buildings, chiseled great works of art into stone, developed a sophisticated calendar, and had a system of writing. However, not all Mayan symbols have been deciphered, and much remains to be learned.

In 1949 the Mexican archaeologist Alberto Ruiz was working in the Temple of the Inscriptions at the archaeological site of Palenque. Like most Mayan temples, the temple itself was built on top of a large mound, or pyramid. The name of the temple is taken from the extensive inscription on a wall of the temple that tells of the kings of Palenque up until the time the temple was built.

Unlike most temples, the floor of this sanctuary was covered with paving stones. One of these stones had some holes along the edge, filled with stone plugs, which suggested that the stone was made to be lowered into position. Knowing that caches of religious objects often lay underneath the floor of temples, Ruiz had the paving stone removed and discovered what appeared to be a rectangular hole filled with rubble. After the top layer of rubble was removed, the workers found that the rubble filled a steep staircase that descended into the depths of the pyramid.

In 1952 the workers finally reached the bottom of the staircase to find a large stone blocking the passage. Eventually, they were able to reach the end of the passage and entered a room in which was found a large stone sarcophagus richly carved with Mayan pictures and writing. They were stunned by the beauty of the sarcophagus, especially the cover, which is one of the most important pieces of carving in Mayan prehistory (Figure 3.2). The cover was removed to reveal the skeleton of a man.

Many archaeologists believe that the skeleton is that of the greatest king who ever ruled Palenque. His name was Hanab-Pakal, Pakal the Great, or Lord Shield, and he died at the age of 80 on August 31, 683, after having ruled for sixty-seven years.

The sarcophagus lid measures twelve by seven feet. As we in the twenty-first century look at this carving from the seventh century, especially if we have never

FIGURE 3.2 *The Mayan Cosmos.* This carving is a symbolic representation of the Mayan cosmos. The carving is found on the sarcophagus cover in the Temple of the Inscriptions, Palenque, Mexico, the burial site of Hanab-Pakal, who died in 683.

encountered Mayan art before, we probably recognize only a few elements—perhaps a reclining figure and a bird near the top. Of course, if we were aristocratic Mayas living in the seventh century, the meaning of all of these elements would be known to us. Our fathers would have taken us to the temple precinct to show us the various motifs carved into the stone and to explain their meaning. As aristocrats we also would undoubtedly have attended religious classes or received tutoring from the priests.

This carving is important to modern scholars because it is a visual representation of the Mayan cosmos. We cannot explain all of the elements, and limited space here prevents us from offering a complete explanation of what we do know, but let us examine some of the elements as examples of how symbolic representations are used to create a virtual supernatural world.

We know that we are in sacred territory because of the various symbols that appear to be floating in the background, elements such as bones, shells, flowers, and beads. These elements are associated with the supernatural power that is found all around us. Near the base of the carving is an image of a skeletal snake. The skull of the "White-Bone-Snake" has been slit and spread out. The open jaws of the serpent form the portal that connects the world of the living with Xibalba, the world of the dead. We see Pakal at the moment of his death descending into the serpent's jaws as he moves from the world of the living into the world of the dead.

Behind the figure of Pakal, appearing to be growing out of the serpent's jaw, is the Cosmic Tree, which is the central axis of the world. The tree is rooted in the underworld; behind Pakal is the Middle World, which is the world inhabited by people; the upper parts of the tree reach into the heavens. Many of the representations in the upper portion of the tree represent constellations and heavenly bodies. For example, what appear to be branches that end in square-nosed serpents, flowers, and other symbols represent the Milky Way. The bird perched at the top of the tree is the companion of one of the gods involved with the creation of the world. We know this because of various symbols found carved on the bird, such as a necklace, and the "ribbon" in its beak.

The carving shows Pakal descending into Xibalba. There he will undergo a series of trials followed by his resurrection as a god. Associated with Pakal is a sacrificial bowl that is carved with the symbol that represents the sun. Like the sun that moves into Xibalba at sunset and is resurrected at dawn, so does Pakal move into the Underworld to be resurrected as a god. After his death the priests would enter into an altered state of consciousness (see Chapter 5) and contact Pakal's spirit. In fact, along the side of the staircase leading to his tomb is a pipe made of brick. This is a **psychoduct,** through which Pakal's spirit moves from the tomb into the temple sanctuary during rituals.

Other important symbols on the sarcophagus refer to blood. Blood was an important symbol both in terms of tracing bloodlines (as is done around the sides of Lord Pakal's sarcophagus) and because of the importance of bloodletting. At important rituals the ruler would pierce his penis with a stingray barb, and his consort would pierce her tongue and pass a string with thorns attached through her tongue (see p. 114). The blood would bleed onto strips of paper made from the bark of a tree. The blood-soaked strips would be burned, the smoke being seen as an offering to the gods. It was believed that this bloodletting would consecrate the event and call the gods into attendance. Several blood-related symbols are found on the sarcophagus, including platters used for blood offerings.

The Meaning of Color

As we saw with the sarcophagus of Lord Pakal, religious art can be quite complex. There are many important elements in artistic representation. One of these is color. Although today we see the statues and carvings of the Romans and the ancient Mayans in white marble or the color of stone, we know that at the time these statues and carvings were made, objects of stone were often covered with paint.

Colors have cultural meanings. In weddings American brides wear white. Irish folk wisdom dictates the following:

Married in white, you have chosen all right.
Married in red, you'd better be dead.
Married in yellow, ashamed of the fellow.
Married in blue, your lover is true.
Married in green, ashamed to be seen.
Married in black, you'll ride in a hack.
Married in pearl, you'll live in a whirl.
Married in brown, you'll live out of town.

These meanings do not necessarily apply to other cultures. For example, sometimes white may be avoided because of its association with death. In Chinese culture, brides wear red.

Many scholars have studied color terminology. English has eleven basic color terms: *red, orange, yellow, green, blue, purple, brown, pink, black, white,* and *gray.* These are the colors that children learn in preschool. We also define colors more narrowly within these basic categories by using combined terms (such as red-orange) or specialized terms (such as lavender and turquoise).

All peoples in all societies, except individuals with some form of color blindness, see the entire visible spectrum of colors, but the color spectrum is not divided up into natural units of color. All languages have ways of dividing up this spectrum into arbitrary categories that are labeled by linguistic forms. However, the actual number of basic color terms and how the visible spectrum is actually divided vary from culture to culture. Generally, languages of industrial societies tend to have a greater number of basic color terms than do languages spoken in less complex societies.

A color term, a word such as *blue,* is a symbol. In this case the word *blue* refers not to a physical object, but to a particular segment of the color spectrum, or, as a physicist might define it, a range of wavelengths of light. When speakers of different languages are asked to identify the range of colors covered by a particular color term, we see a great deal of variation. Symbols, including color terminology, are arbitrary and learned; they are parts of cultural traditions. For example, the Navaho think of the ideal blue as turquoise. The stone of that color not only is important in jewelry making, but also has religious importance. To the Navaho "blue is the color of celestial and earthly attainment, of peace, happiness, and success, of vegetable sustenance."[2]

Yoruba Color Terminology.   The language of the Yoruba of Nigeria in the Guinea Coast culture area has only three basic color terms. Each term covers a much larger part of the color spectrum than do English color terms. *Funfun* includes what English speakers call white, silver, and pale gray. *Pupa* covers what English speakers would label red, pink, orange, and deep yellow. *Dúdú* includes black, blue, purple, green, dark browns, red-brown, and dark grays.

In the English language colors evoke emotions. We say that a sad person is feeling blue; when angry, we see red; a jealous person is green with envy; a coward is yellow. The Yoruba also associate colors with particular temperatures and temperaments. For example, *funfun* is associated with coolness, age, and wisdom; *pupa* evokes hotness; *dúdú* is dark and warm.

The supernatural world of the Yoruba is populated by many spiritual beings called *orisha*. (The *orisha* will be discussed in greater detail in Chapter 8.) Obatala, the king of the *orisha*, an ethical and merciful deity, is linked to the color *funfun*, the color of wisdom and respect. Objects associated with Obatala are frequently colored white, and he is sometimes called the "King of the White Cloth." In contrast, Sango is associated with the color *pupa.* He rules thunder and lightning and is proud and quick-tempered, and his images are often colored red. Ossosi, who is associated with hunting, is introverted and unstable. He is linked to the color *dúdú,* green and blue. The messenger of the gods is an *orisha* named Esu-Elegba. He is the intermediary between the people and the gods and ancestors and is the first deity addressed in rituals. Representations of Esu-Elegba are usually done in black and white or, in Yoruba color terminology, *funfun* and *dúdú.* These are contrasting colors and represent the god's unpredictability. Artistic representations of Esu-Elegba in carvings, paintings, and embroideries primarily use these two colors. A Yoruba seeing such a representation can identify the *orisha* in part by the colors being used.

Sacred Self, Space, and Time

Symbols are also used to create sacred realities: supernatural worlds, sacred spaces, sacred divisions of time, and interpretations of self.

Symbolic Alterations to the Human Body

All peoples have cultural images of themselves. These images serve to separate humanity from the rest of the animal world, an expression of **anthropocentrism.** These images also serve to distinguish a particular society from other societies; this is an expression of ethnocentrism. Or one segment of a society will distinguish itself from other segments, such as gender, age, occupational groups, and social categories. People will change the physical appearance of their bodies to conform to these cultural images. Although many of these are secular, many such changes in the human body occur in ritual, as we will see in Chapter 4.

Although Americans may be amused by the appearance of other peoples, Americans, like other peoples, change their appearance to conform to cultural images. There are many ways to alter one's appearance. Perhaps the simplest is to wear particular items of clothing. For example, concepts of fashion identify one's occupation, as when physicians in a hospital wear white coats and have a stethoscope around their neck or when priests wear clerical collars. An individual might alter his or her clothing to conform to different social roles. For example, a student might wear a T-shirt and blue jeans to class in the morning and change to a suit and tie for his afternoon job. American women might put on makeup, dye and process their hair into particular styles, and put various types of jewelry around their neck and on their arms and fingers. Men might also dye and process their hair and beards and wear various types of jewelry.

Symbolic expressions such as clothing are temporary, of course, as is hairstyle. The application of some type of pigment on the body is another way of temporarily changing the appearance of the body. The application of body paint frequently occurs in religious ritual and serves a variety of functions, such as symbolizing elements of the supernatural. This can also serve to separate the religious practitioner and participants from the remainder of the community. However, many peoples apply body paint in nonreligious contexts, as when an American applies eye shadow and lipstick.

Permanent Alterations of the Human Body.   People also do things that permanently alter the appearance their bodies. American women and men may bore holes into their earlobes to hang earrings. **Infibulation,** or piercing, is a fairly common cultural practice, although what is pierced varies. Some Americans pierce parts of the body other than the earlobes, such as the nose, eyebrow, lips, tongue, nipples, and even genitals. Body piercing often proclaims membership in a particular social category or group or is an expression of separation and dissatisfaction with mainstream values. A society matron might pierce her ears to wear fashionable earrings; her rebellious child might pierce his nose or eyebrow as a symbolic act of rebellion or as a means of identifying with the youth culture.

Of particular interest is the practice of tattooing. Tattooing is found in many traditional societies throughout the world, where tattoos are often a way of marking social identity or membership in a particular social category, such as religious practitioner. The history of tattooing in American and European cultures can be traced to the voyages of James Cook in the eighteenth century. Many of Cook's sailors were tattooed during their stay in Tahiti, and the word *tattoo* is derived from the Tahitian word *ta-tu,* meaning "to mark or strike."

The social implications of tattooing in Western society have varied. At times it has been a fad among the aristocracy or members of particular social groups, such as sailors, gangs, and prisoners. In this context a tattoo served as a mark of social identity. At other times tattooing has been a way to express dissatisfaction with the social order and was a way to distance oneself from the mainstream society.

Basically, tattooing involves piercing or cutting the skin and then introducing a pigment into the wound. In contemporary Western societies this is done with an electronic device, but the principle is the same. Depending on what part of the body is tattooed, the process can be quite painful. As we will see in Chapter 5, pain itself can play an important role in ritual and religious experiences.

In societies where people wear little or no clothing, tattooing and other alterations of the body serve the same purpose as clothing does in American society. Changes in social position are more frequently signified by an alteration of the physical body—say, a tattoo—than by a change in costume.

The total list of what people do to alter their appearance is really remarkable. It includes piercing (infibulation) and stretching. Once the ear is pierced, the hole may be enlarged so that a plug can be inserted, or weights may be attached so that the earlobe will be stretched. A few societies pierce the lower lip and insert a round plate. Closely related to tattooing is **cicatrization** or scarification. This is frequently seen in peoples with dark skin on which tattoos would not show well. In scarification a pierce of skin is raised and cut, and some material, such as ash, is rubbed in to encourage the production of scars. Closely related to cicatrization is branding, in which the scars are created by burns.

Some societies see white teeth as resembling the teeth of animals. To create a boundary between humans and nonhuman animals, teeth are often knocked out, filed into various shapes, or colored, most often blackened. Other body parts can be removed, most frequently a finger joint. The skeleton can also be altered. This process usually begins in childhood when the bones are more pliable than they are in the adult. An example is the old Chinese custom of foot binding. The child's foot is cut and bent backward and bound. The result is a deformed foot that is quite small. Bound feet were said to be erotic, as was the way women with bound feet walked. Moreover, a woman with bound feet could not walk very far and was therefore unlikely to engage in extramarital liaisons.

Another example is found among the Karen Padaung of northern Thailand. Here the necks of women are covered with concentric metal rings that give the appearance of an elongated neck. Actually, the neck is not being lengthened. The rings are pushing down the clavicle, or collarbone, giving the appearance of an elongated neck. Although this custom has died out in most communities, it is still found in areas visited by tourists who pay money to take pictures of such women. Another practice that also altered the skeleton was the British and American custom of corseting, which was popular in the nineteenth century. Girls would wear corsets from a young age to produce a thin waist. This resulted in a dislocation of many of the internal organs and a weakening of the back muscles that made it difficult to walk long distances.

Our final example involves the skull. The bones of the skull in infants are quite pliable, and pressure on these bones will cause them to deform. Sometimes such deformation results unintentionally from various practices such as a flattening of the back of the head in infants bound on cradleboards for an extended period of time. (Today some American children are also developing a similar flattening of the back of the head due to the preferred practice of consistently placing infants on their back to sleep.) In other societies, such as the Maya, the heads of infants born into high social classes were deliberately bound to alter their shape. Though not always affecting the skeleton, we need to mention implants and plastic surgery. Although these procedures are frequently used to correct congenital or accidental damage to the body, they are also used to alter the body to fit some preconceived valued image of the human body. Finally, circumcision and other genital alterations will be discussed in Chapter 4.

Body Modification in Religious Practice. In contemporary American society most body modifications are done for nonreligious reasons. Yet in small-scale societies and in some segments of American society, such physical acts are tied to religious practice. For example, male circumcision is an important element in Judaism and Islam. This type of alteration is commanded in the religious text and also serves to physically and permanently mark an individual as a member of a particular religious group. Other modifications of the body are done to mark an individual as having become a religious specialist—they are marks of initiation into a religious status.

Many Americans are drawn to tattoos for religious reasons. Many tattoos have a religious theme, such as an ornate cross. Some people get mortuary tattoos done on their body in remembrance of a loved one who has passed away. Many Americans who participate in New Age or Neo-Pagan subcultures are also drawn to tattoos. New Age imagery, including astrological symbols, is common in tattoo art.

As we will learn in Chapter 4, the act of body modification often becomes an important element in ritual. First, such symbols mark participation in and completion of particular rituals. A Maasai man from East Africa who has been circumcised as part of a coming-of-age ceremony can participate in many activities that were prohibited prior to the ritual, such as sexual activity. Because circumcision in the second decade of life can be extremely painful, circumcision also symbolizes bravery and manhood in general. Also pain itself has great meaning and is a means for entering an altered state of consciousness such as a trance.

Finally, body imagery becomes a way of transforming an individual into something else. A priest or dancer covered with body paint in a particular pattern not only plays the role of the particular deity in the ritual, but might actually be thought to become the deity.

The Meaning of Time

All of the examples of symbols we have examined thus far have been things that we can directly see as part of some physical artistic endeavor, whether it is a shape or a color. Yet not all things symbolic are physical. People also handle nonphysical entities symbolically. Our example will be the cultural handling of time.

What is time? People see time as being made up of recurring units that are based on real physical events such as the rotation of earth on its axis (a day), the journey of the moon around the earth (a month), and the travel of the earth around the sun (a year). We also can divide a day into phases based on the position of the sun (morning, afternoon, and evening). Human activities are organized by particular parts of the day, certain days of the week, or certain times of the year.

Humans also create units of time that are not based on real astronomical events such as the rotation of the earth. These units appear to be arbitrary. A week in our culture has seven days. Why not five, as is common in parts of Central America and Africa? Why not eight, as was found among the ancient Inca of the South American Andes? And why not sixteen, as is found among the Yoruba of Nigeria? The seven-day week of Western society is derived from the cultures of the ancient Near East and perhaps came from the division of the approximately 28-day lunar cycle into four quarters. In other words, concepts such as "a week" are nonphysical symbols that stand for particular periods of time. Many of these periods do not exist in the real world, but only in the human mind.

Time is an important element of religious rituals. Many rituals are performed at specific moments of time, often as part of a ceremonial cycle. As we will see in the next section, time often has important symbolic meaning.

The Mayan View of Time.   The passage of time had a deep religious significance for the ancient Maya of southern Mexico and Central America, and they had a very complex view of time. They developed several systems of marking time that intersected with one another to form a very complex calendar. Like many peoples the Maya had a calendrical system based on the solar year consisting of about 365 days. The Maya divided their year into eighteen months of twenty days and a nineteenth month of five days. Each month was named, and each day within a month was numbered. A particular day was named by a combination of its numerical position within the month and the name of the month.

Although the solar year is a natural unit that is determined by the movements of the sun in the sky throughout the year, many cultures divide the solar year into varying segments of time. However, the Maya developed a second kind of year of 260 days that was constructed from a cycle of twenty day names and a second cycle of thirteen numbers. A particular day was known by a number and a day name. The twenty-day cycle of day names and the thirteen-day number cycle are interconnected like teeth in two large gears. The same combination of day name and number occurs every 260 days.

The two calendar systems ran simultaneously, and a specific day is named after its position in both calendars, which results in 18,980 unique combinations of days. It takes fifty-two years to go through all of these combinations and to start over again. The end of a fifty-two-year cycle and the beginning of the next was an important ceremonial event in Mayan religious life. The fifty-two-year cycle has no astronomical basis but is a part of Mayan culture, a part of how they understood their world. And this was just the beginning. The Maya recognized several other cycles, such as that based on the movements of the planet Venus in the sky.

Thus each day from the beginning of time in the Mayan calendar was unique and was designated by a sequence of notations based on the various calendars. When a child was born, the child was taken to a priest who used the designation of the day of the child's birth to predict the child's future. Important events, especially those surrounding the ruler, were scheduled to fall on days that were considered to be particularly auspicious. Thus to the Maya time was much more than just a flow of days and years. Time had an important religious meaning.

Rituals and Calendars in Modern World Religions.   There are many other examples from modern world religions of the importance of time and calendars. Many rituals are performed according to a temporal cycle. Such rituals are termed **periodic rituals.** They often commemorate the anniversary of important events in the history of the religion. Because of the importance of setting the date of the celebration correctly, many religions continue to use calendars that are older than the one most commonly used in the Western world.

In Islam, Ramadan is the ninth month of the Muslim calendar, which is the month during which the Qur'an was sent down from heaven to Mohammad. The month of Ramadan is a time for worship and contemplation. During this time Muslims follow many constraints on their daily lives, such as not eating or drinking during daylight hours. At the end of the day the fast is broken with prayer and a meal. The *Laylat-al-Qadr* (the Night of Power) is celebrated on the evening of the twenty-seventh day of Ramadan, as the night when Mohammad first received the revelation of the Qur'an. According to the Qur'an, this is also the night when God determines the course of the world for the following year. The end of the fasting, and of the month of Ramadan, is celebrated for three days in *Id-al-Fitr* (the Feast of Fast Breaking).

Another example of periodic rituals being set to older calendars is the *Yamim Nora'im* (Days of Awe), or Jewish high holy days, which are observed for a ten-day period between the first and tenth days of the month of Tishri, the seventh month of the Jewish calendar. *Rosh Hashanah* (Jewish New Year) marks the beginning of this time period, and *Yom Kippur* (Day of Atonement) marks the end. These are considered to be the most important of all the Jewish holidays and are the only Jewish holidays that are purely religious and not based on any historical or natural event.

The high holy days are a time for penitence and prayer during which Jews are given time to repent of their sins against God and ask God for forgiveness. On *Rosh Hashanah,* God judges the people and records His judgment in the Book of Life. However, there is a ten-day reprieve until *Yom Kippur,* when the Book is closed and sealed. *Yom Kippur* itself is a day for fasting and prayer.

Other times, not related to a specific calendar, may also have religious significance. A common example is the time following a death. In Judaism this period of mourning is called *shiva. Shiva* begins as soon as the mourner has returned from the cemetery and lasts for seven days. During this time the mourner remains at home and does not participate in any of his or her normal activities, such as work or school. Friends and relatives visit the home of the mourners and often bring food.

Sacred Time and Space in Australia

The religious systems of the Australian Aborigines are focused on expressions of sacred time and space. To understand these systems we must examine the concept of **totemism.** A simple definition of a **totem,** as it is frequently used, is that of a symbol or emblem of a social unit. A special relationship is said to exist between a group or individual and its totem, which is frequently, but not always, an animal. American culture possesses many such emblems. They are found primarily in athletics as mascots and in business as logos. Many athletic teams are named after animals—such as bears, bulldogs, eagles, and panthers—and the selection of a team's mascot often reflects those characteristics of the animal that are deemed important for players to display in that particular sport. Because athletic teams are supposed to be strong, aggressive, and competitive, the choice of a mascot that manifests these

features is obvious. Yet to think of totems simply as mascots and logos is very su-
perficial. The idea of totems, or totemism, is actually much more complex than it
first appears.

Many late nineteenth century and early twentieth century anthropologists
were very interested in totemism. In their evolutionary theories totemism represented a primitive stage, perhaps the original stage, of religious thought. Totemism has been described from many parts of the world, including North America,
Africa, and Australia.

The term *totem* comes from the Ojibwa language of Canada, in which the
word *ototeman* can be translated as "He is a relative of mine." This refers to particular animal species, known as totems, that become associated with Ojibwa
clans, a type of kinship group. The clans are given the name of the totem.

Totemism and the Dream Time in Australia.   Perhaps the best-known examples of totemism come from Australian aboriginal groups. The totemic system has
many components, including totemic symbols, myths, and a sacred landscape.

In contrast to isolated sacred sites, which are often the sites of pilgrimages,
indigenous peoples live on a sacred landscape. The places described in their myths
are places that exist in their own physical world—a stream, a cave, a mountain.
And their origin stories tell of the creation of this landscape and the heavens and
the creation of the plants, animals, and people who inhabit the landscape.

The creation myths of the Australian Aborigines begin in the dim past during
the Dream Time with the creation of an earth without features, an earth devoid of
mountains, rivers, and plains. Supernatural creatures then appeared on the earth.
These creatures of the Dream Time appeared from under the earth or, among
coastal groups, on rafts. They then traveled over the landscape, creating the world
as we see it today—the physical world, the plants, the animals, the people—as well
as the customs that govern people's lives. They then left the surface of the earth or
turned themselves into some object in the landscape, such as a boulder or hill. The
places that are associated with particular mythological beings—the places of emergence, places that play important roles in acts of creation such as water holes and
caves, and finally the creatures themselves turned into natural objects—are today
sacred spaces that play important roles in religious rituals. The landscape in which
the Aborigines live is a canvas on which their mythology is written, and various
features of this landscape and the heavens serve to define the nature of humanity.
It is a link to the past, to their history.

The stories of the Dream Time establish special relationships between humans and animals, for both types of creatures are descendants of the same supernatural being that was neither human nor animal. Thus the tie of kinship is
extended to the animal world and, through the stories of the journeys of the creatures of the Dream Time, to the rest of the living world as well as the physical landscape. These animals, plants, and natural objects are the totems of the community.
Any particular place, be it a water hole or a hill, can be associated with a particular story and can be claimed as part of the religious heritage of a particular group
of people.

Within a community different groups of people share different totems. Totems exist for bands, clans, the sexes, and even individuals. Claiming a totem brings with it special obligations. One is a prohibition against eating the flesh of one's totemic animal. It is acceptable for other members of the community, even your spouse and children, to eat of your totem, but not for you because you share a special relationship with the totemic species. However, the flesh of one's totem may be consumed as part of a ritual. There are many other rules that are part of the special relationship between an individual or group and its totem.

Members of a totemic group have responsibilities to perform religious ceremonies, including initiation ceremonies. These rituals often involve offering of blood and visits to sacred sites. A very important type of ritual is called an **increase rite.** The purpose of these ceremonies is to assist the totem in successfully surviving and reproducing so as to provide a food resource for other members of ones community.

Totemic affiliations also organize Australian society. Although the Aborigines have a very simple technology, their social organization is extraordinarily complex. Specific clans are associated with particular totems. There are rules regulating who can marry whom. For example, one cannot marry someone from one's own clan and other related clans. Complex rules often define the affiliation of one's children as well as the appropriate social behaviors between different classes of kin.

The determination of the group into which a child is born can be complex. In some groups it is determined by rules of kinship. In many groups the pregnancy is thought to be the result of a totemic spirit, perhaps residing in a sacred water hole, entering the womb of the woman. The husband and other elders will question the woman to determine which spirit from what totemic group entered her womb to determine that child's affiliation. In some groups the identity of the spirit is revealed in the father's dream. On death the individual's soul returns to the totemic well.

At some point young men are initiated into manhood. These initiation rituals involve the learning of ritual knowledge, including the ability to look at and handle totemic objects. These rituals also involve some type of alteration of the body, such as circumcision or the knocking out of a tooth. When visiting sacred places described in the Dream Time stories, wounds are opened or new wounds are made on the body, and a person's blood is allowed to fall on sacred objects.

Australian Aborigine culture has a rich tradition of symbolic religious art. This art includes arrangements of stones, decoration of sacred objects, bark paintings, and rock art. Sacred spaces, especially caves and rock overhangs, are decorated with paintings and engravings, some going back well over 10,000 years. Many of these were done by men as representations of totemic creatures, objects, and events; others were thought to have been completed by the totemic beings during the Dream Time. Some are said to actually represent the totemic being who turned to stone or became a painting on a wall.

Murngin Totemism.   Today much of the culture of the Australian Aborigines has been lost owing to depopulation and the influence of Western culture. Early descriptions of Aborigine peoples offer a rare glimpse into their lives. One of these early reports is that of W. Lloyd Warner, who lived among the Murngin between 1926 to 1929.[3] They lived in the northern and eastern regions of Arnhem Land in the north of Australia.

Murngin society is composed of several clans, which are a type of kin group. Each clan is associated with a specific territory as well as several totems. Within each territory is one or more sacred water holes that play an important role in Murngin religion.

A sacred water hole can be a well or spring, a small lake, or a section of a creek or river. There are two classes of water holes. One class consists of water holes that are not sacred. Although they are associated with a lower order of totems, objects and symbols associated with these totems may be seen by women and uninitiated boys. For example, women may bathe or gather foods in areas near these water holes. The second group of water holes, *narra* wells, are sacred. They were made by higher totems. Only initiated men may approach these areas. The water holes are sacred in two ways. First, many are sites where important events occurred during the Dream Time. Second, totemic spirits reside there.

Beneath the clan water hole, residing in waters under the earth, dwell the ancestors of the Dream Time and totemic spirits. The spirits have the form of very small fish. A spirit will then appear to a man in a dream and ask the man who his wife is so that the spirit may enter her womb. A father may also know of this by some peculiar action of an animal. (Although the Murngin believe that it is the entrance of a totemic spirit into the womb of a mother that causes pregnancy, they are very much aware of the biological cause of pregnancy. However, it is the mythological cause that is of social importance.) If an infant dies, its spirit returns to the water hole and, after a period of time, returns to the womb of the same mother. When any other person dies, his or her spirit goes back to the water hole, where it remains a spirit forever.

Murngin mythology is very complex and consists of many interrelated stories and rituals. One of the important myth cycles is the one that tells the story of the Djunkgao sisters. These mythological sisters appeared on a raft, walked over the landscape with their two yam sticks (long, pointed sticks used to dig food out of the ground), and then disappeared beneath the earth. As they traveled, various plants and animals were "named" or created. They made the islands off the coast, and they made totemic emblems, the sacred objects that are used in ritual. For example, at one of the water holes the sisters "squatted down there and a stone *ranga* fell out of the womb of the younger sister. This stone can be seen a short distance from the well. Anyone can go touch it. That stone is bigger than a house. . . . The stone is called the *bir-ta* (black stone)."[4]

The Symbolism of Music and Dance

Dance and music play special roles in religious rituals. The degree to which dance and music are included in ritual is quite variable. Some rituals simply include a song; others focus on an elaborate performance of a myth in song and dance. Dance and music can be thought of as symbols as stories are told through movement and through music motifs.

The Symbolism of Music

Music is a key element in ritual. Music may simply set the mood for a ceremony or music may actually be the primarily vehicle by which religious stories are told and by which people communicate with the gods. Music fulfills many roles during religious rituals. Music is used to teach, to express or engender emotional states, to produce altered states of consciousness, to please the supernatural powers, or to make contact with them.

An important function of music is the facilitation of memorization. In nonliterate societies large amounts of narrative must be committed to memory. Anyone who has had to memorize a piece of prose in school knows how difficult this can be. Poetry is easier to memorize than prose because poetry has rhythm and rhyme. The easiest of all to memorize are the lyrics to a song. For this reason narratives and prayers are frequently chanted or sung.

Of course, music also sets the mood for a ritual. The organ setting the mood for a funeral, a choir singing a medieval chant, the rejoicing of a gospel hymn—all illustrate the power of music to set the ambience for ritual. We use music in a similar way for secular purposes. Compare the music you would select to listen to while studying with the music you would play when having friends over for a party or a date for a romantic evening. Movies continually use music to set the emotional tone. We know when to be happy, sad, or frightened on the basis of the music on the soundtrack.

Many early Christian missionaries understood the influence of music and brought pianos and organs with them to remote areas of the globe. A small organ might have been played in a crude brush church set in the middle of a tropical rain forest. However, these missionaries were making the assumption that the various types of music that we produce reflect universals in moods and emotions.

A somber hymn played on an organ reflects the sadness of a funeral, and a romping gospel hymn expresses the joy of closeness with God. We could assume that Euro-American religious, military, or love music will evoke the same emotional response in all societies throughout the world. This assumption, however, turns out not to be true. In reality, Euro-American music often fails to convey its intended meaning to non-Westerners, and native musical idioms fail to move outsiders. Of course, the meaning of music is symbolic, and as such, it is part of the learned traditions of a culture.

Realizing this basic fact, many missionaries and many contemporary musicians are writing music in traditional idioms and are discovering and importing tribal musical traditions into contemporary music. This is an example of **syncretism**, the fusion of elements from two different cultures. For example, the well-known Congolese composition *Missa Luba* is a Catholic Mass sung in Latin but set to music elements and instruments of the Kongo tribe of Democratic Republic of

Congo (formerly Zaire). African drumming, Australian Aborigine songs, and Native American flute playing have all been integrated into new musical experiences.

Instruments are very important elements in music, and an unbelievable array of musical instruments can be found throughout the world. We can divide instruments into four basic types. **Idiophones** are instruments that are struck, shaken, or rubbed. Common examples are rattles, bells, wooden drums, rasps, bullroarers, marimbas, and xylophones. **Membranophones** are instruments that incorporate a taut membrane or skin. These include drums. **Cordophones** are instruments with taut strings that can be plucked or strummed, hit, or sawed. These include harps, zithers, and violins. Finally, we have **aerophones,** in which air is blown across or into some type of passageway, such as a pipe. These include whistles, pipes, didjeridus, flutes, and trumpets.

In some cultures the actual musical sounds may be interpreted as sounds of the supernatural. The sound may be produced either vocally or instrumentally. One example of this is the Tuva (Siberian culture area). For the Tuva spiritual power is found in nature. These spirits manifest themselves both through physical appearance and by the sounds they make or that can be made through human interaction. Examples would be the sound of running water or the echo of a human voice from a cliff. The way for humans to make contact with supernatural powers is to imitate their sounds. Caves, in particular, are important for this purpose. Caves are sites of supernatural power and can be used to contact the spirits of the earth. The type of vocal sounds the Tuva use is also interesting. They are known for a technique called *xöömei,* or "throat-singing." A single vocalist using this technique is able to produce two distinct pitches at the same time.

For other cultures sounds produced by musical instruments have religious significance. The best-known examples in the anthropological literature are the didjeridu of the Australian Aborigines and the molimo of the Pygmies of the Ituri Forest of Central Africa. These are very simple aerophones that are essentially nothing more than long pipes, usually of wood. The sounds of these instruments are said to be the sounds of spirits. Initiated men play these instruments out of sight of the women and children, who are told that the sound is the actual voice of the spirits. The true nature of the sound is revealed to young men as part of initiation rites.

The Symbolism of Dance

The use of dance is not common in American religious rituals, but in many religious traditions dance is an important means of symbolically representing the supernatural world and telling religious stories. Of course, dance does not exist in isolation. Dance is usually performed to music, frequently involves the chanting or singing of words, and involves the manipulation of physical symbols such as costumes and masks, sets, and props.

Culture consists of patterned, traditional behaviors. We can define dance as a system of patterned, traditional movements. These movements, involving the whole body or sometimes just a part of the body such as the hands, are symbolic in that they have culturally determined meanings. Characters in well-known stories are identified by their traditional movements, such as their way of walking and moving their arms, as well as by their costumes, masks, and so forth. In societies that lack systems of writing, dance becomes an important vehicle for telling sacred stories to the community. For example, among native Hawaiians, hula dances told the stories of the gods and goddesses.

The Kwakiutl of the North American Northwest Coast culture area say that a human family line was created when the ancestor of the group came down to earth, took off his mask, and became human. Carved animal masks are an important religious art form for the Kwakiutl and frequently are worn by the dancers who retell important mythic stories. Dance, however, goes far beyond the telling of stories. Dances can act as offerings, and many deities like to be entertained. Dancers also can become conduits of supernatural power. The Kwakiutl masked dancers, for example, become the being whose mask is worn for the duration of the ritual.

In many cultures gods and spirits enter the human body and take over its functioning. The particular movements during possession identify the god within the body and may actually provide communication between the deity and the human participants. Possession is an important feature of Vodou. During a Vodou ritual a song is sung to summon a particular god. When the god arrives, he or she possesses one of the dancers. A common metaphor is that the dancer is a horse on which the deity rides. Which god has possessed a dancer can be deduced by the dancer's movements and actions. We will discuss the Vodou religion in more detail in Chapter 10.

Early in the history of Islam, a group who was most interested in the mystical aspects of the religion broke off to form the Sufi. One of the most important of the Sufi mystics was a man named Mevlana Rumi, who lived in the thirteenth century Ottoman Empire. Rumi founded the Mevlevi Order and revived the practice of whirling. The members of the Mevlevi Order are often called "whirling dervishes" by people in the West. They wear long white skirts that billow out as the dancers, their arms extended in the air, continue to turn. Through this whirling, the dancers seek to become one with God.

The Tewa, a Pueblo group from the Southwest culture area, say that they dance to "seek life," "regain life," or "renew life." Many symbolic references to this theme of new life can be found in the movements of the dancers, the costumes that are worn, and the songs that are sung. Dancers lift their arms upward to symbolize the welcoming of rain; lower their arms to indicate digging, planting, or harvesting; and move their arms from side to side to symbolize rainbows or clouds. Costume designs are also symbolic. Long tassels represent raindrops; woven headdresses contain depictions of squash blossoms or embroidered layers of clouds. The songs that accompany the dances make references to dawn, youth, flowers, and growing corn. The Tewa practice agriculture in a very arid environment, so references to rain and items associated with rain such as clouds, thunder, and rainbows are important symbols of life.

Tewa dances are generally held in open plazas where performers can be in contact with the earth. The dancers array themselves in long, parallel lines and move in unison to the beat of one or more drums. The dancers themselves may sing, or a chorus of singers standing nearby may accompany them. Before the dance, the participants prepare in a kiva. A **kiva** is an underground room that is entered from a hole in the roof. When the dance is about to begin, the dancers emerge from the kiva and move to the plaza. This is a symbolic reference to the Tewa origin story that tells how the first people emerged from a world below into the present world.

Symbolism among the Asmat: Art, Music, and Dance

We have examined several types of religious symbolism. However, art, music, and dance do not exist as isolated elements—another illustration of holism. The following example will show how all of these elements interact as a part of a religious system.

The Asmat live on the southern coast of Irian Jaya, an Indonesian province that is the western half of the island of New Guinea. They call themselves the "tree people"; their environment is composed of water, mud, and wood.

Although the Asmat practice farming, their main source of food is the starch that is obtained from the pith of the sago palm, a noncultivated tree. Every four days or so, a group of men locate and cut down a sago palm. The processing of the palm is laborious as the men remove the internal pith, which is then processed into sago flour.

Culture adds meaning to the natural world. The sago palm is a species of tree. It is used as a source of food. It also provides building material and wood for carving. Yet to the Asmat the palm is much more than a plant. It is thought to be like a woman. The white pith inside is like mother's milk and is a life force. The Asmat were headhunters, and cutting down a sago palm is like taking a human head. In cutting down the sago, men attack it, and in removing the starch, they butcher it.

As in a great many societies, death is explained in terms of the supernatural. Death can be the action of a god or spirit or an action of another person through witchcraft or sorcery. The Asmat believe that death is caused by enemies, either as a result of being killed directly by a weapon on a raid or through sorcery from afar. In either case the spirits of the dead demand revenge. The presence of an unavenged spirit poses a great danger to the village. In former times revenge was extracted by taking the head of an enemy.

The taking of heads is supported by Asmat mythology. The Asmat believe that the universe originated when a god beheaded his brother. This was an act of creation as the blood spurting outward from the body of the god created the universe. The cutting off of heads and the heads and skulls themselves are important elements in Asmat religion. Many symbols of head hunting are found in Asmat wood carvings. For example, a common symbol is the female praying mantis, an insect that bites off the head of her mate during copulation.

In mortuary rituals a head of an enemy is taken, a step that is usually skipped in today's world. Next, a relative of the deceased hires a wood carver to create a tall *bis* pole, which, when erect, stands fifteen to twenty feet tall (Figure 3.3). As the carving progresses, the community moves the spirit of the dead relative into

FIGURE 3.3   Bis *Poles*. Group of Asmat *bis* poles that have been discarded following a *bis* ceremony.

the pole. This is accomplished by drumming and dancing. (This is similar to the myth that the first humans were carved in wood and the god drummed and danced life into the image.) Finally, the spirit is sent to an island, where the souls gather awaiting rebirth.

Conclusion

To conclude our discussion of symbolism, we need to tie together several concepts that we have explored thus far. We discussed myths and the concept of worldview in previous chapters. Now we need to examine the strong connection between worldview, myth, and symbols. Symbols are often based on specific episodes that are recounted in myths, and they represent a specific worldview. An example we already discussed was the Tewa practice of beginning dances by emerging from a kiva to symbolize the emergence at the beginning of the world. We will reexamine some of the other symbols we have already discussed to explore these connections.

We know that bloodletting was an important part of Mayan religious rituals and that the sarcophagus of Lord Pakal contains blood symbolism. The reason for this is found in the origin story as told in a document known as the *Popul Vuh,* a seventeenth century book that recounts the history of the Maya. In the *Popul Vuh* we are told that the reason why the gods created people was to have a kind of living creature who would worship them. As they prepare to create human beings, the gods say, "So now let's try to make a giver of praise, giver of respect, provider, nurturer."[5]

This reflects the worldview of the Maya that there exists a reciprocal relationship between the Mayan people and their gods. The world was brought about by a sacrifice by the gods, but it will continue to exist only if the Mayans in turn sacrifice for the gods. The smoke produced by burning cloths soaked with blood was seen as providing nourishment to the gods.

The image of Pakal descending into the underworld to be reborn also refers to a portion of the *Popul Vuh.* The story tells of twins, Hunahpu and Xbalanque, who disturb the Lords of Death by playing a ball game. They are summoned to Xibalba to participate in a series of trials, but they are able to defeat the Lords of Death through their cunning and are then reborn.

In a similar way the Christian cross is based on the story of the crucifixion of Jesus found in the Christian Bible. The symbol of the cross also expresses the Christian worldview: that the death of Jesus provides the opportunity for salvation.

> And when they were come to the place, which is called Calvary, there they crucified him, and the malefactors, one on the right hand, and the other on the left. Then Jesus said, Father, forgive them, for they know what they do. And they parted his raiment, and cast lots (Luke 23:33–34).

> And one of the malefactors which were hanged railed on him, saying, If thou be Christ, save thyself and us. But the other answering rebuked him, saying, Dost not thou fear God, seeing thou art in the same condemnation? And we indeed justly; for we receive the due reward of our deeds; but this man hath done nothing amiss. Then he said unto Jesus, Lord, remember me when thou comest into thy kingdom. And Jesus said unto him, Verily I say unto you, Today shalt thou be with me in paradise (Luke 23:39–43).

> For God so loved the world that he gave his only begotten Son, that whosoever believeth in him should not perish, but have everlasting life (John 3:16).

Another example of the connection between symbol, myth, and worldview is the yin-yang symbol (Figure 3.4). This symbol is based on the Taoist worldview of the importance of balance and harmony. The Taoists believe that there are two

FIGURE 3.4 *Yin-yang.* According to Taoist belief, *yin* is the female element and *yang* is the male element in the universe.

interacting forces in the universe, called *yin* and *yang*. *Yin* is the female element, associated with coldness, darkness, softness, and the earth. *Yang* is the male element and is associated with warmth, light, hardness, and the heavens. The two elements are opposites but mutually dependent, and they need to be in equilibrium. *Yin* and *yang* are believed to be present in every aspect of the world. Yet each holds the seed of the other that expands and becomes the other.

In an ancient Chinese creation story *yin* and *yang* were held together in a cosmic egg until the struggle of the opposing elements cracked the shell. A creature called P'an Ku took form inside the egg. P'an Ku is sometimes referred to as the child of *yin* and *yang* or as the giant of Chinese mythology. P'an Ku emerges from the egg and goes about creating the world, in several versions fashioning the earth using an adze or a hammer and chisel. But the creation of the world is not complete until P'an Ku dies, whereupon his body gives rise to various elements. His skull becomes the dome of the sky, and his flesh becomes the soil of the earth. His bones become rock; his blood, rivers; his breath, the winds; his eyes, the sun and the moon. The fleas and parasites on his body became the ancestors of modern human groups.

These connections between symbol, myth, and worldview will continue to be important as we add one more element to the mix: ritual. In the next chapter we will discuss rituals and the ways in which they are intimately connected with symbols, myth, and worldview.

Summary

A symbol is something that stands for something else. Symbols enable us to talk about things that are not immediately in front of us and to create our own realities. They are important elements in religious practice, and religious rituals center on the manipulation of symbols.

Symbols can appear in many forms. Language is symbolic in nature, since various speech sounds are used to create combinations that have meaning. Yet there is nothing of the referent that is inherent in the sound combination—its meaning is part of a cultural tradition. Recitation of religious narratives is an important feature of religious practices. Religious ideas also can be expressed in art that may contain many symbolic elements. Much artistic representation is arbitrary in that the nature of the symbol does not always communicate its meaning. Simple examples are the swastika, the pentagram, and the cross. Although an outsider might have difficulty understanding a piece of religious art, a member of that culture would have no such difficulty.

Music and dance are also symbolic and are important elements in religious ritual. Musical elements suggest emotions and have symbolic meanings. What is considered to be religious music in one community might not be in another. Dance, composed of music, movement, costume and masks, props and sets, is often used to tell religious stories in societies where such stories are not written down. All of these elements—language, art, music, and dance—interact to provide rich religious experiences.

Suggested Readings

Norine Dresser, *Multicultural Celebrations* (New York: Three Rivers Press, 1999).
[This is a practical book on the appropriate etiquette for celebrations in various ethnic traditions in the United States, useful in our multicultural society.]

Carl G. Liungman, *Dictionary of Symbols* (New York: Norton, 1991).
[This is one of several compilations of symbols that are useful reference tools.]

Gananath Obeyesekere, *Medusa's Hair: An Essay of Personal Symbols and Religious Experience* (Chicago: University of Chicago Press, 1981).
[A psychological anthropologist examines the use of symbols by Sri Lankan ascetics.]

Clinton R. Sanders, *Customizing the Body: The Art and Culture of Tattooing* (Philadelphia: Temple University Press, 1989).
[A look at the American tattooing culture.]

Fiction:

Rudolfo Anaya, *Bless Me Ultima* (New York: Warner Books, 1999).
[In a story filled with religious symbolism, a boy grows up in New Mexico in the 1940s.]

Suggested Web Sites

http://symbols.net
A comprehensive listing of web sites that deal with symbols in various contexts including religion.

www.pauahtun.org/basic.html
An introduction to the Mayan calendar.

www.asmat.org
The American Museum of Asmat Art.

www.lib.washington.edu/music/world.html #native
A list of web sites related to ethnomusicology, folk music, and world music from the University of Washington.

http://home.att.net/~wegast/symbols/symbols.htm
Symbols in Christian art and architecture.

Study Questions

1. Logos and trademarks are examples of symbols that are important in American society. Select some examples and show how they express a particular emotion or idea about the product being advertised.

2. Historically, symbols can be very powerful and can evoke great emotions. This is especially true of religious symbols. List some religious and political symbols, and describe what roles they have played in human history.

3. Color has meaning in all cultures. How are colors used in American society to convey meaning? What are some of the social rules that determine the use of color in our society (e.g., a bride wears white)? Do you know of any differences in the meaning of color in other cultures?

4. How are totemism and the concept of Dream Time a social charter for Australian Aborigine cultures? How do you think these cultures would react to the presence of non-Aborigine cultures, such as those represented by missionaries?

5. Many American organizations are identified with particular animals. For example, colleges and professional football teams are often associated with a mascot, usually some kind of animal. What animals are usually used as college and team mascots? Why are those particular animals used and not others? When you go to a football or

baseball game, what ritual activities revolve around the mascot animal? How does this differ from an Australian totem?

6. What kinds of body alterations do you observe in your own school or place of employment? Why do your friends and co-workers alter the appearance of their bodies? Are any of these alterations of a religious nature?

7. Describe the role of music in American culture. In what situations do you find music being played? Why is music played in these situations?

8. Choose a religious symbol that you are familiar with and describe its meaning. How is this symbol connected to the myths and worldview of the culture in which it is found?

Endnotes

1. J. Church, *Language and the Discovery of Reality* (New York: Random House, 1961), quoted in Oliver Sacks, *Seeing Voices* (New York: Vintage Books, 1990), p. 36.

2. G. A. Reichard, *Navaho Religion: A Study of Symbolism* (Princeton, NJ: Princeton University Press, 1977), p. 206.

3. W. Lloyd Warner, *A Black Civilization*, Revised Edition (New York: Harper & Row, 1958).

4. Ibid., p. 329.

5. D. Tedlock (translator), *Popul Vuh: The Definitive Edition of the Mayan Book of the Dawn of Life and the Glories of Gods and Kings* (New York: Simon & Schuster, 1985), p. 79.

4

Ritual

The alarm clock rings. You reluctantly jump out of bed and begin your morning routine. This routine might include showering, shaving or putting on your makeup, reading the newspaper, and eating breakfast. You probably do the same things in the same order day after day—or at least on weekdays. This patterned, recurring sequence of events may be termed a **ritual.**

The term *ritual* can refer to any repetitive sequence of acts. Psychologists use the term when referring to repetitive compulsive activity, such as the ritual of washing one's hands dozens of times a day. A class might begin with the ritual of calling role and making announcements. However, when the ritual involves the manipulation of religious symbols such as prayers, offerings, and readings of sacred literature, we call it a **religious ritual.**

Ritual and Myth

In some ways a ritual resembles a play. A play consists of actors, words, sets, and props presented in a set way according to a script. And a play is a reflection of the culture of a society and that society's worldview.

A public religious ritual also consists of actors (shamans and priests, for example), words (perhaps a prayer, a spell, or a sermon), sets (such as an altar), and props (such as candles, religious books, or masks) and may contain music and dance as well. Smaller-scale rituals, such as that performed by a shaman affecting a cure, also have many of these elements, although here the similarity to a play is not as strong. Of course, a religious ritual is much more than a play. Its primary purpose is not to entertain—although in some societies rituals are an important form of entertainment—and the audience is an active participant.

Two of the most basic elements in religious practices are ritual and myth, and the two are often closely connected. Ritual is often based on myth in that the instruction to perform the ritual may lie within the myth. The myth provides the elements for the development of the ritual. There is some debate over which came first. Myth is reflected in ritual, and ritual often gives rise to myth.

A society's mythology consists of stories that reflect the underlying world-view of the society. Although few people in a community can articulate in a philosophical or theological manner the basic themes and underpinnings of their religious system, everyone is familiar with the myths of their religion and accepts the basic truths of the religious system. This is also true of rituals.

Many rituals, though by no means all, are public rituals in which an entire community is involved to some degree. Ritual activities symbolize the particular beliefs and values of that community. A ritual is the vehicle by which basic ideas, such as the definition of good and evil and the proper nature of social relationships, are imparted to the group. However, there is much more to rituals than the transmission of knowledge and rules. Participation in ritual signals acceptance of these values.

Unlike other forms of discourse—reading this book, for example, or listening to a lecture—people attending a religious ritual usually are familiar with the ritual and understand what it means. Perhaps they have read a commentary or attended a Sunday school class that discussed the meaning of the ritual. Thus participation in the ritual signals a public acceptance of the basic tenets of the religion. The mere fact that the activities that take place within the ritual are well known and accepted lends a sense of stability to the society and imparts a sense of social unity. Also, the fact that the elements of the ritual are repeated on a regular basis lends a sense of validity and sacredness to the religious system.

The Basics of Ritual Performance

A survey of the ethnographic literature reveals an astonishing diversity of religious rituals. The first step is to develop some basic concepts for describing rituals. Here we will discuss classifications that address the why and when of a ritual performance.

Prescriptive and Situational Rituals

There are many terms that we can use to describe rituals. For example, rituals may be prescriptive or situational. **Prescriptive rituals** are rituals that are required to be performed. The requirement may be set forth in a religious text ("Remember the Sabbath day, to keep it holy [Exodus 20:8]"), may be required by a deity or a religious authority, or may simply be based in tradition.

Other rituals are performed because of a particular need of an individual or a community. These are called **situational rituals** or **crisis rituals.** Such rituals often arise spontaneously, frequently in times of crisis. A community might hold a spontaneous ritual for a group of men and women from the community who are going off to war or engaging in some dangerous activity. The tragedy of September 11, 2001, in the United States gave rise to many situational rituals—some as simple as flying a flag, others more complex, such as the setting up of informal altars where people laid flowers, lit candles, and left photographs. Many churches and temples scheduled special situational rituals to address the concerns of the community.

Periodic and Occasional Rituals

Another way of describing rituals is to identify them as being performed on a regular basis as part of a religious calendar or being performed when a particular need arises, such as a marriage or a death. The former are called **periodic rituals** or **calendrical rituals;** the latter are called **occasional rituals.** The classification of rituals as prescribed or situational is separate from their classification as periodic or occasional. Thus a particular ceremony—a Sunday morning church service, for example—is both prescribed and periodic.

Periodic rituals may be performed daily or several times a day, as in the daily prayers (*salaht*) of Islam. (Muslims pray at dawn, midday, midafternoon, sunset, and nightfall, as commanded by the prophet Mohammad, which makes prayer a prescribed ritual as well.) Periodic rituals may be performed weekly, such as the Jewish ritual of the lighting of candles that occurs on every Friday evening to mark the start of the Sabbath or the celebration of Sunday Mass in the Catholic Church. They also include the annual celebrations of Easter, Passover, and Ramadan.

Another example of a periodic ritual is Diwali, the Festival of Lights, one of the most important festivals in India. It was originally a Hindu festival, but its observance has spread, and it is celebrated as a public holiday throughout India. Diwali is celebrated on the darkest night (the new moon) of the month of Kartik. During the festival, oil lamps are lit, and firecrackers are set off. The ritual is associated with several important mythical events. One such story is the return of Rama, his consort Sita, and his brother Lakshmana to their kingdom of Ayodhya after a fourteen-year exile. To celebrate their return, the people of Ayodhya are said to have lit up their houses with oil lamps. The lights that are associated with this festival are said to symbolize the removal of spiritual darkness.

The celebration of Diwali was probably originally related to the harvest season. Many periodic rituals are aligned with the phases of the agricultural cycle. This is the basis of the timing of many religious rituals in the Jewish and Christian religious calendars. The most important rituals are associated with the periods of sowing and harvesting.

For example, Passover is a Jewish commemoration of the exodus of the Israelites from Egypt. However, many historians believe that this holiday was also originally a spring agricultural festival. This can be seen in many of the symbolic foods associated with the Passover *Seder*, or ritual meal, such as parsley. Exactly seven weeks after the Passover holiday is Shavuot. Shavuot is also known as Yom Habikkurim, or "the Day of the First Fruits," and commemorates both the beginning of the wheat harvest and the giving of the Ten Commandments to Moses at Mount Sinai.

Occasional rituals are rituals that are performed for a specific purpose when a situation arises that requires the ritual to be performed. Many occasional rituals are associated with nature and the impact of nature on the agricultural cycle. These include rituals to control an infestation of insect pests or to bring rain, which are performed when crops are threatened by insect pests or when rain does not come. Occasional rituals are also associated with important events in the life of an individual. These include rituals marking birth, marriage, and death, which will be discussed in more detail later in the chapter.

A Classification of Rituals

Our next step is to group the subjects of our study, in this case rituals, into a manageable number of categories. This can be very difficult when the variation is great, and any classification is to an extent arbitrary. Here we will discuss many of the different kinds of rituals using some of the categories developed by Anthony F. C. Wallace.[1]

Technological Rituals

Technological rituals are rituals that attempt to influence or control nature, especially in activities that affect human activities and well-being. The success or failure of human endeavors such as hunting, fishing, and farming is influenced by the vagaries of nature. Game animals might not be located, fish might fail to take the bait, the lack of rain might cause a crop to wither and die. Because these events affect the very survival of a people, all societies attempt to influence or even to control nature so as to ensure the success of the hunt, fishing expeditions, or cultivation. Examples of technological rituals include hunting and gathering rites of intensification, protective rituals, and divination rituals.

Hunting and Gathering Rites of Intensification.   The function of **hunting and gathering rites of intensification** is to influence nature in the quest for food. Although the name refers to hunting and gathering activities, these rituals also extend to other economic activities such as fishing, herding, and farming. They include periodic rituals that follow the seasonal cycle and occasional rituals performed in response to some crisis such as lack of rain. They may initiate the hunting of particular animal species as they migrate at different seasons through a traditional territory. At the start of a fishing trip, such rituals are performed to ensure success in locating fish. Rituals accompany the preparation of the soil, the planting of seeds, the protection of the growing crop from the elements and wild animals, and the harvest.

Among hunting and gathering peoples the commencement of the time when particular wild foods are available is often marked by ritual. On a practical level, these rituals serve to regulate the gathering of that food. The premature gathering of a particular type of fruit, for example, might negatively affect the total amount of fruit that is available. They also reaffirm the rights of particular social units to specific foods and areas of food gathering. These rituals are frequently referred to as "first-fruit ceremonies." Among the Cahuilla of the southern California desert, individuals would be sent out to gather small amounts of food. Food left from the winter stores would be added, and members of each kin group would eat a ritual portion of the food in a ceremony thanking the supernatural for providing the food in a ceremony that lasted three days and three nights.

Fertility is a central theme in this group of rituals, be it the successful sprouting and growth of crops in the spring or the birth of wild animals, without which people would go hungry and societies would die. When people are successful in the hunt, rituals are performed to thank the animal for allowing itself to be caught.

The Lakota are a Native American tribe living today in the north-central United States. In the early nineteenth century they were hunters of the buffalo. Today, although wild herds of buffalo have disappeared from the plains, the Lakota manage herds of captive buffalo and sell their meat as a major source of income. Occasionally, an uncontrollable animal must be killed, which today is accomplished by a shotgun rather than a bow and arrow. But when the animal has died, the hunters gather around the body and perform a simple ritual to thank the buffalo for permitting itself to be killed, thus ensuring the continuous success of the enterprise.

The Inuit, who live on the Arctic coast, depend on seals for their survival. The myths and rituals of the Inuit reflect this connection. The creation of seals is the subject of an important creation myth.[2]

Long ago, there lived in the Arctic a young and beautiful woman. Many men were presented to her as prospective husbands, but she rejected them all, until one day a handsome stranger came to her family's camp. He had many dogs and finely crafted hunting tools, and he promised her a life of comfort. She could not resist, and she left with him for his land across the sea, only to find on her arrival that she had been deceived. Her betrothed was in fact a seabird, and his dwelling was a hovel. When her father came to rescue her, they escaped in his boat across the calm sea. But her seabird husband's spirit, angered by this, pursued them and whipped the icy sea into a raging storm. In midocean in a small boat, the father feared for his life and, to appease the bird, cast his daughter overboard into the wave-tossed waters. But she clung relentlessly to the gunwale of his boat. Determined to release her grip, the father cut off her fingers at the first knuckle; the pieces fell into the sea and became the ringed seals. Still she held on. Then he cut all her fingers at the second joint, and those pieces swam away as bearded seals. Other pieces of her fingers became walruses and whales. That is how seals were created, and that young woman became Nuliajuk, the Mother of the Sea. . . . To this day she lives at the bottom of the sea and controls all the animals in her watery domain.

The success of a seal hunt among the Inuit depends on the benevolence of the Mother of the Sea. If important customs are neglected, she can cause many difficulties for hunters such as storms or breaking up of the ice. She might also keep the seals out of the reach of the hunters. The Inuit believe that Nuliajuk is at her happiest when her hair is neat, and the misbehavior of people is seen as tangling her hair. Because her fingers were cut off and became the seals, she cannot tend to her hair herself and it is the role of the shaman to visit her in her home at the bottom of the sea to comb her hair and thereby appease her.

The traditional Inuit belief is that seals have a soul, and many Inuit hunting customs and rituals are designed to show respect for the seals. One example is the practice in many Inuit groups of placing fresh water into the mouth of a dead seal before it is butchered. Some groups believed that a seal that was given a drink was more likely to return again as another seal for another drink, but the general belief across the groups was that the drink would appease the spirit of the seal.

In the words of an Inuit, Peter Irniq, "Inuit were extremely respectful toward seals. My father used to catch a seal and put it into our iglu. Before my mother skinned the seal she would put a piece of ice in her own mouth to melt, then let the meltwater fall into the dead seal's mouth. She said this was to make sure the seals under the ice will not be thirsty. She did this every time. It's a spiritual belief, done out of respect for the seals."[3]

Protective Rituals.   There are numerous potential dangers that accompany risky activities. Imagine traveling in a small dugout canoe out on the ocean, out of sight of land, looking for productive fishing grounds, with no real ability to predict the weather more than a few hours in advance, if that. **Protective rituals** usually accompany such activities, and they may be prescriptive in that they are routinely performed at the start of a dangerous activity or occasionally in response to a gathering storm.

These are rituals designed to protect the safety of the people who are involved in dangerous tasks. Protective rituals are also performed in response to some unexpected threat to the success of an economic endeavor. Such threats might include an infestation of insect pests threatening to destroy a crop, floods and droughts, sick animals in a herd, and many other potential crises too numerous to name.

The ocean trading journeys of the Trobriand Islanders of New Guinea are dangerous. There are numerous concerns, including ensuring the seaworthiness of canoes and the desire for good weather. These voyages are accompanied by a great number of rituals. The canoe captain is not only an expert on navigation and weather prediction, but also a ritual specialist, performing rituals throughout the voyage. As an example, some of rituals that are performed before the launching of a canoe are rituals for expelling the heaviness out of a canoe, rituals to make the canoe more seaworthy, and rituals to make the canoe fast, in part by making other canoes slow.

Rituals for the protection of boats on the open ocean are common among seagoing peoples. The Vikings christened a new ship by "blooding the keel," which involved a ritual human sacrifice in which a person was tied to the keel of the boat, to be crushed beneath it when the boat was launched. The Western practice of christening a new ship by breaking a bottle of champagne still carries with it the idea of a blessing from God, and the person who does the christening enters into a special relationship with the ship.

Protective rituals are also used for other modes of transportation. Among the Yoruba of Nigeria in West Africa, Ogun is the god of iron. More recently, Ogun has also become associated with cars and trucks. It is common for taxi drivers to decorate their cars with his symbols and even on occasion to offer an animal sacrifice to him asking for his protection.

Often it is not actual control that is needed. Foreknowledge of natural events that affect the success of economic efforts can lead to preventive measures, be they technical (building a fence to keep wild animals out of the field) or ritual. Such ceremonies assist communities in selecting the best time to plant or the best place to locate game or fish. Rituals that seek information are referred to as **divination rituals.** Divination will be discussed in detail in Chapter 6.

Therapy Rituals

Of all tragedies that may befall a people, perhaps the most disturbing and disruptive are illnesses and accidents that lead to incapacity or death. All peoples have theories about the cause of illness and accident, and these are associated with techniques, including rituals, for dealing with them.

There are a number of methods for dealing with accidents and illnesses that are technical rather than religious. For example, many traditional healers know how to set bones, and many of the plant materials that are administered as medicines have been found to have genuine medical value. The anthropological study of medicinal plants is part of the study of **ethnobotany.** Such studies have led to the development of several drug therapies. Some plant material has been known for centuries to have some pharmaceutical properties, such as digitalis from the foxglove plant, which is used to treat heart problems. Most recently, the drug taxol, derived from the bark and needles of the Pacific yew tree, has been used for the treatment of ovarian cancer. Northwest Coast Native American tribes traditionally treated a variety of diseases with medicines derived from this tree.

Many illnesses cannot be dealt with through technology, especially in traditional societies. Various theories of illness give rise to many types of cures that include ritual. Rituals that focus on curing are called **therapy rituals.** These are among the most important rituals found in many societies. The type of ritual will depend on the cause of the illness, with the cause frequently being discovered by means of divination. Some of the supernatural causes of illness and their treatment will be discussed at length in later chapters, but Table 4.1 lists those that are most frequently encountered.

As we discussed in Chapter 2, the Navaho worldview stresses the importance of balance and harmony. When this balance is upset, something bad, usually

TABLE 4.1   *Causes and Treatment of Supernatural Illnesses*

Cause of Illness	Therapy Ritual
Object intrusion	Massage and sucking to remove object
Spirit intrusion	Exorcism
Soul loss	Soul retrieval
Breach of tabu	Confession
Witchcraft	Anti-witchcraft rituals
Spirits and gods	Sacrifices and offerings

illness, will be the result. Balance is upset by human actions, and the specific nature of the transgression will determine how the illness will manifest itself. The Navaho have separate specialists for diagnosis and treatment. Diagnosis is done by hand tremblers, who are generally women. The healers are usually male.

The entire family or even the entire community will gather together for the therapy ritual, which lasts anywhere from one to nine days. Prayers, medicine, songs, herbs and sand paintings are used to restore balance and harmony and thus cure the illness. An important element in Navaho rituals is the sand painting (Figure 4.1). The Navaho word for sand painting is *ikaah*, which means "a summoning of the gods." They believe that if a prayer is offered with a good heart and is correct in every detail, the gods are compelled to answer it. If they do not answer, there must have been some imperfection in the sand painting or the ceremony.

The sand painting itself depicts a specific portion of the complex Navaho mythology. Usually, this is a story of a hero who encounters some misfortune, but

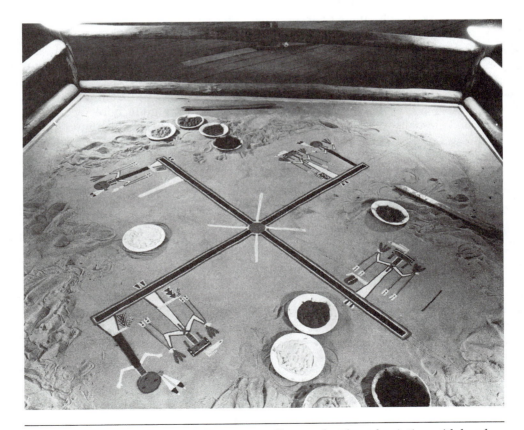

FIGURE 4.1 *Navaho Sand Painting.* A partially completed sand painting with bowls of ground, colored rock, shows the image of a swastika.

with help from others, usually a supernatural being, the hero recovers and learns how to heal the same problem in others. The story also is recounted in long, complex chants. This example again shows the relationship between ritual, myth, and worldview.

Anti-Therapy Rituals

Anti-therapy rituals are rituals that bring about illness, accident, or death. When directed towards a member of one's own community, the behavior is clearly anti-social. The person responsible needs to be identified, usually through divination, stopped, and punished. However, when directed toward an enemy, an anti-therapy ritual may support an objective of the society. Among the Yanomamö of northern South America, warfare is carried out with spears and arrows, as well as through ritual activities that send illness-causing spirits into the bodies of their enemies.

Bone pointing is an anti-therapy ritual performed by Australian Aborigines that may be referred to as a **cursing ritual.** The sorcerer points the bone at his victim while reciting a death spell. The victim then becomes ill and dies unless a therapy ritual can be performed. Another anti-therapy ritual was described in Chapter 1 for the Fore of New Guinea. A sorcerer takes something connected to the victim, such as a piece of clothing, and places it in a bundle, recites a spell, and puts the bundle in the cold, muddy ground. As a result, the victim becomes ill with the disease *kuru*.

Ideological Rituals

The next group of rituals serves to maintain the normal functioning of a community. These are termed **ideological rituals.** They delineate codes of proper behavior; define good and evil, moral and immoral; and articulate the community's worldview. They assist people and the community in getting through times of change and times of crisis. They facilitate the orderly running of the society. They tend to be conservative, sanctioning the social order.

An important type of ideological ritual is the **social rite of intensification.** These are very familiar rituals. They are usually prescribed and periodic and include the weekly Sunday morning church service found in most Christian denominations, the Jewish Sabbath rituals, and the daily prayer or *salaht* of Islam. They also include major annual rituals such as the Christian Easter and the Jewish Rosh Hashanah. Elements that are frequently found in social rites of intensification that are most familiar to us include the reading of sections of the sacred text; a sermon, commenting on some aspects of the sacred text, commentary on current crises, or a discussion of moral issues; and prayers to the deity.

Some rituals have aspects that can be classified in more than one category. A good example of this is a funeral ritual, which is often both a rite of passage for the individual who has died (discussed in the next subsection) and a rite of intensification for those who remain. A death is a time of crisis for the group. The funeral ritual brings people together and reaffirms the existence of the social group and its values. This is seen most clearly when we examine the rituals surrounding the death of a chief or king. The death affects the entire community and ushers in a period of potential instability. In the absence of a strong leader the group may be vulnerable to internal strife. Enemies may take advantage of both the lack of strong leadership and the fact that the focus of the community is on the death.

Among the Swazi of the East African Cattle culture area, the death of a king has the potential of precipitating a major crisis. The prosperity of the Swazi nation is bound up with the health and virility of the king, and during his life the king must avoid all contact with death. He may not visit a grave or touch a dead body and may mourn the passing of a close relative for only a few days. Individuals living in his household are removed from the homestead when they become very ill so that they will not die in the king's presence. The death of the king is kept secret until a council of kin has made the selection of an heir. Only after the heir has been installed as the new king will the burial of the old king proceed. Following the period of mourning, rituals are held to rejuvenate and revitalize the Swazi nation.

Another example of the element of a social rite of intensification in a funeral ritual is the Jewish practice of reciting the *kaddish*. The *kaddish* is known as a mourner's prayer, but variations on this prayer are recited at many other times, and the prayer itself actually says nothing about death or mourning. This prayer actually is a reaffirmation of faith in the face of a great loss. The prayer begins, "May His great Name grow exalted and sanctified in the world that He created as He willed. May He give reign to His kingship in your lifetime and in your days, and in the lifetimes of the entire family of Israel, swiftly and soon. May His great Name be blessed forever and ever." Similarly, the simple practice of gathering at the home of the mourner after a funeral service can be seen as reaffirming important group ties.

Rites of Passage

Another important type of ideological ritual is the **rite of passage.** A society consists of a number of individuals who are related to one another and interact with one another in complex ways. We can think of a society as being composed of a series of positions, each one defined in terms of appropriate behavior, rights and obligations, and relationships to one another. Each position is known as a **status.** Examples of a status include mother, husband, teacher, blacksmith, mayor, and priest. Of course, a person can occupy more than one status. One person can be a mother, a wife, and a teacher, depending on the social context. Here we are using the term *status* to refer to a social position, not to the relative placement of each position in the society. The term **rank** is used for this latter purpose.

When a person changes his or her status in the society—becomes an adult, marries, enters a profession, or attains political office—the individual alters his or her social relationship with other members of the society. In addition, such changes might require that the individual dress in a new way, speak in a different fashion, and behave toward certain people in new ways. Making these changes can be difficult for the individual. They often are marked and facilitated by rites of passage.

Rites of passage imprint the change in a person's social status on the minds of the participants and grant community approval or legitimacy for the change. In a literate society such as ours, all one truly needs is a legal piece of paper. A couple can fly to Las Vegas or go to the local courthouse and be married with a brief ceremony, without the presence of family or other community members. It is the marriage license, not the ceremony, that establishes the legality of the change in status and inserts the event in the legal record of some political unit. This is not the case in nonliterate communities, where the combined witnesses and participation of family and community are required. Most couples in Western culture choose to get married in this manner as well.

Some rites of passage are very familiar. These include rites marking a person's progression through the life cycle. All cultures have terminology to refer to the phases of one's life—infant, child, adult, and senior, for example. However, these divisions of the life cycle are more formal and clear-cut in some societies than in others. As a person moves from one category to the next, the event may be marked by ritual.

The life cycle begins with birth ceremonies designed to ensure the safety and well-being of the child. Through these rituals the child becomes an integral part of the community. However, in societies with a high infant death rate, the introduction of the child to the community may be delayed. A child may be kept in isolation and is considered a nonperson until his or she survives for a certain period of time. In traditional societies the child might then be presented to the family and other members of the community, receive a name, perhaps be passed over the smoke of a fire and have strings tied around his or her wrists to prevent the child from falling ill.

Examples of birth rituals in our society are baptism in Catholicism, by which the child becomes a member of a Catholic community, and the Jewish circumcision ceremony whereby a male child becomes a member of the Jewish community. In Judaism this ceremony is referred to as a *Berit Mila* (often called a *bris*). *Berit* means covenant and *Mila* means to cut, so a *Berit Mila* cuts the covenant with God. The ritual is a prescriptive one and is based on a passage from Genesis:

> And God said to Abraham, "As for you, you shall keep my Covenant, you and your descendants after you throughout their generations. This is My Covenant which you shall keep, between Me and you and your descendants after you: Every male among you shall be circumcised. You shall be circumcised in the flesh of your foreskin, and it shall be a sign of the Covenant between Me and you. He that is eight days old among you shall be circumcised; every male throughout your generations." (Genesis 17:9–12)

The circumcision is performed by a ritual specialist, known as a *mohel*. The ritual also includes a formal naming of the child. For girls the ceremony is called a *Brit Bat* (or Covenant of Daughters) and includes the naming portion only.

The next major transition is that from childhood into adulthood. These coming-of-age ceremonies include confirmations, *quinceañeras,* bar mitzvahs, and bat mitzvahs. Other important life cycle ceremonies are marriage and death rituals. In addition to life cycle ceremonies, rites of passage mark initiation into social groups (such as fraternity initiations) or religious or political office (such as a presidential inauguration).

The Structure of a Rite of Passage.   A familiar example of a rite of passage is the American wedding, which actually consists of a series of rituals performed over a period of time. Although there is considerable variation among various segments of American society, there is a general pattern found in many weddings. We will use this example to describe the structure of a typical rite of passage.

Anthropologists identify three phases in the typical rite of passage. The first phase is called **separation.** In this phase the individual is removed from his or her former status. In some rituals this is an abrupt separation of the individual from the community; in others it may take place over a longer period of time.

In the American wedding the separation phase is actually a series of events that take place over the period of time preceding the ceremony. A typical wedding cycle might begin with an engagement party. Next follows a number of planning and preparation activities, frequently involving wedding specialists. Although these are usually thought of as practical, logistical activities, they often take on the characteristics of ritual in that they consist of traditional activities. These include the selection of a wedding dress, costuming the wedding party, selecting and mailing invitations, signing up with a gift registry, attending wedding showers, the rehearsal, and the rehearsal dinner. The final event in the separation phase is when the bride walks down the aisle and bids farewell to her parents and, in some ceremonies, is formally "given away" by her father and/or mother or other close relative.

The second phase is the **transition** phase. During the transition phase several activities take place that bring about the change in status. In the American wedding ceremony this phase lasts from only a few minutes to over an hour. This is relatively short when compared with rites of passage found in other societies, in which the transition phase can last months or even years.

At the conclusion of the transition phase the person conducting the American wedding ceremony often will introduce the newly married couple to the congregation as "Mr. and Mrs." Thus begins the final phase, **incorporation,** during which the couple reenters normal society, though in a new social relationship. This phase includes the reception or party celebrating the marriage. The incorporation phase usually lasts several hours, although in many groups it is considerably longer. After the reception there is often a series of additional activities, such as a display of gifts and the writing of thank-you notes.

All of this can be quite daunting and very expensive. Of course, in our society a couple can fly to Las Vegas or go to the local courthouse and get the piece of paper and skip most of the traditional activities. However, many couples and their families are very uncomfortable with this and will follow such an official wedding with some type of celebration to reaffirm the marriage, such as a reception or perhaps a second wedding ceremony attended by friends and family.

Coming-of-Age Rituals.   A ritual that frequently assumes great importance in traditional societies is the coming-of-age ritual, which marks the transition from childhood to adulthood. An example is the rite of passage that accompanies **menarche,** or a girl's first menstruation. Menarche is only one physiological event within a complex cycle of events we call puberty that extends over several years. However, menarche is a very definite, easily observed event. Because puberty is so well marked in females, the ritual is sometimes an individual ritual rather than a group ritual.

The announcement of first menstruation by a girl to her mother may initiate the separation phase. In many cultures menstrual blood is considered polluting and dangerous to the men. Menstruating woman may be segregated in a menstrual hut or a special, enclosed area of the dwelling. Female coming-of-age rituals may also occur as a group ritual. In this case the ritual usually occurs several years before the onset of puberty to ensure that the ritual is completed before the onset of menstruation.

A Yanomamö girl who is menstruating for the first time hides in a simple enclosure built in the corner of her dwelling. The transition period lasts three days, during which the girl sits on the floor eating little. She shaves her head and removes her ornaments in an effort to look as unattractive as possible. This is done to prevent evil spirits from seducing the girl and taking her away to be married, leaving behind her dead body. At the end of this period she is incorporated into the community. She cleans herself, and puts on a new apron and ornaments. She is now considered to be an adult female member of the community.

Initiation rituals for boys are often more elaborate than those for girls. Because boys lack a clearly defined physiological event to mark the onset of puberty, the timing of male initiation is fairly arbitrary. Male initiation rituals are usually group rituals in which all of the boys of a certain age range in a community are periodically rounded up to go through the ritual as a group.

Male initiation ceremonies are usually characterized by relatively short separation and incorporation phases. The separation phase may be very sudden, as when masked dancers tear the boys away from their families without warning. The incorporation phase may simply be a reintroduction of the boys, now occupying their new status as men, to the community, followed by feasting.

Transition and Liminality.   Initiates in the transition stage, especially in those rituals in which this stage lasts for a significant period of time, are in an out-of-the-ordinary situation. They have shed their previous identification and place in society but have yet to take on the mantle of the new status. Their ambiguous position and the fact that they are marginal to their society—often in a real sense if they are removed to a special camp away from the village—are represented symbolically.

An often-encountered metaphor for a rite of passage is the cycle of death and rebirth. Separation is symbolized by death, and incorporation by rebirth. The period of time between death and rebirth is a time of mystery during which the initiate undergoes a metamorphosis from one kind of human being to another. Just as the process of change within an insect's cocoon is hidden from view and therefore mysterious, the activities surrounding the transitional phase may be hidden from view from women and uninitiated boys.

Initiates within this transition period are said to be in a liminal state. **Liminality** is the state of ambiguous marginality during which the metamorphosis takes place. As such, it is symbolically represented by a number of attributes. Victor Turner provides us with a list of features that characterize the liminal state. The first column in Table 4.2 lists some of the properties of liminality, which are contrasted in the second column with the normal state.

An important feature of the state of liminality is summed up by the term *communitas.* Within this state not only is there a sense of equality, but the mere fact that a group of individuals is moving through the process together brings about a sense of community and cameraderie. This is what occurs in the Islamic *hajj,* in which all pilgrims wear the same white garments and perform the same rituals regardless of wealth or social standing. The sense of belonging transcends the tremendous ethnic diversity of the pilgrims who gather together from all over the world.

TABLE 4.2 *Characteristics of Liminality*

Liminality	*Normal State*
Transition	State
Communitas	Structure
Equality	Inequality
Anonymity	Systems of nomenclature
Absence of property	Property
Absence of status	Status
Nakedness or uniform clothing	Distinctions of clothing
Sexual continence	Sexuality
Absence of rank	Distinctions of rank
Humility	Just pride of position
Disregard for personal appearance	Care for personal appearance
Unselfishness	Selfishness
Total obedience	Obedience only to superior rank
Sacredness	Secularity
Silence	Speech
Simplicity	Complexity
Acceptance of pain and suffering	Avoidance of pain and suffering

Source: Adapted from Victor Turner, "Liminality and Communitas," in *The Ritual Process: Structure and Anti-Structure* (Chicago: Aldine, 1969), pp. 94–113, 125–130.

In many traditional societies the boys who are initiated together form very close bonds and will usually remain close friends throughout their lives. In some African societies this group of males will form a formal group known as an **age set.** Age sets cut across other group boundaries, such as clans and lineages, and create solidarity between groups that often are opposed to one another. Age sets serve a number of functions and may serve as important social units, such as military units.

Members of an age set may move together through various age grades. An **age grade** is a specific status defined by age, such as warrior or elder. We can think of a system of age grades as a classification of an individual into age categories. An individual or a group such as an age set will move through a series of age grades during his or her life. Here the distinction is more complex than just a transition from child to adult, and rites of passage often mark the entrance into each age grade.

Gururumba Rites of Passage.   Among the Gururumba of New Guinea a group of boys are initiated at the same time, whenever there are enough boys who are of the right age. In many cultures in New Guinea there is residential segregation of the sexes, men living together in a men's house and women living separately with their children. Women and children are not allowed to enter the men's house. The initiation begins when the boys are taken from their mother's house and taken to the men's house for the first time. The boys sit around a fire in the middle of the men's house. They wipe off their sweat with a stick, an act that is seen as the wiping off of the pollution acquired during their years of living with women.

The boys are subjected to both psychological and physical hazing, including having bamboo sticks put up their noses to make them bleed and sugarcane put down their throat to make them vomit. Both of these practices are done by adult men, and the boys will later learn to do this for themselves.

A large part of the liminal period is spent learning the things they need to know to be men. For the Gururumba this includes sacred knowledge that is known only to men. Previously, the boys would sometimes hear a noise that they were told was a large predatory bird coming to eat them. After being admitted to the men's house, they learn that the sound is actually a flute. Learning to play the flutes is part of the process that makes them adults. The boys spend months in the forest in specially constructed houses learning to play the flutes. When they have accomplished this, they are presented to the community as men.

Apache Rite of Passage.   The coming of age ceremony for Apache (Southwest culture area) girls is a periodic ritual, held every July. The ritual lasts four days, mirroring the four days of creation. For the duration of the ceremony the girls are seen as reincarnations of the culture heroine White Painted Woman. The Apache say that White Painted Woman first appeared as a young girl, arriving from the east. She grew to adulthood, during which time she was associated with the south. As she grew older, she was associated with the west, the direction taken by those who die. As a very old woman she was associated with the north. However, after she died, she appeared again the next day as a young woman in the east. Thus White Painted Woman symbolizes the cycle of women's lives. The girls wear special costumes that contain many items symbolic of White Painted Woman.

Every evening there is singing and dancing. On the first night the songs refer to the first day of creation and so on until the last evening. The ritual that is performed on the fourth night is called *pulling the sun*. This ritual must be carefully planned and timed. The ritual specialists, known as singers, sing four sun-pulling songs, moving their hands, which have been painted with sun symbols, into different positions. As the last verse of the song is sung, the singers raise their hands over their heads. As the last note is sung, the sun rises over the mountains and falls on the singers' raised hands.

After this ritual is completed, the girls run back to the places where they are staying during the ritual, but they are not seen doing this because four large poles that were erected at the start of the ceremony now come crashing down, causing the other people to turn and look at the source of the noise. The next time the girls are seen, they are adult women. As the final component, the girl's singer comes to the girl to recite her genealogy to her. The Apache are a matrilineal society, tracing kinship through the women. The singer places three small bits of food in the girl's mouth, and her godmother places a fourth bit of food. This symbolizes the girl being fed by all the women, of all time, of her tribe.

American Secular Rites of Passage.   In the United States we find a number of secular rites of passage and other nonreligious activities that have many of the characteristics of rites of passage. One that has been studied is basic military training, which has many of the characteristics of coming-of-age rites in tribal societies. The recruits are physically removed to an isolated and special place, the military base, where they shed their civilian clothing, have their hair cut, and are issued a standardized uniform. Civilian occupational specializations and socioeconomic ranks become irrelevant. The actual training has many of the features of transition, including the development of communitas, equality, total obedience, acceptance of pain, and many other features of liminality listed in Table 4.2. Graduation from basic training would be the beginning of incorporation. However, there is one major difference between military training and tribal coming-of-age rituals. After completing military service, the individuals often return to the status they occupied before induction and undergo a period of readjustment during which they discard their military identity.

Another example is the experience of a patient entering a hospital. Separation begins when the patient enters the hospital and has his clothes taken away from him and is given a standardized "uniform." The actual medical procedures represent transitions as the individual is in some way changed. Some of the experiences of the patient resemble features of a liminal state. Discharge represents incorporation. However, unlike the typical rite of passage, the process seldom results in a permanent change of status that is acknowledged by the society, except perhaps in the case of permanent disability.

Alterations of the Human Body

As we saw in Chapter 3, one way of symbolically representing a changed social status is through altering the appearance of the individual (Figure 4.2). Although this change is often a change in clothing or hairstyle, it frequently is a more permanent change in the outward appearance of the body. The value of body alteration, especially where little clothing is worn, is that the change in status is permanently visible and unlikely to be faked.

Rites of passage frequently include some type of activity that changes the physical appearance of the body and, in the process of producing the alteration, creates a situation in which the individual must endure a painful procedure. Being able to have one's body cut, pierced, tattooed, and scarred without showing pain is often a critical element in rites of passage. The experience and acceptance of pain is an important feature of liminality. The pain makes the new status more valuable and increases one's pride of membership. This pain may also play a major role in developing an altered state of consciousness (see Chapter 5).

The forms that alterations take during rites of passage vary considerably, but one area of interest is the frequent occurrence of alterations of the genitals. This is certainly not foreign to Western societies. What is **circumcision,** as found in Judaism and Islam, but a form of changing the appearance of the male genitalia?

Male genital alteration, including, but not limited to circumcision, is a widespread practice that usually signifies membership in a particular social unit or attainment of a particular social status. But there is a great deal of variation in the details. One variable is the age of the boy when circumcision occurs. The Jewish *bris* is done on the eighth day of life; among the Maasai of East Africa circumcision marks the movement from childhood to manhood and is done during the

(a)   (b)   (c)

FIGURE 4.2   *Alterations of the Human Body.* (a) Maori (New Zealand) facial tattoos, early twentieth century; (b) Mangbetu (Democratic Republic of the Congo) woman with elongated head holding infant with ropes bound around head; (c) American from San Francisco showing tattoos, pierced nose, and pierced and stretched earlobes.

teenage years. The acceptance of pain during circumcision is an essential part of the Maasai coming-of-age ritual.

In some parts of the world, female genital alteration is as common as male circumcision. It is practiced in many traditional Islamic and even Christian societies. Although sometimes associated with Islam, it is not a part of the Islamic religion and represents a pre-Islamic cultural practice. The practice actually includes several different procedures. What is literally termed female circumcision corresponds to male circumcision and involves removal of the clitoral foreskin. The second form, **clitoridectomy,** involves the removal of the whole clitoris as well as parts or all of the labia minora. **Pharaonic circumcision** is the oldest form and is attributed to the time of the ancient Pharaohs, and it is the most radical of the procedures. It involves complete removal of the clitoris and the labia minora and majora; the two sides of the wound are then stitched together, leaving a small opening.

Reasons given for this practice vary from group to group. In some cultures girls must have this done to be acceptable marriage partners. This procedure ensures virginity and is seen as preserving both the honor of the girl and that of her family. In other cultures aesthetics are important, and uncut genitals may be seen as ugly and uncared for.

Revitalization Rituals

The final type of ritual that we will examine is the **revitalization ritual.** These rituals are associated with revitalization movements. Revitalization movements include nativistic movements, which focus on the elimination of alien customs and a return to the native way of life, and messianic movements, which involve the participation of a divine savior in human flesh. These rituals are often associated with social movements and usually develop within a context of rapid culture change. We will discuss revitalization rituals in detail in Chapter 10.

Pilgrimages

In Chapter 2 we looked at stories that tell of the creation of the earth and of humankind. In particular, we read the story of creation in Genesis and the story of creation as told by the Navaho. One difference between the Judeo-Christian and Navaho stories is that the former takes place at a location that, although believed to have existed, cannot be located on a modern map or visited by tourists. The Garden of Eden may be a supernatural place or a place whose location has been lost. In either case it is far removed from the immediate landscape of people who read the narrative.

By contrast, the Navaho live in the midst of the landscape of the creation. As they move through their world, they point to mountains, streams, and rock formations that are mentioned in their myths. The landscape is a constant reminder of their mythological past, and they interact with this past on a daily basis.

All religions are associated with sacred places that are mentioned in their religious stories, places associated with important events in the past. The Muslims have the Ka'ba in Mecca; the Jews have the Temple wall in Jerusalem; Christians have places in Jerusalem that are recounted in the story of Jesus; Buddhists have relics of the Buddha that are housed in particular temples; Hindus have the River Ganges. These are important focal points for religious practice.

There are also sacred places where miraculous events have taken place in more recent times. In Mexico the story is told of a native who was baptized into the Catholic Church in 1525 and became known by his Christian name of Juan Diego. According to legend, in 1531 an image of the Virgin Mary appeared to Juan Diego and left a likeness of herself on his cloak. The cloak bearing the image resides today in the Basilica of Our Lady of Guadalupe in Mexico City (Figure 4.3). The basilica has become a major sacred site. People come to this

FIGURE 4.3 *Our Lady of Guadalupe.* Painting of Our Lady of Guadalupe on the wall of the Atotonilco Sanctuary in the State of Guanajuato, Mexico.

site for many reasons, including the seeking of cures for illness. Juan Diego was made a saint of the Catholic Church in 2002.

A journey to a sacred place is often referred to as a **pilgrimage.** A pilgrimage can also be a series of rituals that are associated with a sequence of sacred spaces. In terms of our classification of rituals, each ritual in the sequence of rituals is a social rite of intensification, although therapy rituals are often included. In fact, the purpose of a pilgrimage may be to seek a supernatural cure for an illness.

However, a pilgrimage often can be seen as a rite of passage. Such a journey may be a requirement of a religion, and a person returning from a pilgrimage may have achieved a new status or position in the community. The experience of participating in a pilgrimage may include the three phases beginning with separation (traveling from one's home to the sacred place or to the beginning of the journey to several sacred places). During the rituals that occur at a sacred site or series of sites the pilgrim is in a liminal state that is characteristic of the transition phase. Finally, at the end the individual reenters the everyday world, often with some symbol of having participated in the pilgrimage.

One of the best-known pilgrimage sites to which individuals travel is that of Lourdes, France. From February through July 1858 Bernadette Soubirous witnessed a total of eighteen apparitions of the Virgin Mary at a grotto near the town of Lourdes. Today the grotto is the site of pilgrimages by Catholics seeking a cure from illness.

Pilgrimages also may involve the visitation of a number of related sites. One of the best known of such pilgrimages, and certainly one that involves large numbers of participants, is the Islamic *hajj.* This involves a prescribed visit to a series of sacred sites with specific ritual activities occurring at each one. The *hajj* is described in Box 4.1.

The Huichol Pilgrimage. The Huichol are a Native American people living in the Sierra Madre Occidental of central Mexico (Meso-American culture area). A key element of their religious traditions is the annual journey of over 300 miles to Wirikuta, an area located east of their villages. This is a sacred journey. It reenacts the journey of the Ancient Ones, the Huichol ancestors, that took place during the creation of their world.

During the dry season, between October and February, small groups of pilgrims, each led by a shaman, leave their villages to travel to Wirikuta. Many objects are collected and prepared for the journey, including candles, small yarn paintings, coins, and special arrows. Each pilgrim assumes the role of one of the Ancient Ones. This is more than play acting, for they become the gods they represent. The shaman leading the pilgrimage becomes Grandfather Fire.

As the Huichol pilgrims journey on foot (or today partly by bus or truck), they visit a number of sacred sites, such as water holes and caves. At each of these places the story of the journey of the Ancient Ones and their visit to the sacred place is told. Offerings are made, and prayers are recited, as social rites of intensification are performed.

BOX 4.1 • *The Hajj*

One of the Five Pillars of Islam, which form the framework of Muslim life, is the *hajj*, or the pilgrimage to Mecca. All Muslims who are able to do so are expected to make the pilgrimage to Mecca at least once in their lifetime. The *hajj* begins on the eighth day of *Dhul-Hijjah* (month for Hajj), the twelfth month of the Islamic year, and lasts for as long as six days. Every year, more than two million pilgrims from all over the world go to Mecca during this month. The *hajj* includes a series of rituals and symbols that are intended to bring the pilgrim as close as possible to God. A common act during the *hajj* is a constant repetition of the *Shahadah*, or statement of belief. This creed states that *"La ilaha ill-Allah Muhammad-un Rasulu-llah"* ("There is no God but Allah, and Mohammad is the Messenger of God").

Although there is some variation, what follows is a basic description of the sequence of events that make up the *hajj*. Before entering Mecca, the pilgrims stop at designated places outside the city to conduct cleansing rituals. As part of this cleansing, men cut their nails, trim their beards, and put on a white seamless garment. (Women also wear white, but no particular dress is prescribed.) By wearing this special clothing, all pilgrims become alike, symbolic of the Islamic belief that all Muslims are equal before God regardless of social status or wealth. This garment is also like a burial shroud, which symbolizes dying or turning away from earthly life to devote all attention to God.

The pilgrims then move into the Great Mosque, which can hold up to 500,000 pilgrims at a time. Here the pilgrims walk around the Ka'bah seven times. The Ka'bah is a black stone that stands fifteen meters high, engraved with the sacred names of Allah. It was already a sacred object in Mecca before the time of Mohammad. The Qur'an says that Abraham and Ishmael together built the Ka'bah, and it is also thought to be the site of Adam's original place of worship.

The pilgrims then travel to the plain of Mina, three miles from Mecca. According to the Qur'an, Mina and other sites such as Arafat are places where the word of God was revealed through Mohammad. After going to Mina, the pilgrims move on to the Arafat Valley, where Muslims believe Mohammad delivered his last sermon. The pilgrims gather stones and return to Mina. The stones are thrown at the *Jamraat*, three pillars that represent places where Satan tried to tempt Abraham from following the path of Allah. This act is symbolic of Abraham throwing stones at Satan when he tried to dissuade Abraham from sacrificing his son. Also related to this event is the ritual sacrifice of a sheep. This is seen as a reminder of Abraham's willingness to sacrifice his own son, even though God's mercy allowed the substitution of a ram. The meat is distributed to family, friends, and the needy. Finally, the pilgrims return to the Great Mosque to again circle the Ka'bah.

After completion of the rituals the pilgrims reenter normal life. They cut their hair, feast, and may engage in sexual intercourse. On returning home, they often wear special clothing, are given a special title, and assume important positions within their communities.

Finally, they reach the sacred land, where they find the peyote cactus, the "footprint of the deer." After being ritually "killed" and after offerings have been made, the cactus is collected and eaten. Peyote contains a hallucinogenic. The Huichol believe that by eating the peyote, they see what the gods see.

Religious Obligations

There are a number of simple religious ritual acts that are usually performed by an individual or a small group such as a family. A Christian says grace before eating a meal. A Jew entering a building kisses the mezuzah, a small case attached to the door frame in which lies a parchment with verses from the Torah. A Buddhist lights a candle in a household shrine.

There are other ceremonial obligations that might not involve obvious ritual activity but do entail a series of obligations and avoidances of particular objects, foods, and activities that are found in daily life. For example, virtually all cultures have certain foods that are served only on ceremonial occasions. Other foods may be forbidden to all members of the community or certain members of the society at particular points in time.

Many cultures have complex systems of food prohibitions. These prohibitions may apply to the entire community, or they may apply only to individuals of a particular age, gender, or social position. For example, among the Yanomamö of Venezuela and Brazil a couple must avoid eating certain foods during the wife's pregnancy. This includes the prohibition against eating porcupine, otter, and turtle meat. If either the husband or wife eats this forbidden food, they believe that the woman will miscarry.

Tabu

In a society some objects and people may be off limits and are said to be **tabu.** The term *tabu* also refers to inappropriate modes of interpersonal behaviors. These are often phrased in terms of pollution. It would bring dishonor, bad luck, or some other negative result for a person to have contact with someone or something that is tabu.

Things that are sacred can be thought of as possessing supernatural power and are therefore off limits to most individuals. Contact with the supernatural can be dangerous. Priests must perform rituals to safeguard themselves and the community against this danger. This is not malicious power. It is neutral, like electricity. If you stick a wet finger into an electric socket, you will receive a large jolt of electricity, and perhaps you will die. The electricity is not evil, but it is powerful. When properly harnessed, it can be used to light our homes, run machinery, and so forth.

One of the most sacred objects in the Torah is the ark that carried the stone tablets from Mount Sinai to Jerusalem to be installed in the Temple. The journey of the ark to Jerusalem was not a simple one, and many of the episodes that occurred on this journey illustrate how dangerous the ark was. Not only was the ark a sacred object, but also God had declared that only Aaron and his descendants were allowed to touch it. On one occasion, as the ark approached the threshing floor of Nacon, the oxen that were pulling the cart that carried the ark stumbled. One of the followers, Uzzah, reached out to steady the ark. After all, it would have been a sacrilege to let the ark fall to the ground. Yet we are told that Uzzah reached out his hand to steady the ark, "And the anger of the Lord was kindled against Uzzah; and God smote him there for his error; and there he died by the ark of God" (2 Samuel 6:7). In other words, Uzzah's death was not the result of some evil activity. In fact his steadying of the ark was a good thing; but his contact with such a holy object, in the absence of ritual, resulted in his death.

Objects and spaces that are tabu are dangerous, and contact with them can bring bad fortune, illness, and even death to the transgressor along with other members of the family or community. Frequently, the response to breaking a tabu is thought to be automatic rather than being at the decision of a deity. Sometimes nothing can be done to save the individual who has broken the tabu, but often there are ritual means of mending the situation.

Mana and Tabu in Polynesia.   The concept of tabu in Polynesia can be seen in the etiquette surrounding the chief. Again, this relates to the idea of things that possess supernatural power being seen as dangerous and often best avoided. In Polynesia this supernatural power is described by the term **mana**. Mana is an impersonal supernatural force that is found concentrated in special places in the landscape, in particular objects, and in certain people.

In some cases it is possible for an individual to gain or manipulate mana, thus tapping into a source of supernatural power that then can be used for some purpose. Frequently, mana is granted to a person by a supernatural being. In Polynesia mana comes from the gods. The chief, as a direct descendant of the gods, has the most mana, followed by his relatives and so on down through the hierarchy. Mana does flow from one thing to another, but it is part of the chief's role to be a reservoir and conductor of mana.

However, because of the chief's great amount of mana, he constitutes an involuntary menace to those around him, who have a lesser capacity for mana. Thus many tabus are in place to protect others from this power. Not only is it tabu to touch the chief himself, but because the chief's mana also runs into everything he uses, it also is dangerous to use his furniture or even use his fire to cook with. In some places the chief was even carried around on litter because if he walked on a path with his own feet, the path became forever dangerous, or tabu, to commoners.

Jewish Food Laws

Kashrut is the Jewish law regarding what foods can and cannot be eaten and how foods must be prepared. *Kashrut* comes from the Hebrew root *Kaf-Shin-Resh*, meaning fit, proper, or correct. The more commonly known word *kosher* comes from the same root. Kosher foods are those that are proper according to the *Kashrut*. Food that is not kosher is referred to as *treyf*. Although some have tried to analyze these rules in terms of early health regulations, Jews who observe these dietary laws do so because the Torah (the Hebrew Scriptures, including the books of Genesis through Deuteronomy) says to do so. No other reason is necessary. (Rules similar to the Jewish dietary laws are also found in Islam, in which permitted foods are *halal* and prohibited foods are *haram*.)

The rules for keeping kosher include eating only land mammals that have cloven hoofs and chew their cud. ("Whatsoever parteth the hoof, and is cloven-footed, and cheweth the cud, among the beasts, that shall ye eat" [Leviticus 11:3].) This is why eating pork is not allowed.

Even animals that are allowed to be eaten must be slaughtered ritually. This ritual slaughter is known as *shechitah* and is performed by a ritual specialist, a *shochet*. The ritual slaughter is done by a quick, deep stroke across the animal's throat with a perfectly sharp blade. This method is seen as being the most humane method of slaughter possible. It ensures a rapid and complete draining of the blood as well, which is also a kosher rule. The prohibition of the consumption of blood is the only dietary law that has a reason given in the Torah: The life of the animal is contained in the blood. ("Moreover ye shall eat no manner of blood, whether it be of fowl or beast, in any of your dwellings. Whatsoever soul it be that eateth any manner of blood, even that soul shall be cut off from his people" [Leviticus 7:26–27].)

Many of these obligations serve to provide a social identify to a group and to clearly separate that community from its neighbors. They also serve to separate different subgroups from one another in a multicultural society. For example, members of a particular group might wear special clothing that marks them as a member of that group, such as a wearing a turban or other head covering, or might alter the appearance of their body, such as growing a beard. Particular behaviors and food prohibitions also serve as symbols of group identity and as barriers to social interactions between different social units. If you cannot eat with someone, it becomes difficult to engage in close social interactions. Such prohibitions play important roles in defining religious groups and keeping them intact.

The Amish Way of Life

The Amish are a series of Christian communities found throughout the United States and in Ontario, Canada, with major concentrations in Pennsylvania, Indiana, and Ohio. As you travel though a region that has an Amish population, it is easy to identify the Amish by their distinctive mode of dress. Dress reflects the Amish values of simplicity and equality. For example, women wear solid-colored dresses without any decoration, even buttons, and they wear a white organdy cap on their head. Other customs may include personal appearance. Amish men, for example, all wear beards but no mustache. There are also a number of behavioral restrictions.

The Amish adhere to rules and customs that are seen by outsiders as old-fashioned, such as the use of horse-drawn buggies and farm equipment and the prohibition against the use of electricity or a telephone in the home. The Amish organize themselves into a series of districts, each with its own bishop. Each district is independent of the others in terms of their interpretation of the rules. The rules and prohibitions of behavior are part of an oral tradition known as the *Ordnung*. The *Ordnung* can be changed but only after considerable discussion and on the authority of the district's bishop. The rules may vary from one district to another, some districts being seen as more conservative than others.

Conclusion

In the last few chapters we have introduced many basic concepts in the study of religion, such as worldview, narratives, symbols, and rituals. As we progress through the book and discuss new ideas and practices, it is important to keep in mind how these different elements are related to one another. We discussed in the last chapter the connection between worldview, symbols, and religious narratives. In this chapter we added ritual to the mix.

We defined a religious ritual as a repetitive, patterned act that involves the manipulation of religious symbols. In Chapter 3 we discussed how religious symbols are often based on specific episodes recounted in religious narratives and that they represent a specific worldview. On another level we see that rituals are often reenactments of, or directly reference, specific religious narratives. In the examples in this chapter we saw that Navaho sand paintings represent important religious stories, that the Huichol pilgrimage retraces the path of the Ancient Ones as told in religious narratives, and that the Jewish Passover ritual is based on the book of Exodus, just to name a few.

Ritual itself is an essential component of religious practice. The ritual expresses important worldviews through the retelling of sacred narratives and the manipulation of fundamental symbols. Participation in a ritual is usually a group event and constitutes an expression not just of the beliefs of the group, but also of group solidarity. In the next chapter, in our discussion of altered states of consciousness, we will further discuss the important psychological impact of rituals. In the words of Anthony Wallace, "Ritual is religion in action; it is the cutting edge of the tool. . . . It is ritual which accomplishes what religion sets out to do."[4]

Summary

A religious ritual is a standardized, repetitive sequence of activities that involves the manipulation of religious symbols such as prayers, offerings, and readings of sacred literature. Rituals are often based on and are sanctioned in myths that articulate the underlying worldview of a culture, and these tenets are embedded in the rituals that are performed by a society. Prescriptive rituals are ones that are required to be performed by some religious authority; situational rituals are performed because of a particular need of an individual or a community. Periodic rituals are performed as part of a religious calendar; occasional rituals are performed when a particular need arises.

There are many types of rituals. Technological rituals attempt to influence or control nature, such as hunting and gathering rites of intensification that influence nature in the quest for food, protective rituals that serve to protect individuals in some dangerous or unpredictable activity, and divination rituals. Therapy rituals are healing rituals; anti-therapy rituals are performed to bring about illness and death. Ideological rituals serve to maintain the normal functioning of a society. These include the familiar social rite of intensification that reinforces religious and social beliefs and values and the rite of passage that marks an individual's movement from one status to another. Rites of passage include birth, coming-of-age, marriage, and death rituals as well as many secular rituals such as graduations and inaugurations. Three phases can usually be identified within a rite of passage: separation, transition, and incorporation.

In addition to these there are many small rituals and obligations that are demanded of adherents of particular religions. This includes the concept of tabu. Things that are tabu are separated from the society and are often considered to be sacred.

Suggested Readings

Donald B. Kraybill and Marc A. Olshan, *The Amish Struggle with Modernity* (Hanover, NH: University Press of New England, 1994).
[A series of essays describing the issues surrounding the maintenance of Amish customs in a world of change.]

Mark J. Plotkin, *Tales of a Shaman's Apprentice* (New York: Viking, 1993).
[The story of an ethnobotanist's search for new medicines in the Amazon.]

Tepilit Ole Saitoti, *The Worlds of a Maasai Warrior* (Berkeley, CA: University of California Press, 1986).
[An autobiography of a Maasai from Tanzania.]

Marjorie Shostak, *Nisa: The Life and Words of a !Kung Woman* (New York: Random House, 1981).
[The story of the life of a !Kung woman from the Kalahari Desert of southern Africa told both in her own words and in the words of the author.]

Suggested Web Sites

http://tahtonka.com/religion.html
Native American arts, humanities, and culture.

http://home1.gte.net/rattan/wedding.htm
The significance of rituals performed at a Hindu wedding.

www.ummah.net/hajj/rituals
How to perform the ritual of *hajj*.

www.ou.org/kosher/primer.html
Kosher laws.

http://amish.net
Comprehensive site of information about the Amish.

Study Questions

1. Rituals are an important part of academic life, be they graduation ceremonies or pregame pep rallies. What are some of the rituals that are performed at your school? Are any rituals performed at your workplace? How would you classify these rituals?

2. Disasters often precipitate religious rituals. Describe some of the ritual activities that immediately followed the September 11, 2001, tragedy. What kinds of rituals were they? What functions did they serve?

3. Discuss a rite of passage that you have attended. Identify and describe the three phases.

4. When one enters a hospital as a patient, one's clothes and personal property are taken away and one is treated in a fashion that is very different from how one is treated outside the hospital. Do you think that a hospital stay can be considered a rite of passage? Why or why not? If so, can the three phases be identified?

5. How is adulthood defined in American culture? At what point is an American considered an adult? Is there a rite or several rites of passage that mark this transition? How does the lack of a formal marker of adulthood complicate this transition?

6. Many religions mandate specific ritual obligations. How do these obligations function in society? How do they influence interpersonal relationships between members of different religious groups?

7. If you have a chance, observe individuals from a particular religious group. Describe differences in dress and other behaviors. Would you label these ritual obligations?

Endnotes

1. A. F. C. Wallace, *Religion: An Anthropological View* (New York: Random House, 1966).

2. Excerpts from *The Sacred Hunt.* Copyright © 2001 by David F. Pelly. Published in Canada by Greystone Books, a division of Douglas & McIntyre Ltd. Reprinted by permission of the publisher. U.S. rights courtesy of the University of Washington Press.

3. Ibid., p. 28

4. A. F. C. Wallace, op. cit., p. 102.

5

Altered States of Consciousness and Religious Specialists

Religion is a system of beliefs and behaviors that deals with the relationship between humans and the sacred supernatural. The way in which humans interact with the sacred supernatural is largely through the performance of rituals. Some rituals are fairly simple and are performed by most adult members of a community; other rituals are quite complex and require specialized training to perform. Other rituals require the performer to have special abilities, such as being able to directly contact the supernatural. Because of this, religious specialists are found in many societies. These are individuals whose role is to perform rituals and to interact with the supernatural world.

In interacting with the supernatural world, an individual may have mental experiences that transcend ordinary experiences, such as a trance. Such experiences are called *altered states of consciousness*. This chapter will discuss altered states of consciousness and religious practitioners.

Altered States of Consciousness

A religious experience is a subjective one that manifests itself on an emotional and psychological level. These emotions range from fear and anxiety to a generalized feeling of well-being to a profound experience in which a person feels an association with supernatural power or a supernatural entity such as a spirit or a god. These experiences and emotions make up an important element of religious practice. They include **altered states of consciousness.**

In its simplest sense an altered state of consciousness is any mental state that differs from a normal state. For example, daydreaming or the feeling that comes from drinking a little too much alcohol are examples of mental states that can be subjectively identified by the individual, and/or seen by observers, as being different from that individual's normal, alert mental state. Although everyone experiences altered states of consciousness to some degree, in both religious and nonreligious contexts, in many cultures these states are encouraged and are interpreted by the culture as important religious experiences.

Entering an Altered State of Consciousness

Altered states of consciousness can be brought about by a number of physiological, psychological, and pharmaceutical factors. The experiences encountered in an altered state will vary according to the factor that is responsible for the state as well as the physical condition and the expectation of the individual. A representative list is presented in Table 5.1.

Perhaps the most familiar are states of meditation and trance. A person can enter these states by ceasing all activity and reducing stimuli. For example, in passive meditation one seeks a quiet place without any distracting noise or activity and sits quietly. Many people experience a state of total relaxation in many nonreligious situations, such as lying on a beach or floating in a pool.

Altered states of consciousness can also be achieved through more severe enforced isolation, such as that which occurs in solitary confinement or self-imposed isolation. People who seek enlightenment or contact with a god or spirit might deliberately isolate themselves in a cave or in the middle of a desert or plain.

Another way of entering an altered state is to concentrate on an object or sound, as in active meditation. The sound might be a chant or repeated sequence of words, the monotonous beat of a drum, or the sounds of nature such as the crashing of waves on a beach or the sound of a waterfall.

In marked contrast to situations of quiet concentration or elimination of stimuli are altered states of consciousness that are produced by sensory overload and

TABLE 5.1   *Some Features of Altered States of Consciousness*

Difficulty concentrating, poor memory, impaired judgment

An increase in the feeling of power and control

Weakness, numbness, blurred vision

Hallucinations and visions

Feeling of timelessness, a speeding up or slowing down of time

Expression of extreme emotions, detachment and lack of emotions

New meanings attached to objects and experiences, belief of a gain of insight

Loss of control, feeling of helplessness

Parts of the body appear to be enlarged, heavy, detached, shrunken

Increased acuteness of the senses

strenuous motor activity. For example, the Mevlevi Order, or "whirling dervishes," in Near Eastern cultures achieve an altered state though continuous and monotonous movement that often leads to a state of exhaustion. Many religious rituals are accompanied by loud music, singing, and energetic dancing.

Changes in body chemistry can also lead to changes in one's mental state. Such changes can be brought about by fasting, dehydration, and sleep deprivation. This is perhaps why fasting is so common in many societies. Muslims fast from sunup to sundown during the month of Ramadan, and Jews fast on Yom Kippur. Several Native American cultures call for a young person to seek a guardian spirit. This search often involves a lack of food, water, and sleep. These factors, in addition to isolation and discomfort, will likely result in a vision that is part of a spiritual experience.

Drugs can also be used to attain an altered state of consciousness. In Chapter 4 we discussed the pilgrimage of the Huichol of Mexico. The use of peyote is a key element in their religious practices; it is used to contact and interact with supernatural powers in rituals that are an integral part of their pilgrimage. Although peyote is a controlled substance and its possession is illegal in the United States, it is legally used by the Native American Church (Box 5.1) as a sacrament in much the same way as Christians and Jews were able to use sacramental wine during the period of Prohibition. In all of these cases the substance is used to create a religious experience as it is defined by the culture. Table 5.2 lists various categories of drugs that produce an altered state of consciousness.

Sacred Pain.   Altered states of consciousness can also result from pain. Pain is a common theme in religious traditions. Pain may be a punishment, as in the Christian legacy of Eve bringing forth children in pain ("in sorrow thou shalt bring forth children" [Genesis 3:16]) or the Hindu consequences of bad karma. Pain may be seen as purifying, as with the ascetics and monks who cause themselves pain of the flesh in this life to avoid greater torment of the soul in the next life. Pain is sometimes an enemy or maybe even a weapon, as with Christ's battle on the cross. Finally, pain may be seen as transformative or as a source of supernatural power— Pain purifies and is used to achieve exorcism.

In our society we tend to think of pain as a very individualistic and even isolating experience. However, religious pain is often shared pain. Sometimes this sharing is vicarious. Christianity provides many examples of the importance of vicarious suffering, including the sacrifice of Christ on the cross, the existence of hell, the public executions of witches and heretics, and the ability to imitate the suffering of Christ through **stigmata.**

Many rituals use pain that is either self-inflicted or inflicted by others. For example, some funeral rituals involve self-mutilation on the part of mourners (Chapter 7). Self-inflicted pain is also effective because before performing the act, people often become very focused, concentrating on the act. They may also have undergone a period of purification before the act that might include fasting or lack of sleep.

Among the ancient Maya, male rulers would use small obsidian blades to perforate the foreskin of their penises, and women would perforate their tongues and

BOX 5.1 • *The Native American Church*

The late nineteenth century was a difficult time for the Native American population of the United States. The tribes were losing land, their traditional lifestyles were disappearing, disease had decimated many native communities, and the official policy of the U.S. government was to destroy Native American culture and to assimilate the Native American populations into the general American culture. Religion became one method of coping with this stress, and out of the chaos developed a series of religious movements known by anthropologists as nativistic movements. (These movements will be discussed in detail in Chapter 10.) Many of these movements combined both native and Christian elements, an example of syncretism.

Some of these early movements involved the use of the hallucinogenic cactus peyote. Peyote grows in northern Mexico and southern Texas and has a long history of use in religious ritual. The ritual use of peyote slowly moved into the Native American populations, where it is referred to as **peyotism.** Some of these groups stress Native American beliefs and rituals; others combine Native American elements with those of

Christianity that were introduced by missionaries. They also tend to be **pan-Indian** in that they incorporate elements and draw membership from many different tribes. Familiar elements of ritual include meditation, revelation, prayer, and the use of native plant materials—for example, tobacco and sage.

For some groups that utilize Christian elements, peyote plays a role similar to that of the sacramental bread and wine of the Christian Mass. The peyote is believed to contain the power of God, and to ingest the peyote is to absorb God's power. Members of the Native American Church say that this enables them to have a direct experience of the supernatural.

The first Native American Church was incorporated in Oklahoma in 1918, followed by others. The reactions of the various states to the use of peyote have been mixed. In some situations it was tolerated; in others individuals were tried and convicted for using a banned substance. Finally, in 1978, Congress amended the American Indian Religious Freedom Act to legalize the use of peyote as a sacrament in Native American Church rituals.

TABLE 5.2   *Drugs That Produce an Altered State of Consciousness*

Category	Examples	Effects
Euphoria	Morphine	Reduces mental activity and induces a sense of well-being
Phantastica	Marijuana, peyote	Causes visions, illusions, hallucinations, delirium
Inebriantia	Alcohol	Produces a state of intoxication; brings about an initial phase of cerebral excitation followed by a state of depression
Hypnotica	Xanax	Sedatives or sleep producers; may cause insensibility to pain
Excitania	Analeptics, coffee, tobacco	Mental stimulants
Tranquilizer	Librium, Thorazine, Valium	Reduces anxiety and mental tension, produces a state of mental calm

FIGURE 5.1 *Mayan Carving.*
Carving on Lintel 24, Temple 23,
Yaxchilán, Mexico, shows Lady Xoc
pulling a rope through her tongue as
her husband, Shield-Jaguar, holds a
torch. The ritual took place on
October 28, 709, celebrating the birth
of Bird-Jaguar.

draw strings, often studded with thorns, through their tongue (Figure 5.1). The
blood would fall onto strips of bark-paper lying in a ceremonial bowl. The blood-
soaked paper then would be burned as an offering. The intense pain and blood loss
would bring about visions that were interpreted as the entrance of gods and ancestors into the presence of the ruler.

In Chapter 4 we examined rites of passage that included coming-of-age rituals. These rituals often include tattooing, scarring, and circumcision. Because many
of these operations are quite painful, the ability to withstand pain has become an
important element in these rituals. The subject often enters an altered state of consciousness in the course of undergoing such painful procedures. This altered state
of consciousness often makes it possible to withstand the pain that is being inflicted.

Certain levels of pain have an analgesic quality (such as when the dentist
shakes your lip before giving you a Novocain shot or when you rub the elbow you
just banged on something hard). Pain can also induce a euphoric state, through the

body's production of natural opiates, and may be related to experiences of dissociation or trance. The voluntary ordeals to which shamanic initiates and ascetics submit themselves may be related to this effect. This is also the goal of many participants in modern Western body modification subcultures who practice such things as hook hangings.

Pain is also closely linked to emotion and sense of self. In modern Western medical practice, pain is often seen as being very disruptive and devastating to a person's life and sense of self, isolating the individual in his or her own private world. However, pain can also be experienced as healing and transformative. In these cases pain is often experienced as the catalyst for strengthening the person's sense of self. Instead of being isolating, the pain experience may reinforce the person's connections to both the social and supernatural worlds. Prime examples of changes in identity that occur through pain experiences are possession and exorcism, both of which will be discussed in later chapters.

A pilgrimage (see Chapter 4) often involves sacred pain that may be interpreted as a sacrifice, an imitation of the suffering of a god, a penance, a test, and so on. Again, such pain is related to an altered state of consciousness. One example comes from the pilgrimage to Sabari Malai in South India. The pilgrimage follows the path of the god Lord Ayyappan, son of Shiva, and his encounter with, and defeat of, a female demon. Pilgrims commit themselves to celibacy, moderate eating, walking with bare feet, and sleeping on the ground. The pilgrimage is a forty-mile journey, walked barefoot over sharp stones and hot sand. The pain of this is seen as an essential part of the pilgrimage, the goal of which is becoming one with Ayyappan. Following is a description by E. Valentine Daniel of the experience of pain on this pilgrimage:[1]

> One tells oneself, "I shall walk on this side or that" or "Look! There's a patch of grass. Let me go walk on that. It will make my feet feel good, even though the patch is only three feet long." During this phase, one is able to differentiate between the pain caused by the blisters under one's toenails and those on one's heels. Then again, one is able to distinguish between the pain caused by blisters, wherever they happen to be, and the pain arising from strained calf muscles and tendons. . . . The headaches caused by the heat of the noon sun and the load of the *iru muti* can be distinguished from the pain resulting from the straps of the knapsack biting into one's shoulders.
>
> Sooner or later, however, all the different kinds of pain begin to merge. . . . The experience of pain makes one acutely aware of oneself (ego) as the victim, and the outside (undifferentiated as roots, stones, and hot sand) as the pain-causing agent. . . . With time, pain stops having a causative agent, and ego is obscured or snuffed out because it has nothing to contrast itself with or stand against. . . . There is a "feeling" of pain, of course, but it is a sensation that has no agent, no tense, and no comparative. . . . Pain is the only sensation belonging to the eternal present.

The Role of Altered States in Religious Practices

The interpretation of the changes in mental state when one is in an altered state of consciousness is largely a cultural interpretation. In other words, culture places meaning on our experiences. A buzz from drinking several alcoholic drinks is amenable to several interpretations. Some are secular: "I've had a little too much to drink, and I'm feeling tipsy." Some people, experiencing the identical reaction, might interpret that same feeling as "I feel as if a spirit has entered my body." The objective feeling may be the same, but the subjective interpretation may be very different.

Many of the effects achieved in an altered state, especially those brought on by drugs, can and do result in behavior that is maladaptive, antisocial, and sometimes even dangerous. Such reactions, in addition to crimes committed to obtain drugs, have resulted in social constraints limiting their use. Which drugs are considered illegal is a function of how society views them. For example, although sometimes leading to antisocial behavior and death, the use of tobacco and alcohol is accepted in our society. On the other hand, altered states of consciousness may be adaptive and may play important roles in religious practice where and when they are considered appropriate.

The religious interpretations of altered states of consciousness generally fall into two categories. First, supernatural power, usually in the form of spirits or gods, enters the person's body, a phenomenon that we call **spirit possession.** An individual can control the spirit within his or her body to accomplish certain goals, or the spirit that possesses a human body can use that body to heal or to divine the unknown, often without the knowledge or the memory of the possessed person. However, possession by an unwanted spirit can bring about illness that may be cured by exorcism rituals.

The second common religious interpretation of an altered state of consciousness is that a person has entered a trance state because the soul has left the person's body. The experience of the individual in the altered state is then associated with the experiences of the soul, which is operating in a supernatural realm.

Altered states frequently play an important role in healing, for both the healer and the patient. Healing is facilitated, and in some cases even accomplished, through suggestibility, emotional catharsis, and feelings of rejuvenation. For example, when possessed by a spirit, the healer may use the supernatural power of the spirit to remove the cause of the illness, often by sucking the offending spirit out of the patient's body. When an illness is diagnosed as the loss of the soul, the healer sends his or her soul on a voyage to retrieve the lost soul of the patient.

The most common idea of religious altered states, though, is the idea of achieving a **unitary state.** A unitary state is one in which the individual experiences a feeling of becoming one with the supernatural, however this is conceived of by the community. For some this is becoming one with God or a spirit; for others it may be expressed as becoming one with a generalized supernatural force. We saw an example of this in our discussion of the Sabari Malai pilgrimage, the goal of which is a unitary state with the god Lord Ayyappan.

The idea of the unitary state is often one of the major components of a religious ritual or even an entire religious system. A common religious theme is that humans were once at one with the supernatural but somehow became separated. The goal of many religious practices is to regain that unity. This theme can be seen in many familiar religions. For Christians Jesus provides the pathway back to God; for Buddhists following the teachings of Buddha allows an individual to attain oneness with the universe; for Muslims reconciliation is possible through submission of the will to Allah.

In previous chapters we discussed symbols, narratives, and the importance of religious rituals. However, it is only with a discussion of altered states of consciousness that a true appreciation of the power of rituals can be reached. Narratives provide a basis for belief, but it is only with ritual that these ideas are turned into experiences. A religious altered state in a way offers visceral proof of the existence of the supernatural. These experiences move the supernatural from the realm of abstract belief into that of a lived reality.

The Biological Basis of Altered States of Consciousness

In the first chapter of this book we discussed the importance of the holistic approach of anthropology and the distinction between insider (emic) and outsider (etic) perspectives. For example, members of a community may perceive altered states as spirit possession and soul loss. We will now discuss altered states from an etic, biological perspective.

One example is the work that has been done on migraines by neurologist Oliver Sacks and others.[2] The term *migraine* is generally used to describe a type of headache, but migraines are also associated with nausea and other symptoms that can incapacitate the individual. One symptom associated with migraines is an aura, a type of hallucination. Although auras are most often visual, they may also involve distortions of other senses.

Culture plays a major role in how the patient interprets an aura. A modern migraine sufferer might experience a visual aura as pathological, a condition that makes it difficult to function—for example, to drive a car. (An aura that consists of floating lights, for example, can severely interfere with normal vision.) The same visual experience could be interpreted as a vision. In fact, descriptions of visions were written down and illustrated by Hildegard of Bingen, a nun and mystic who lived from 1098 to 1179. Her descriptions and drawings match contemporary descriptions of auras by migraine patients. Thus a particular experience may be experienced as a medical condition or, if the culture interprets it that way, a mystical experience.

Of course, migraine auras are not consciously induced, as many religious altered states are. New research in neurobiology has focused on how rhythmic, ritualized behavior affects certain parts of the brain. For example, in situations in which a fast rhythm is being used, such as with vigorous singing and dancing, the **sympathetic system** or arousal system of the brain is driven to higher and higher levels, ultimately becoming overstimulated. When this happens, the brain essentially selectively shuts down, and certain areas of the brain stop receiving the neural input that they normally receive and on which they depend to function normally.

One area that shuts down is a structure in the brain known as the **orientation association structure.** This is the part of the brain that enables us to distinguish ourselves from the world around us and to orient ourselves in space. These are tasks that we normally take for granted because our brains are functioning well, but the inability to perform these tasks can cause huge difficulties for people who have sustained damage to this part of the brain. Imagine trying to sit down in a chair if you could not tell where you ended and the chair began or if you did not know where exactly your body was.

The orientation association structure becomes deprived of new information because of the selective shutdown response to overstimulation of the arousal system. The result of this is a softening of the boundaries between self and other. This might be responsible for the unitary state reported by participants in many rituals.

Other research has focused on the emotional impact of repetitive motor behaviors, including what are referred to as marked actions, or actions that are different from normal ordinary movements, such as a slow bow. Other studies have looked at the impact of smell, such as that of burning incense. What is important to note is that these studies have found that it is not possible to get the exact same effects as are seen with ritual behavior just by chemically stimulating the right area. It is only with the merging of beliefs and behaviors that the full effect is achieved.

Ethnographic Examples of Altered States of Consciousness

The best way to demonstrate the role of altered states of consciousness in ritual is to examine specific ethnographic examples.

The Holiness Churches.   Altered states of conscious occur in rituals in American society, although they often are not seen as altered states. Meditation is common to a number of American religious practices. While it is highly developed in Buddhism, it is also found in Christian rituals, as when a person in silent prayer enters a state very much like meditation. Another example of an altered state of conscious in American religious traditions can be found in many evangelical churches. Long periods of prayer and ecstatic singing often lead to mental states that are manifested in convulsive dancing or speaking in tongues.

The Holiness Churches are a series of independent churches that are found primarily in Appalachia, most predominantly in West Virginia. This area of the United States was once highly dependent on coal mining. It was a relatively isolated, economically depressed area. Although some of this is true today, the isolation is breaking down, and life is improving. However, many Holiness Churches still survive. Each church is independent, yet individuals will frequently visit several churches in the region. The rituals do not follow a set pattern, although many elements are highly traditional, and the sequence of activities is determined largely by the elders of the church community.

During the service several members of the congregation enter an altered state of consciousness. The state is entered through intense concentration in prayer and with loud music with a repetitive beat; no drugs are used. Individuals speak in tongues, dance energetically, and even enter trancelike states. In some Holiness

Churches participants in an altered state will pick up poisonous snakes and drink poison. Entrance into an altered state is a highly desired religious experience and is interpreted as being filled by the Holy Ghost. This is an example of a unitary state. These practices are based on a specific portion of the Bible:

> And he [Jesus] said unto them, Go ye into all the world, and preach the gospel to every creature. He that believeth and is baptized shall be saved; but he that believeth not shall be damned. And these signs shall follow them that believe; In my name shall they cast out devils; they shall speak with new tongues; they shall take up serpents; and if they drink any deadly thing, it shall not hurt them; they shall lay hands on the sick and they shall recover (Mark 16: 15–18).

San Healing Rituals. The Ju/'hoansi are a subgroup of the San, a hunting and gathering people occupying areas of the Kalahari Desert in southern Africa (Khoisan culture area).[3] Their way of life has been the subject of many ethnographic studies. Several times a month a group gathers around the fire for a night of singing and dancing as a part of a healing ritual. They believe in the presence of healing energy residing within the body of certain individuals, the *n/um k"ausi,* or medicine owners. This healing energy, or *n/um,* heats up as the *n/um k"ausi* dance around the fire. The healer soon feels the *n/um* coursing through his or her body. The healer feels power and energy and experiences visions. Moving around the fire, the healer lays trembling hands on the bodies of the members of his community or rubs his sweat, thought to be imbued with *n/um,* on their bodies (Figure 5.2).

The Sun Dance of the North American Plains. The Sun Dance was a major communal religious ritual practiced by many tribal groups in the North American Plains culture area, including the Arapaho, Blackfeet, Cheyenne, Crow, Kiowa, and Sioux. Although each group had its own particular customs and variations, there were certain elements that were common across the different cultures. The Sun Dance usually took place near the summer solstice and represented the theme of renewal.

A Sun Dance lodge would be constructed with a large pole in its center. The individuals who were the main participants would fast for the three or four days of the ritual. During this time the participants would dance while continuously blowing on eagle-bone whistles. In some groups, such as the Sioux and Cheyenne, there was an additional important element to the Sun Dance. Dancers in those cultures would be pierced through the chest or shoulder muscles with a skewer or eagle's claw, which would then be tied to the center pole. The dancers had to pull back until the skewer was torn free. The fasting, dancing, and pain all would result in an altered state of consciousness for the dancers. Participants often reported having visions during the ritual.

Drug-Induced Altered States

The use of drugs to induce an altered state of consciousness is practiced by many societies. As with any altered state of consciousness, this can have both adaptive

FIGURE 5.2 *San Healing Ceremony.* Healing ritual of the /Gwi band, a subgroup of the San, southern Africa. The men begin to dance around the women, who are singing around a fire.

and maladaptive expressions. For example, a drug addict may be unable to maintain a home, a job, or normal social relationships as a consequence of his or her addiction. In discussing drug-induced altered states, it is important to recognize the difference between secular drug use, which is often extremely maladaptive, used for escapism, and leads to many personal and social problems, and ritual drug use, which is highly controlled and generally adaptive. We will return to this issue after we examine a few examples of ritual drug use.

Religious Use of Drugs in South America.   The use of drugs is ubiquitous in South American traditional societies. For example, anthropologist Napoleon Chagnon describes his first meeting with the Yanomamö of Venezuela:[4]

> The entrance to the village was covered over with brush and dry palm leaves. We pushed them aside to expose the low opening to the village. The excitement of meeting my first Yanomamö was almost unbearable as I duck-waddled through the low passage into the village clearing.
>   I looked up and gasped when I saw a dozen burly, naked, sweaty, hideous men staring at us down the shafts of their drawn arrows! Immense wads of green

tobacco were stuck between their lower teeth and lips making them look even more hideous, and strands of dark-green slime dripped or hung from their nostrils—strands so long that they clung to their pectoral muscles or drizzled down their chin. We arrived at the village while the men were blowing a hallucinogenic drug up their noses. One of the side effects of the drug is a runny nose. The mucus is always saturated with the green powder and they usually let it run freely from their nostrils.

After Chagnon spent some time with the Yanomamö and was able to look deeper into their culture, he began to understand the role of these practices in their religious system. The Yanomamö world is populated by tiny, humanlike spirits called *hekura*. One's supernatural power depends on one's ability to entice the *hekura* into the chest, which is visualized as a world of rivers, mountains, and forests. To accomplish this, one must take *ebene,* which is a hallucinogenic snuff made of several ingredients. The snuff is blown into the nose of the individual.

Many ethnographies of South American cultures describe the varied ways in which drugs are used among these peoples. Many of these practices are outlined by Johannes Wilbert, who, while focusing on the use of tobacco in South American societies, also touches on the use of other substances. In these societies a drug is often used in combination with a variety of substances, both collected and cultivated.[5]

The use of tobacco, often mixed with other substances, is common in South American societies. The substances are made into several different forms, and many delivery systems have developed. Of course, traditional societies do not have the option of injection, so the problem is how to get the drug into the bloodstream, where it will move rapidly to the brain.

Substances are efficiently absorbed in parts of the body that are lined with epithelial tissue that contain a high density of blood capillaries. These include the lining of lungs, mouth, throat, digestive system, rectum, nose, and eyes. Tobacco can be smoked, sucked (as in chewing tobacco), or drunk. Some tribes produce a processed form of tobacco with the consistency of a jelly, which is then rubbed on the teeth and gums. Tobacco can be dried and ground into a power and blown up the nose.

Drugs also can be introduced into the rectum by some type of enema device. The advantages of this technique are that it will not irritate the stomach and that the drug will not be lost if the individual vomits. Sometimes the enema device is a simple tube. The drug is then blown into the rectum. Another device makes use of a bulb that can be made from rubber or the bladder of an animal. A painting on a pottery vessel found in a Mayan site solved the mystery of a particular type of pottery vessel that appeared to have no obvious function. The painting shows it being used, with a rubber bulb, as an enema syringe.

Other Ethnographic Examples. The Huichol peyote pilgrimage was discussed in Chapter 4. In addition to peyote, Huichol shamans use tobacco to achieve an altered state of consciousness, generally through inhaling and swallowing large amounts of tobacco smoke. This results in intoxication and produces visions.

During important ceremonial times the shaman might smoke continuously for up to four days.

Peyote and tobacco are often used together and are seen as being connected. The Huichol origin story says that tobacco was created by Deer Person, who later turned into peyote. Tobacco smoking, along with the drinking of various alcoholic beverages, is often done to enhance the peyote experience. The Huichol believe that during these altered states of consciousness they are able to see what the gods see—another example of a unitary state.

Rastafarians are members of an Afro-Caribbean religion that has its roots in Christianity but venerates the former emperor of Ethiopia, Haile Selassie, as the messiah. Rastafarians believe that people of African descent are the Israelites reincarnated and generally focus on issues of race relations. One of their key beliefs is in the coming repatriation of blacks in the Americas to Africa. The Rastafarians are an example of a revitalization movement (Chapter 10), originating in conditions of social and economic deprivation and meant to improve the lives of its adherents through adopting new religious beliefs. Since its beginnings the Rastafarian movement has grown to encompass not just the poor, but also the middle classes, and has spread out from its place of origin, Jamaica, partly through the international spread of both Jamaican people and reggae music.

The Rastafarians stress a philosophy of *ital levity*, which stresses the rejection of Western consumerism and emphasizes living in harmony with nature. This includes eating food that is grown without chemical fertilizers and using herbal remedies. In addition to vegetarianism and not cutting the hair (resulting in dreadlocks), a common Rastafarian religious practice is the smoking of marijuana, or *ganga. Ganga* is sometimes referred to as the "wisdom weed" or "the holy herb" and is seen as a religious sacrament and a way to gain new understandings of self, the universe, and God.

Rastafarians trace the use of *ganga* to several passages in the Bible, including the following: "thou shalt eat the herb of the field" (Genesis 3:18), "eat every herb of the land" (Exodus 10:12), and "Better is a dinner of herb where love is, than a stalled ox and hatred therewith" (Proverbs 15:17).

The Importance of a Ritual Setting.   As was mentioned at the beginning of this section, in a discussion of the religious use of mind-altering substances it is important to distinguish between religious drug use and recreational drug use. The problems associated with recreational drug use, such as addiction, are generally not seen when the usage is done in a religious context. Religious drug use takes place only at certain times and in certain contexts, with defined beginning and end points. The ritual setting channels the experience in important ways.

The importance of this structure and the possible dangers of drug use are often recognized in the insider's perspective as well. For example, the Huichol emphasize the role of the shaman not just to lead them on the peyote pilgrimage, but also to lead them back. They long for the ecstasy of this religious experience but also worry they might not be able to return from it. It is the role of the shaman to guide them safely through the experience. Members of the Native American

Church, who use peyote as a sacrament, also caution against using peyote in anything but a religious context.

Religious Specialists

Although many participants in a religious ritual will enter into an altered state of consciousness, such states are often the purview of religious specialists. Generally speaking, most members of a community can perform religious rituals, as when a family member says grace before a meal. However, the performance of some rituals, especially communitywide rituals, requires special training. This training may consist of learning the sacred texts and the steps in the performance of a ritual, or it may consist of learning how to contact and deal directly with the supernatural world, that is, enter an altered state.

In small-scale societies with relatively simple technologies, rituals usually are performed by most or all of the adult members of the community. However, some individuals may develop a special interest in religious practices and may develop a special ability to contact the supernatural. An example are the healers found among the Ju/'hoansi San, in which half of the men and a number of women become healers. Yet these men and women are full participants in the secular life of the group. Full-time, specialized religious statuses usually do not exist in such societies, because these societies do not produce the surplus of food that is necessary to support full-time specialists. Religious practices are more the concern of the older men, but all may participate on occasion.

As we discussed earlier, religious activities are not clearly delineated from nonreligious activities in small-scale societies. Religious activities are interwoven with secular activities; indeed, the separation between religious and secular is not even made. This is reflected in the lack of full-time religious specialists.

Some societies have developed part-time specialists. These are people who earn their living at some economic task, such as hunting or farming, but who are called on to perform rituals when necessary because of their special knowledge or abilities. Such a person might be paid for his or her services, but many are not.

In larger and more technologically complex societies we see the development of many occupational specializations, including religious practitioners. These religious practitioners may be full-time specialists who derive their income primarily from the performance of religious rituals. Such individuals may be supported by the community, or they may derive their income through payment for services by individuals whom they have helped. For example, religious practitioners may be found in a marketplace, ready to be approached by clients who are in need of services in order to secure economic success for some endeavor or perhaps a cure for an illness. In some societies religious practitioners may attain important political and economic positions.

There are many terms that are used to describe religious specialists. Unfortunately, the terms are not used in a consistent manner. Sometimes it is a problem of translation because the nature of religious practitioners and their activities in many societies might not neatly fit into a defined category in our society or into a category as defined by anthropologists. Also, many terms are not used consistently. For example, the term *healer* can refer to a priest or to a shaman. However, the two major categories that are used to categorize religious specialists are those of priest and of shaman.

Priests

Priests are full-time religious specialists who are associated with formalized religious institutions. These may be linked with kinship groups, communities, or larger political units, and priests are given religious authority by those units or by formal religious organizations. Priesthoods tend to be found in more complex food-producing societies, whereas shamans are associated with technologically simpler ones. Generally speaking, a society will contain either priests or shamans but seldom both. (Here we are using the term *priest* as a generic term that includes a wide variety of practitioners, including minister, rabbi, and imam.)

A priest acts as a representative of the community in dealing with the deity or deities. In this capacity priests are responsible for the performance of prescribed rituals. These include periodic rituals on a ceremonial calendar that is usually tied with the agricultural calendar. A priest also performs rites of passage such as birth and death rituals and weddings, as well as performing rituals in the event of disaster and illness. A priest's skill is based on the learning of ritual knowledge and sacred narratives and on knowledge of how to perform these rituals for the benefit of the community. However, a particular ritual might or might not result in the desired end. A ritual performed for a rain god to end a drought might result in a rainstorm or a continuing drought. But the failure of the ritual to work is not necessarily due to the activities of the priest, but might be due to the will of the deity who has made the decision whether or not to let the rains come.

While priests may contend with important, practical matters, such as the success of crops or the curing of illnesses, they are also associated with rituals with more generalized purposes. These purposes are usually articulated in social rites of intensification and deal with the reinforcement of the belief system and the established ethical code. Priestly rituals legitimize community ventures—for example, the coronation of the British monarch by the Archbishop of Canterbury—and, on a more personal level, establish the legitimacy of a child as a member of the community.

Priests also are individuals who personify the image of the ideal person. They are models of ethics and morality in their communities, and they are held to higher standards of behavior than is the population at large. When a priest fails to live up to these standards, the significance is much greater than when another person fails in the same way. For example, recent revelations of child molestation by Catholic priests are considered exceptionally heinous and shocking.

Priestly rituals usually take place in a space that is set aside for ceremonial activities, which is considered to be sacred space. It is usually a community space as well. It may be an outdoor area or a structure, and the structure may be large enough that the entire community can enter and participate in the rituals. However, in many societies the ceremonial structure—a shrine or a temple—is a place where sacred objects are kept and into which only a priest may enter.

The training of a priest usually involves memorization of vast amounts of knowledge, for the very survival of the community might depend on the priest's competence in the performance of rituals. Individuals become priests for a variety of reasons. Often it is an inherited responsibility, as when a priestly office is passed on from father to son. Many societies have priestly lineages, such as the Levites of the Old Testament, or priestly classes or castes, such as the Brahmins of Hinduism. Sometimes the position of priest is one of great prestige and power, and one enters the priesthood to further one's standing in the community. At the conclusion of training, the priest is formally recognized as a religious authority by the community through a rite of passage, such as an ordination.

Priests also may have received a divine call, sometimes in dreams, visions, or trances. In some societies a person becomes a priest after being cured of an illness. The very fact of being cured may be taken as a sign of divine favor. In other societies the reason for entering the priesthood might be more practical. In Europe in the nineteenth century one of the only ways in which a middle-class man could get an education was by joining the priesthood. Research and teaching would be important components of his responsibilities. It was the custom in some agricultural societies that the oldest son inherited the land, the middle son entered the military, and the youngest son entered the priesthood.

However, no matter what the reason, the novice must have the aptitude and ability to learn the required elements of priestly duties. Although a priest may connect with the supernatural through visions and trances, this ability is not as important as the priest's ability to memorize and perform rituals in the proper manner.

Ethnographic Examples of Priests

We are probably most familiar with priests from our own religious experiences. For example, in Hinduism the future of the world and all people are in the hands of the gods. Therefore the gods must be worshipped. Priests are important as the focal worshippers and intermediaries between people and the gods. Priests play crucial roles, performing public worship for the well-being of all. Priests also conduct important religious actions in the major temples of the high gods, such as Shiva and Vishnu, including burning incense and making offerings.

Many similarities can be found between rabbis, Jewish religious specialists, and ulemas, a type of Islamic religious specialist. In both cases the specialist is primarily a scholar and an interpreter of a system of religious law—the Jewish *halachah* and Muslim *sharia*, respectively. The basis of the status of the rabbi and ulema is their knowledge and expertise in this religious law. Both religions are largely based on a core text, the Torah and the Qur'an. These texts have been greatly expanded by oral tradition, later recorded, which is the basis for further interpretations. Although rabbis often preside at marriages and funerals, this is not necessary; anyone who possesses the knowledge of how to perform the ritual can do so. The specialists are more like experts, who through scholarship and the living of an exemplary life have attained their position. For example, although Judaism stresses the value of studying the religious texts for all males, the existence of a vast amount of commentary and interpretation has in practice restricted the explanation of the sacred texts to a small number of trained specialists. In contrast, the position of the Roman Catholic priest is based primarily on ritual knowledge and control. The priest's authority lies in his sole right to administer the sacraments, including the important rites of passage of baptism, marriage, and last rites. Unlike Catholic priests, the rabbi and ulema do not administer sacraments, control rites, or assume control over congregations.

Aztec Priests.   Aztec society (Meso-American culture area) was based on agriculture and was highly stratified. Priests, who were full-time specialists, ranked very high in this society. They numbered in the thousands and were arranged in a complex hierarchy. The main role of the priests was to serve as intermediaries between the people and the gods. The Aztecs believed that the life of the Sun was about to end and tried to avoid that by providing the sacred food that the sun needed: blood. Human sacrifice on a large scale was an important part of Aztec religion and ritual and was carried out by the priests.

A ritual would begin with a four-day (or some multiple of four) period of preparation. During this time the priests would fast and make offerings of such items as food, cloth, and incense. The ritual itself would be preceded by a dramatic procession. The participants, elaborately costumed and accompanied by music ensembles, would walk to the specific temple of sacrifice. All important rituals involved the sacrifice of either animals or humans.

The ritual human sacrificial victims were called *in ixiptla in teteo,* or deity impersonators, as the belief was that they were transformed into gods. They would be ritually bathed, specially costumed to impersonate the specific deity to whom they were being sacrificed, and taught special dances. A wide range of techniques were used in sacrifice, including decapitation, drowning, strangulation, shooting with arrows, combat, and throwing from heights. Commonly, the victim was led up the temple stairs to the sacrificial stone (*techcatl*). There the victim would be held down by four priests, and the temple priest would cut through the victim's chest to remove the still-beating heart, referred to as "precious eagle cactus fruit." The heart would then be offered to the sun for nourishment. This was sometimes followed by the body's being rolled back down the temple steps, where it was often dismembered, flayed, and eaten.

Zuni Priests.   The Zuni, a pueblo people of the American Southwest culture area, developed religious practices that involved a complex of priests. This complex of priestly societies forms the basis of Zuni religious and political organization.

Young males, rarely females, are inducted into one of the six kiva groups that exist in Zuni society. A kiva is a ceremonial chamber, a sacred space analogous to a shrine or temple. Among the Zuni, kivas are rectangular rooms built above ground. (This is different than the more familiar circular underground kivas found among other pueblo peoples and so commonly seen in archaeological sites.) The six kivas are associated with the six cardinal directions, which include the familiar north, east, south, and west but also the zenith overhead and the nadir underground. Ritual responsibilities rotate among the six kiva groups. The major responsibility of the priests of each kiva group is the accurate performance of rituals. This involves the manipulation of sacred objects and the recitation of prayers.

Zuni society also recognizes many other priesthoods. They include the priests of the twelve medicine societies that both men and women join when they are cured of an illness because of the work of the medicine society. If a man takes a scalp in battle, he joins the warrior society. In a time a man may join a number of priesthoods. The accumulation of ritual knowledge over time is associated with prestige and political authority.

Zuni political authority is vested in a council of priests led by the priest of the sun and keeper of the calendar. Their major concern is with religious matters, such as selecting some of the participants in certain rituals, the placement of occasional rituals into the ritual calendar, and the reaction of the religious organization to natural disasters. They appoint a civil administration to handle nonreligious matters.

Shamans

The distinction between priests and **shamans** is not always a clear-cut one, and there are many religious specialists who fall somewhere in between. Generally speaking, in contrast to a priest, a shaman receives his or her power directly from the spirit world and acquires status and the ability to do things, such as cure, through personal communication with the supernatural. Unlike priests, who are full-time community-based specialists, shamans are part-time independent contractors. The authority of a shaman lies in his or her charisma and ability to heal.

The relationship between a shaman and the community is a personal one. Shamans focus on specific problems, such as those that affect a particular individual or family. Because clients often select a shaman in a particular situation for the shaman's reputation and track record in curing, successful shamans can amass a significant degree of social authority. Because of shamans' ability to directly contact the supernatural, members of their communities often regard shamans with some suspicion. The same powers that enable them to cure sickness could also be used to cause it. Priests do not have this same connection and so are not viewed with the same concern. Priests are capable of causing the same personal evil that we all are, but they have no special abilities to do so.

The method the shaman uses for contacting the supernatural may consist of traditional, standardized methods that fit our definition of ritual. The ritual is only a means for contacting and establishing a relationship with a supernatural entity; the ritual is not an end in itself. The success of a shaman lies not in his or her ability to memorize and perform rituals, but in his or her ability to successfully establish contact and some measure of control over the supernatural.

Because shamans receive their power and authority directly from a supernatural entity, they frequently are chosen by spirits to become a shaman. Perhaps the behavior of a child with regard to sacred objects is interpreted as a sign that he has been selected by the spirits to enter training to become a shaman. Often the call comes in a dream or trance. In some societies a person may deliberately seek a call through inducing an altered state of consciousness. This is most frequent in societies in which shamans achieve some degree of political status. In other societies the task of being a shaman is so difficult and demanding, and the shaman is so marginalized, that individuals do not seek a call. When a call comes—through recovery from an illness, a dream, a trance—the individual might be reluctant to act on it.

It is common that the spirits will call to the future shaman during a particularly difficult time of his or her life, including periods of stress, illness, accident, possession, or near-death experiences. The shamanic initiation often includes the idea that the spirits eat, dismember, or kill the person before he or she can be reborn as a shaman. The spirits are testing the initiate, and the symbolism of death, transformation, and rebirth are very common.

The shaman often undergoes a period of training, usually with an older shaman. Although learning religious knowledge is important, the main purpose of the training is to learn how to make contact with the supernatural, a very dangerous activity, and how to manipulate the supernatural world to achieve some specified end. The candidate establishes a relationship with a spirit familiar, who acts as his or her guide to the supernatural world. The period of apprenticeship may include periods of seclusion, fasting, and the taking of hallucinogens, but the main goal is to learn to enter into and control the experience of an altered state of consciousness.

The shaman's ability to make this soul's journey to the supernatural realm is linked to his or her special abilities at transformation. This is often linked to other ideas of transformation, such as speaking other languages or transforming into animals or other beings. Also common is gender transformation, in which the shaman wears the clothes of, or even takes on some of the social roles of, the opposite sex or is seen as being sexually ambiguous.

Ethnographic Examples of Shamanism

The shaman is found in many cultures across the globe. Here we will look at examples from Asia and North America.

Siberian Shamanism. The term *shaman* actually comes from the Tungus language of Central Siberia, in which it refers to religious specialists who use handheld drums and spirit helpers to help the members of their community. The term was later expanded to include similar religious specialists in other cultures, although some people believe that the term *shaman* should only be applied to these Siberian religious specialists. Siberian shamans performed rituals to heal the sick, to divine the future, and to ensure success in the hunt.

Here the world is seen as being divided into three realms. The upper realm is one of light and good spirits; the middle realm is the home of people and spirits of the earth; the lower realm is one of darkness and evil spirits. It is the shaman's role, while in an altered state of consciousness, to communicate with various spirits. The shaman may also journey to one of the other realms.

One of the main functions of the shaman is healing. This is accomplished in many ways. A shaman can communicate with spirits to learn what they want. He or she can also send off a disease-causing spirit or retrieve a lost soul. A shaman has a spirit familiar or animal souls that help in the shaman's work. These spirits give the shaman his or her particular qualities and powers. It is by having these spirits that the shaman is able to heal, but they also give the shaman the potential to do harm.

Other shamans specialize in using the ability to contact the spirits to help ensure a successful hunt. In this case the shaman will contact the spirits of an animal species and make a deal with them. The animal spirits will supply humans with food, and the humans will eventually supply the spirits with human flesh and blood. This is one cause of human sickness and death. It is the role of the shaman to attempt to minimize the amount of human sickness while trying to maximize the number of animals that will be successfully hunted. A shaman is successful in doing this in part because the shaman has made a pact with the animal spirits through his or her special relationship with the daughter of the elk or reindeer spirit.

Korean Shamanism.   Korean shamans are mostly women. Referred to as *mudang*, these women function largely through the practice of possession. The society believes that certain people have a psychological predisposition for this role. The spirits, in their search for someone to possess, tend to be drawn to individuals whose *maum*, or soul, has already been fractured and therefore been made vulnerable. The potential *mudang* therefore is someone who is experiencing *sinbyŏng*, or possession sickness. The shamanic initiation ritual heals the initiate of the illness. This healing can be achieved only if the initiate accepts her fate as a *mudang* and undergoes the initiation ritual.

Youngsook Kim Harvey recounts the description by a Korean *mudang* of the events that led to her initiation:[6]

> Long before I had any indication of supernatural notification, I found myself feeling excited by the rhythm of the *changgu* ("drum"). I don't remember how I came to feel that way. . . . All I know is that I used to have to be brought back to myself . . . , it happened more and more often. When I heard the *changgu*, I seemed to forget everything instantly and lose all sense of inhibition. I wanted to dance and chant to it. It is this helpless sense of being swept up and away in a weightless sort of way that makes you dance and be a *mudang* in spite of everything else. When you are in that state of mind, you cannot think of anything else. . . . Even now, just talking about it to you makes the temperature rise in me. . . . You can see how people who are possessed by spirits can go insane if they are improperly initiated. . . . You have no way of making use of the feelings that take hold of you.
>
> When you start doing your own *kut* [shaministic rituals], you just feel your spirits stealing into you and taking over; the sensation is incomparable. . . . You just know that you've got the spirits in you . . . that you don't have to worry because

it's them inside you, not you. . . . You're just a medium and you feel marvelous. Otherwise, how could anyone do the things a *mudang* does in her sober mind? You lose all sense of embarrassment . . . all inhibition . . . you are suffused with the feeling, "I'm the number one, the best—there is none else like me in the whole world!"

After initiation the shaman performs many other kinds of shamanic rituals. These include rituals that lead the spirit of a person who has died into paradise, heal illness, bring well-being to a village or family, help for a good harvest, and celebrate important family events such as weddings.

Shoshoni Shamanism.   The Shoshoni are a Native American culture from the Great Basin–Plateau culture area, although some groups were heavily influenced by Plains cultures. Central to Shoshoni religion is the idea of receiving supernatural power, usually through visions or dreams. Spontaneous dreams are probably an older source. After the influence of Plains culture on the Shoshoni and the beginnings of the reservation system, visions became more important, including those obtained through the vision quest and the Sun Dance. The Shoshoni name for the supernatural power acquired by humans in this way, and also for the guardian spirits who grant this power, is *puha.* People with *puha,* visionaries and shamans, are called *puhagan* or "possessors of power."

There is little difference between shamans and other men because most men seek out guardian spirits. Many men can treat minor illnesses. However, only shamans can cure many difficult diseases and are accepted as healers by the community. Shoshoni shamans treat illnesses from a variety of causes, the most common being spirit or object intrusion and soul loss. Traditionally, a Shoshoni shaman would cure soul loss by entering into a trance. During this trance the shaman's own soul would retrieve the lost soul by leaving his body and traveling toward the land of the dead, where lost souls generally went. Many shamans reported this trance state as an out-of-body experience and said that they saw their body lying on the ground while their soul floated away. In cases of spirit or object intrusion the object or spirit would be removed by sucking or by passing feathers or other items over the site to draw out the disease object. Shamans were also believed to have other supernatural abilities, such as divination.

Healers and Diviners

Anthropologists and others have identified many other kinds of religious practitioners. Sometimes these other terms are actually used to refer to priests or shamans, or they include many characteristics of priests or shamans. Sometimes they represent specialized functions that are also found in priestly and shamanistic activities. Some more complex societies have developed an array of religious specialists.

The term *healer* is often used to refer to a priest or shaman, especially when the individual is focused on the curing of illness or accident. However, more specialized **healers** also exist. Many of the activities of healers are similar to those of

American medical practitioners. For example, they may set bones, treat sprains with cold, or administer drugs made from native plants and other materials. Many governments have used traditional healers as conduits for the introduction of new practices in nutrition and public health.

A type of healer is the **herbalist.** Herbalists are specialists in the use of plant and other material as cures. The herbalist may prescribe the materials to be administered or may provide the material as prescribed by a healer or diviner. Various plant materials that are used in tribal societies actually do have medicinal properties. Herbalists are intimately familiar with the various plant materials in the habitat and gather, process, and administer various medicines made from these materials. However, much of the theory of curing is based on principles of magic to be discussed in Chapter 6.

A **diviner** is someone who practices divination, a series of techniques and activities that are used to obtain information about things that are not normally knowable. These may include things that will happen in the future, things that are occurring at the present time but at a distance, and things that touch the supernatural, such as the identification of a witch. Some divination techniques involve the interpretation of natural phenomena or some activity, such as the turning over of cards. Other techniques involve the diviner entering an altered state of consciousness and, while in that state, obtaining the requested information.

Diviners usually focus on very practical questions: What is a good time to plant my crop? Will my investment pay off? Whom should I marry? What is an auspicious day for a marriage? A very important type of information that diviners provide is the causes of illness. The diviner often provides the diagnosis, and the healer provides the cure. Diviners usually, but not always, work for private clients and are paid for their services. Divination is discussed in Chapter 6.

Prophets

A **prophet** is a mouthpiece of the gods. It is the role of a prophet to communicate the words and will of the gods to his or her community and to act as an intermediary between the gods and the people. Although shamans may occasionally function as prophets, in many cases the role of prophet is a separate one. Prophets are found in a wide variety of cultures and include the familiar examples of Moses and Mohammad.

Handsome Lake was a prophet of the Seneca tribe (Eastern Woodlands culture area) during the time when the reservation system was first imposed. In 1799 Handsome Lake became ill and appeared to have died. His body was prepared for burial, but he revived. He said that he had had a vision of three messengers who had revealed to him God's will and told him that he was to carry this message back to his people. Later the same year he received a second revelation in which he was shown heaven and hell and was given moral instructions, which were very similar to Christian ideas. Handsome Lake received further revelations in subsequent years. On the basis of his visions, he preached a revitalization of traditional seasonal ceremonies, strengthening the family, and a prohibition against alcohol.

Handsome Lake's teachings continued to spread after his death in 1815 and ultimately became the foundation for the Longhouse religion.

Ngundeng was a nineteenth century Nuer prophet. The Nuer, a cattle herding people living in the Eastern Sudan culture area, have a history of prophets.

The prophet Ngundeng Bong was born in the late 1830s. Of course, there are no historical records of his life, but there are many stories, especially those told by his family. According to tradition, he was conceived after his mother was past menopause and was born after a twelve-month pregnancy. Ngundeng is said to have spoken to his mother at birth and to possess a number of physical characteristics that were attributed to divine influence. Unlike some prophets who make contact with supernatural power later on in life, Ngundeng was born with that power.

As a young man he had seizures, or altered states of consciousness. He also showed very strange behaviors such as wandering alone in the bush, fasting, and drinking nothing but water for long periods of time. As he began to eat tobacco, mud, grass, and human feces, he became very thin, and his hair grew long and matted. Then he was possessed by a god, who revealed himself to be Deng. Ngundeng, as Deng's prophet, began to make prophecies, and because Deng controlled both life and death, Ngundeng developed a reputation as a peacemaker.

The Nuer believe that prophets are chosen by a god and are then able to predict the future, cure the sick, ensure the fertility of women and cows, influence the growth of a good crop, and so forth. Stories began to circulate about Ngundeng's further ability to take a life through words or even thoughts. The ability to kill was the other side of the coin of controlling life. The god Deng was a life-giver, controlling rain and the procreation of cattle and children, but he was also a god of death. Ngundeng gained a wide reputation for making barren women fruitful and halting epidemic disease. He died in 1906.

Conclusion

So far in this book, we have discussed many of the basic concepts and components of religious systems, such as narratives, worldview, symbols, rituals, and ritual specialists. As we move into the next section of the book, we will shift our attention to supernatural forces and beings. Again, all of these topics are tied together. For example, the conceptions people have of the nature of the gods influence the character of the rituals that will be directed toward the gods. An important factor in a culture's worldview is how and in what ways supernatural phenomena and powers manifest themselves.

Summary

An altered state of consciousness is any mental state that differs from a normal mental state. Altered states may be brought about by a number of physiological, psychological, and pharmaceutical factors, including fasting, lack of sleep, pain, and drugs. The interpretation of what occurs in an altered state of consciousness is largely a cultural one. The religious interpretations generally fall into two categories. First, supernatural power, usually in the form of spirits or gods, enters the person's body, a phenomenon we call spirit possession. An example is possession by the Holy Ghost in the Holiness Church. The second common religious interpretation is that a person has entered a trance state because the soul has left the person's body. The experience of the individual in the altered state is then associated with the experiences of the soul, which is operating in a supernatural realm. One common interpretation is that of achieving a unitary state in which one experiences a feeling of becoming one with the supernatural. Such experiences may have a biological basis.

Most religious systems identify specialists to carry out specific religious functions. Two of the most frequently found specialists are priests and shamans. Priests are full-time religious specialists who are associated with formalized religious institutions and tend to be found in more complex food-producing societies. The priest acts as a representative of the community to the deity or deities and is responsible for the performance of prescribed rituals. The skill of a priest is based on the learning of ritual knowledge and sacred narratives and on knowledge of how to perform these rituals for the benefit of the community. Priestly rituals usually take place in a space that is set aside for ceremonial activities, such as a temple or shrine.

By contrast, a shaman receives his or her power directly from the spirit world and acquires the ability to do sacred things through personal communication with the supernatural. Shamans are part-time independent contractors whose authority lies in their charisma and ability to heal. A Siberian shaman works with a spirit familiar or animal soul that helps the shaman in his or her work of sending off a disease-causing spirit or retrieving a lost soul. Shoshoni shamans treat illnesses from a variety of causes, the most common being spirit or object intrusion, as well as soul loss. Shamans also practice divination.

Another type of religious specialist is the prophet, who is a mouthpiece of the gods. It is the role of the prophet to communicate the words and will of the gods to his or her community and act as an intermediary between the people and the gods.

Suggested Readings

Nicholas Black Elk (as told through John G. Neihardt), *Black Elk Speaks* (Lincoln: University of Nebraska Press, 2000).
[The story of a Lakota shaman living during the years of white settlement at the end of the nineteenth and beginning of the twentieth centuries.]

Ariel Glucklich, *Sacred Pain: Hurting the Body for the Sake of the Soul* (Oxford, England: Oxford University Press, 2001).
[Examines ideas about and uses of pain in religious contexts.]

Autobiographies about Personal Religious Experiences:

Karen Armstrong, *Through the Narrow Gate* (New York: St. Martin's Press, 1995).
[Armstrong, who has written on many religious topics, tells of her own spiritual life, including seven years in a convent.]

Frederick Buechner, *The Sacred Journey: A Memoir of Early Days* (San Francisco: Harper & Row, 1982).
[Autobiography of Buechner's childhood, finding Christ, and becoming a minister.]

Madeleine L'Engle, *The Irrational Season: The Cross-wicks Journal, Book 3* (San Francisco: Harper & Row, 1984).
[L'Engle's journal follows a church year and her own questioning of her faith.]

C. S. Lewis, *Surprised by Joy: The Shape of My Early Life* (New York: Harcourt Brace, 1995).
[Lewis's autobiographical account of his life, including as a Christian and as an atheist.]

Thomas Merton, *The Seven Story Mountain: Fiftieth-Anniversary Edition* (New York: Harcourt Brace, 1998).
[Merton discusses his early doubts, his conversion to Catholicism, and his decision to take life vows as a Trappist monk.]

Fiction:

Carlos Castenada, *The Teachings of Don Juan: A Yaqui Way of Knowledge* (New York: Washington Square Press, 1990).
[The account of an anthropologist learning the ways of a shaman. Presented as fact but believed by some to be fictional.]

Myla Goldberg, *Bee Season* (New York, Doubleday, 2000).
[A girl's participation in a spelling bee sets in motion events that will ultimately lead to the disintegration of her family. Largely about the spiritual quests of all four of the family members.]

Suggested Web Sites

www.sci-con.org
Science & Consciousness Review On-Line Journal.

http://religiousmovements.lib.virginia.edu/nms/Snakes.html
Information and links on serpent handlers.

www.meteoros.de/hilde/hildee.htm
Reproductions and discussion of Hildegard of Bingen's visions.

www.bme.freeq.com/
Body modification e-zine; contains graphic content.

Study Questions

1. Altered states of consciousness include familiar experiences such as dreaming and daydreaming. Describe any such experiences that you have had. How do they fit the description of an altered state of consciousness that is given in this chapter?

2. There are many factors that can lead to an altered state of consciousness that are likely to occur in most people's lives. What are some of these?

3. Tattooing, body piercing, and other alterations to the body that are practiced among some people in today's society are painful procedures. How does the experience of pain become a part of the total experience? You might want to talk with some people who have undergone these procedures.

4. Next time you go to a religious service, pay close attention to any experiences that could be labeled an altered state of consciousness. Describe the experience. What were the conditions that led to the experience? How do the physical layout of the church, temple, or mosque; the presence of ritual objects; and the playing of music help to produce an altered state of consciousness?

5. Religious specialists in American society are often set apart by particular modes of dress, grooming, and general behavior. Some specialists are subject to special rules, such as celibacy in Catholicism. What is the function of setting religious specialists apart from other members of the community? How does this help the individual in his or her function as a religious specialist?

6. Although most religious specialists in American society are priests, some do, on occasion, carry out functions that are more apt to be classified as shamanism. What are some of these?

7. In cases of illness most Americans visit a physician rather than a religious specialist. In what ways does the behavior of a physician resemble that of a religious specialist?

Endnotes

1. E. V. Daniel, *Fluid Signs: Being a Person the Tamil Way* (Berkeley: University of California, 1987), pp. 267–268.

2. O. Sacks, *Migraine* (New York: Random House, 1992).

3. The various symbols other than letters used in San words stand for a variety of clicks that characterize their languages.

4. From *The Yanomamo* 5th edition by N. A. Chagnon. © 1997. Reprinted with permission of Wadsworth, a division of Thomson Learning: www.thomsonrights.com. Fax 800 730-2215.

5. J. Wilbert, *Tobacco and Shamanism in South America* (New Haven, CT: Yale University Press, 1987).

6. Y. K. Harvey, *Six Korean Women: The Socialization of Shamans,* American Ethnological Society Monograph No. 65 (1979), pp. 31–32.

6

Magic and Divination

When most Americans hear the word *magic,* they most likely picture a rabbit being pulled out of a hat or someone on television making an elephant disappear. What is popularly called *magic* we shall call *illusion,* since magic in this sense refers to acts that rely on some sort of trickery and deception. Entertainers in our culture who perform such illusions freely admit that they are manipulating not the supernatural world, but rather human perception. *Magic,* as anthropologists use the term, refers to activities, usually rituals, by which a person can compel the supernatural to behave in certain ways. Closely related to magic are ways of gaining information about the unknown, be it what will happen in the future, what is happening in some faraway place, or the cause of an illness. These techniques are aspects of divination.

Magic and Religion

Magic refers to methods that somehow interface with the supernatural and by which people can bring about particular outcomes. A **magician** is usually a worker in the kind of magic that is on the whole public and good, whereas a **sorcerer** is generally considered an evil figure, one who deals in matters that his or her clients would rather keep secret and one whose work may be downright antisocial. Of course, many other religious specialists, such as healers, use magic in their activities. Sometimes the term *magician* is not used because it implies that there are specialists in magic when in fact most, if not all, members of the community may be well versed in how to do magic.

Early anthropologists were quite ethnocentric when it came to the study of magic. Edward Tylor, who discussed magic in his book *Primitive Cultures,* published in 1871, wrote that magic is a logical way of thinking. The problem is that the logic is based on bad premises. Tylor believed that in tribal cultures the magician takes the same approach as a scientist, but the magician makes a mistake because he assumes a causal relationship that does not exist simply because things appear to be similar.

In addition, Tylor did not include magic in the realm of religion because no spirits are involved, which he considered necessary for his definition of religion. Today anthropologists consider magic to be religious because it is associated with supernatural mechanisms, but this has not always been the case. Earlier anthropologists and some contemporary ones see magic as a separate category from religion.

James Frazer, like Tylor, believed that magic was a pseudo-science, based on direct action. Frazer was a part of the evolutionary school (see Chapter 1) and thought that magic was an early stage that would be replaced by religion. Religion was seen as different from magic because it is based on persuasion of supernatural beings rather than manipulation of supernatural forces. Some evolutionary school thinkers believed that ultimately religion itself would give way to science. Of course, none of this has happened; in most societies magic, religion, and science coexist.

Émile Durkheim (see Chapter 1) also thought that magic could be distinguished from religion, but he focused on the social context. Unlike religious rituals that tend to involve the whole of the community, magic is often centered on the needs and desires of an individual. A farmer wants rain, a young man wants a wife, a woman needs a cure for her illness. In contrast to religious rituals that are carried out for the good of the community, magic is directed at very practical ends as articulated by an individual. Durkheim wrote, "In all history, we do not find a single religion without a church. . . . There is no church of magic."[1] However, generalizations are just that. Magic is frequently used in communitywide public rituals to bring rain or defend the community against an enemy.

Another related difference is seen in the purpose of the magic or religious ritual. Religion is seen as "an end in itself." Malinowski wrote: "While in the magical act the underlying idea and aim is always clear, straightforward, and definite, in the religious ceremony there is no purpose directed toward a subsequent event."[2] Some nonmagical rituals certainly have very specific goals—coming-of-age ceremonies, for example—but many rituals are more generalized, especially social rites of intensification.

The issue of whether or not magic is part of religion or a separate category altogether is largely a function of how religion itself is defined (see Chapter 1). Given the definition that we are using in this book—that religion is the domain of human interactions with the sacred supernatural—magic would be included.

Magic and Science

In industrial societies science provides techniques for dealing with difficult and adverse situations. For example, if someone falls ill, science may provide an explanation (e.g., a bacterial infection) and a course of action to combat the illness (e.g., take an antibiotic).

All peoples have rational means for dealing with difficult and potentially dangerous situations. Although some anthropologists have labeled such activities *science,* it is not science as we use the term in the industrial world. In the scientific community, science is a methodology for coming to an understanding of our world through objective observations, experimentation, and the development of **hypotheses** and **theories.**

Science deals only with **empirical** observations, that is, observations that are made through our senses, such as using vision to examine animal tissue under a microscope. Scientific conclusions also must be **testable.** This means that scholars must be able to develop new experiments and make new observations that will test the validity of a conclusion with the very real possibility that the hypothesis may be false. However, all peoples make detailed observations about their world and sometimes manipulate objects in their environment in order to come to some understanding of their world. All peoples have systems of technology that use rational and practical methods to achieve certain objectives.

As an example, consider a subsistence farmer who is growing crops to feed his family. A lot is riding on his success. Failure to produce an adequate crop could lead to malnutrition or starvation for his family. A subsistence farmer is very knowledgeable about his craft. He is familiar with various types of soils, knows the best time to plant, and knows how to build a fence to keep out wild animals.

However, no matter how carefully and skillfully the farmer performs his task or lives his life, bad things can and do happen. Rains might fail to come, or an infestation of insect pests might destroy his plants. He probably wonders, "Why is this happening to me? What can I do to prevent these things from happening?" To answer these questions, the farmer might turn to religious ritual to invoke the influence of a deity. Perhaps he will present an offering to a god and ask the god to help, perhaps to bring rain. Or he might build a small spirit house in the corner of his field and, by presenting the spirit with food offerings, try to persuade the spirit to take up residence and guard the fields. However, these activities depend on the good will of the god or spirit, who might or might not be inclined to do as the farmer asks.

Another approach is to somehow control the situation directly. Perhaps there is a way in which our farmer can connect to the supernatural world and bring about a desired end. This is what we mean by magic. Magic consists of activities, usually rituals, by which the farmer can automatically produce certain results, such as rain for his crop. There is no god or spirit to convince to help him. All the farmer needs is knowledge of how to perform the magic, and the result—rain or protection from wild animals—will happen.

Magic in the Trobriand Islands

In this section we will discuss the magic of Trobriand Islanders, who live off the western coast of New Guinea, as a means of illustrating basic concepts of magic and magical rituals. This will include magical knowledge, how magic is learned, magical rituals, and the functions that magic serves.

Magical Knowledge

Many peoples do not distinguish in practice between technological knowledge and magical knowledge. The goals of both are very much the same, and one would be ill advised to pay attention to one without paying attention to the other. Just as the farmer would be foolish not to build a fence around his plot to keep out wild animals, he would be equally foolish not to perform the appropriate magical ritual. Both are seen as essential for the successful completion of the task at hand.

The Trobriand Islanders distinguish among three types of knowledge. First there is knowledge of things in the everyday world, which is shared by all or a large group of adult members of the society. This is what a child learns from his or her parents and may be appropriate to one or the other gender. For example, boys might learn how to garden, and girls might learn how to weave mats. This is put to use in the everyday activities that are a part of the normal pattern of living.

A second form of knowledge is more specialized and is shared with a limited number of individuals. This includes expert knowledge that is necessary for task specializations, such as sailing or woodcarving. This form also includes knowledge of particular magical rituals that tend to be learned by many members of the society.

The highest level includes knowledge of the most complex and valued technological skills, such as canoe building, as well as knowledge of myths, songs, and dances. These skills are important to the community, and a person who has such skills is called *tokabitam,* "man with knowledge." This level of knowledge includes knowledge of important magic, such as rain magic and garden magic. This knowledge is of great importance to the community, and the relatively few people who possess such knowledge are very important people, in terms of both prestige and wealth, because the services of such people are paid for.

Learning Magic

Although many forms of magic are well known among adult members of a community, much magical lore is the private property of individuals. The most common way to obtain magic is to learn it from one's parents, grandparents, or other kin. Thus certain types of magic frequently are associated with particular family lines. Sometimes the magic is owned by a more remote relative or a nonrelative. In this case the person who desires the magic will purchase it from its owner.

A Trobriand Islander who wants to learn particular magic will present a series of gifts over time to the owner as a way of convincing the individual to bestow that knowledge. It is to the advantage of the owner of the magic to spread the learning process over a long period of time, thus maximizing the amount of gifts given. Sometimes the owner dies before all of the magic has been transferred to the student. In such cases the magic might not be effective because the transfer of the magic is incomplete.

Sometimes the owner of the magic dies before beginning the transfer process or, for some reason, does not want to share the knowledge. This is how magic disappears from the community. For example, Malinowski, who studied the Trobriand Islanders between 1915 and 1918, provided details of particular garden magic (see Figure 6.1). This magic disappeared because it was not passed on to the next generation. However, garden magic is very important, and influential members of the community were able to purchase different garden magic from peoples

FIGURE 6.1   *Trobriand Island Garden Magic.* Tokunaya performs a magic ritual in a yam garden on the Trobriand Islands.

living on islands to the south. Today many young men travel to the capital of Papua New Guinea to find work. After several years they return, bringing gifts of manufactured goods as well as magic that was purchased from tribes living on the large island.

Magical Ritual

A key component of a magical act is the words that are spoken—the **spell.** The spell is often an oral text that is transmitted without change from generation to generation. The slightest deviation from its traditional form would invalidate the magic. Because spells usually are passed down unchanged, they often come to be recited in an archaic form of the language and might include words that no longer have meaning or, if the magic comes from a different cultural group, may even be spoken in a foreign language. In the Trobriand Islands the ritual must be performed exactly. The slightest slip in the ritual, such as a minute omission in its performance or a seemingly insignificant change in its sequence, invalidates the magic. This is not the case in all societies. Among the Azande of the Sudan, for example, magical rituals are variable, and the spell is unformulated.

Magical rituals usually contain material objects that are manipulated in set ways. Sometimes a special material or object is required for the magic to work; at other times familiar objects are manipulated. Another aspect of ritual is the condition of the performer and the conditions of the ritual. Rituals can often be performed only at special places and at special times. The performer must often observe certain restrictions, such as abstention from sexual intercourse and avoidance of certain foods (see Box 6.1).

Magic involves the direct manipulation of the supernatural. There is a sense of control. If one performs the ritual correctly, one will automatically obtain the desired result. The magician does not have to convince a deity to bring about the result. Magic compels the supernatural to bend to the person's wishes, and success is seen as inevitable (provided one knows the right formula). Other religious rituals assume that supernatural powers are free agents that might or might not grant requests. (In many societies gods can be manipulated, bribed, or tricked but not controlled.)

The Function of Magic

Malinowski noted that Trobriand Islanders did not use magic in lagoon fishing because it is not dangerous. However, open-sea fishing is dangerous and is accompanied by extensive rituals designed to assure safety and success. He writes: "We do not find magic wherever the pursuit is certain, reliable, and well under the control of rational methods and technological processes. Further, we find magic where the element of danger is conspicuous."[3]

However, Annette Weiner notes that although lagoon fishing is relatively safe, there are other reasons to perform magic in the lagoon environment. She writes: "They 'turn' to magic, not out of psychological distress over a physical environment out of control, but when it is essential that they produce a large catch that must be used for an important exchange that has social and political consequences. To control the actions of the wind and the fish is ultimately proof of one's ability to control an exchange, thereby providing a measure of control over others."[4]

A similar connection between magic and uncertainty can be found in athletics. Of course, skill and practice play a major role in athletic prowess, but poor athletes sometimes do exceptionally well, while great athletics will hit a patch of "bad luck." Since much is riding on performance, athletes frequently attempt to control "luck" through magical behavior.

Anthropologist and former professional baseball player George Gmelch describes magical behavior among athletes.[5]

On each pitching day for the first three months of a winning season, Dennis Grossini, a pitcher on the Detroit Tiger farm team, arose from bed at exactly 10:00 A.M. At 1:00 P.M. he went to the nearest restaurant for two glasses of ice tea and a tuna fish sandwich. Although the afternoon was free, he changed into the sweatshirt and supporter he wore during his last winning game, and one hour before the game he chewed a wad of Beech-Nut chewing tobacco. After each pitch during the

BOX 6.1 • *Trobriand Island Magic*

Bronislaw Malinowski described the role of magic in the building of a canoe among the Trobriand Islanders. The tree that is to become the canoe is found in the inland forest. The tree is cut down, and the bark is removed; men come out to pull the log from the forest to the village. Of course, it is a practical matter to make the log as light as possible, so the branches are removed, and the log is cut to the appropriate length.

In addition, the proper magic is performed to further reduce the weight of the log. A piece of dry banana leaf is put on top of the log. The builder beats the log with a bunch of dry *lalang* grass and says, "Come down, come down, defilement by contact with excrement! Come down, defilement by contact with refuse! Come down, heaviness! Come down, rot! Come down, fungus!"[a] The heaviness and slowness, due to all these magical causes, are drawn out of the log. This bunch of grass is then ritually thrown away. This is the heavy bunch—it takes into it the heaviness of the log.

Another bunch of *lalang* grass, seared and dry, is beaten against the log. This is the light bunch, which imparts lightness into the log and speed to the canoe. The builder says, "I lash you, O tree; the tree flies; the tree becomes like a breath of wind; the tree becomes like a butterfly; the tree becomes like a cotton seed fluff."[b]

Malinowski also described garden magic.[c] Despite all the knowledge, skills, and hard work that are put into gardening, bad things can happen. Rain might fail to come, or insect pests might destroy a crop. To deal with these seemingly uncontrollable problems, the farmer turns to magic.

In farming, good fertility and a good crop are attributed to the skill and knowledge of the farmer and the superiority of his magic. There is a clear distinction between work that must be performed manually and work performed through magic.

Together, they make up a complex gardening system.

The Trobriand Islanders recognize many types of soils; they discriminate between many varieties of yams; they build fences to keep out pigs. "All these practical devices they handle rationally and according to sound empirical rules."[d] The islanders are very clear about what tasks are considered work and what are considered magic. The construction of a spirit house is strictly magic, but weeding is work. Work and magic are essential to the success of a garden. Good luck, a better-than-expected result, is confirmation of the strength of the magic; bad luck, a poor crop, points out a deficiency in the magic.

Malinowski describes many garden rituals. For example, this is part of a ritual that occurs before a field is cleared of brush: In the morning the men gather together around the magician, a religious specialist, who fasts until the completion of the ritual. The men, dressed and bodies painted for the special occasion, pick up their axes, which have been magically prepared. They march to the garden, where the magician takes his hereditary wand of office in his left hand and his axe in his right hand and enters the garden. He cuts a small sapling and recites a spell:[e]

> This is our bad wood, O ancestral spirits! O bush-pig, who fightest, O bush-pig from the great stone in the *rayboag*, O bush-pig of the garden stakes, O bush-pig drawn by evil smells, O bush-pig of the narrow face, O bush-pig of the ugly countenance, O fierce bush-pig. Thy sail, O bush-pig, is in thy ear, thy steering-oar is in thy tail. I kick thee from behind, I despatch thee. Go away. Go to Ulawola. Return whence you have come. It burns your eyes, it turns your stomach.

The sapling, which is then thrown into the forest, stands for evil influences and the bush-pig, which causes damage by digging up gardens. This ritual is followed by others, creating a cycle of rituals that parallels the work that must be accomplished to secure a bountiful harvest.

[a]B. Malinowski, *Argonauts of the Western Pacific* (New York: Dutton, 1961), p. 129.

[b]B. Malinowski, op. cit., p. 130.

[c]B. Malinowski, *Coral Gardens and Their Magic* (New York: Dover, 1978), first published in 1935.

[d]Ibid., p. 77.

[e]Ibid., p. 100.

game he touched the letters on his uniform and straightened his cap after each ball. Before the start of each inning he replaced the pitcher's rosin bag next to the spot where it was the inning before. And after every inning in which he gave up a run, he washed his hands.

When asked which part of the ritual was most important, he said, "You can't really tell what's most important so it all becomes important. I'd be afraid to change anything. As long as I'm winning, I do everything the same."

Where do these ritual behaviors come from? They come from what appears to be an association between an activity and a result. Most people do not believe in coincidence. The juxtaposition of a behavior with a desired result—the eating of a tuna sandwich before a game in which the pitcher pitches a perfect game, for example—is seen in terms of one causing the other. The pitcher will from that point on religiously eat a tuna sandwich before each game as a method of ensuring success. Gmelch notes that such rituals are found most frequently in those areas that are most difficult to control and are therefore most influenced by random fluctuations of success, such as pitching. This behavior among baseball players closely resembles the behavior of Trobriand Islanders engaging in fishing or trading voyages on the open ocean.

Rules of Magic

Magic does tend to follow certain principles. These were first described by James Frazer in his book *The Golden Bough* originally published in 1890. Frazer articulated the **Law of Sympathy,** which states that magic depends on the apparent association or agreement between things. There are two parts to the Law of Sympathy. The first is the **Law of Similarity,** which states that things that are alike are the same. The second is the **Law of Contagion,** which states that things that were once in contact continue to be connected after the connection is severed. The Law of Similarity gives rise to **homeopathic,** or **imitative magic,** and the Law of Contagion give rise to **contagious magic.**

Homeopathic Magic

Homeopathic or imitative magic assumes that there is a causal relationship between things that appear to be similar. The similarity can be physical or behavioral. The most familiar kind of homeopathic magic is **image magic.** This is the practice of making an image to represent a living person, who can then be killed or injured through doing things to the image, such as sticking pins into the image or burning it. The first may cause pain in the body of the victim that corresponds to the place on the image where the pin was stuck; burning the image might bring about a high fever. Animals drawn on the walls of Paleolithic caves with arrows through them might be an example of image magic. Here the artist is creating the hunt in art. Depicting a successful hunt will bring about a similar outcome in the real hunt.

There are many examples of behaviors that imitate a desired end, causing the end to occur. Sometimes these are found embedded within rituals that are not specifically seen as magic rituals. An example is the increase ceremonies of the Australian Aborigines. These are essentially fertility rituals that function to facilitate the successful reproduction of the totem animal (see Chapter 3). They are performed annually and are seen as essential parts of the animals' life cycle. The men who perform the ritual draw sacred designs on their bodies and place various objects on their persons. In this way the men become the totem animal in a magical sense. Their behavior, which is often expressed in dance, brings about a sympathetic behavior in the actual animal. For example, the acting out of the copulation and birth of an animal species will translate into reproductive success for those animals.

The principle of sympathy explains many folk customs, including those in American society. Folklorist Wayland D. Hand has collected many examples, such as walnuts being good for the brain.[6] After all, does not the shell resemble a skull and the meat inside resemble the brain?

Many of the practices that are labeled "alternative medicine" or "homeopathic medicine" in American society are based on the Law of Similarity. Traditional herbal medicine is often based on the **doctrine of signatures.** This is the belief that signs telling of a plant's medical use are somehow embedded within the structure and nature of the plant itself. Some believe that God provided these signatures so that people could ascertain the use of particular plants in healing. For example, red cloverhead is used to treat problems of the blood, as is the red sap of the bloodroot. Indigestion is treated by several yellow plants associated with the yellow color of the bile that is often vomited up. The fused leaves of the boneset plant are used, as the plant's name suggests, to heal broken bones.

Similar analogies appear to be the basis of many food prohibitions observed by pregnant women among the Beng of the Ivory Coast, West Africa. A pregnant woman is told not to eat meat from the bushbuck antelope, which has a striped coat. If she does, her child will be born with striped skin. During pregnancy a women should give herself enemas using a particular vine that has slippery leaves; then the infant will move quickly through the birth canal during birth. The soon-to-be new mother is also told that her behavior during her pregnancy will be reflected in her child, especially negative behaviors. A pregnant woman who steals will have a child with the long arm of a thief. Some Americans think that if the mother is anxious or nervous during pregnancy, the baby will be nervous and fussy.

Contagious Magic

Contagious magic is based on the premise that things that were once in contact always maintain a connection. An example of contagious magic from our own culture is the rabbit's foot. The rabbit is a successful animal, but not because it is intelligent. It is a prey animal for a wide variety of other animals, but some rabbits survive. This must mean that the predators are not always successful. Because rabbits are not smart, they must be lucky. If we carry a part of this lucky animal, the luck will rub off on us.

The following example comes from New Guinea. If a man has been hit in battle by an arrow, his friends will bind up the wound and put a cool poultice on it to keep the fever down and make him comfortable. They will also put a poultice on the arrow, which they have taken out of the wound, because it was connected with the wound, and this too will help with the cure. The enemy who fired the

BOX 6.2 • *Magic and the Determination of Longitude*

The use of magic was proposed to solve one of the major navigational problems of the eighteenth century: the need to establish longitude so that ships would be able to locate themselves on a map and thereby not only find their destination, but also accomplish this without running into rocks or land. The British Parliament passed the Longitude Act of 1714, naming a prize of millions of pounds for a practical and useful method of determining longitude. Needless to say, a great number of "interesting" ideas were submitted. In her book *Longitude,* Dava Sobel writes about some of the proposals that were submitted.

It became apparent that if one knew the time where one was and compared it with the time in London, one could calculate longitude. Local time can be determined by the point at which the sun is directly overhead. Keeping track of London time was a bit more daunting. This led to the invention of the chronometer, an extremely accurate clock, so that the navigator knew at all times what time it was in England.

However, it is another idea, presented in 1687, that interests us here. A powder, said to have been discovered in France, was reputed to heal something at some distance. So, for example, if the bandages removed from a wound were treated with the powder, the wound would heal more rapidly. However, the powder was painful to the body of a person to whom it had been applied. The idea of using this as a timekeeping device was very simple: Take a wounded dog aboard a ship but keep some of the dog's bandages from the wound in London. Every day, at noon, have someone dip the bandages into the healing powder. This would make the dog yelp on board the ship, thereby informing the captain that it was noon in London.

Source: D. Sobel, *Longitude* (New York: Walker, 1995).

arrow, however, is likely to be practicing counter-magic. Back in his camp he will keep the bow near the fire and twang the string from time to time because the bow fired the arrow that made the wound, and through this connection he can send twinges of pain.

Wayland Hand notes that there are many examples of American folk medicine that are based on the principle of contagion. Many of these involve transference of the disease into some object. The object could then be disposed of, thus curing the illness. Warts could be cured by rubbing a penny on the wart and then burying the coin. One cure for whooping cough was to tie a caterpillar in a band around the neck of the child. The illness disappeared as the caterpillar died, the disease having been successfully transferred to the animal.

We also see the principle of contagion in modern American society with the collection of, and prices paid for, anything used by a celebrity. A sweaty shirt thrown by one of your professors into the classroom would get a very different reaction than a shirt that had been worn by, and thrown by, your favorite rock star or actor.

Anything connected with the person can be used in contagious magic. If you can get hair, a nail cutting, or even a belonging (such as clothes), you can do your worst to the person it came from. In fact, a hair from your enemy's head is likely to be the first thing any sorcerer would ask you for before taking on a contract to liquidate the enemy. You can attack someone through his or her footprint, name, shadow, or reflection (although the latter also involves soul beliefs).

Why Magic Works

Not all magic is directed or purposeful. It is possible to set something in motion without being aware of it, without deliberately performing a ritual. For example, if you break a mirror, you set in motion events that will result in bad luck. This is why many people are careful not to step on a crack in the sidewalk and not to let a black cat cross their paths. You have not offended a deity who is extracting punishment. You have unwittingly pressed the wrong button and the result—bad luck—will automatically happen.

This perceived relationship between doing something and what appears to be a result of that action is the basis of much behavior in all societies, including our own. I find a coin on the sidewalk that I place in my pocket. The next day something good happens—I unexpectedly receive a raise. In the world of logic and science the juxtaposition of two events does not necessarily imply causality. It does not suggest that the presence of the coin in my pocket is responsible for my good fortune. It is most likely simply coincidence and nothing more.

However, the human mind frequently sees coincidence as evidence of causation. A student wears a particular shirt to a final exam and earns a grade of A in spite of not having had enough time to study. Although doing well can be attributed to hard work, there is always an element of uncertainty. A student might study hard for an exam yet find a question on material that, for some reason, was not studied very extensively—bad luck. Or the question might just happen to be exactly on the material that was well prepared—good luck. When good luck happens, it is often attributed to some outside entity, such as a piece of clothing or object that was being worn or carried that day, or perhaps to the fact that the student behaved in a particular way before the exam—drinking a particular beverage in a particular location, for example.

Tylor addressed the question of why people believe that magic works. The answer is because magic appears never to fail. There are several reasons for this. First, magic often attempts to bring about events that will occur naturally. Rain magic works because it will eventually rain. Rain magic often is performed at the end of the dry season, when rain is badly needed. Of course, the onset of rains normally follows the end of the dry season. However, the practitioners of such magic do not see it that way. The rain comes not naturally, but as a result of the ritual. The proof is very simple: You perform the ritual, and it rains. We could perform an experiment and try to convince a community not to perform rain magic to see what would happen, but to people who depend on their crops for survival this would be a very foolish thing to do. In addition, humans are very resistant to changing their beliefs, even when presented with evidence to the contrary.

This observation is important in understanding the use of magic and other healing rituals in curing illness. In our society over 90 percent of all illnesses, including colds and fevers, will eventually disappear, with or without treatment. Therefore in the vast majority of illnesses a cure will naturally follow the ritual. Again we have to assess the juxtaposition of the ritual and the end of the illness—a case of cause and effect.

People do not generally ask impossible things of magic. Magic to bring rain at the end of the dry season or to make a garden grow is likely to work. Magic to enable a student to pass an exam without studying or to be able to fly off the roof of a building is likely to fail. No one tries to grow his or her garden by magic alone. There is a natural world that demands a natural response (you must plant correctly and weed and water your garden), and there is a supernatural world that demands a supernatural response (you must make sure no supernatural harm comes to your garden and try to gain supernatural help for its success).

Of course, if you do not get the expected results, it could be because you did not do it right; the failure is with the magician, not the magic. In fact, if the belief is that the ritual must be performed without error for it to succeed, failure of the ritual is direct evidence that the magician made an error. Also, someone else could be doing counter-magic; one person's failure is another person's success. Or magic might be performed by two opposing entities, and the more powerful will prevail over the weaker. For example, one village might be using magic to kill members of another village, while people in the latter village might be performing magic to prevent illness and death. Thus warfare is being conducted on a supernatural plane.

Finally, there is the issue of selective memory. We do not remember everything that happens to us. Some things are etched in our memories; other things are quickly forgotten. Successes, even if infrequent, are remembered and are thought of as proof that something works. Memories of failures, even if common, quickly fade with time.

However, there are documented cases of magic working, especially death magic (i.e., magic is worked against someone who then dies). Is there a physiological basis for such deaths? This issue is discussed by Harry D. Eastwell among the Australian Aborigines of Arnhem Land.[7] Eastwell notes that the basis of such death by magic often is the result of an extreme state of fear. Such fear gives rise to many symptoms, such as agitation, sleeplessness, and sweating. This is further exacerbated by the belief on the part of the victim and his or her family that death is inevitable. Thus as symptoms increase in intensity, the family withdraws support because the patient is seen as socially dead. Because the individual is socially dead, the family will not provide food and water and will often begin funeral rituals before death has occurred.

Magic among the Azande

One of the most detailed studies of a religious system of a small-scale society is that of the Azande conducted by E. E. Evans-Pritchard in the 1920s and 1930s.[8] The Azande live in the southern Sudan, Congo culture area, which at the time Evans-Pritchard worked was a British colony. Here we will examine Zande magic; later in this chapter we will look at Zande divination. We will return to the Azande in Chapter 9 when we discuss witchcraft.

Among the Azande magic involves the use of objects, usually of plant material, called *medicines*. A medicine is an object in which supernatural power resides. To access this power, to change a piece of wood or plant material into medicine, requires ritual. The object, which may be consumed in the ritual or kept intact for long periods of time, then becomes the center of magical rituals.

There are large numbers of plants from which medicines are derived. Sometimes the association between the nature of the plant and its use is clearly based on the Law of Similarity. This is recognized by the Azande, who point out that a particular plant is used because of its resemblance to something that is associated with the purpose of the magic. A good example is a particular fruit that is full of a milky sap. The fruit resembles the breast of a woman with a young child. A drink is made from the root of the plant and is given to a mother who is having difficulty producing enough milk for her infant.

The thousands of available medicines can be placed in a series of categories based on their purpose. There are those that control nature, such as rain. One is used to delay sunset so that the person will have time to reach home before dark. Many medicines are associated with horticulture and hunting. For example, medicines are used to direct the flight of a spear or an arrow into the prey and to protect the hunter from dangerous animals. Craftsmen, such as blacksmiths, have their own magic to aid in their task. Some medicines are used against witches and sorcerers. Magic is used to bring about success in love and to guarantee a safe journey. An important function of magic is to avenge murder, theft, and adultery. Finally, diseases are cured by using specific medicines.

There are several ways in which the medicine is used. For example, plant material may be burned and, using oil, made into a paste that is then rubbed into incisions made on the face or torso; or the medicine may be made into an infusion that is drunk. A man may make a whistle out of a particular variety of wood and keep this whistle tied around his waist. He blows it in the morning soon after waking up as a protection against misfortune. This very simple type of ritual is very common. But even more important rituals tend to be performed privately so that an enemy will not know that it is being performed and use other magic to interfere with the effects of the ritual. In some cases a man might not want others to know that he owns a particular medicine. He does not want to be pestered by kin to perform the magic for them.

Zande magic rites are not very formal, nor are they usually public. There are a number of ritual actions that need to be performed; yet the order of their performance will vary. Although there are some public rituals, such as war magic performed by a chief, most magic is performed by a single individual for his or her immediate need.

The ritual itself is usually quite simple. It involves manipulating the medicine and reciting a spell. The spell is not formal. The individual simply addresses the medicine and tells it what he or she wants done. Unlike magical spells in other societies, power does not reside in the spell. Rather the power resides in the medicine, and the spell is simply a way of waking up the power and giving the power instructions. The manner is quite informal; the only requirement is that the instructions be clear. If the medicine is handled correctly and the instructions are clear, the magic will work. Another requirement is the observation of a number of tabus, although which tabus are observed vary widely. Commonly, they include abstention from sexual activity and the avoidance of certain foods. If the tabu is not observed, the magic will fail.

Sorcery is magic that is worked for illegal or antisocial ends. Whether or not a particular medicine is good or bad often depends on context. For example, magic that is worked to kill someone out of spite is bad. It is worked in secret in the dead of night. If a person who works bad magic is discovered, he or she will be killed. On the other hand, lethal magic that is legally sanctioned is good magic. This includes magic used to kill witches and sorcerers. Anything that disrupts the life and happiness of someone is sorcery. Sorcery also can be dealt with by counter-magic and antidotes.

Sorcery among the Fore

Although magic is used for a variety of reasons to increase the probability of success and control the uncertainties of life, magic can also be used in antisocial ways to interfere with the economic activities of others and to bring about illness and even death.

The Fore of New Guinea believe that the disease *kuru* is caused by sorcery (see Chapter 1). The sorcerer steals food remnants, hair, nail clippings, or excrement from the victim. He makes a bundle with leaves and some sorcerer's stones and places the bundle in cold, muddy ground. He then beats the bundle with a stick and calls the victim's name, reciting the following spell: "I break the bones of your arms, I break the bones of your hands, I break the bones of your legs, and finally I make you die."[9] The location of the bundle in cold, muddy ground suggests the deep chill felt by immobilized *kuru* patients. The use of something from the victim, such as hair, is an example of contagious magic. The Fore attempt to prevent *kuru* by attempting to deprive the sorcerer of the materials he needs. Much day-to-day behavior involves the hiding of hair clippings, parings, feces, and food scraps.

The Fore recognize many diseases, some of which correspond to diseases recognized by Western medicine. They are usually seen as the result of sorcery. Many magical techniques use materials that were once in contact with the victim, as in *kuru*, but many use special poisons that are placed where the victim will make contact with it, such as on a trail. In *nankili*, or pleurisy (a lung condition), the sorcerer makes bone needles out of the bones of pigs, cassowary, or possums. He blows smoke on the bone needles to make the needles fly into the victim's body.

Wiccan Magic

Wicca is a **Neo-Pagan** religion, meaning that it is a revival of pre-Christian religious practices. Although there is great variation within the Wiccan religion, magic is often a central element of ritual. Practitioners see their magical knowledge and rituals as a continuation of thousands of years of folk magic, which was often lost or pushed underground by the spread of Christianity. Wiccans also borrow freely from the magic traditions of various cultures around the world.

The magic ritual usually consists of a stated goal, the manipulation of specific objects, and the observation of special conditions, such as place and time. However, the core of the ritual, what is often considered the "real magic," is movement of energy, which takes place within the practitioner. The magician builds up this energy within herself or himself, and it is released at the right time to bring about the goal of the spell.

Wiccan magic is based on the worldview that there is a power that exists in all things. Through rituals (involving such things as music, dance, visualizations and the manipulation of objects) this power can be awakened and concentrated and can be set to affect a particular goal, which is the purpose of the spell. The power can also be moved from one person to another or between humans, places, and objects. As this power moves to its intended target, it will have an effect on that target.

Popular objects used in Wiccan spells include crystals, herbs, oils, candles, images, runes, and specific foods. The symbolism of color is also used, as are chanting and creative visualization. The religion is closely connected to nature, and the working of magic spells might require a consideration of the weather, season, lunar phase and/or time of day. The goal of such magic is often very practical and meant to help with everyday challenges such as relationships, health, protection, money, and employment. Magic is to be used when all else fails and in conjunction with more mundane efforts. For example, the belief is that just doing magic to get a job will not help unless you also take practical measures, such as sending out resumes. Because each individual's personal power is limited, it should not be used lightly.

As we will see in Chapter 9, Wiccan moral rules are such that magic is to be used only for positive purposes. Wiccans often say that they respect life, respect the earth, and respect the power too much to do magic for evil.

Divination

In the previous section we examined the subject of magic, techniques for directly and automatically bringing about desired results through supernatural mechanisms. People use magic for a variety of purposes, such as bringing rain, curing illness, and ensuring fertility. Another way of dealing with the uncertainties of life is to anticipate them. As the saying goes, "Knowledge is power." If we only knew what the future holds for us or what is happening at the present time in places and situations that are hidden from us, decision making would certainly be easier. We could see the consequences of our actions and learn about unknown variables that affect our lives.

Techniques for obtaining information about things unknown, including events that will occur in the future, is known as **divination.** The word *divination* comes from the same root as the word *divinity.* This implies that divination has to do with the supernatural.

The nature of many forms of divination is magical. Such magical rituals are used to manipulate the supernatural world in order to provide information. In other words, the ends of a magical ritual can be a physical occurrence, such as the coming of rain, or information, such as who will win the Super Bowl.

Of course, supernatural beings—ancestors, spirits, and gods—also may have access to unknown information. Many divination techniques involve contact with such supernatural entities, as when a medium contacts the spirit of a deceased individual or when a shaman falls into a trance.

Other forms of divination are based on the idea that the world consists of things and events that are interconnected with one another. We saw this same worldview for the workings of magic. In magic it is based on the manipulation of perceived connections between things; in divination it is based on observing these connections. For example, many people believe that the movements of the planets, sun, and moon are in some way ultimately connected with a person's life and that an understanding of these movements enables one to learn about the future. There is much information in nature, and those who are knowledgeable and observant often make accurate predictions. For example, a change in wind direction during a particular time of the day can foretell the coming of rain. This is a very rational approach, one that leads to planning. But the relationship between some signs is not obvious and, in fact, might not be based on a scientific point of view. The interpretation of such signs falls into the area of divination.

Forms of Divination

There are many ways of accomplishing an act of divination. To understand these methods better, we can classify various techniques into a number of categories.

A basic characteristic of divination techniques is that some are **inspirational** and others are **noninspirational.** Inspirational forms of divination involve some type of spiritual experience such as a direct contact with a supernatural being through an altered state of consciousness, usually possession. This form of divination is sometimes referred to as **natural** or **emotive divination.** Noninspirational or **artificial** forms are more magical ways of doing divination and include the reading of natural events as well as the manipulation of oracular devices. (The term *oracle* usually refers to a specific device that is used for divination and can refer to inspirational or noninspirational forms. Examples are the poison oracle of the Azande, to be described shortly, and a contemporary American toy called the Magic 8 Ball.)

We also can divide divination techniques into **fortuitous** and **deliberate** types. Fortuitous forms happen without any conscious effort on the part of the individual. One sees a flight of birds overhead or unexpectedly falls into a trance and has a vision. Deliberate forms are those that someone sets out to do, such as reading tarot cards or examining the liver of a sacrificed animal.

Using these two ways of classifying divination techniques, we can create four categories: fortuitous noninspirational, deliberate noninspirational, fortuitous inspirational, and deliberate inspirational, as shown in Table 6.1.

TABLE 6.1   *A Classification of Methods of Divination with Examples to Be Described*

	Noninspirational	*Inspirational*
Fortuitous	Apantomancy	Necromancy
	Omens	Oneiromancy
	Ornithomancy	Possession
		Presentiments
		Prophecy
Deliberate	Aleuromancy	Medium
	Astrology	
	Dowsing	
	Flipping a coin	
	Graphology	
	Haruspication	
	Magic 8 Ball	
	Ordeals	
	Ouija board	
	Palmistry	
	Phrenology	
	Scapulamancy	
	Tarot cards	
	Tasseography	

Divination Techniques

There is a wide variety of divination methods. We will review a number of these, but, of course, this cannot be an exhaustive list.

We will begin with dreams, which are a common form of divination. Dreams are often thought of as visits from spirits or visions of journeys taken by one's soul during sleep. Either way, an individual establishes a connection with the supernatural world. All you have to do is to be able to interpret what you experience in the dream. Much of the dream experience is symbolic, which often makes dreams difficult to interpret. Sometimes the interpretation is something you can do on your own, but at other times it requires a specialist. The interpretation of dreams is termed **oneiromancy.**

In American society you can purchase a book to help you interpret your dreams. One such book lists the following examples of the meanings associated with the presence of animals in dreams.[10] Dreams of bats flying during the day are a sign of reassurance and calm, but bats flying during the night signify a problem. A bull is a sign of tough competition. Riding a horse is a sign of happiness, but a black horse signifies grief. Dreaming about monkeys is a warning that you are surrounded by lies and deceit. And so it goes for thousands of dream experiences that are interpreted as signs telling of what is to be.

These interpretations of dream content are based on Euro-American dream symbolism. However, dreams may be interpreted differently in non-Euro-American cultures. Some scholars see two basic categories of dreams. One is the individual dream, which is the type familiar to us, the kind that comes from inside of the dreamer. In some societies, however, the source of the dream may lie outside of the dreamer. These are the culturally patterned dreams that often are deliberately sought—in a coming-of-age ritual, for example. Sometimes the individual simply waits for the appropriate, culturally demanded dream to occur, often encouraged by a shaman or parent. Other dreams may be induced by fasting, isolation, and so forth.

Whatever the source of the dreams, they often are a source of information, which classifies them as a divination method. Often an ancestor will appear in a dream and prescribe for the dreamer a cure for illness or a warning of what is to come. Guardian spirits and totems may let themselves be known through dreams. Or a spirit may appear in a dream informing the individual what his lot in life is, such as a call to a career as a shaman or priest. Or a dream may be a visit from the soul of a recently deceased relative informing the dreamer of a particular desire of the soul. Failure to meet this desire might result in illness and perhaps death.

Presentiments are feelings that a person experiences. They suggest that something is about to happen, such as a feeling of dread or an impending disaster. In some societies a warrior on a raid will return to the camp or village on feeling a presentiment that is thought to be an omen of his impending death on the raid. The warrior will be thought of not as a coward, but as a prudent individual.

Body actions include such things as sneezing, twitching, and hiccupping. Such activities can be interpreted in many ways, and interpretations of the same action differ from culture to culture. Some American examples are as follows: If you sneeze before breakfast, you will receive a letter that day. If you sneeze six times, you will go on a journey. If you hiccup or your ears are burning, someone is talking about you.

The term **necromancy** is used in various ways. Generally, it refers to divination through contact with the dead or ancestors. In ancient Greek society, when a person died under suspicious circumstances, the body was brought into the temple for close examination. It was believed that signs on the body were attempts of the spirit of the dead to communicate what happened and who did it. In most cases a diviner enters a trance in an attempt to communicate with the dead.

Knowledge can be derived from the observation of living or dead animals. This includes **omens,** fortuitous happenings or conditions that provide information. There are a large number of examples as well as a very extensive vocabulary that describes them. Here are only a few.

One can gain information from the observed behavior of animals. **Ornithomancy** involves reading the path and form of a flight of birds, and **apantomancy** refers to a chance meeting with an animal, such as a black cat crossing one's path. (Many cultures attribute good and bad fortune to various animals that one comes upon. Among the Nandi of East Africa, if a rat crosses one's path, that is good, but if it is a snake, that is bad.)

An animal does not have to be alive to be used for divination, and it is sometimes a sacrificed animal or part of an animal that is examined for answers to questions. **Haruspication,** the examination of the entrails of sacrificed animals, was part of the ceremonies opening a session of the Senate in ancient Rome. In another technique a dried scapula or shoulder blade from an animal skeleton, such as a sheep, or even from a human skeleton is dried. Sometimes the question is written on the bone. The scapula is then placed in a fire, and the pattern of burns and cracks is read by a specialist to determine the response. This is called **scapulamancy.**

Many physical entities of the natural world are "read" for information. **Astrology** is based on the belief that all of the stars and planets, as well as the sun and moon, influence the destiny of people. Modern astrology is based on an ancient interpretation of the mechanics of the organization of an earth-centered solar system. Other techniques observe the winds and the movement of water. Infrequent appearances of natural events, such as earthquakes and comets, are said to portend evil events.

There are many other forms of divination that are familiar to most Americans. These include **aleuromancy,** the use of flour (as in fortune cookies); **dowsing,** in which a forked stick is used to locate water underground; **graphology,** handwriting analysis; **palmistry,** the reading of the lines of the palm of the hand; **phrenology,** the study of the shape and structure of the head; and **tasseography,** the reading of tea leaves. Other familiar forms of divinations are mechanical types that include the manipulation of objects (see Box 6.3). A good example is flipping a coin. This is the most common type in American society and includes the Ouija board, Magic 8 Ball, and tarot cards. Other types of mechanical devices are used in other societies. For example, in many divination systems a series of objects, such as shells and bones, are thrown and the pattern formed by these objects is read (Figure 6.2).

BOX 6.3 • I Ching: The Book of Changes

The *I-Ching*, or *The Book of Changes*, is a Chinese divination text that is thousands of years old. The methods described provide much more than just yes/no answers and are seen not so much as foretelling the future, but rather as revealing what the person needs to do to live in harmony with the forces of the universe that control the future.

In Chapter 3 we discussed the concepts of *yin* and *yang*, the two interacting forces in the universe. *Yin* is the female element and is associated with coldness, darkness, softness, and the earth. *Yang* is the male element and is associated with warmth, light, hardness, and the heavens. The two elements are mutually dependent and need to be in equilibrium.

In the *I Ching*, *yang* is represented by a single line (—), and *yin* is represented by a broken line (— —). A set of three lines produces eight patterns or trigrams. Each is named and is associated with nature: heaven, earth, fire, water, thunder, wind, mountain, and lake. In addition, each is associated with a number of characteristics. For example, K'un, represented by three broken lines, is the earth and is associated with the color black and the animal the cow. K'un is gentle, passive, and nurturing. Two sets of trigrams are then put together to form the sixty-four hexagrams.

There are many techniques of casting a hexagram. Some methods are quite complicated and involve much ritual. One commonly used method involves the throwing of three coins. The outcomes of six throws identify the six lines in the hexagram. A more elaborate method of casting the hexagram is to use a set of yarrow stalks.

Each hexagram can be read on several levels. First, each of the six lines, which can be *yin* or *yang*, has meaning. Second, one can examine the pair of trigrams. However, most important are the meanings assigned to each of the sixty-four hexagrams.

In some techniques of casting, there are four types of lines: old *yin*, young *yin*, old *yang*, and young *yang*. Old *yin* and old *yang* are changing lines. While the original hexagram is used to provide insight into the present, when the changing lines change to the opposite form, information is provided about the future. Thus if the top two lines are old *yin*, they will change into *yang* creating a second hexagram.

As examples, here are brief descriptions of three hexagrams. The hexagram that is composed of six solid lines (*yang*) is named Heaven. "This hexagram is a good omen for an important occasion of state, an imperial sacrificial rite." The hexagram named Small Castle is composed of five solid lines and one broken line third from the top. "The image of heavy clouds promising rain that has not yet arrived conveys a mood of expectation and anxiety. There is a sense of impending storm." Finally, the hexagram named Peace consists of three broken lines on top and three solid lines at the bottom. "Some small sacrifices may be called for in order to attain your larger goal. Generally favorable."

Source: K. and R. Huang, *I Ching* (New York: Workman, 1987).

Inspirational Forms. Inspirational divination is a form in which an individual has direct contact with a supernatural being, be it an ancestor, a ghost, a spirit, or a god. This is usually accomplished through an altered state of consciousness. **Possession** can be either fortuitous or deliberate. **Prophecy** is fortuitous in that the prophet receives information through a vision unexpectedly, without any necessary overt action on the part of the individual.

FIGURE 6.2 *Divination.* Divination is practiced in South Africa by throwing objects, including pieces of bone, on a mat.

A familiar example of prophecy is Moses. The book of Exodus tells that Moses was tending his father-in-law's flock and one day led them to the edge of the desert. An angel of God appeared to Moses from within a burning bush. God told Moses to lead the Israelites out of Egypt, but Moses at first did not want to go. He replied, "Who am I, that I should go to pharaoh, and that I should bring the children of Israel out of Egypt?" God replied, "I will be with you" (Exodus 3).

Deliberate possession involves an overt action whereby the individual falls into a trance. Such people would be called **mediums.** Communication from the deities through possession, usually of a priest, is a very common feature of many religious systems.

Ordeals. **Ordeals** are painful and often life-threatening tests that a person who is suspected of guilt may be forced to undergo, such as dipping a hand into hot oil, swallowing poison, or having a red-hot knife blade pressed against some part of the body. Ordeals can be thought of as a trial by divination performed on the body of the accused. In some cultures, including past European and American cultures, ordeals were an important part of criminal trials.

Among Kpelle of Liberia, trials are conducted through the use of the hot knife ordeal. The ordeal is conducted by a specialist, who is licensed by the government. The specialist will heat a knife in a fire and first pass the knife over his own body to show that the ordeal is valid because he himself is not burned. Then the knife is stroked over the body of the accused. If the individual is burned, he is guilty.

Ordeals can rely on the idea, as in Christian Europe, that an ordeal reflected the judgment of God, who would punish the guilty and save the innocent. In most cases it seems that the fact of guilt or innocence itself acted in some magical way to affect the ordeal. For example, in a trial by fire only the guilty would be burned.

It might appear that in ordeals it is the guilty who suffers, but this is not always the case. In trial by water it is the innocent who runs the risk. The idea is that the pure element of water would reject the impure, being happy to accept and drown an innocent person but would cast up and reject an impure body such as that of a witch or a criminal. This was extensively used against accused witches. The accused was tied up and tossed into the water. She had a rope on her with a mark at a certain length. If she sank to this point, she was innocent. She would be pulled up and turned loose—if she could be resuscitated. A medieval text reads:[11]

> Consecration to Be Said over the Man. May omnipotent God, who did order baptism to be made by water, and did grant remission of sins to men through baptism: may He, through His mercy, decree a right judgment through that water. If, namely, thou art guilty in that matter, may the water which received thee in baptism not receive thee now; if however, thou art innocent, may the water which received thee in baptism receive thee now. Through Christ our Lord.

Fore Divination

We have already discussed the Fore of New Guinea and the effects of the disease *kuru* in their lives (see Chapter 1). The Fore believe that sorcery is the cause of the disease. Therefore an essential element in curing *kuru* is the identification of the sorcerer. The most common divination technique uses a possum as a vehicle for supernatural revelation. The victim's husband, brothers, and husband's age mates place some of her hair clippings in one small bamboo tube. In another tube they insert the body of a freshly killed possum. Striking one bamboo against the other, they call the name of the supposed sorcerer and then place the bamboo containing the animal in the fire. The guilt of the accused is established if the possum's liver, the locus of its consciousness, remains uncooked. After divination they do not openly accuse a specific person of sorcery, but the suspected sorcerer is subjected to further tests or death magic.

The Fore also consult healers, who usually belong to distant communities and even non-Fore groups. These "dream men," whom we would label mediums, enter altered states of consciousness through the rapid inhaling of tobacco and the use of other plant materials that produce trances and hallucinations. Information is also gleaned from dreams. Such diviners are then able to identify sorcerers.

Oracles of the Azande

Zande oracles have been described in great detail by Evans-Pritchard. The best known are *iwa*, the rubbing-board oracle; *dakpa*, the termite oracle; and *benge*, the poison oracle.

The oracle that is most often used is *iwa*, or the rubbing-board oracle. This is a relatively inexpensive and easy-to-use oracle that can be consulted very quickly. There are many situations in which some answer is urgently needed, such as the sudden onset of an illness, decisions about going on a journey, questions about interpersonal relationships, and a myriad of minor questions. Many older men carry *iwa* on their persons, ready to consult it at a moment's notice. If a man has not acquired or learned to use the oracle, it is quite easy to find a friend or relative who has.

The rubbing-board oracle takes many shapes, but it is relatively small and is always made of wood with a flat, round or oval "female" surface and a "male" piece or lid that fits on top. After being carved, the object becomes an oracle only after it has been rubbed with medicines and buried in the ground for a few days to permit the medicines to work. The female surface is treated with plant juices, and the male lid is moistened with water. As the lid is moved back and forth, it will either move smoothly or stick to the female surface. The sticking is usually interpreted as a yes answer; moving smoothly is interpreted as a no answer.

Iwa is manufactured and used by humans and therefore is thought to be prone to error. Although it is sometimes inaccurate, this fact is balanced against the ease of use and the fact that a large number of questions can be asked of this oracle within a very short period of time. It often serves as the first step in the process that leads to the use of more reliable, albeit more expensive and complex, oracles.

A greater level of reliability is given by *dakpa*, the termite oracle. Just about any man, and sometimes a woman, can consult *dakpa*. All one has to do is to find a termite mound and then take two branches from two different trees and place them into the mound. The next day one removes the two to see which one or both has been eaten by the termites. Of course, the process is slow—one has to wait over night—and because only few questions can be asked at any one time, its use is quite limited. However, it is considered to be reliable, primarily because it is not manufactured by humans, the agents of the oracle being termites that are not influenced by the same things that influence a person.

Without question the most important Zande oracle is *benge*. When it is consulted or sanctioned by a chief, the results may be used as evidence in legal proceedings. It is used in all important legal and social situations and directs the Azande on what to do in major crisis situations.

The poison that is used is a red powder that is manufactured from a forest creeper and mixed with water to become a paste. The liquid is squeezed out of the paste into the beaks of small chickens, which are compelled to swallow it. Generally violent spasms follow. The doses sometimes prove fatal, but just as often the chickens recover, and sometimes they are even completely unaffected by the poison. From the behavior of the chickens, especially by their death or survival, Azande receive answers to the questions they place before the oracle.

The creeper does not grow in Zandeland. It takes a long, difficult journey through the territory of other tribes to procure the poison. This, in part, accounts for the high value the Azande place on the poison oracle. The oracular consultation takes place away from the homesteads where the oracle can be consulted in secrecy without interference from witches. The equipment includes the poison and a basket of chickens. The Azande raise chickens but do not regularly slaughter them for food except on very special occasions. Eggs are not consumed but are permitted to hatch.

The oracle is owned by older men. This ownership conveys authority and prestige, but older men will consult the oracle for younger kinsmen as an obligation of kinship. Women are excluded from any contact with *benge*.

It takes experience and skill to become a good operator of the oracle, to judge the amount of poison to be given the chickens, and to observe and interpret the behavior of the chickens. At the start of a consultation the operator, who has observed a number of tabus, prepares the poison. A second man will pose the questions. The operator twirls a grass brush in the liquid poison and squeezes the brush so that the poison runs into the throat of the chicken. Then the questioner begins to address the poison for several minutes, and more poison is given to the chicken. Then the operator takes the chicken in his hand, jerks it back and forth, and finally places it on the ground. The operator and questioner watch as the animal dies or survives. Depending on the way in which the question was phrased and the instructions that are given to the poison, the death or survival of the chicken provides a yes/no answer to the question. We will discuss *benge* further when we discuss Zande witchcraft in Chapter 9, since the poison oracle is the principle method of determining the identity of a witch.

Bunyoro Divination

The Bunyoro of Uganda (East African Cattle culture area) consult a diviner when they are in trouble and want to know what caused the trouble and what to do about it. Problems include suspected sorcery or witchcraft, barrenness, impotence, and frequent miscarriages. Usual causes are sorcery by a living person, activity of a ghost, or agency of one of the numerous nonhuman *mbandua* spirits. Two common types of divination among the Bunyoro are various mechanical forms (which involve the manipulation of material objects) and spirit mediumship.

The most common mechanical method involves the use of cowrie shells. The tops of the shells are cut off so that they will lie flat in an up or down position. The diviner whispers a question and instructions to the shells and then drops them on the ground. The answer is determined by the pattern made by the thrown shells. Some standard interpretations include the following: If the shells fall with the cutoff side up, the prognosis is good; if one shell falls onto another shell, someone will die; if the shells are scattered, someone is going on a journey; three or more shells in a line indicate a safe return.

The Bunyoro also have a traditional cult of spirit mediumship. Powerful spirits may be present, and modesty and respect are appropriate. The diviner is dressed in a distinctive and striking costume with a special headdress. Once the spirit has possessed the body of the medium, it is possible for individuals to speak directly to the spirit, asking specific questions and receiving specific answers.

Astrology

Quite likely the most popular divination technique practiced in the United States today, astrology has a history stretching back thousands of years. The basis of astrology is the assumption of a causal relationship between celestial phenomena and terrestrial ones, or the influence that the stars and planets have on the lives of human beings. Astrology can be used to examine the life of a specific individual or to divine events of importance to the whole community. The origins of astrology appear to have been in Babylonia and spread from there to Greece, Rome, and Egypt; from there to Iran and India; and then on to Central Asia, Tibet, China, Korea, and Japan.

Astrology in Babylonia was the most common form of divination. However it was not done on an individual basis, but rather for the well-being of the entire community. The casting of horoscopes did not occur until the fifth century B.C.E., rather late in the history of Babylonian astrology. Other important innovations included dividing the ecliptic of the sun's orbit around the earth into twelve zones of thirty degrees each.

Crucial to Babylonian astrology was the idea that the movements of the celestial bodies represented the will of the gods. Therefore by reading the signs in the heavens, the future could be divined. The sky was seen as containing the "mansions" of the three principal gods: Anu, Enlil, and Ea. These gods governed the "celestial paths" or three belts that ran along the equator, the Tropic of Cancer, and the Tropic of Capricorn. Each of the planets was also identified with a specific deity. For example, the planet Jupiter was associated with Marduk, and Venus was associated with the goddess Ishtar. Ultimately, a god was linked to, and was seen to rule over, each month. Importantly, this was closely linked with the activities of the agricultural cycle.

From Babylonia astrology spread to Greece, Rome, and Egypt, where it was developed far beyond what the Babylonians had achieved. Hipparchus is credited with discovering the position of the equinoxes around 130 B.C.E., thus laying the foundation for the horoscope as we now know it. One of the most significant contributions to astrology on the part of the Greeks is this attempt to chart an individual's destiny by looking at things such as the position of the stars. From the Greeks we also get the fully developed zodiac. Each of the twelve zones was linked to a particular animal (e.g., Saturn with a goat, Mars with a ram, Venus with a bull). From Greece astrology spread to India and Iran and throughout much of Asia.

In Europe, Greek astrological knowledge was revived only with the translation of Arabic texts in the twelfth and thirteenth centuries. There was a large renewal of interest in the subject in Western Europe during the fifteenth and sixteenth centuries. Up until the rise of modern science in the sixteenth century, astrology and astronomy were intertwined. With the discoveries of Copernicus, Galileo, and Kepler, astrology lost any scientific basis and became separate from astronomy.

Astrology is extremely popular in the United States today. Even people who do not believe in its divinatory abilities generally still know what their sign is and at least a little of what is associated with that sign. For example, both of us are Geminis, one born in late May and the other in early June, albeit a generation apart. Gemini is ruled by Mercury and symbolized by the twins. The twin symbolism is supposed to relate to the dual, creative, versatile, and complex nature of those born under this sign. Less flattering descriptions include unpredictable, restless, and confusing to others. Gemini is also considered to be a masculine, outer-directed, and active sign. One of three air signs, Gemini is associated with being free-thinking, intellectual, and communicative. Of course, an individual horoscope could be done for each of us that would also take into account the specific day and time of our respective births.

Conclusion

Although magic at first appears to be an exotic topic, practiced by those in foreign places, in reality magical thinking is a very human way of thinking and is practiced at some time or another by every one of us. The logic of magic not only is the result of our normal mental processes, but also answers our need to have some control over our lives. Magic gives us control and divination gives us knowledge—two of the major functions of religion.

Magic deals with supernatural forces and thus is a religious phenomenon. In the next two chapters we will turn to what may be more familiar domains of religion and anthropomorphic supernatural beings.

Summary

Magic refers to activities by which a person can compel the supernatural to behave in certain ways. Key components of magical acts are the words that are spoken or the spell and objects that are manipulated in set ways. Magical rituals usually can be performed only at special places and at special times. The performer must often observe certain restrictions such as abstention from sexual intercourse and avoidance of certain foods. A magician is usually a worker in the kind of magic that is on the whole public and good, whereas a sorcerer deals in matters that are evil and antisocial.

Frazer articulated the Law of Sympathy, which states that magic depends on the apparent association or agreement between things. There are two parts to the Law of Sympathy. The first is the Law of Similarity, which states that things that are alike are the same. The second is the Law of Contagion, which states that things that were once in contact continue to be connected after the connection is severed. The Law of Similarity gives rise to homeopathic or imitative magic, and the Law of Contagion to contagious magic.

Tylor addressed the question of why people believe that magic works. The answer is because magic appears to never fail. There are several reasons for this. Because magic always works, failure must be due to the inadequacies of the magician. Magic usually attempts to bring about events that will naturally occur; people do not generally ask impossible things of magic. Finally, there is the issue of selective memory.

Techniques for obtaining information about things unknown, including events that will occur in the future, is known as divination. Inspirational forms of divination involve some type of spiritual experience, such as a direct contact with a supernatural being through an altered state of consciousness. Noninspirational forms are more magical ways of doing divination and include the reading of natural events as well as the manipulation of oracular devices. Fortuitous forms simply happen without any conscious effort on the part of the individual; deliberate forms are those that someone sets out to do. Examples of divination include omens, presentiments, possession, prophecy, ornithomancy, oneiromancy, necromancy, astrology, dowsing, flipping a coin, ordeals, palmistry, phrenology, and reading tarot cards.

Suggested Readings

Tahir Shah, *Sorcerer's Apprentice* (New York: Time Warner, 2002).
[Shah's travels across southern India to find and learn the art of magic from one of India's greatest practitioners.]

Paul Stoller and Cheryl Olkes, *In Sorcery's Shadow* (Chicago: The University of Chicago Press, 1987).
[The story of Stoller's work with sorcerers in the Republic of Niger.]

Stuart Vyse, *Believing in Magic: The Psychology of Superstition* (New York: Oxford University Press, 1997).

[Examines the psychological and cognitive reasons behind magical thinking.]

Fiction:

Ursula K. LeGuin, *A Wizard of Earthsea* (Emeryville, CA: Parnassus Press, 1968).
[The life story of a powerful wizard growing up in the fantasy world of Earthsea.]

Gregory Maguire, *Wicked: The Life and Times of the Wicked Witch of the West* (New York: HarperCollins, 1995).
[The story of the Wizard of Oz told from the point of view of the Wicked Witch of the West.]

Suggested Web Sites

www.bartleby.com/196
An on-line copy of James Frazer's *The Golden Bough*.

www.era.anthropology.ac.uk
Spider divination of the Mambila people of West Africa, including simulation.

http://skepdic.com/
Discussion of divination methods from *The Skeptic's Dictionary*.

www.lib.umich.edu/pap/magic/
Traditions of Magic in Late Antiquity exhibit from the University of Michigan.

Study Questions

1. In gambling, we know that the result of a throw of a pair of dice is a random event, yet gamblers believe that various behaviors can influence the results. This is an example of magical thinking. What does this mean?

2. Someone gives you a "lucky charm" that you place in your pocket, and soon afterward sometimes very good happens that you attribute to the charm. Is this an example of magic? Explain.

3. Can you think of any examples of magical thinking in your own life?

4. "Magic always works." Is this statement true? Explain.

5. There are two major types of magic: homeopathic magic and contagious magic. How are they similar and how are they different? Provide some examples of each type as used in the area of healing.

6. What are some of the divination devices that one can buy in an American toy store? Classify each and explain how it works.

7. One could argue that the use of divination—astrology, for example—is harmless entertainment. Are there negative consequences of living one's life relying on astrology and fortune telling?

Endnotes

1. E. Durkheim, *The Elementary Forms of the Religious Life* (New York: Collier Books, 1961), p. 60.

2. B. Malinowski, *Magic, Science and Religion and Other Essays* (Garden City, NY: Doubleday, 1954), p. 38.

3. Ibid., p. 17.

4. A. B. Weiner, *The Trobrianders of Papua New Guinea* (Fort Worth, TX: Harcourt Brace, 1988), p. 8.

5. G. Gmelch, "Baseball Magic," *Transaction*, 8 (1971), pp. 39–41, 54. Courtesy of G. Gmelch.

6. W. D. Hand, "Folk Medical Magic and Symbolism in the West," in A. Fife, et al. (eds.), *Forms upon the Frontier*, Utah State University Monograph Series 16, no. 2 (1969), pp. 103–118.

7. H. D. Eastwell, "Voodoo Death and the Mechanism for Dispatch of the Dying in East Arnhem, Australia," *American Anthropologist*, 84 (1982), pp. 5–17.

8. E. E. Evans-Pritchard, *Witchcraft, Oracles and Magic among the Azande* (Oxford, England: Clarendon, 1937).

9. S. Lindenbaum, *Kuru Sorcery: Disease and Danger in the New Guinea Highlands* (Palo Alto, CA: Mayfield, 1979), p. 65.

10. R. Grant, *The Illustrated Dream Dictionary* (New York: Sterling, 1991, 1995).

11. From E. F. Henderson, *Select Historical Documents of the Middle Ages* (London: George Bell, 1910), pp. 314–317.

7

Souls, Ghosts, and Death

The late nineteenth century anthropologist Edward Tylor introduced the concept of animism, a belief in spirit beings that animate all living things (see Chapter 1). Although the spiritual nature of living things can be thought of as a generalized supernatural power, it is seen most frequently as supernatural beings of various kinds. Some supernatural beings live within animals, plants, and natural physical features; others live as independent beings. Some supernatural entities are closely associated with humans, being human in origin; others, like gods and spirits, are usually separate from humans in origin. This chapter will study the former type of supernatural beings, those that are thought to be the supernatural mirror of animate beings, primarily humans, or are transformed human beings.

Important among these are soul and ghosts, which are supernatural manifestations of individuals living and dead. Death rituals, including funerals, are important to societies because they perform many critical functions both for the deceased and for those who remain.

Souls and Ghosts

The belief in the existence of a spirit entity residing within a person appears to be a natural one that grows out of simple observations about life. A human being does certain things, interacts with people in certain ways, and has a distinct personality. What is responsible for this? On the other hand, a person temporarily ceases to be an active being during sleep or when in a faint or coma; during sleep a person dreams; during ritual a person enters a trance. A person permanently ceases to be an animated being in death.

The Soul

The term **soul** is used to label the noncorporeal, spiritual component of an individual. Although many people are familiar with the presence of spirits within non-human animals, most scholars reserve the term *soul* for the spirits that inhabit the human body. Usually, each individual possesses a soul that takes on the personality of the individual (or perhaps the individual takes on the personality of the soul). The soul usually has an existence after death, at least for some period of time.

When one dreams, it is as if one's soul leaves the body and travels rapidly through space and time. It meets up with all sorts of people, including the souls of relatives who have died. In some groups it is considered dangerous to wake someone up suddenly, for there might not be enough time for the soul to return from its travels, and the soul might be lost. On the other hand, it is not a good idea to murder someone in his or her sleep since the person's soul is absent. It is better to wait until the victim is awake and the soul has returned.

We see a person sleeping, lying inert, devoid of activity and personality. We make the same observation when one faints or goes into a coma. Some believe that when a shaman enters a trance, the shaman's soul has left the shaman's body to travel to a supernatural world. Illness may be caused by the soul having left the body. Death is the permanent withdrawal of the soul from the body. The existence of a soul that survives death is reinforced when a loved one feels the presence of the deceased or experiences visits from the deceased in dreams.

Variation in the Concept of the Soul.   Although the concept of a soul can be found in all cultures, the soul takes on a great many forms. The soul may be envisioned as a full-sized duplicate of the living individual, or it may be small and reside somewhere in the body. Where? Perhaps in the liver, the chest, the heart, or the brain. The soul may exist as a person's shadow, so one must be careful where one's shadow falls. Or the soul may be reflected in a mirror, which is why beings without souls, such as vampires, have no reflection. When seeing a photograph for the first time, some people see the image as the soul that has been captured by the photographer.

Many people think of different kinds of souls that reside within the body. One soul might be responsible for a person's animation and will disappear at death. This soul, or life force, may be reincarnated into other living beings. Another soul might be a spirit that is that individual's personality. Different souls may be associated with different parts of the body, or one soul may come from the father's family and another from the mother's.

For example, in Haitian Vodou there are three spiritual components associated with the physical being. One of these is a spirit known as the *mét-tét,* or "Master of the Head." Its identify is discovered through divination. The *mét-tét* may possess the individual. The other two spiritual components can be seen as souls. The *ti-bonanj,* or "little angel," is a person's consciousness and ego. When the body dies, the *ti-bonanj* stays nearby for a while and then moves on to heaven, where it has little more to do with the living. The *gwo-bonanj,* or "big angel," comes from the ancestral spirits and is returned after death. It is a part of Bondye, the "High God," and is a person's life force that determines, in part, his or her character and intelligence. If a person has lived a good life, the person's memory will be kept for many generations, and his or her *gwo-bonanj* may be prayed to.

You may be born with souls, but other souls may be acquired during your lifetime. The Jivaro of Ecuador (Amazon culture area) believe that a person has three souls. Every person is born with a *nekas,* or the soul that is the life force. The second soul, the *aruntam,* has to be acquired through a vision. The Jivaro see this life as false and the spiritual world as real. Only by acquiring an *aruntam* can a person enter into the real, spiritual world. Acquiring this soul is also believed to give a person power, intelligence, and self-confidence. The third soul, the *miusak,* is the "avenging soul." If a person's *aruntam* is killed, the *miusak* will avenge the death. It is this belief that gives rise to the practice of headhunting. The *miusak* is believed to reside in the head, and capturing and ritually shrinking the head are believed to neutralize it.

In some cultures the soul is created anew for each child. Beliefs differ as to when and how the soul enters into the child. For example, the Roman Catholic belief that the soul enters the child at conception has influenced their position on such issues as cloning. In other cultures the soul may have a previous existence before it starts a new life.

Among the Beng of West Africa the soul has been living in a place called *wrugbe* with the ancestors before being born. For this reason a baby will be bathed with the same kind of soap that is used to bathe the dead—both are moving from one world to another. It takes some time for the child to actually leave *wrugbe,* an event that is marked by the umbilical cord falling off. If a child dies before this time, a funeral will not be held. Because the child never left *wrugbe,* it did not really die.

Souls, Death, and the Afterlife.   The concept of a soul is very closely tied to ideas about death. As Nigel Barley writes, "notions of what it means to be dead are always part of a more general idea of what it means to be a living human being in the first place and funerary behaviour and beliefs around the world read like an extended discussion of the notion of the person."[1]

As far as anthropologists are aware, there are no cultures that do not have a soul-like concept and no cultures that do not believe that this soul survives the death of the body, at least for some period of time. Where there is a belief in multiple souls, the different souls may have different destinations after death, including surviving for different lengths of time. In most cultures the idea of the soul after death is based more on continuity with life than with immortality, as is common in the West.

Souls that live after death may spend some time near their family, often until the funeral is completed, and then may travel some place else or be reincarnated. One of the functions of funeral rituals is to aid the soul in its journey. Sometimes these journeys are dangerous and difficult, and a soul might perish on the journey or might end up in a not-so-nice place. In some religious systems the duration of a soul's residence after death is finite, and the soul is reborn in another individual or, in the case of **transmigration,** into the body of an animal.

The ability of a soul to survive its journey to the land of the dead after death may depend on the quality of the person's life before death. In such societies the life is judged, and the threat of failing to "pass the test" to enter paradise can act as a means of social control. On the other hand, in many groups all souls make it to wherever souls go after death, or only those who have memorized particular rituals or who have had elaborate funeral rituals. It is not always the good that successfully make the journey; often it is the wealthy and powerful.

Where is the land of the dead, and what is it like? The final destination of the soul is usually at some distance from the place where the person lived. It is often located at a known geographic place, such as a mountaintop or island, or a place that is "over the horizon." Often it is located in a place that is not considered a part of the normal physical world, such as in the sky or under ground. Although we in the West tend to think of the physical afterlife as a paradise, in many cultures it is surprisingly similar to the physical community on earth. In the afterlife the dead socialize, hunt, and have sex. However, there is no illness, and the dead interact with their ancestors.

Not all souls go to the same afterlife. Many people have special places for souls depending on certain attributes. For example, warriors who have died in battle, women who have died in childbirth, or suicides might go to a special space. There may be special places for the souls of certain social classes or occupational groups, such as shamans. For example, Valhalla was the special place for Viking warriors who died a good death, that is, died in battle. In this case both social status and manner of death were important.

Examples of Concepts of the Soul

In this section we will examine soul beliefs in several societies, including the Yup'ik of Alaska, the Yanomamö of South America, and the Hmong of Southeast Asia, as well as Roman Catholic, Hindu, and Buddhist conceptions.

Yup'ik Souls.   Many religious systems believe in the recycling of souls. Among the Yup'ik of western Alaska a newborn has the soul of someone who has recently died in the grandparental generation, after whom the child is named. After death the soul remains nearby for a period of time and then leaves to await rebirth. Thus the immortal soul recycles through time from the beginning of the earth.

In Yup'ik culture animals also possess immortal souls that are a part of a cycle of birth and rebirth. However, this cycle is based on a reciprocal relationship between humans and animals that is based on how each treats the other. For example, if a seal perceives that the hunter is adhering to the rules of Yup'ik society and its relationship to the animal world, the seal will permit itself to be killed. Its flesh will provide food for the hunter and his family, and the seal's soul will, if treated properly by the hunter, return to the sea to be reborn again.

On death the soul of the seal retracts to its bladder. The Yup'ik collect all of the bladders from the seals killed during the year. They are inflated and hung throughout a five-day festival and then are shoved through a hole in the ice into the water, where the souls are eventually reborn.

Yanomamö Spirits and Souls.   The Yanomamö (Tropical Forest culture area) believe in a complex of souls. The main part of the soul becomes a *no borebö* at death. The Yanomamö cosmos is composed of four layers. The living Yanomamö live on the third layer, and on death the *no borebö* moves up to the second layer, where it moves down a trail until it encounters a spirit named Wadawadariwä. The spirit asks the soul whether it has been stingy or generous. If the soul replies that it has been stingy, it is sent to a place of fire, but if it has been generous, it joins the ancestors. One would assume that the possibility of being sent to a place of fire would act as a constraint on negative behavior during life, but Wadawadariwä is thought to be somewhat stupid and will accept what the soul tells him, which is why everyone is generous and is sent to the village of the ancestors.

Another aspect of the soul is the *bore*, which is released during cremation. It remains on earth and lives in the jungle. Some *bore* possess bright glowing eyes and will attack people who are traveling through the jungle at night.

The third aspect of the soul is the *möamo*, which lies within the body near the liver. Shamans will use their powers to remove the *möamo* from the body of their enemies, who will become sick and die. Much of the activity of shamans is divided between stealing the souls of enemies and recovering the souls of members of their own community.

In addition, everyone has a *nonoshi*, or animal, which is born each time a human child is born and will develop and grow along with the child. The animal is the person's double, and what happens to one will happen to the other. When either the person or his or her *nonoshi* dies, the other dies. The most common *nonoshi* for males are large birds, and the most common for females are land animals.

A person's *nonoshi* lives far away. Therefore a person has no physical contact with his or her own *nonoshi*. Still it is possible for someone else living where the *nonoshi* lives to kill the *nonoshi*, usually by accident: then the person associated with it dies. If possible, the dead person's relatives will seek vengeance by killing the murderer. Every once in a while, hunters will encounter an animal that shows unusual behavior. Such an animal is either an evil spirit or someone's *nonoshi*. It is never killed and certainly never eaten.

Hmong Souls.   The Hmong are a people living in the mountainous regions of Southeast Asia. Large numbers of Hmong from Laos immigrated to the United States after the end of the Vietnam war.

The Hmong believe that a person possesses a number of souls—some sources say as many as thirty. Health is the result of a balance between the physical body and its souls. When one or more of the souls are lost or stolen, the person falls ill.

A soul may be frightened out of the body by a traumatic event, or it may be stolen by a spirit. Anne Fadiman, in her book *The Spirit Catches You and You Fall Down*, tells the story of a Hmong family living in Merced, California.[2] The story centers on a little girl, Lia. One day Lia's sister came into the house and slammed the door, frightening Lia's soul out of her body. The loss of the soul resulted in an illness, which the Hmong call by a phrase that translates as "the spirit catches you and you fall down." The spirit being referred to is a soul-stealing spirit. This illness is diagnosed as epilepsy in Western medicine.

Curing such illnesses falls to the shaman. The shaman enters an altered state of consciousness to search for the lost soul and, if it is found, will return it to the patient's body. If the soul was stolen by a spirit, the shaman will negotiate with the spirit for the return of the soul. Gifts will be offered, and the soul of a sacrificed animal will be offered in exchange for the soul of the sick individual.

After the birth of a child its placenta (afterbirth) is buried under the dirt floor of the house. The word used by the Hmong for the placenta can be translated as "jacket," and it is thought of as a piece of clothing. At death the soul travels back to the place where the person's placenta was buried and puts on its placenta jacket. This allows the soul to travel on the dangerous path to the place where the ancestors live. If the soul fails to locate its placenta jacket, it will wander for eternity, never to be reunited with its ancestors.

The Soul in Roman Catholicism.   The doctrine of the Roman Catholic Church states that after death the destiny of each soul is determined by God, based primarily on the person's behavior during life. The main issue is the presence of sin, which is defined as a moral evil. People who are free of sin and are perfectly pure will go to Heaven, where they will be with God and will experience perfect happiness. Although God is considered to be omnipresent, Heaven is considered to be His home; in general it is conceived of as being in the sky.

Souls that are in a state of grace but in need of purification go to **Purgatory.** The word *Purgatory*, comes from the Latin *purgare*, meaning to make clean or to purify. Purgatory exists for those souls who die with lesser faults for which the person had not repented or for which the penalty was not entirely paid during the lifetime. For example, venial sins are considered a consequence of human frailty and are considered pardonable, requiring only temporary punishment. These sins can be dealt with by time spent in Purgatory. This is necessary because nothing less than the perfectly pure can enter Heaven.

People who die in mortal sin or with original sin are relegated to eternal punishment in Hell. A mortal sin is an act that is contrary to Divine law and separates the sinner from God; original sin is the sin of Adam in Genesis, which is washed away by baptism. Hell is a place of punishment and eternal torment for the damned, including both humans and demons. Hell is usually conceived of as being within the earth. In the Bible it is described as an abyss and a place to which the wicked descend. Because its inhabitants are estranged from God, they are placed as far away from His home and His light as possible.

The Soul in Hinduism and Buddhism.   In Hinduism there is a belief in an immortal, eternal soul that is born again and again in different bodies, a process called **reincarnation.** Although the bodies differ each time, the self—its distinct personality—remains unchanged. A rebirth might not be into a human body, and birth as a human is seen as a precious and rare opportunity.

The Hindu idea of reincarnation is closely tied to the concept of **karma.** Karma concerns an individual's actions and the consequences of those actions. One's life is what one has made it, and every action, thought, and desire—be they good or bad—will affect one's next life. The life one lives now is the consequence of past actions. This cycle of birth, death, and rebirth in this world is known as Samsara. The ultimate goal is to escape from Samsara and achieve *moksha*, or liberation from the limitations of space, time, and matter. Because the achievement of salvation is difficult and complex, an individual will require multiple lifetimes to achieve it. Although there is no mobility within a single lifetime, how the individual accepts and lives during that life will determine the level for the next reincarnation.

Although Buddhism is similar to Hinduism in some of its of ideas, Buddhist concepts of the soul, reincarnation, and karma differ in important ways. Buddhists do not believe in an immortal soul or a conscious personality that continues on. What is referred to as a soul, Buddhism conceives of as a combination of five mental and physical aggregates: the physical body, feelings, understandings, will, and consciousness. These make up the human personality, and this is what is caught up in the endless cycle of birth, death, and rebirth.

The Four Noble Truths state that life is imperfect and inevitably involves suffering. This suffering originates in our desires but will cease if all desires cease. The way to do this and to achieve release from the cycle is to follow the Eightfold Path, which consists of right understanding, right thought, right speech, right action, right livelihood, right effort, right mindfulness, and right meditation. A person who does this can achieve Nirvana. The goal of Buddhism is not to go to some blissful heaven, but to extinguish desire and craving and escape from the suffering of this life.

Buddhists also have the concept of karma, the belief that all of one's actions, good or bad, help create one's personality. This process continues even after death. Rebirth is seen as the transmission of karma. Buddha compared this process to a flame that passes from one candle to the next. However, it is only the flame of karma that is passed on, not a continuous personality. The Wheel of Life (Figure 7.1) shows

FIGURE 7.1 *The Wheel of Life.* A painting of the Wheel of Life on a monastery wall in Nepal.

the thirty-one planes of existence, conceived of by some Buddhists as psychological metaphors and by others as reality. These planes of existence include hells, hungry ghosts (beings tormented by unsatisfied desires), animals, humans, and gods. Humans proceed around and around this wheel, repeatedly experiencing suffering, unless we are freed into Nirvana. Following on the flame metaphor, *Nirvana* means to extinguish, or to put out the flame of the candle.

Ancestors

One possible fate for a soul is that it becomes part of the group of supernatural beings that are important to the living: ancestors. Anthropologists have often used the term **ancestor worship** to describe the beliefs and behaviors surrounding the veneration of ancestors. However, the use of the term *worship* is falling out of favor because a number of researchers think that the ancestors are respected and attended to but not really "worshipped."

The importance of ancestors to a culture is a reflection of the importance of kinship, generally kinship beyond the immediate family. Even after death a person is still a valued member of the kinship group, one who reinforces ideas of social roles and contributes to social harmony and social solidarity. In some cultures the ancestors act as a moral force, punishing their descendants for misbehavior.

However, not all souls become ancestors—or at least not ancestors who receive any ritual attention. For example, in societies in which descent is figured through men, mainly males may become ancestors. If a woman in such a culture were to become an ancestor, this would be determined by her relationship to a man, for example, by marriage or through her children. Although most ritual activity concerning ancestors is a family matter, in Africa it is common for the ancestors of chiefs or kings to be considered responsible for things that concern the entire community, such as rain, and therefore will be recognized by everyone.

Yoruba Ancestors

Among the Yoruba of West Africa ancestors play very important roles in the continued welfare of their descendants, and much of their religious practices, including the maintenance of shrines and the performance of rituals, are centered on them.

The Yoruba identify two broad classes of ancestors: family ancestors and deified ancestors. Of those who die, only a limited number become family ancestors. Ancestors are individuals who led noteworthy lives while alive. They lived to an old age and lived a good life, and their descendents are willing to perform the required rituals. It is one of the most important tasks of the family head to perform proper rituals for the family ancestors. The maintenance of good relations with the ancestors is important for the continued well-being of the family, for the ancestors possess power to bring good or ill to their descendants. The ancestors provide guidance and protection for the family but will punish family members who do not behave as they should and do not fulfill their obligations to the dead. Deified ancestors are those with great powers and are worshipped at shrines throughout the region. In fact, such ancestors may be thought of as gods with human origins.

The *egungun* are spirits who have traveled from the land of the dead to visit the living. In ritual the ancestors are often represented by the *egungun* dancers, who become conduits between the living and the ancestors. An *egungun* dancer is a man who wears a long grass robe and a wood mask with a human or animal face. Several days after a funeral, the *egungun* goes to the house in which the person has died and tells the relatives that the deceased has arrived in the land of the dead and is doing all right. Food is then given to the *egungun* and his followers.

On death an individual travels to the land of the dead. If the person has been good in life, he or she will lead a pleasant existence, but those who behaved badly will suffer. One of the rewards of living a good life is to be remembered. As long as they are remembered, dead people are able to act as intermediaries between the gods and the family. The ancestors often contact their living family in dreams or through the aid of the *egungun*. *Egungun* may appear at times when the family needs advice and at the annual festival.

Tana Toraja Ancestors

The Tana Toraja are a horticultural people living in small villages growing rice and raising water buffalo and pigs in the mountains of Sulawesi, Indonesia. Ritually, their world is divided into the smoke-ascending part and the smoke-descending part. This division exists in both the physical and supernatural worlds. The smoke-ascending part is associated with the rising sun in the east, the *deata*, and health and fertility rituals. The *deata* are gods and spirits that are associated with nature. They are found in mountains and rivers, trees and animals, and the roofs of houses; they exist in the stars, clouds, rain, and mist. The smoke-descending dominion includes the *nene* or ancestors and the *bombo* or souls of people who have recently died. This realm is associated with the setting sun in the west and with death rituals. Through ritual the *bombo* are transformed into *nene*, and the *nene* can be transformed into *deata*.

The smoke-ascending and smoke-descending realms must be kept separate, and this requirement lies at the heart of much of Torajan ritual. Ritual also includes the offering of food, such as rice, and the sacrifice of animals. This ritual activity is known as "feeding the gods." It pleases the gods, and they will, in turn, come to the aid of the people.

The Torajans clearly separate physical death from social death. The definition of the moment of death in a modern industrial society has been made difficult because of life-prolonging machines (see Box 7.1). For example, the brain might cease functioning, but the heart is kept artificially beating. In Torajan society physical death is associated with the cessation of breathing and heartbeat. Yet it is not as simple as that because when breathing and heartbeat cease, when physical death has occurred, social death has not, for death is stretched out over an extended period of time. This is a good example of how culture reinterprets natural events—in this case, death. When a person is physically dead, the individual is not

BOX 7.1 • *Determining Death*

Determining when a person is dead is not as simple as it seems. Such a determination is a cultural interpretation of a series of biological events. In the eighteenth and nineteenth centuries many people feared that they would be declared dead when they in fact were not. Some coffins of the time were outfitted with pull cords attached to outside bells so that if a person was buried alive, they could signal those on the outside by pulling on the cord. This fear of being buried alive lessened with the development of new technologies, such as the stethoscope.

The modern debate on the determination of death has focused on the heart versus the brain. Are you dead if you have no brain activity but your heart is still beating? This debate has been influenced by the question "Which is the seat of the soul: the heart or the brain?" Modern medicine has defined death as the cessation of brain activity, leading to the existence of "beating-heart cadavers" from which organs can be procured for transplantation into another individual. However, many families still deny consent for organ donation, fearing that the person is not really dead yet. Although the EEG prevents misdiagnosis of brain death, people have difficulty seeing someone whose heart is beating as really being dead. Thousands of people are on waiting lists for organ donation, and many die each year while waiting for organs to become available.

Another interesting phenomena associated with organ donation is the claim by some heart transplant recipients that they take on some of the qualities or personality traits of the donor. Such a belief is clearly rooted in cultural beliefs about the soul.

said to have died, but is said to have a fever or to be sleeping. This knowledge is important because at this point, all smoke-ascending rituals are forbidden. In terms of the supernatural, the process of dying is a process whereby the *bombo* (soul) begins to separate from the physical body.

The social pronouncement of death does not take place for weeks and, in the case of very important people, even years. The dead body is wrapped in a cloth or put in a wood coffin and placed along the south wall of the house with the head to the west, which is the direction that is associated with smoke-descending rituals. The corpse, which may or may not be partially embalmed, is said to be asleep. During this time the decaying body is still referred to as a person with a fever. Offerings of food and drink are made to the dead person. People greet the dead person when they enter the house, and they converse with the dead, keeping him or her up to date about what is happening to the family and the community. During this time the *bombo* of the deceased stays close by and watches the preparations for its funeral. Soon the *bombo* has the power to cause trouble or to bring blessings to the family.

Torajan funeral rites are complex and important smoke-descending rituals that move the *bombo* into the next world, where it is transformed into a *nene* (ancestor). At the start of the funeral the sound of a gong formally announces the death. Sacrifices are made, and the body is moved to the west wall with its head pointing south, which is the direction in which it will travel to the afterlife.

The next day the body is wrapped in cloth, and an effigy is made on which the family hangs the personal possessions of the deceased. A few weeks later a water buffalo is prepared, and the body leaves the house along with household items and provisions for the soul's journey. The body is moved toward the burial site along with the effigy, which is usually a frame of bamboo but is carved of wood for an important person. Now the rituals begin that will separate the physical corpse from the *bombo*. The buffalo is sacrificed, and the corpse is buried in a limestone cliff. If the effigy is carved of wood, it is placed on a ledge in the cliff along with other effigy figures.

The *bombo* has now become a *nene* (ancestor), and it begins its journey southward to Puya with the guardian buffalo. However, suicides, lepers, and people who did not play according to the rules of society are not allowed to enter Puya. The life of a *nene* in Puya is very much like one's life while breathing. The *nene* has the same social rank as in life and is still wealthy or poor. The *nene* keeps an eye on the family to be sure that it is being properly honored. The *nene* has the power to bring aid and blessings as well as harm.

Some time after the funeral the descendants perform the rituals to transform the *nene* into a *deata* (god). Whereas the *nene* lives in the smoke-descending realm, the *deata* moves to the smoke-ascending realm. The *deata* joins the other spirits in the trees, mists, and sky and continues to watch over its descendants, who continue to offer sacrifices.

Ancestors in China

A major feature of Chinese culture is the veneration of ancestors. The deceased souls of ancestors are believed to remain closely concerned with the activities of living family members. The family's founding ancestor and the recently deceased are of the utmost importance, and respect must be paid to them. If the ancestors are treated with proper respect, they will give aid to their descendants. However, if they are ignored, the ancestors will cause problems. Divination (see Chapter 6) is often used as a way to receive messages from the ancestors.

The importance of ancestors in Chinese culture was emphasized by Confucius in the sixth century B.C.E. Confucius reinterpreted the ancient Chinese custom of ancestor veneration as an extension of the very important value of filial piety, or the respect due parents from their children. He encouraged the practice of the traditional rites honoring the ancestors. The basic theme of much of Chinese ritual is reciprocity. In the rites for the ancestors this is expressed by leaving offerings of food, in return for which the ancestors will grant favors. Ancestral shrines with tablets containing the names of the recent and notable dead are maintained in the house, and rituals are practiced there as well as in temples.

Bodies and Souls

As we have seen, the concept of the soul is intimately connected with death. Although the soul animates the living body, the soul also has a life beyond that of the physical. In this section we will look at cases in which the soul and body are disconnected but one or the other remains closely connected with the world of the living. These include ghosts, vampires, and zombies.

Souls without Bodies: Ghosts

The distinction between a soul and a **ghost** is not always a clear one. They are both manifestations of an individual after death. A soul is essentially good. It might hover around its corpse and the family after death, but eventually it goes somewhere else or is reincarnated. However, souls can bring misfortunate to the family if they are neglected or the family fails to perform the appropriate funeral rituals. By contrast, a ghost is essentially a negative force and tends to remain in the vicinity of the community. Ghosts can bring about illness and other misfortune; therefore, they have to be dealt with.

Dani Ghosts.   When someone among the Dani of New Guinea dies, a supernatural element called the *mogat* leaves the body. The *mogat* remains near the community and the family and becomes a ghost.

Dani ghosts will alert the community to enemy raids, thereby performing a service. However, ghosts are generally troublesome, and they are held responsible for a wide range of misfortunes, including accidents and illnesses of both people and pigs. The Dani are reluctant to travel in the dark for fear of being accosted by ghosts. However, these problems can be dealt with by rituals designed to placate the ghost, and, in truth, the Dani show more fear of ghosts in stories than they do in their everyday activities.

A major function of a funeral is to make the ghost happy and to keep it away from the community. The ghost of a person who has been killed in war is especially dangerous. It must be given a "fresh-blood" funeral, which is much more elaborate than the regular funeral given for a person who dies in other ways. The ghost of a person who is killed in war is also placated by the killing of an enemy.

There are many ways to keep ghosts happy and to control the negative influence of ghosts. An essential element in Dani ceremonies is the killing of pigs during feasts, and food is always given to the ghosts. (Although the food, especially pork, is set aside for the ghosts, eventually someone will eat the ghosts' share.) The Dani build small structures called ghost houses in several locations both within and outside the village as a place where the ghosts can live.

Bunyoro Ghosts.   The Bunyoro live in the East Africa Cattle culture area, and much of their religious activities centers on relationships with ghosts. Ghosts are one of three significant causes of illness, the others being sorcery and the activities of spirits. When illness strikes, a Nyoro will use the services of a diviner to determine the cause of the illness. If the misfortune is due to a ghost, the diviner will then proceed to identify the ghost. Generally, a ghost causes trouble for someone who is close to it and who has offended it in some way. A ghost will bring misfortune to an individual's relatives and descendants as well.

The Nyoro ghost is the disembodied spirit of a person who has died. It is a transformation of the soul. It is seen as being left by a deceased person but not being the deceased person per se. Unlike ghosts in Western cultures, Nyoro ghosts are never seen except in dreams. Ghosts are essentially evil and are associated with the underworld as well as with specific places, such as their graves. However, on the positive side, a ghost of a man may come to the aid of his son and descendants.

There are many ways in which a person can deal with ghosts. For example, there are techniques for capturing ghosts, and once captured, the ghost can be destroyed or removed from the community. Other rituals keep the ghost away from the family. However, many ghosts remain in the community and will periodically possess the victim or a close relative, thereby entering into direct communication with the living. Often the ghost will form a relationship with a living person, who will periodically sacrifice a goat to it and build a special ghost hut for it to live in.

The belief in ghosts plays important roles in Nyoro society. It gives the Nyoro an explanation for things that happen, such as illness, as well as methods, through ritual, of dealing with these problems. The Nyoro also believe that a ghost will cause trouble if it was treated poorly while living. This belief encourages people to behave properly toward family members so as to avoid problems after that person dies.

Japanese Ghosts.   Japanese religious practice is a complex mixture of folk beliefs, Buddhist, Shinto, and Tao influences and influences from cultures outside of Japan, especially China. Throughout Japan there is a belief in a variety of supernatural beings, the less savory ones including what Western writers call ghosts, demons, and goblins, among others. Not only are these spirits found among the peasants of the countryside, but they also appear in urban centers and have been immortalized in plays and art.

Many Japanese believe that at death an individual is transformed into an impure spirit. At specified intervals over the next seven years the family performs various rituals of purification as the spirit becomes an ancestral spirit. As an ancestral spirit, it watches over the family and helps in time of crisis. However, during the seven-year period the impure spirit floats between the land of the living and the land of the dead. During this time it is important that the family perform the required rituals and make offerings; if this is not done, the spirit will hover close to the living, often in the form of a ghost, and cause misfortune. Also, if an individual dies under conditions of great emotional stress, the spirit will remain in the world of the living as a ghost and haunt the individuals who are responsible for its anguish. Many folktales tell of murder victims and unrequited lovers who are so distraught at the moment of death that they remain on earth as ghosts.

Ghosts are frequently depicted in traditional Japanese art. For example, some drawings show a female ghost "with long straight hair and waving or beckoning hands. Pale clothing with long, flowing sleeves was draped loosely about the seemingly fragile figure, and the head and upper part of the body were strongly delineated. From the waist down, however, the form was misty and tapered into nothingness."[3]

Bodies without Souls: Vampires

Vampires are familiar creatures to Americans. Countless books, movies, and television shows have featured vampires and vampire hunters as their main characters. However, the vampire is a creature that was considered to be real throughout much of Europe, primarily in parts of Eastern Europe.

Much of our American vampire lore is based on Bram Stoker's novel *Dracula*, published in 1897. Stoker based his book loosely on the historical figure of Vlad Tepes, or Vlad the Impaler, but Stoker made numerous changes. Tepes was a Romanian prince, not a count, who ruled in Walachia, not Transylvania, and who was never viewed as a vampire by the local population. In fact, Tepes is a local hero in Romania.

The vampires of tradition bear little resemblance to the Count Dracula of Stoker's novel. Vampires were more likely to be shabbily dressed peasants than elegant counts. So who or what is a vampire? A vampire was believed to be someone who had recently died but who had returned to bring death to others.

The interest in vampires and the documentation of cases of vampirism began in the eighteenth century when parts of Serbia and Walachia were turned over to Austria. Austrian patrol officials began recording the local custom of exhuming dead bodies and "killing" them. An important case comes from the Serbian village of Medvegia in the 1730s. The following is a translated report of the case:[4]

> a local haiduk [a type of soldier] named Arnold Paole broke his neck in a fall from a hay wagon. This man had, during his lifetime, often revealed that, near Gossowa in Turkish Serbia, he had been troubled by a vampire, wherefore he had eaten from the earth of the vampire's grave and smeared himself with the vampire's blood, in order to be free of the vexation he had suffered. In twenty or thirty days after his death some people complained they were being bothered by this same Arnold Paole; and in fact four people were killed by him. In order to end this evil, they dug up this Arnold Paole forty days after his death . . . and they found that he was quite complete and undecayed, and that fresh blood had flowed from his eyes, nose, mouth, and ears; that the shirt, the covering, and the coffin were completely bloody; that the old nails on his hands and feet, along with the skin, had fallen off, and that new ones had grown; and since they saw from this that he was a true vampire, they drove a stake through his heart, according to their custom, whereby he gave an audible groan and bled copiously.

In reality, much of the evidence for the return of Paole and others as vampires can be easily explained by anyone with knowledge of how corpses decompose. For example, as the corpse decays, it becomes bloated with gas. This results in a red coloration of the skin and the appearance a full abdomen. The gas also pushes blood into the mouth. When the villagers staked Paole and reported that he groaned, what they most likely heard was the release of this gas. Although his corpse appeared not to have decomposed, this also is not unusual. Corpses actually decay at varying rates, and burial itself delays decomposition. In fact, all decomposing bodies would show these "vampire" features. However, only the bodies of those suspected of vampirism were ever dug up and "killed."

Paul Barber points out that the people who were most likely to be labeled vampires were likely to have been considered difficult, unpopular, or great sinners during their lifetime. He suggests that a belief in vampires provided an explanation for unexplained deaths, especially from epidemic diseases and other unfortunate events. Even better than just an explanation, the attribution of misfortune to vampirism also provided a course of action: The vampire could be "killed."

Bodies without Souls: Zombies

Zombies are the "living dead"—corpses that have been raised from their graves and animated, usually for evil purposes. Although zombies are known from other cultures (see the discussion of the Berawan in this chapter), they are most closely associated with the island of Haiti and the religion of Vodou (see Chapter 10). In contrast to vampires, who are believed to bring death and are therefore feared, zombies themselves are not to be feared. Again, this is contrary to Hollywood's popular renderings of them as brain eaters. The fear associated with zombies is the fear of being made into one. Zombies are seen as soulless creatures, animated for a life of slavery on a plantation.

There are a few documented cases that, although controversial, seem to show that zombification actually occurs. These involve people whose death and burial were documented and who were then observed to return. On the basis of these cases a Haitian psychiatrist named Dr. Lamarque Douyon requested the help of an ethnobotanist to track down the zombie powder. Dr. Douyon thought that the victim was given a drug that made him or her appear to be dead. After the burial the person who had administered the powder would dig up and revive the victim. Dr. Douyon received help from Wade Davis, then a graduate student at Harvard University. Davis's account of his research was published in 1985 in the book *The Serpent and the Rainbow*, which was later made into a movie.[5]

Davis claims that he was able to acquire some of the zombie powder and analyze it. The key ingredient turned out to be pieces of dried puffer fish. Puffer fish is considered a delicacy in Japan, where only specially licensed chefs are allowed to prepare it owing to the poisonous nature of the fish. A small amount of the poison is considered exhilarating. It causes tingling of the spine, prickling of the lips and tongue, and euphoria. Still, several dozen Japanese people every year get tetrodotoxin poisoning from eating puffer fish, and some die. A victim of this kind of poisoning is likely to make a full recovery if he or she survives the first few hours. So why do Haitian poisoning victims end up zombies but Japanese victims do not?

Davis pointed out the importance of cultural context and expectations. Haitians who practice Vodou believe that it is possible for a powerful priest to control the part of the soul known as *ti-bonaj*. This soul is associated with a person's personality and individuality. When the person's *ti-bonaj* is captured, the person is deprived of will, and his or her body can be held as a slave. These beliefs are necessary underpinnings to the zombification phenomena. Davis also suggested that the threat of zombification is used as a social control mechanism.

Davis's theory is very controversial, as are some of his research methods. Some question whether he paid for the zombie powder and participated in the exhumation of the corpse. Even more damaging is the inability of others to find tetrodotoxin in samples of the powder or to verify how the powder would work. In all, Davis's work remains unproven but provides an interesting hypothesis.

Death Rituals

Death rituals or funerals can be thought of as rites of passage whereby an individual moves from the status of living to that of dead (or another postdeath state such as ghost). The loss of a member of the community, especially an important member, can be very traumatic. If the deceased was a productive individual—a farmer, craftsman, or political leader—his or her passing can have a significant impact on the family and community. We can think of a death as a disruption of the social fabric of the family and community that needs to be mended. Death rituals also provide a way of channeling behavior in what can be a highly emotional state. Funeral rituals provide explanations for death and for what happens after death. In these functions, funerals are acting very much like social rites of intensification.

However, death rituals differ in many ways from other rites of passage. One of the most striking features is the presence of the body of the deceased. Even if the body does not play a role in the ritual itself, it is present, and something must be done about it.

Funeral Rituals

Funerals permit and channel expressions of grief. All people feel grief, but it can be manifested in many ways. In some societies there are specific times when it is appropriate to express grief and times when it is not. Some societies, including British and American societies, emphasize control of one's emotions. Grieving is often done privately, not in public, even at the funeral service. The length of time that is set aside for grieving is often limited, and after a period of time, the close relatives are expected to once again take up their lives. Even when grieving is publicly conducted and is very boisterous, it is still limited in time, and its expression is culturally channeled.

Among the Murngin of Australia funeral rituals actually begin before death. The family and band gather around the dying person and begin to wail and sing song cycles to comfort the dying. The songs also provide instructions to the soul so that it will make it to the totemic well and not cause difficulties for the family. Although some of the emotional energy of the men is directed toward revenge for the death (death is usually caused by sorcery or fighting), grief is more explicitly expressed by the women, who take sharp sticks or stone knives and cut their heads so that they bleed.

Earlier, we described the funeral rituals of the Torajans of Indonesia as part of the discussion of ancestors. Here we have a good example of the cultural expression of grief and how the outward expression of grief does not always coincide with the internal emotion of grief. In Tana Toraja there is a strong cultural pressure not to show one's emotions and to keep sadness and anger hidden from others. The Torajans believe that such emotions are bad for one's health and are disruptive to interpersonal relationships. Even in the face of what appears to be an emotionally charged event, people appear very calm. However, in the context of death Torajans can and are expected to express grief.

Torajan funerals are very elaborate and lengthy and involve a lot of people over a long period of time. During the lengthy funeral there are particular times when it is appropriate to cry and wail. Wailing is loud and expresses both grief and sympathy for the family of the deceased. Wailing occurs when people are near the body or an effigy figure, and they sometimes cover their faces and touch the body. Between the time the person physically dies and the beginning of the funeral, when the corpse is kept in the house, wailing does not occur, and the family remains calm. When the funeral begins, which might be several months later, people once again cry and wail.

Funerals are for both the living and the dead. Frequently, the fate of the soul depends on the proper rituals being performed correctly by the family. Thus while rituals may comfort the living, they may explicitly function to move the soul out of the community to some other place, such as a "land of the dead."

Often the most important issues are to protect the living by separating the living from the dead and to move the soul away from the living community so that it cannot cause harm. There are many ways in which living and dead are separated. Often the personal property of the deceased is destroyed. This eliminates anything that might attract the soul and encourage it to stay. The Nuer, a pastoralist group in East Africa, quickly bury the body and obliterate the grave so that the soul cannot find its body and therefore will leave. Other ways of moving the soul are to frighten it with firecrackers, as was done in China, or to build some type of barrier that ghosts will not cross.

The need to protect the community from ghosts is made very explicit in funeral rituals of the Dani of New Guinea. Karl Heider describes a Dani funeral and writes: "In every way, explicit and well as implicit, the funeral acts shout out to the ghosts: 'See this! See what we do for you!' And then, although this part is not so often said in words: 'Now go away and leave us in peace!' "[6]

Disposal of the Body

The focal point of most funeral rituals is the corpse, and one of the most important activities in a funeral is the process of disposing of the corpse. In some societies it is truly a disposal, for it is thought that as long as the body is intact, the soul will not leave. Some rituals involve very rapid disposal, and the body itself plays a very minor role in the funeral. In other societies the corpse is the centerpiece of the funeral, and the disposal of the corpse may be extremely elaborate.

Perhaps the most common means of disposing of a body is burial. In analyzing burials, there are many variables that we can look at such as where the body is buried. Often there is a sacred place for burials, such as a cemetery or cave. A cemetery may be restricted to a particular ethnic group or social class or people characterized by a particular cultural feature such as occupation or cause of death.

Warriors who die in battle or women who die in childbirth are often buried in special areas. (American culture provides special cemeteries for members of the military, for example.) Some cemeteries contain unmarked graves; others contain very elaborate tombs.

However, bodies are not always placed in special places. Often they are buried near the house or even under the floor of the house. This occurs frequently when the soul becomes an ancestor and the family wishes to keep the ancestor close by. In some cultures burial takes place quickly, often within twenty-four hours; in others the body may be kept for several days or even longer before burial. This is especially true if some type of preservation is practiced and the body plays an integral part in the ritual.

The body can be simply wrapped in a blanket or cloth, and sometimes the blanket or cloth has special designs and may be prepared early in life. The body can be placed in a wood coffin of various shapes and designs or in pottery vessels. The position of the body may be influenced by the size and shape of the container. A body can be stretched out in a coffin (most frequently on its back but sometimes on its side or stomach) but would be bound in a fetal position if placed in a pottery vessel. Sometimes the body is oriented in a particular direction with the head often positioned in the direction of some sacred place.

Often the body is prepared in some way before being placed in a container or in the ground. The body may be decorated or clad in special clothing. Sometimes the body is painted. Sometimes it is preserved in some way, by embalming, smoking, drying, or **mummification.** Grave goods may be placed in the grave, ranging from simple mementos to elaborate grave goods. And the grave goods may include sacrificed animals or sacrificed people.

The African Burial Ground

Much of our knowledge of history comes from written documents. Written records, however, document only a few segments of society, usually the important and literate, and those activities, such as shipping, that require that careful records be kept. Answering specific historical questions will send the researcher to archives, genealogical records, and old newspapers. But what about the uneducated, the poor, and the disenfranchised? Although they might have played important roles in society, their very existence remains poorly documented.

Our understanding of American slavery before the Civil War is very spotty, since most slaves could not read or write (letters and diaries are important sources of information) and their activities were not documented by scholars. However, information about this group can be gleaned from the archaeological record.

We normally do not think of slavery in northern cities, yet slaves in New York City in the eighteenth century made up a significant portion of the population at that time. And people die and need to be buried. People of European ancestry built churches with adjacent cemeteries within the city limits, but those on the fringes of society, such as slaves, had to bury their dead on land outside of the city limits that was set aside for this purpose.

A cemetery containing the remains of slaves was discovered in New York City in 1991 when contractors started to excavate a lot for a new government office building in lower Manhattan. Located at Broadway and Reade Street, it is known today as the African Burial Ground (Figure 7.2).

This cemetery dates from the eighteenth century and was in use until 1795. At this time it was located several miles outside the limits of a city that was considerably smaller than it is today. Archaeologists have excavated only a small portion of the cemetery because buildings stand on most of it. Yet over 400 skeletons were removed for analysis and later reburied.

What information can be gleaned from an analysis of a cemetery? Let us begin by examining the skeletons themselves, a task that is performed by **forensic anthropologists,** specialists in the analysis of the human skeleton. We know that over 90 percent of these skeletons exhibit features that suggest African ancestry. Many of the New York slaves at this time came directly from Africa or the West Indies. The high infant and child mortality rates are documented by the fact that about half of the total are skeletons of children twelve years of age or younger. About 40 percent of these children are infants. The death rate of children was high in all segments of society at this time, but the infant and child death rates in the slave population were much greater than those of the general population. Historical records show that slave owners did not provide adequate food and shelter for

FIGURE 7.2 *The African Burial Ground.* Archaeologists excavate the eighteenth century burial ground located in front of the Javits Federal Building in lower Manhattan in 1991.

children of their slaves because of the high cost, and disease and malnutrition are evident in the bones. We also have evidence of the brutal workload of adult slaves. Many of the adult bones show evidence of muscle strain and tears as well as fractures from lifting and carrying heavy loads.

Besides the skeletons themselves there is much evidence of cultural practices. Many of the teeth have been filed and modified in some way, a custom that was common in western and central African cultures. Most, but not all, of the bodies were buried in wooden coffins. The most common artifacts recovered were shroud pins, which held together the cloth used to wrap the bodies. Some cultural items were placed into the coffin with the body, including jewelry, glass beads, and coins.

The coffins were oriented with the heads to the west. We do not know exactly what this means, but several explanations have been suggested, including a belief that on the Day of Judgment the bodies would sit upright in their graves with their eyes to the east, the direction of the rising sun and the direction of Africa, their homeland. Although only about 400 graves were excavated, it has been estimated that as many as 10,000 people were buried in the cemetery throughout the eighteenth century. The government office building was never constructed on the site, and the lot has been turned into a memorial park.

Secondary Burials

Funeral rituals sometimes include two burials. The first takes place at death and involves burial or some other disposition of the body. The second takes place at a later time, perhaps months or years later. This second phase often marks the end of the mourning period and commonly involves digging up, processing, and reburying the body in some way. This is sometimes related to conceptions of the soul and the idea that what happens to the body mirrors or in some way affects what happens to the soul after death.

Murngin Death Rituals.   Among the Murngin of Australia, each kin group is associated with one or more sacred water holes, where totemic spirits live (see Chapter 3). The spirit comes out of the water hole, often in a father's dream, and asks the father to point out its mother; the spirit then enters its mother's womb. If a baby dies, its spirit returns to the water hole, becomes a spirit once again, and waits to be reborn. When an adult dies, the spirit returns to the totemic well, where it will always remain a spirit, never again to be reborn.

After death has occurred, totemic designs are painted on the body, which becomes the centerpiece of singing and dancing. It is then carried to the grave. The grave is a symbol of the sacred well, and the body is placed into the grave, laid out straight with the face down. Then the grave is filled in.

After two or three months or more, the body is exhumed. Any remaining flesh is then removed from the bones, and the bones are washed. Some of the small bones, such as finger bones, are kept as **relics** by close relatives. The cleaned bones are placed on bark paper and made into a bundle. The bones are watched over for several months. A coffin is then made from a tree trunk that has been hollowed out by termites that is carved into its proper shape. The bones are broken up with a stone and placed into the log. The log is left to rot, and the bones are left to decay.

Berawan Death Rituals. The Berawan of Borneo (Southeast Asia culture area) believe that after death the soul is divorced from the body and cannot reanimate the already decaying corpse. However, the soul cannot enter the land of the dead because it is not yet a perfect spirit. To become one of the truly dead, it must undergo a metamorphosis. As the body rots away to leave dry bones, so the soul is transformed into spirit form. As the corpse is formless and repulsive until putrefaction is completed, so the soul is homeless. It lurks miserably on the fringes of human habitation and, in its discomfort, may afflict the living with illness.

The decaying body is feared—not because of the process of rotting, for that releases the soul of the deceased from the bonds of the flesh, but because of the possibility that some malignant spirit of nonhuman origin will succeed in reanimating the corpse. Should this occur, the result would be a monster of nightmarish appearance, invulnerable to the weapons of humans, since it is already dead. Eventually, the soul passes to the land of the dead, and the mortal remains—the bones—join the bones of the ancestors in the tomb.

Cremation

Cremation is not as common as burial, yet many cultures practice cremation for a variety of reasons. Sometimes it is a reaction against the process of decay, which is thought to be a highly dangerous process. It is also a way to destroy the corpse so that the soul is cut off from its former body. In modern industrial societies cremation is becoming more popular as land becomes more and more valuable and crowded and less land is available for cemeteries. Also, cremation is more economical than burial, and cremation becomes more popular as the cost of burial increases.

Among the Yanomamö, after a person has died, the body is decorated. It is then brought to a pile of firewood that has been set up in the open area in the middle of the community, and the body is burned. The smoke from the fire is thought to be contaminating, and bows and arrows are washed afterward. Children and the ill leave the village while the body is being cremated to avoid contamination from the smoke. After cooling, bits of unburned bones and teeth are removed from the ashes and saved in a hollow log.

The Yanomamö are **endocannibalistic anthropophagers.** The term *endocannibalism* refers to the eating of one's own people, and *anthropophagers* refers to the eating of human bodies. (We have already seen the example of ritual eating of noncremated bodies among the Fore, described in Chapter 1.) The cremated bones are pulverized and placed into several small gourds. Later a series of memorial rituals will be performed in which the ground ashes from the gourds will be added to a plantain soup and consumed. The Yanomamö say they do this so that the dead will find a home in the bodies of the living. They are horrified by our unfeeling practice of leaving the dead to rot in the ground—a good reminder of cultural relativism.

Mummification

In some cultures, such as those that practice cremation, it is important to destroy the body to release the soul. Other cultures stress the importance of maintaining the integrity of the body after death. The American practice of embalming is not intended so much to preserve the body for all time as to prevent decay during the funeral period and to permit the display of a lifelike body. Other peoples, however, stress the need to prevent decay of the flesh for all time. Besides embalming, some peoples smoke the body or preserve the body in salt or oil.

To the ancient Egyptians death was the next step in a continuation of life. To participate in this new life, the body had to be preserved. The Egyptians developed a process of mummification that by New Kingdom times (ca. 1570–1070 B.C.E.) was able to thoroughly preserve the body.

The process of mummification was complex and time-consuming and could be practiced in its complete form only by the important and wealthy. The first step was to thoroughly remove as much of the water in the body as possible by burying it in the mineral natron for seventy days. The internal organs were removed and preserved in jars, and the body cavity was filled with resin-soaked linen. The body was then wrapped in additional linen, and hot resin was painted on the wrapping to form a hard layer. Finally, the entire body was wrapped in a cast made of linen and plaster.

Exposure

Another possibility is to expose the body to the elements or to be consumed by animals. This very effectively and quickly reduces the body to just bones. In some cases the bones would then be collected for further processing or burial. Again the disposal method may reflect soul beliefs—in this case the belief that once the soul has departed the body, the physical body itself is unimportant. Among the Inuit, who live in the Arctic, exposure was largely done out of necessity, because the ground was unsuitable for burial.

Some North American societies placed the body up in a tree or on a high platform, where it would be exposed to the elements. Sometimes the body would be placed in a cave, and in the hot, arid climate of the American Southwest the body would become a natural mummy. In Tibet we find sky burials, in which the body was consumed by birds. Perhaps this type of body disposal developed because of the difficulty of digging a grave in the hard ground and the scarcity of fuel for cremation. Special areas were set aside for sky burial where the body was cut into pieces and the bones smashed to be consumed by vultures.

American Death Rituals in the Nineteenth Century

In early nineteenth century America a person would most likely die at home, especially in rural areas, surrounded by family, friends, clergy, and perhaps a physician. Death often was a public affair, and the "audience" showed concern about the medical and religious condition of the dying person.

Once death occurred, the close members of the family took responsibility for the preparation of the body for burial. This was done primarily by female family members rather than by a professional undertaker. The body was ritually washed and groomed, and a cloth or shroud was wrapped around the body. Finally, the corpse was placed in a coffin. The coffin was most likely made after death to the measurements of the person, although some people prepared shrouds and coffins for themselves before their death.

The body stayed in the home for one to three days in the parlor. Furniture was removed, mirrors were covered, and black crepe was hung. If the weather was warm, ice was often placed around the body to slow decay. Family members would keep a vigil by the body, and people would come to the house to view the body, recite sections from the Bible, socialize, and eat.

Finally, after a brief service the family and friends formed a procession, and the coffin was carried to the gravesite. Early in the century, especially in rural areas, the body would be buried on family land. However, as communities grew, burials more frequently occurred in cemeteries. If the distance between the home and the cemetery was short, the coffin would be carried; later this was replaced by the hearse, a horse-drawn carriage specially built for this purpose that could be rented from a livery stable. Sometimes the procession stopped at a church for a public funeral service and perhaps a final viewing of the body before continuing on to the graveyard. The body would finally be buried in the ground or placed into an aboveground tomb.

Things changed during the Civil War, during which more than 600,000 men died. (This is a very large number, especially when compared with the 57,777 who died during the Vietnam War and the 405,399 who died in World War II.) After a battle there were so many corpses that it was not possible to give them the respectful treatment that was expected during other times. However, attempts were made to give the bodies a proper burial if at all possible and to mark the graves so that relatives could locate the bodies later. Moreover, many families wanted the remains shipped home to be buried with proper ceremony in the family plots, and they would provide money for this purpose. In 1862 Congress authorized the establishment of military cemeteries, and twelve were created during that year near major battlefields, forts, and hospitals. These included Arlington National Cemetery across the Potomac River from Washington, D.C., on the estate that had belonged to the Confederate General Robert E. Lee.

Sometimes a family member would locate a grave that was located near a battlefield, remove the remains, and ship them home. A thriving business developed in metal, cement, and marble coffins that would preserve the remains for a time. However, the most significant development in the area of corpse preservation was the increasing use of embalming, a process that did not occur in the local funeral when a person died in his or her own bed.

Embalming was practiced beginning in the 1840s to preserve medical cadavers. It was not until the Civil War that this process became widely used in the general population to preserve the bodies of those who had died in battle so that they could be shipped home for proper burial. Undertakers who specialized in embalming set up shops near hospitals and army camps and in tents next to battlefields. Thus a new form of burial practice was introduced into American culture.

American Funeral Rituals Today

American society is very heterogeneous, and we must take note of the tremendous variation in funeral practices, especially among recent immigrants. However, we can describe what might be called a "traditional American funeral."

Today most Americans die in hospitals or nursing homes. When the individual is formally pronounced dead, the care of the body passes from the medical to the ritual specialists: the clergy and the funeral director. The death is announced in the obituary section of the local newspaper as word spreads by mouth throughout the network of family and friends. The body is then removed to the funeral home, where it is prepared by embalming. (Not all bodies are embalmed. Orthodox Judaism, for example, prohibits embalming; the bodies are refrigerated, and burial takes place soon after death.)

The purpose of embalming in America today is not to preserve the body for eternity, as in the case of Egyptian mummification, but to hold off the start of decay until the funeral is completed and to give the body a lifelike appearance for purposes of display. Americans feel that it is necessary to view the body to demonstrate that the individual is indeed dead. This makes the death seem real. Americans will go to great lengths to recover bodies for this purpose. In the case of major disasters, expensive recovery operations are mounted for the purpose of recovering remains, which then become the focal point of death rituals.

Before the funeral ritual there is often a viewing, at which the body is put on display. There is little formal ritual at a viewing, yet there are what appear to be standards in the objects that are displayed (such as flowers and photographs), people dressing in somber colors, and words that are said to the survivors. People often sit or stand around and tell stories of the deceased.

Americans have relatively little experience with death compared with members of other societies and are often ill at ease in its presence. Commonly, an American will not attend his or her first funeral until adulthood. In other societies children would be present throughout a person's illness, death, and funeral. Americans also use a special vocabulary for things associated with funerals that is thought to be more acceptable than more traditional terms—*funeral director* for undertaker and *casket* for coffin, for example.

The viewing is followed by the funeral ritual, which may be religious or secular. American funeral rituals are relatively short, usually lasting a half hour to a full hour. Typically, friends, neighbors, and coworkers will take a few hours off of a normal working day to attend the funeral before returning home or back to work. These rituals are relatively quiet, since there is little outward expression of grief. The casket is then taken in procession to the gravesite, where there is usually a short graveside ritual. Often the mourners leave the gravesite before the grave is filled in. This is followed by an informal gathering of family and friends at a family member's home that includes informal feasting and conversation, usually with little or no ritual.

In recent times some changes have been seen in American practices around death. Cremation has become a popular alternative to burial, and the growth of grief recovery therapy shows a new recognition that American funerals and American culture do not always provide the best means of coping with such events. Even modern technology has had an impact, with email condolences and web sites honoring the deceased becoming more common. (See Box 7.2 for a discussion of roadside memorials.)

Days of Death

Festivals that emphasize death and frame it as a concept are found cross-culturally. The one that is most familiar to Americans is probably Halloween, although few Americans know much about the origins and religious underpinnings of what has become a secular day of costumes and candy.

BOX 7.2 • *Roadside Memorials*

Unlike a formal, structured funeral that takes place in a space designated for death and mourning, roadside memorials are informal and mark the spot where the death occurred rather than the final resting place for the body. These memorials can be found not just all over the United States, but all over the world. The memorials vary but generally consist of a cross and flowers, pictures of the deceased, and other personal items.

These public markers of private grief are most commonly found at sites of traffic accidents and usually appear quite quickly after the incident. Some are temporary, but some last for years and may be tended to and added to during that time. The memorials tend to mark deaths that are sudden and unexpected. In addition to those found at sites of traffic accidents, such impromptu memorials were seen at Columbine High School following the shootings there, at Buckingham Palace after the death of Princess Diana, and near the sites of the Twin Towers and the Pentagon after September 11, 2001.

Roadside memorials in the United States are not uncontroversial. For some they involve the issue of freedom of speech; for others they violate the separation of church and state (an overwhelming majority of the memorials contain crosses). There is no federal law governing the memorials, and states have dealt with the issue in different ways. Here the concern is generally one of traffic safety, as the displays might interfere with traffic or distract other drivers. Three states—Colorado, Massachusetts, and Wisconsin—ban roadside memorials. Other states allow the displays but may remove them if they are thought to interfere with traffic. Some states, such as Texas and Florida, have official memorials that can be purchased from the state Department of Transportation. In the summer of 2003 the state of Alaska passed a bill to legalize homemade memorials for anyone who dies on the road.

Halloween

In essence, the holiday of Halloween has its origins as a case of culture contact, a theme that will be discussed in more detail in Chapter 10. The basis of this holiday is an ancient Celtic festival called Samhain. Samhain was New Year's Day and was celebrated on November 1. The Celts believed that during Samhain the gates that normally separate the worlds of the living and the dead were opened, and the souls of those who had died during the past year could then move into the otherworld. To celebrate the day, special foods were prepared as offerings, and people dressed up as spirits and wild animals.

With the conversion of Ireland to Christianity in 300–400 C.E. many local religious beliefs and practices were redefined. In a practice that continues to this day, Christian missionaries were encouraged to reframe local customs in Christian terms. November 1 was soon declared All Saints Day, as a day to honor the Christian saints, particularly those who did not otherwise have a feast day. The day before All Saints Day, October 31, became known as the Eve of All Saints, or the Even of All Hallows, which was shortened to Hallow Even or Halloween. However, the meaning of All Saints Day was not at all related to the original Celtic holiday, and it was not very successful in replacing it.

Around 900 C.E. the Christian Church added the holiday of All Souls Day on November 2. This holiday honors all of the people who have died during the past year and is much closer in meaning to Samhain. Many of the traditional beliefs and customs of Samhain were preserved, including the idea that night was a time for the wandering dead, the offering of food and drink to masked revelers, and the lighting of bonfires. Stylized representations of death, including skeletons, are common.

Day of the Dead (Dia de los Muertos)

The Mexican Day of the Dead is also associated with the Catholic holidays of All Saints Day and All Souls Day on November 1 and 2. Much like Halloween, the Day of the Dead is associated with cultural contact. This time the influence comes from the Aztec culture. The Aztecs set aside a month (which would correspond to the end of July and early August in our calendar) to honor the dead. The festivities were overseen by Mictecacihuatl, or the "Lady of the Dead." Later, Spanish priests moved the celebration to coincide with All Saints Day and All Souls Day.

In what is often referred to as the "folk Catholicism" of Mexico, the dead are seen as intermediaries between the living and God. The Day of the Dead is a time of family reunion, for all family members living and dead, and is an expression of family continuity. This is not seen as macabre or as a solemn event but as a celebration. During the first week in November, shops offer many special items for this celebration. Included are many representations of skeletons, elaborate wreaths and crosses, and *papal picado,* or tissue paper cutouts. Food items are also popular, including special bread called *pan de muerto* and skulls and coffins made out of sugar.

An altar is set up in the home with pictures of saints, candles, incense, vases of flowers, and portraits of the deceased. Offerings of food and drink are made to the dead, especially food that was a favorite of that person while he or she was alive. Gravesites are decorated, and a feast takes place in the graveyard (Figure 7.3). The souls of children return first and then those of adults. The souls do not physically consume the food but are believed to absorb its essence.

Tomb Sweeping Day (Qing Ming Jie)

Related to the Chinese focus on the importance of ancestors is the Chinese holiday of *Qing Ming Jie*. The name translates as "clear brightness," but the holiday is usually referred to as Tomb Sweeping Day. The holiday takes place in early April and is associated with the renewal of spring as well as with respect for the dead. On this day, gravesites are cleaned and tended to. Offerings are made to the dead, including food and goods made of paper. The paper will be burned to transfer the item to the deceased. These offerings will help to ensure the goodwill of the ancestors.

As with the Day of the Dead, the entire family participates. In recent years even family members not living in the area have been able to participate through web sites set up by a few local graveyards. People can visit an on-line memorial hall to pay their respects to the dead.

FIGURE 7.3 *The Day of the Dead.* A woman in Michoacan, Mexico, decorates a grave during *Dia de los Muertos.*

Conclusion

Issues of life and death are of central concern for the domain of religion. What makes us alive? What happens to us when we die? Can my soul exist without my body? Can my body exist without my soul? Although cultures will answer these questions differently, humans must universally come to some sort of understanding and explanation of these phenomena. The belief in some sort of soul, for example, appears to be universal, as is the idea that the soul survives the death of the body, at least for some time. A belief in a soul explains many things for us, such as an individual's life force and unique personality and what happens to that personality when all that remains is a corpse. So important to us are the souls of other people that they often remain a part of the world of the living, numbered among the beings that populate the supernatural world. In the next chapter we will turn our attention to other supernatural beings: gods and spirit beings.

Summary

The belief in the existence of a spirit entity residing within a person appears to have grown out of observations of sleep, coma, and death. A soul is the noncorporeal, spiritual component of an individual. Usually, each individual possesses a soul that takes on the personality of the individual and has an existence after death. During life the soul may leave the body. Dreams are seen as adventures of the soul, and illness may be caused by an absence of a soul that must be retrieved by a shaman. Death is the permanent withdrawal of the soul. How the soul is perceived varies widely, including the number of souls, the size of the soul, and where the soul is located in the body. The soul may retain its identify after death for a limited time or eternity. The destination of the soul after death may depend on the behavior of the person during life, the social status of the individual, or perhaps the way in which the person died. Funeral rituals may assist the soul on its journey to the land of the dead and serve to protect the living from any negative influences of the soul. Sometimes the soul returns and animates another individual, a concept termed reincarnation.

One possible fate for a soul is that it becomes part of the group of supernatural beings known as ancestors. Even after death a person is still a valued member of the kinship group and reinforces ideas of social roles, contributes to social harmony and social solidarity, and punishes descendants for misbehavior.

Ghosts are negative forces that remain in the vicinity of the community after death. They can bring about illness and other misfortune, although their role is sometimes ambiguous. In contrast, vampires and zombies are creatures that have no souls. Vampires are believed to be individuals who have recently died, usually before their time, and have returned to bring death to others. The body of an alleged vampire will be exhumed and "killed" or destroyed in some way. Zombies are corpses that have been raised from their graves and animated. They are not necessarily feared, because the main reason for their existence is to provide slave labor.

Death rituals or funerals are rites of passage that move the individual from the status of living person to that of ancestor or other postdeath status. Funerals vary among cultures in a number of ways: the form of the expression of grief, the role of the ritual in terms of what will happen to the individual in the afterlife, the ritual ways in which the family and community separate themselves from the dead to avoid contamination or illness, how the living are reorganized in society to accommodate for the absence of the deceased, and the method of disposal of the corpse.

Many cultures allow for the return of the spirits of the dead at special times of the year. A familiar example is Halloween, which is based on an old Celtic holiday when the gates that normally separate the worlds of the living and the dead were opened and the souls of those who had died during the past year could then move into the otherworld. The early Church transformed this celebration into All Saints Day and All Souls Day on November 1 and 2, respectively. The Day of the Dead (*Dia de los Muertos*) in Mexico is also associated with these Catholic holidays. The family, including both the living and the dead, gather together for celebration. *Qing Ming Jie* (Tomb Sweeping) in China is a day on which graves are tended and offerings are made to the dead.

Suggested Readings

Paul Barber, *Vampires, Burials and Death: Folklore and Reality* (New Haven, CT: Yale University Press, 1988).
[Looks at European folklore about vampires and the scientific explanations for some of the phenomena.]

Nigel Barley, *Grave Matters: A Lively History of Death around the World* (New York: Henry Holt, 1995).
[A look at how different cultures define and react to death.]

Wade Davis, *The Serpent and the Rainbow* (New York: Touchstone, 1985).
[An ethnobotanist's experiences in Haiti searching for the "zombie drug."]

Gary Laderman, *The Sacred Remains: American Attitudes toward Death, 1799–1883* (New Haven, CT: Yale University Press, 1996).
[Presents the history of mortuary practices in the United States in the nineteenth century.]

Peter Metcalf and Richard Huntington, *Celebrations of Death: The Anthropology of Mortuary Ritual* (Cambridge, England: Cambridge University Press, 1991)
[A cross-cultural study of the rituals that accompany death.]

Fiction:

Piers Anthony, *On a Pale Horse* (New York: Ballantine Books, 1983).
[Book 1 of the Incarnations of Immortality series. The main character kills the Incarnation of Death and is forced to fill the position.]

Margot Livesey, *Eva Moves the Furniture* (New York: Henry Holt, 2001).
[Eva grows up with two companions whom no one else can see.]

Alice Sebold, *Lovely Bones* (New York: Little Brown, 2002).
[Narrated by a fourteen-year-old girl who has been murdered and is now in heaven, watching her family.]

John Richard Stephens, *Vampires, Wine and Roses* (New York: Berkeley, 1997).
[A collection of short stories, excerpts and poems about vampires by many authors, including William Shakespeare, Arthur Conan Doyle, Lord Byron, Voltaire, Woody Allen, and Bram Stoker.]

Suggested Web Sites

www.africanburialground.com
Office of Public Education and Interpretation of the African Burial Ground, U.S. General Services Administration.

www.ancientegypt.co.uk/mummies/home.html
A site that explores mummification from the British Museum.

www.loc.gov/folklife/halloween.html
A discussion of Halloween from the American Folklife Center of the Library of Congress.

www.deathonline.net/index.cfm
An Australian Museum on-line exhibit on death.

http://altreligion.about.com/library/weekly/aa102202a.htm
Death rituals from around the world.

www.grief-recovery.com
The Grief Recovery Institute web site.

Study Questions

1. With the growth of urban centers, American funerals have moved out of the family context into the commercial world. As in any commercial venture, a special vocabulary develops that replaces many familiar terms. Look up some web sites for funeral homes and cemeteries, and examine the vocabulary that is used. What terms are used today in place of older terms such as *undertaker, coffin, corpse,* and *death*? What other examples can you find?

2. We can divide methods for disposing of the body into two main categories: those that preserve the body or part of the body and those that result in the complete disappearance of the body. Is there any correlation between these two categories and how a religion views death and the afterlife?

3. Discuss the practice of cryogenics as a method of handling a body after death. How is cryogenics similar to mummification?

4. Describe the customs surrounding the festival of Halloween in contemporary American society. Do you see any religious elements in this festival today? What elements that are secular today are derived from religious elements in the past?

5. Many Hollywood movies show images of ghosts, vampires, and zombies. How do these images resemble or differ from these entities as they appear in actual religious systems?

Endnotes

1. N. Barley, *Grave Matters: A Lively History of Death around the World* (New York: Henry Holt, 1995), p. 27.

2. A. Fadiman, *The Spirit Catches You and You Fall Down* (New York: Noonday, 1997).

3. B. Jordan, "Yurei: Tales of Females Ghosts," in S. Addiss (ed.), *Japanese Ghosts and Demons: Art of the Supernatural* (New York: George Braziller, 1985), p. 25.

4. P. Barber, *Vampires, Burial, and Death* (New Haven, CT: Yale University Press, 1988), p. 16. Copyright © Yale University.

5. W. Davis, *The Serpent and the Rainbow* (New York: Touchstone, 1985).

6. K. Heider, *Grand Valley Dani: Peaceful Warriors,* Third Edition (Fort Worth, TX: Harcourt Brace, 1997), p. 132.

8

Gods and Spirits

Ghosts, ancestors, and vampires are transformed human beings. However, there are many supernatural beings that generally do not have human origins. These supernatural beings include **gods** and **spirits.** Although we recognize these as two separate types of supernatural entities, this division is to some degree arbitrary. Generally speaking, gods are individualized supernatural beings, each with a distinctive name, personality, and sphere of influence that encompasses the life of an entire community or a major segment of the community. Spirits are generally less powerful than gods and usually are more localized. Frequently, they are collections of nonindividualized supernatural beings that are not given specific names and identities.

Supernatural beings are usually a crucial aspect of a religious system; many anthropologists have defined religion by the presence of such beings. Myths describe the actions of such beings, and their behavior may be seen as a model for human behavior. Rituals are often directed toward superhuman beings, to placate, praise, or make requests.

Spirits

Nonindividualized spirits include the leprechauns of Ireland, the jinns of the Middle East, and the kami of Japan. There are also spirits that are individually recognized, such as a guardian spirit, an ancestral spirit, and a shaman's spirit helper. In contrast with gods, spirits are less powerful and are more focused on a particular individual, family, or group of specialists.

Whereas gods may live in a remote location, such as Mount Olympus, the home of the Greek gods, spirits live in the human world, interacting with humans and concerned about what humans are up to. Spirits often exhibit complex personalities. They may be friendly or harmful. They provide protection, success, and luck but also are blamed for minor mishaps. One can ask for their assistance, since they are closely connected to people and are involved in everyday human affairs. Offerings, entertainment, and attention will promote the development of a beneficial relationship between people and the spirit world. But ignoring their presence or, worse yet, doing something to harm or offend them can have negative consequences, such as the loss of a crop, infertility, illness, or the death of a child.

Because spirits live in the human world, they often reside in various physical objects—some natural, others human-made. Places of special beauty or unusual characteristics, such as a sacred grove or a waterfall, are said to be inhabited by spirits. Such places may also be considered dangerous. They may be venerated, and people will often travel to such places to seek solutions to problems or to ask favors of the spirits. Unusual natural objects—such as a remarkable or strange stone or plant—may contain a spirit, as might a human-made object such as a statue or a **shrine.** Sometimes special structures are built and spirits are enticed to take up residence in them to provide protection or good luck to the builder.

The Dani View of the Supernatural

The Dani live in the highlands of New Guinea, in the Indonesian province of Irian Jaya, which comprises the western half of the island. This description of spirits is based upon a study of the Mulia Valley Dani.

The study of Dani religion brings the paired concepts of emic and etic into clear focus (see Chapter 1). Because the Dani themselves seldom articulate their belief system, it becomes exceedingly difficult for an outsider to learn about Dani religious practices from an insider, or emic, perspective. As is the case with many religions, to the outsider, Dani religion appears to be confusing and illogical. Questions about rituals and beliefs are greeted either by silence or by the familiar "That is just the way we do things" or "This is the way our fathers did it." Sometimes the question elicits a specific myth.

The anthropologist, using an outsider or etic perspective, can attempt to understand the underlying structure and logic of Dani beliefs and practices, although the Dani themselves might not understand or accept this structure and logic. For example, anthropologist Douglas James Hayward notes that the Dani appear to organize their world into complementary pairs.[1] Their physical landscape is divided into cultivated and noncultivated land, and animals are divided into those that live in association with people and those that do not. Their society is organized in terms of a system in which all individuals are placed into one of two social groups that intermarry with one another. Using the principle of complementary pairs, Hayward divides the Dani supernatural world into several categories by using three criteria: Are the beings physical or spirit? Are they beneficent or malevolent? Are they close or far away?

The beings that inhabit the Dani world are either spirit or physical ("truly present"). Physical beings are mortal and are subject to the laws of nature. They include people, animals, and plants. Spirit beings are immortal and are not subject to the laws of nature. However, this classification does not necessarily correspond to our dichotomy between spirit and physical. For example, the sun is believed to be a real woman and thus a physical being, albeit one with unusual abilities.

The identification of a being as beneficent or malevolent also is not as easy as it first appears, for the categorization of a being as beneficent or malevolent often depends on context. For example, ghosts are spirits of the recently deceased that linger near the village in which they once lived, reluctant to leave. If the community fails to perform funeral rituals in a satisfactory manner, the ghost becomes disappointed and may cause trouble for the community. Although ghosts have a negative influence on Dani life, they also can be beneficent. Ghosts are consulted in divination ceremonies. They also warn the community of the approach of an enemy raiding party.

The focus of Dani rituals is aimed at those spirit beings that live close by and play significant roles in their lives. This includes close beneficent spirits such as guardian spirits. Everyone has a guardian spirit, but whereas boys are introduced to their spirits during initiation rituals, women never get to know their guardian spirits.

An important group of close beneficent spirits is spirits associated with nature. These include forest spirits, rain spirits, and flood spirits. The *weya* spirits control the rains. When they become violent, they send lightning storms, and trees that have been struck by lightning are evidence of their presence and power. However, they are classified as benevolent beings because they bring the rain.

Included among the close malevolent spirits are forest spirits and swamp spirits. In the forest lurk male forest spirits, who seduce women who travel alone through the forest. The forest also contains female forest spirits, who seduce men by taking the form of their wives and girlfriends. Sexual intercourse with such a spirit brings about death for the man (unless a pig has been sacrificed) as well as the birth of a child that looks exactly like a human child but only has half a human soul.

Many close malevolent spirits are associated with illnesses. These spirits often are identified with particular animals. For example, a spirit associated with frogs causes illnesses characterized by cold, clammy hands and feet; a spirit associated with owls bring about sore throats; and a spirit associated with lizards is responsible for the swelling of the limbs and joints.

Remote malevolent spirits live in other people's territories. They are a danger only when someone brings a spirit with him or her into Dani territory. When returning home from a journey, the traveler closes the trail behind him by placing a "spirit restrainer," composed of clumps of grass on sticks. The spirit cannot go beyond or around the restrainer and therefore cannot follow the traveler home.

Apart from the enemy, the only other malevolent nonspirit beings are a community of little people who live in the sky. Being lazy, they stole food from their neighbors' gardens rather than growing it themselves. They were finally driven out by the Dani and climbed into the sky. Eventually, they learned how to farm. However, these little people like to urinate on their former enemies during rains. Men do not like to go out of doors on days when it is raining or misty.

Guardian Spirits and the Native American Vision Quest

An important element in many Native American cultures is direct contact with supernatural beings and supernatural power. An example is the vision quest, in which the individual enters into an altered state of consciousness, makes contact with the world of spirit beings, and receives a gift of supernatural power. The spirit beings that are encountered in these visions are often referred to as guardian spirits. An individual, usually male, may attempt to make contact with a guardian spirit either as part of a coming of age ritual or continually throughout his adult life, as a means of attaining protection, guidance, and identity. According to their worldview, it is only through the attainment of this connection with the supernatural and the receipt of supernatural power that a person can be successful in life.

Among the Ojibwa of the Great Lakes area, the vision quest is carried out at puberty. However, children begin preparing early in life with periodic fasting. They are given instruction in how to induce a vision and how to recognize and reject a bad vision. At the appropriate time the boy is led into the forest to a platform that has been constructed in a tall pine tree. He is left there alone to fast until he receives his vision. The vision is interpreted as a journey into the supernatural world. The boy is shown the path his life should take and the spirit beings who will be his guardian spirits. He is also told of certain objects that he can acquire that will serve as physical symbols of his relationship with the guardian spirits. After a successful vision quest the boy assumes the status of an adult man.

Among the Wind River Shoshoni of Wyoming a vision quest is undertaken not just at puberty, but throughout life. Supernatural power can be attained from guardian spirits in visions and in dreams. In the vision quest the supplicant, usually male, rides to a place with rock drawings in the foothills. After cleansing himself in a creek or lake, he goes to the rock ledge beneath the drawings. Naked except for a blanket, he waits for the vision. The vision is brought on by a combination of fasting, enduring the cold, sleep deprivation, and smoking tobacco. What is actually seen varies but commonly includes trials to be overcome before the spirit appears, often as an animal, to bestow supernatural power. The spirit frequently gives the man specific instructions, such as wearing a special item or avoiding certain people or behaviors. For example, a deer spirit that gives the gift of speed while running might instruct the man to wear a deer tail sewn on his clothes or on a ribbon around his neck. Among the Shoshoni, a man can acquire several guardian spirits to aid him.

Jinn

The Qur'an tells of God's creation of three types of conscious beings: humans made from clay, **angels** made from light, and **jinn** made from fire without smoke. Jinn are normally invisible, but they can make themselves visible, and in doing so, they often take the form of a human or an animal. Once visible, they can alter their shape and features at will. Jinn are born, live, and die; they marry, mate, and have families. Some have great powers; others do not. Many are specifically known and named; others occur as a part of an unnamed collective of spirits. Like people, jinn have different personalities, some good and some bad. They may lie and deceive people; they enjoy playing tricks and kidnapping people; and they often tempt humans into sexual intercourse.

Sometimes a person can forge a special relationship with a jinn, and then the jinn becomes a source of special powers. For example, a person can enter into an alliance with a jinn and become a powerful magician. The Genii of the Aladdin story is a jinn, and the stories of the *Arabian Nights* are largely stories involving jinn. But generally, people try to keep a distance between themselves and jinn because, more often than not, jinn are troublemakers. People will frequently recite verses from the Qur'an or avoid situations that attract the attention of jinn. This is the origin of many tabus surrounding blood, childbirth, and marriage, since these are situations that are very attractive to jinn. The very existence of jinn causes people to be careful, yet they also provide an explanation for illness and bad luck.

Spirit Possession in the Sudan. Anthropologist Janice Boddy describes the presence of jinn in the small Arabic-speaking village of Hofriyat in the northern Sudan.[2] The Hofriyati recognize three types of jinn. White jinn have little effect on humans, while black jinn, or devils, are dangerous, and possession by black jinn often leads to serious illness and death. However, the most frequently encountered are red jinn called *zairan* (singular: *zar*). The red color symbolizes an association with blood and fertility. *Zairan* are capable of causing illness. Such illnesses must be dealt with, but they are seldom fatal.

The world of the *zairan* parallels the world of humans. *Zairan* belong to different religions, occupations, and ethnic groups, and they exhibit a range of behaviors, some good and some bad. In other words, they are very much like humans, mixing both good and bad traits, but generally they tend to be amoral and capricious. The Hofriyati recognize jinn that are identified as representing diverse ethnic and social groups. Some are Europeans, West Africans, Ethiopians, Arabs, and so forth, representing outside groups with which they have had contact in the past. Yet there are no *zairan* who resemble the Hofriyati themselves.

Spirit possession occurs when a *zar* enters the body of a woman. Most possession occurs in women of childbearing age, and close to half of the adult women in the community are possessed. In these communities the life of a woman is very restricted. Physically, she remains within the high walls of the family compound, where she is segregated from the men, eating and even sleeping in separate quarters. Her worth and happiness depend on her fertility and her ability to produce sons. The production of sons and their survival are women's tasks, and men are not to blame in the case of failure. A woman who does not have children, miscarries, or has only daughters or whose children die young is accorded a very low position in the society. She may be divorced by her husband or may have to accept a co-wife in the marriage.

Therefore there is a great deal of anxiety in marriage, and this anxiety often leads to depression. In this case a woman may be possessed by a *zar*. However, it also is possible that the *zar* is responsible for the misfortune surrounding her reproductive life. Once the *zar* has entered her body, she will continue to be possessed from that time on.

Although *zar* possession is a lifelong condition, it would not be accurate to describe this possession as an illness. After a time it is possible for a woman to enter into a lifelong relationship with a *zar* through possession. During ceremonies each *zar* is drummed into each woman in turn; the woman then goes into a trance. Through this relationship the woman regains a measure of well-being, although she must constantly pay attention to the wishes of the spirit by attending posses-sion ceremonies on a regular basis. The possessed woman must also meet certain demands of the spirit. She must eat certain foods, wear gold and clean clothing, avoid anger, and manifest other ideal feminine behaviors. As long as the relation-ship continues, the woman will maintain a "cure." From the spirit's point of view, this relationship gives it access to the human world. Once it possesses its host, the *zar* will be entertained and can engage in various activities.

When she is not possessed, a woman will participate in singing and drum-ming. Such all-female rituals provide an important outlet for otherwise isolated women. They are much more than curing rituals. They are also enjoyable social events in a world where such social activities are relatively rare.

Christian Angels and Demons

Angels and demons are spirit beings that appear in Judaism, Christianity, and Islam. In these monotheistic systems angels act as mediators between god and human beings. Angels are often represented as agents of revelation, executors of divine will, or as witnesses to divine activity. Angels appear in both Greek and Jewish writings but tend to play a limited role. In the New Testament of Chris-tianity angels are frequently mentioned. ("And there appeared an angel unto him from heaven, strengthening him" [Luke 22:43].)

However, much of the popular Christian belief about angels comes not from the Bible, but from the sixth century writings of Saint Dionysus. In his work *The Celestial Hierarchy* he established a rank order of angels that included, in descend-ing order, seraphim, cherubim, thrones, dominations, virtues, powers, principali-ties, archangels, and angels. Belief in angels is widespread in modern American society. A poll conducted in 2003 found that 78 percent of Americans surveyed said they believed in angels.[3] Despite these numbers, there is little consensus on exactly what angels are or how they look. Descriptions range from a glowing light to a very human appearance, or perhaps the presence of the angel is felt but not seen. In general, angels are said to appear to help people in need, often as workers or messengers of God.

At the other end of the spectrum are **demons.** Although frequent mention is made of demons in the Christian Bible, no one passage gives a full account of their creation or workings. However, several Church writings have been published that clarify the Church's teachings on this subject, such as the decrees of the Fourth Lateran Council from the Catholic Church in 1215. Here it says that both the Devil and the demons were originally angelic creatures, created by God as good, inno-cent beings. They became evil by their own actions. Satan and his minions rebelled against God and, after a battle with the good angels, were cast from heaven. Satan and the demons are believed to be closely associated with human evil, including the temptation of Eve in the Garden of Eden and their dominion over hell.

One common activity of demons, as described in the New Testament, is de-monic possession. This was considered a major cause of strange behaviors by hu-mans and much of Jesus' healing ministry involved performing demonic exorcism.

BOX 8.1 • *Christian Demonic Exorcism in the United States*

Possession as a source of illness that requires exorcism for healing is found cross-culturally, including in the modern United States. Many of the cases are in a Christian religion. As is discussed in this chapter, the Christian belief in demons and demonic exorcism is taken directly from the New Testament. There we learn that Satan and his demons harass, torment, and possess humans. This possession sometimes is shown in new skills or strength that the person then has (by virtue of the demon). In general, possession was described as an illness, and much of Jesus' healing ministry involved performing demonic exorcism. In the New Testament, Jesus is able to perform exorcisms by merely demanding that the demons leave; his disciples do the same in the name of the Jesus. ("And in the synagogue there was a man, which had a spirit of an unclean devil, and cried out with a loud voice, Saying, Let us alone; what have we to do with thee, thou Jesus of Nazareth? art thou come to destroy us? I know thee who thou art; the Holy One of God. And Jesus rebuked him, saying, Hold thy peace, and come out of him. And when the devil had thrown him in the midst, he came out of him, and hurt him not." [Luke 4:33–37])

In his book *American Exorcism: Expelling Demons in the Land of Plenty*, Michael Cuneo argues that the phenomenon of Christian demonic exorcism is both influenced by and reflects wider American culture. For example, he cites the great influence of the book and later film *The Exorcist* in the early 1970s. Following the release of *The Exorcist* and other popular books, the reported incidence of demonic possession and requests for exorcism greatly increased. The film depicted a specifically Catholic event. However, official Catholic exorcisms were—and are—difficult to come by. Although the Catholic Church does believe in demonic possession and the need for exorcisms, these are seen as rare events. The priest is advised

to be skeptical and look for other causes first, such as mental illness. The exorcism ritual can be officially performed only with permission of a bishop.

However, some exorcisms were available through unofficial channels, particularly right-wing priests who did not agree with the modernization of the church following the Second Vatican Council in the early 1960s and among charismatic Catholics. In the 1970s and 1980s exorcism rituals also became popular in other Christian religions, particularly among people belonging to a religious movement called neo-Pentecostalism or the charismatic renewal. In general, members of this movement were seeking a more personal and dramatic religious experience. This experience was called baptism in the Holy Spirit and was believed to be associated with various spiritual gifts (or charisms), such as speaking in tongues, prophesy, and healing. Part of this healing was exorcisms—or deliverance ministries, as they were often called. The demons involved were often personal demons such as demons of lust, anger, resentment, and addiction, as well as demons of specific illnesses, such as cancer.

Exorcism also became popular with certain groups of evangelical Protestants, particularly in the early 1980s. Cuneo estimates that there are at least 500 to 600 hundred evangelical exorcism ministries today and that the number might even be two or three times this amount. The 1980s were also a time of the growth of psychotherapy within American evangelicalism. One of the main concerns of this new therapy movement was Satanic Ritual Abuse (SRA), and there was a general concern with Satanic cult activities in the United States during this time. It should be noted that although the Satanist movement does exist, its numbers and activities have been greatly overstated, and the Federal Bureau of Investigation has reported that there is no evidence of SRA in the United States.

Cuneo points out that the exorcism movement fits in very well with other cultural ideas that were popular in the late twentieth century in the United States. Like other self-help regimens and therapies of the era, the exorcism movement teaches that people are victims and not responsible for the bad things in their lives. Demons are to blame in much the same way that more mainstream therapies blame the ubiquitous "dysfunctional family." Cuneo writes, "Exorcism may be a strange therapy, it may be the crazy uncle of therapies, but it's therapy nonetheless. And no less than any of the countless other therapies in the therapy-mad culture of post-sixties America, it promises liberation for the addicted, hope for the forlorn, solace for the brokenhearted. It promises a new and redeemed self, a self freed from the accumulated debris of a life badly lived or a life sadly endured."[a]

As was said in Chapter 4, religious healing can be very effective, and this is often the case with exorcism as well. From an outsider's perspective the ritual attention paid to the afflicted person alone is likely to be helpful.

[a]M. Cuneo, *American Exorcism: Expelling Demons in the Land of Plenty* (New York: Doubleday, 2001), p. 273.

("And he was casting out a devil, and it was dumb. And it came to pass, when the devil was gone out, the dumb spake; and the people wondered." [Luke 11:14].)

In the period roughly between the fifteenth and seventeenth centuries, Christian demonology reached its peak. Beliefs about demons were elaborated and had much social influence. Ornate doctrines were produced detailing the hierarchies, invocation, methods, and exorcism of demons. This was the era of the infamous Witchcraze (see Chapter 9), during which there was a particular interest in **incubi** and **succubae.** Incubi and succubae are, respectively, male and female demons who have sex with humans while they sleep. Sex with an incubus was said to be responsible for the birth of demons, witches, and deformed children.

The belief in demonic possession is still common today among conservative Christians, both Catholic and Protestant. For many of these groups a belief in the inerrancy of the Bible requires a belief in demons and demonic exorcism, since they are mentioned so frequently in the New Testament. See Box 8.1 for a discussion of Christian exorcism.

Gods

Generally speaking, gods are more powerful than spirits. They possess great supernatural power and control or influence major forces of nature, such as the wind, rain, and fertility. Gods are personalized individuals with names, origins, and specific attributes. Some gods are associated with social and political units such as clans and villages. The number of gods found within a religious system varies from one to over a thousand.

Gods are **anthropomorphic;** that is, they resemble people in their physical appearance and personalities. They are born, marry, and sometimes die. They love and lust, are wise and dull, loving and hateful, generous and miserly. Some are sympathetic to human beings; others are hostile. And like humans, gods can be influenced by gifts in the form of offerings and sacrifices and by praise and flattery, and sometimes they can be tricked.

The behavior of humans on earth reflects the orders and commandments of the gods. Gods set up codes of behavior and punish people who do not observe them. They may prescribe that certain ritual activities be performed and bring down misfortune when they are not. Some gods are very concerned about the fate of human beings and will establish close relationships with them and have a great influence in human lives.

Within a particular religious system the gods as a collective make up a **pantheon.** Usually, the gods within the pantheon form a hierarchy with a **supreme god** at the top. They are related to one another in various ways, often making up a large family unit characterized by family relationships, such as those seen in the Greek pantheon (Figure 8.1). The community of the gods often mirrors human society. If the human society is highly hierarchical and warlike, so is the society of the gods.

The gods within a pantheon have specific spheres of influence and control. Sometimes there is a relatively small number of gods, each controlling a rather large slice of human activity. Sometimes there are a great many gods, each highly specialized. For example, instead of a single god associated with agriculture, the Roman pantheon had a rather lengthy list of gods who were responsible for very specific activities within the farming cycle (Table 8.1).

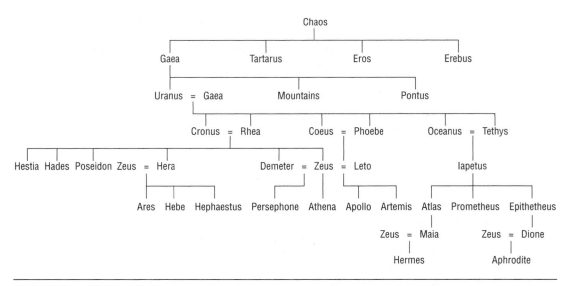

FIGURE 8.1 *The Greek Pantheon.* This diagram portrays the relationships among the better known gods and goddesses of the Greek pantheon. Unlike human families, gods and goddesses are able to marry brother to sister and to produce children without a mate.

TABLE 8.1   *The Roman Gods and Goddesses of Agriculture*

Deity	Responsibility
Seia	The sprouting of the seed
Segesta	The shoots coming through the soil
Proserpina	Forms the stalks
Nodotus	Forms sections of the stem
Volutina	Forms protective sheath around seeds
Patelana	Later removes sheath around seeds
Lacturnus and Matuta	Ripening of grain (at two stages)
Flora	Makes plant blossom

Types of Gods

Although there is a tremendous variety of gods that can be listed, certain types seem to appear over and over as we move from society to society. **Creator gods** are responsible for the creation of the physical earth and the plants and animals that live on it. Creator gods can be very powerful deities and often occupy the top rung of a hierarchy of gods. Creation is not necessarily the work of a single god. Often various aspects of creation are divided among several gods, or, usually after the creation of the physical earth, different gods are responsible for the creation of specific types of plants and animals or the plants and animals that occupy a particular area. This includes the creation of people.

However, sometimes the creator god creates the world and then withdraws from active interactions with the world. These **otiose gods** are too remote and too uninterested in human activities to participate in the activities and fate of humans. Therefore rituals are seldom performed to influence and to ask favors from such gods. Sometimes these gods maintain interest in humans through lesser, intermediary deities.

A common form of supernatural being found in cultures in many diverse areas is the trickster (see Chapter 2). By its very nature the trickster is difficult to pin down. Ambiguity is one of its major characteristics, which often makes it difficult to define. Most often male, the trickster is able to transform himself into a series of beings—human, animal, and deity. The various parts of his body may detach themselves or be severed from the body. In some trickster stories he is seemingly destroyed by being burned, crushed, or disemboweled—yet he is able to reassemble himself. Often the trickster is a creator who is responsible for bringing many technologies, customs, and activities into the world, such as fire, healing, and magic. While on the one hand he is powerful, courageous, and creative, he is also vindictive, selfish, cowardly, and destructive. Perhaps his two most frequently mentioned characteristics are gluttony and lust; he has a voracious appetite for food and sex. He is always finding ways to find and steal food and is never sexually satisfied. Among the best-known tricksters are those of North America, such as Raven, Coyote, and Hare. (Box 2.5 tells a story of a West African trickster and Box 2.6 tells a story of the Haida trickster.) Many examples of trickster stories are also known from the San peoples of South Africa.

The trickster figure plays a number of roles in human societies. The stories point out human frailties through satire, since the trickster represents the antithesis of what it is to be human and places human society in its position in an environment that is not always stable and predictable. Sam Gill writes, "In Trickster is embodied the human struggle against the confinement felt by being bound to place, even with the obvious necessity of such definition in order to prevent chaos. In many of his adventures, Trickster permits people to experience the vicarious thrills and freedoms of a utopian existence. But his folly reveals the very meaning of the boundaries that give order to human life."[4] The trickster may also find a place in situations of contact and social conflict. In San society the trickster is frequently seen as a participant in society who flouts society's rules. In many stories the trickster finds himself interacting with the nonnative, dominant population, in which case the stories become protest and resistance stories in which social situations are reversed and the trickster outwits the dominant individual.

In many ways a pantheon resembles a human society, often with a division of labor. Specific gods are associated with the forces of nature, human fertility and the human life cycle, economic activities, and war. Specialized deities are called **attribute gods.** (The Roman gods associated with agriculture are examples of attribute gods.) The relative importance of such gods depends largely on the importance of various activities within human society. For example, if a society is very warlike, the war gods may occupy important positions in religious rituals.

Gods and Society

Émile Durkheim (see Chapter 1) first proposed the idea that religious symbolism marks as sacred important institutions of human society that are necessary for the group's survival. Durkheim's approach is a functionalist one, seeing religious and other cultural phenomena as serving some essential purpose in maintaining the society. In his analysis of gods he points out that the powers commonly attributed to gods are similar to those of society: creating sacred times and spaces, designating moral rules and punishing offenders, existing above all individuals, requiring sacrifice. Values that we learn in society, such as obligation, loyalty, respect, and hierarchy, are mirrored in our relationship with supernatural beings.

The imagery that is used for gods, such as their anthropomorphic nature, is taken from social categories and statuses. Gods are rulers, fathers, mothers, daughters, and sons. We relate to them through social interactions in ways learned in society. Whatever the themes are in a particular culture will be reflected in the nature and domains of the gods. The values and concerns of a culture are projected onto the gods themselves, and the behavior of humans toward the gods is an expression of the social behaviors valued by that culture.

BOX 8.2 • *Games and Gods*

Among the many expressions of a culture's worldview are the games that are played. For example, are games of chance favored over games of strategy? Do games rely on physical skills or on mental skills? These and other characteristics of games are associated with particular features of a culture. Here we will look at the connection between games and religion.

John Roberts, Malcom Arth, and Robert Rush classified games into three categories: games of strategy, games of chance, and games of physical skill.[a] They found that games of chance, such as dice games, are associated with religious activities. On the simplest level, success at a game of chance may be attributed to aid received from the supernatural, either magical in nature or through supernatural beings. The authors argue that games of chance are "exercises in relationships with the supernatural."[b] They tested

this idea by looking at the nature of supernatural beings in societies where games of chance were the most prevalent type of game played. The dimensions they explored included how aggressive or how benevolent supernatural forces were seen to be and how easy it was to coerce these beings. They hypothesized that gods in these societies would be seen as more benevolent than aggressive and as being relatively easy to coerce. The hypothesis was upheld in their sample of societies. As an interesting side note, the lack of reference to games of chance in the Hebrew Bible suggests that this God was more aggressive than benevolent and not easily coerced.

The study concluded that "games of strategy may be related to mastery of the social system; games of chance may be linked with mastery of the supernatural; and games of physical skill are possibly associated with the mastery both of self and of environment."[c]

[a]John M. Roberts, Malcolm J. Arth, and Robert R. Rush, "Games in Culture," *American Anthropologist*, 61 (1959), 597–605.

[b]Ibid., p. 602.

[c]Ibid., p. 604.

In a similar vein, British anthropologist Robin Horton suggests that supernatural beings function to extend the realm of social relations.[5] Again, the focus is on gods as anthropomorphic beings who reflect human behavior. Horton suggests that the behavior of the gods provides a model for humans. Horton explored his ideas by looking at various African religions. Although a high god is found in almost all of these religions, the nature of this god ranges from an otiose god to one who is in active control of the universe. Horton thought that two variables explain much of this variation.

The first variable is how often people in that society encounter other peoples and the world in general outside their own local community. Horton thinks that lesser gods are associated with the interpretation of events occurring in the immediate area while a high god is more important for interpreting that immediate world in relation to the greater world beyond the local area. With this greater level of contact, issues that people face are more likely to be seen as being part of just being human. Thus the greater the contact a society has with the larger world, the greater the need for a high god who has universal features and is associated with humanity in general rather than just with a local group.

The second variable proposed by Horton was the degree to which an individual's status in the society is **ascribed** or **achieved.** An ascribed status is one that is given to an individual based on attributes over which they have no control, such as gender and family line. Horton proposed that because an individual's status is determined solely by the community, ideas will focus on lesser gods who themselves are focused on local issues. In contrast, where status is based on an individual's personal achievements, the individual is, at least in part, independent from the community. Therefore explanations of personal success and failure are more likely to reference a high god who rules over a wider realm.

Horton suggests that these variables help to explain the openness of Africa to Islam and Christianity. He correlates the arrival of missionaries in Africa with the opening up of local communities to the wider world and an increase in emphasis on achieved versus ascribed status.

The functionalist perspective was also tested in a 1974 study by Guy Swanson.[6] In the study, Swanson looked at fifty different societies to see whether social characteristics of a group are predictive of their religious beliefs. Here we will look at two of the predictions he tested that concern the number and nature of supernatural beings.

First, Swanson looked at religious systems in which there is a high or supreme god who is higher than all other supernatural beings. In Swanson's study, this could be either the only god in the system or the ruler of a pantheon of gods. The essential element was that this god rules over a hierarchy with at least two levels of supernatural beings below it. Swanson reasoned that, on the basis of Durkheim's work, such a religious hierarchy was more likely to be found in a society that also had a decision-making hierarchy that contained at least three different levels. In a kin-based society, for example, this could include families, lineages, and clans (a lineage contains many families, and a clan contains two or more lineages). His study supported this hypothesis. The belief in a supreme god was found in 78 percent of societies with three levels and 91 percent of those with four or more levels but in only 11 percent with only one or two levels.

Swanson also looked at polytheistic systems in which no one god is considered to be supreme. Although they are superior to spirits, each god rules over a particular domain, and none is superior to another. Because these gods are attribute gods, Swanson realized that the presence of this type of god would be connected to the degree of specialization in a society. He found that the number of specialists is positively correlated with the number of such gods.

Sigmund Freud (see Chapter 1) and psychosocial anthropologists have a similar perspective. For example, Freud thought that religion as a whole can be seen as a symbolic expression of relationships between children and their parents. This can especially be seen in the nature of gods. We think about nature anthropomorphically, and so there is a god of thunder, a god of the mountains, a god of the river, and so on. We then project human qualities, particularly those of parents, onto them. For example, if parents are punitive, so are the gods; if parents are indulgent, so are the gods.

Cultural Examples of Gods

In the following section we will look at two societies and their gods. The Yoruba of West Africa are an example of a system with an otiose god and a multitude of intermediary deities that interact directly with the people. With the Ifugao of the Philippines we see the development of an extraordinarily large pantheon. Each of the numerous attribute gods is associated with a very narrow slice of human life.

The Gods of the Yoruba.   In Chapter 3 we examined the color naming system of the Yoruba and how it applies to the deities called the *orisha*. The Yoruba live in the southwestern region of Nigeria and the Republic of Benin in West Africa. Through the slave trade and more recently immigration, Yoruba culture has spread into the New World. Theirs is an ancient culture, and their religious concepts are found throughout a number of city-states, each associated with a particular urban center. The urban center of Ife is of special importance, for it was here that the first acts of creation were performed. It was here that Olodumare sent the gods to create the earth.

The Yoruba cosmos is divided into two realms: Orun, heaven or sky, and Aiye, the earth, the realm of the living. Residing in Orun is the Creator Olodumare, gods known as the *orisha,* and the ancestors. Olorun is the high god and the source of all supernatural power, but he is remote from the people and is not approached in rituals, an example of an otiose god. He is contacted through the intermediaries, the *orisha.*

There are a large number of *orisha.* Some are acknowledged throughout the Yoruba region; others are associated with a particular region, village, or even family group. The *orisha* are anthropomorphic and display human emotions. They are not inherently good or evil, but manifest complex behaviors and can act in a good or evil way, depending on the situation and the context. The *orisha* make themselves known through possessing a devotee, who then moves in a characteristic manner associated with the god. The person will also wear special clothing and hold certain objects. Worship of particular deities is associated with shrines and altars that contain objects that are placed there to please the gods and to show one's devotion. The *orisha* are examples of attribute gods. Each is approached in ritual because of a particular problem. Table 8.2 lists the best known of the *orisha.*

Gods of the Ifugao.   The Ifugao are a mountain-dwelling people living in the western mountains of Luzon in the Philippines (Southeast Asia culture area). They were studied by R. F. Barton in the early part of the twentieth century.[7] The Ifugao are well known as a culture with one of the largest known pantheons. Barton listed 1,240 deities but believed that there were as many as 1,500. These deities are grouped into forty classes, although the classification is quite inconsistent. Yet the Ifugao have no supreme or creator deity. Like most supernatural beings, Ifugao deities are immortal; they are often invisible; they are able to change their shape; they can transport themselves instantly through space; and so on. Although the deities can be grouped by their characteristics and powers, each does have its own specific place in the pantheon. Just as in the world of humans, the best way to get

TABLE 8.2 *Some Yoruba* **Orisha**

Orisha	Domain	Characteristics	Symbolic Representation
Esu-Elegba	"Guardian of the Threshold," first god to be addressed in ritual; intermediary between people, their ancestors, and the gods	Unpredictable, trickster	Hooked beaded stick; red and black
Obatala	King of the *orisha*	Ethical, merciful, patient, composed	White sheet, white beaded cane; white
Ogun	Rules over metal, technology, and war	Aggressive, bold	Beaded machete, metal implements; green and dark blue
Orisa Oko	Agricultural deity, judges antisocial behavior, disease, and poverty, interprets Ifa divination		Iron beaded staffs, flutes; red and white
Osanyin	Forest deity and god of herbalistic medicine		Represented as a puppet with a squeaky voice; iron staff topped with birds; colors of the forest
Osoosi	Hunter god	Quick, strong, aggressive, intellectual	Hunter's hat, powder horns, bow and arrow; green and blue
Osun	Goddess of freshwater streams; sustains life	Youngest *orisha*, beautiful and vain, deceitful	Round fan, crown and beaded apron; crystal yellow gold to opaque chartreuse
Sango	God of thunder and lightning	Proud, aggressive, quick-tempered	Double-bladed axe, gourd rattle, zigzag motif representing lightning
Yemoja	Ruler of the river Ogun, mother of many *orisha*, symbol of motherhood	Calm, serious, dignified	Round fan, crown; crystal white and crystal blue or green

along with the gods is to bribe them. A prayer without a sacrifice is useless because the sacrifice is treated specifically as a payment.

As an example, one of the classes is translated as the "Paybackables." The name is derived from a word used for a payment in an economic exchange. The Ifugao believe that they used to have trading relations with these deities in the past and have received from the deities a great deal of their culture. This is the largest of the classes and includes a rather broad range of deities, including nature gods, deified heroes and ancestors, and technological gods. An important god in this class is Lidum, a deity who taught the Ifugao many of their rituals.

Barton lists 168 "Paybackables." An example is the deities that are involved with the activity of weaving. They include "Separator of Seeds from Cotton," "Separator of Defective, Lumped Fibers," "Fluffer," "Spinner," "Draw Out of Thread on Spindle Bob," "Black Dyer," "Red Dyer," "Yellow Dyer," "Winder into Ball," "Weaver's First Helper Who Receives the Ball and Passes It Back and Forth," "Second Helper Who Passes Ball around the End Stick," "Scrutinizer (who sees that the job of setting up the loom is done right)," and—well, you get the general idea.

A rather interesting class of deities is the "Convincers." These gods bend a person's will to that of the person who invokes them. This process is called by English-speaking Ifugao *convincing.* To fulfill religious obligations, an Ifugao must borrow things to sacrifice. The loan is usually very difficult to get repaid, and the Ifugao have developed many behaviors, including bullying and bluffing, to get the loan repaid. For example, if a debtor has publicly refused to pay a debt and therefore cannot pay it without losing face, the one to whom the debt is owed will call on the god Amobok, who will weaken the debtor's resolve and get him to pay back the debt in secret, thereby saving face.

There are many other important classes of deities. These include gods of reproduction, messenger deities, gods associated with various illnesses, gods associated with death, divination deities, gods of war, guardians of property, and many, many more.

Goddesses

Goddesses have been important figures in many religious systems, although how important they were for the earliest religions is a matter of some debate. Some scholars believe that early human religions centered on fertility, a lunar cycle as opposed to a solar one, and the worship of a goddess. This is largely speculative and based on findings of small carvings of female figures with exaggerated characteristics thought to be connected to fertility (Figure 8.2). Although matriarchy, or rule by women, never existed in the past, the role of women in these prehistoric foraging societies was almost certainly greater than that in contemporary agricultural and industrial societies.

Some believe that goddess worship continued in Europe until a few thousand years before the Common Era. At this time the Indo-Europeans invaded from the East and brought with them many new developments, including a belief in male gods and the exploitation of nature. Some argue that goddess worship and the new god worship gradually combined to produce the polytheistic pagan religions of the Romans, Greeks, and Celts.

With the development of the monotheistic religions, discussed later in the chapter, the goddess was further suppressed, as these latter religions conceived of god in largely male terms. Although all three of the monotheistic religions contained some egalitarian sentiments in their origins and texts, all have also been interpreted at one time or another in very **misogynistic** terms.

Three important goddesses are Ishtar of the ancient Near East, Isis of ancient Egypt, and Kali in Hinduism. We will also discuss the Virgin Mary in Catholicism,

FIGURE 8.2 *Venus of Willendorf.* A prehistoric female fertility figure from an archaeological site near the town of Willendorf, Austria.

although her classification as a goddess is certainly debatable and comes entirely from an etic perspective. Goddess worship has also seen a resurgence with the growth of the Wiccan religion, which will be discussed in Chapter 9.

Ishtar (Ancient Near East).   The goddess Ishtar was worshipped for thousands of years in Mesopotamia. Seen as both invincible in battle and a source of fertility, Ishtar was one of the paramount national deities. However, she was also very important to commoners and was very involved in their lives.

In the natural environment of Mesopotamia, winds, rain, drought, and flood were all common. This contributed to a worldview in which these inconsistencies in nature were seen as being a reflection of violent conflicts among the gods; both the environment and the gods were seen as being unpredictable. All events, both natural and social, were a result of the activity of the gods. The only way to ensure adequate food, victory in warfare, health, and so on was proper performance of rituals and sacrifices for the gods and goddesses. The deities themselves are good examples of anthropomorphic attribute gods.

Among the gods and goddesses in the pantheon, Ishtar is supreme in her power over fate, as recounted in the Epic of Gilgamesh. In this story Ishtar made sexual advances toward King Gilgamesh, which he rejected. In response, Ishtar asked the supreme god, An, to send the bull of heaven to destroy Gilgamesh and his city, Uruk. Ishtar threatened that if she did not get her way, she would release the dead from the netherworld. In her role as a fertility goddess, she also promised that she would ensure that there would be enough food to eat after the bull's destruction.

Sexuality was an important aspect of Ishtar, as seen in the sacred marriage rites. The rites took place between the king and an **avatar** of Ishtar, probably her high priestess. Unlike the Egyptian pharaohs, who were themselves seen as divine, this king was seen as a mortal who was the intermediary between the community and the gods. His relationship with Ishtar was seen as the source of his power and the guarantee of his success. The goddess was shown as dominating the situation as she selected the ruler who was privileged to cohabit with her. This union was seen as explicitly sexual, although it resulted not in offspring, but in the fertility of the land and success in battle.

Isis (Ancient Egypt).
Women occupied a relatively favorable position in ancient Egyptian society. The pharaoh was seen as the son of the sun god, and his queen was not only consort to the divine king but the mother of the divine prince. Women were also important in the religious realm, the pantheon containing a number of prominent goddesses.

Isis was probably the most important deity of the Egyptian pantheon for the average Egyptian. She was called the "Great Mother" and the "Queen of Heaven" and was associated with family. Her most common representation was as a mother, seated, suckling her son Horus on her lap. It is as the devoted wife and sister of Osiris and mother of Horus that she is best known, as is shown in the following myth:

> This is the story of two brothers, Osiris and Set. Set was jealous of Osiris, who was pharaoh, and killed him by throwing him into the Nile in a sealed box. Osiris's wife, Isis, was distraught, and searched all of Egypt for the box containing her husband's body. With the help of her magic she eventually found the box and brought Osiris back to life for a short period of time, during which they conceived the child Horus.
>
> Eventually Set found Orisis's body and tore it into fourteen pieces and scattered the pieces over Egypt. Isis, seeing what Set had done, found thirteen of the pieces, all but his phallus. Carrying out the ritual of rebirth, she gave Osiris eternal life.
>
> Horus grew up into a young man. He challenged his uncle Set for the throne of Egypt. Tiring of the conflict, the gods soon convened a Council of the Gods and had Horus and Set present themselves before them. The Council declared Horus as

the rightful pharaoh. Set was sent away from the land and Osiris became the god of the dead. Thereafter, the pharaohs of Egypt were acknowledged as the god Horus on earth and as the sons of Osiris and Isis.

Isis was often characterized by her wisdom, her insight into the mysteries of life and death. Through her words she was able to resurrect Osiris, although he ultimately went to the netherworld and not to earth.

Although Isis was originally closely associated with the royalty, she became associated with nature as her significance grew and became diversified. Her influence spread; she was present in Rome and Greece. Around 300 B.C.E. the religion of Isis had developed into a **mystery religion** that involved secret and sacred rites. One had to be initiated into the religion to gain the wisdom and salvation that the goddess could offer. The influence of Isis peaked during the third century C.E., when her popularity made her a serious competitor to the Christian church.

Kali (Hinduism).   The worship of a feminine aspect of the divine has a long history in India, probably dating back to pre-Vedic ancient peoples. (The Vedas are religious texts that are the foundation of much of modern Hinduism. They were written down by the middle of the first millennium B.C.E., although they had existed in oral form much earlier.) The goddess remains important today. She is often associated with creativity and nature, in particular great trees and rivers. The Ganges River, for example, is considered to be a sacred and very powerful female presence, and its waters are considered to be purifying. Pilgrims will bathe in its waters, and the cremated ashes of the dead are placed in the river so that the waters will wash away their sin.

The goddess is worshipped in many forms, including local deities at the village level. The great goddesses include Durga, associated with ultimate light and benevolent power, and Kali, who is the divine in its fierce form. Kali means the "Black One," and she is depicted as dark skinned and naked, standing on a corpse, dripping with blood, and carrying a sword and a severed head. She wears a girdle of severed hands and a necklace of skulls (Figure 8.3). Kali is said to have an insatiable thirst for blood, and at her temples animals are beheaded as a sacrifice to her.

Despite this fierce appearance, Kali is not evil. Although she is a fearsome destroyer to those who do evil, she is the loving and compassionate mother to her devotees. In Hinduism the divine is seen as encompassing both creation and destruction. Death and birth are linked together in an endless cycle.

Kali symbolizes transformation. The sword that she carries is used to cut away impediments to the realization of truth. She destroys ignorance and brings knowledge. Her garland consists of fifty severed heads to represent the fifty letters of the Sanskrit alphabet. Thus the garland represents knowledge and wisdom. The severed hands are also symbolic. Hands are the principal means by which work is done and therefore symbolize the action of karma. The hands have been severed, showing that the binding effects of karma have been overcome. Kali blesses the devotee by cutting him or her free from the cycle of karma.

FIGURE 8.3 *The Hindu Goddess Kali.* A fierce goddess, Kali destroys those who do evil, but also brings wisdom and transformation to her devotees.

Kali is often depicted as dancing wildly with the god Shiva. Shiva is sometimes known as the Lord of the Dance and, like Kali, is known as destructive and horrific. Some stories describe their dancing as threatening to destroy the world with its savage power. Gradually, Kali became known as one of Shiva's chief spouses. In art she is often shown standing or dancing on his naked and prostrate body. As she dances, her energy flows into him and brings him life. This image of Shiva and Kali shows Shiva as the passive potential of creation and Kali as his Shakti, or feminine creative principle.

Mary (Roman Catholic).   Christianity is a monotheistic religion and, as such, cannot be said from an emic perspective to have a goddess. However, throughout Christian history Mary has played an important role, and devotion to her has developed in different ways. From an etic perspective she might be considered to be a goddess.

The height of devotion to Mary occurred during the medieval and baroque periods in the modern Orthodox and Roman Catholic traditions. Although Mary was never described as a goddess, she was held in such high esteem that she was certainly seen as more than merely a woman. She was set above the saints and, as the mother of God's son, was seen as only a little lower than God. She played an important role as an intermediary between people and God and Jesus. This was not true of the Protestant religions, which have tended to minimize the place of Mary. In fact, devotion to Mary was one of the major issues of the Protestant Reformation.

According to the gospel of Luke, Mary was a young virgin who was engaged to a man named Joseph. She was visited by the angel Gabriel, who told her she had been chosen by God to be the mother of a son conceived by the Holy Spirit. This moment is celebrated in Christian **liturgy** as the Feast of the Annunciation, and from this time forward Mary was called by the title of Virgin.

All of the stories of Mary in the Bible revolve around her son. The Gospel of Luke tells the story of Mary visiting her relative Elizabeth, who was pregnant with John the Baptist. As Mary approached Elizabeth, John the Baptist (in Elizabeth's womb) "leaped for joy" (Luke 1:44) and Elizabeth said to Mary, "Blessed are you among women, and blessed is the fruit of your womb" (Luke 1:42). These words, the words of the angel Gabriel at the Annunciation, and an additional sentence composed by the Catholic Church were later combined to form the Hail Mary, the prayer that is repeated in saying the rosary: "Hail (Mary) full of grace, the Lord is with thee, blessed art thou amongst women and blessed is the fruit of thy womb, Jesus. Holy Mary, Mother of God, pray for us sinners now and at the hour of our death. Amen."

In the book of Revelation a passage that is normally interpreted as referring to Mary describes her as "a woman, clothed with the sun, with the moon under her feet, and on her head a crown of twelve stars" (Revelation 12:1). This woman is also said to be stepping on a serpent, which is seen as symbolic of Mary overcoming the curse brought on humans by the first woman, Eve. In the language of Revelation, Mary is the "Queen of Heaven."

The importance of Mary is shown in many different ways. First is the celebration, not only of the Annunciation (on March 25), but also of Mary's birth and death. She is shown in countless works of art, and many churches have been dedicated in her name. Shrines and pilgrimage sites associated with Mary were found not only in medieval Christianity, but in modern times. Examples are pilgrimage sites at Lourdes in France, Guadalupe in Mexico, and Fatima in Portugal, at each of which an apparition of Mary occurred.

Similarities between Mary and some of the Near Eastern pagan goddesses have also been noted. (For example, Isis is also referred to as "Great Mother" and "Queen of Heaven" and is depicted seated and holding her son.) Mary fits nicely into the role of these goddesses as protectors and sustainers. Some researchers think that devotion to Mary is actually derived from earlier worship of the Mother Goddess. Despite the fact that technically, all Mary can do is offer intercession for the protection of God, she is often directly addressed for protection. If not a goddess, Mary certainly plays an important role in the Christian understanding of God.

Monotheism: Conceptions of God in Judaism, Christianity, and Islam

Most of the religions that we have discussed and most religions that have existed in the world have been **polytheistic,** that is, they recognize many deities. However, most Americans are more familiar with the **monotheistic** (a belief in one god) religions of Judaism, Christianity, and Islam. These three religions share some of the same history in addition to the concept of a single God. All three have also had to struggle with the philosophical issues inherent in a belief in only one God, particularly one that is seen as **omnipotent** (all-powerful), **omniscient** (all-knowing), and all good. These include the problem of reconciling an omniscient God with human free will and reconciling an all-good and omnipotent god with the existence of evil.

All three religions have also conceived of the nature of God differently. Although most Americans say that they believe in God, for example, this is really a statement that has meaning only in context. We will now examine a little of the history of these three religions and how they have conceived of the nature of God.[8]

Judaism.   The ultimate theme of Judaism is monotheism. Judaism believes that the Jews have been chosen by God to enter into a special relationship with Him, much like that of child to parent. However, many scholars argue that we should not assume that the earliest Jews—for example, the patriarchs Abraham, Isaac, and Jacob—were in fact monotheists.

The patriarchs appear to have shared many of the religious beliefs of their pagan neighbors in Canaan and might not have even shared the same god among themselves. Many different names are used for God in the Tanakh, the Hebrew Bible. Some scholars argue that these were actually names of different gods. For example, the god of Abraham might have been El, the high god of Canaan. (The name *El* is preserved in many Hebrew names such as El Elyon, or Most High God.) The name *Yahweh* is also used, and he is called the "God of our Fathers" by the Israelites. However, Yahweh might have been a different God from El. It has been suggested that Yahweh was originally a warrior god who was worshipped in Midian (what is now Jordan).

When Moses made the covenant with God on Mount Sinai, the Israelites agreed to worship Yahweh alone. The covenant did not say that Yahweh is the only god who exists, although that concept developed later. Even the Ten Commandments take the existence of other gods for granted, such as in the commandment that "Thou shalt have no other gods before me" (Exodus 20:3).

Worship of a single god while ignoring the others was an unusual step in a polytheistic world, where it was dangerous to ignore possible sources of supernatural power. The history of the Israelites, as described in the Tanakh, shows that they were often reluctant to make this move, despite the covenant. It appears that Yahweh had been a warrior god and was very helpful in such matters, but He was not seen as a specialist in other areas, such as fertility. When the Israelites settled in Canaan, they turned to the cult of Baal, the Canaanite fertility god, for such matters. It was difficult for the masculine Yahweh to replace goddesses such as Ishtar and Asherah, who still had a great following among the Israelites, especially among the women. The Prophets of the Tanakh continually had to remind the Israelites of the covenant. All of the early prophets, such as Elijah, focused on the sin of idolatry.

The Tanakh tells that the people had become so corrupt and idolatrous that God permitted the King of Assyria to successfully invade the country. Assyria took most of the Israelites to live among the gentiles in Assyria, where they lost their ethnic identity (and are referred to as the Ten Lost Tribes of Israel). Later, Jerusalem was captured by King Nebuchadnezzar of Babylonia, the Temple in Jerusalem was destroyed, and the people were taken to exile in Babylonia. There they were referred to as Jews, or people from Judah.

This was an important turning point in Jewish history. Some believed that their religion could not be practiced outside of the Promised Land because the Temple, which had been the center of worship, had been destroyed. From this, though, grew the idea of a more pure monotheism—the idea that Yahweh is the only God.

In many ways the monotheism of the Jews was different from the pagan religions around it. The other gods of the ancient Middle East, such as Baal and Marduk, were not involved in the everyday lives of the people. Their actions occurred in a sacred time and space, although these actions did ultimately affect human beings. The God of Israel, however, was an important power in human lives and was intimately involved in the ongoing history of the Jewish people. The pagan religions were generally tribal, limited to a specific people and a specific place. The God of Israel promised that he would protect Jacob and his people when they left Canaan and traveled to a strange new land. This conception of God was very pragmatic.

The way in which God is characterized changes over time in the Tanakh. In the story of Abraham, God, described in a very anthropomorphic way, visited Abraham in his tent and shared a meal with him. Later in time, God appeared to Moses in the much more dramatic form of a burning bush and insisted on distance. Later prophets were visited by angelic messengers, or sometimes they heard a divine inner voice. In the later rabbinic tradition God was presented as even more transcendent and even less anthropomorphic.

The early stories of God depict Him as a very partisan tribal deity, often cruel and violent. He demanded the sacrifice of Abraham's son Isaac, and He visited horrific plagues on the Egyptians. Later He was transformed into a symbol of transcendence and compassion, and in all three of the monotheistic religions discussed in this section, God became an inspiration for social justice.

In the years after the destruction of the second temple by the Romans in 70 C.E., the rabbis stressed that God was intimately present with humans and was in even the smallest details in life. They did not focus on constructing doctrines, but described God as an essentially subjective experience. To this day, Judaism considers theological ideas about God to be a private matter for the individual, for any official doctrine would limit the essential mystery of God. The rabbis also began the important tradition of interpretation and commentaries on religious texts.

Thus there is a fair amount of room in Judaism for individual opinions on such important matters as the nature of God.

Christianity.   Out of Judaism came the new religion of Christianity. Jews at the time of Jesus, under Roman rule, were expecting a Messiah. However, as now passionate monotheists, they expected this Messiah to be human, a descendant of King David, not divine. The term *son of God* had been used previously in Jewish stories and expressed intimacy with God; it was not to be taken literally. Although few Jews of the time accepted Jesus as the Messiah, many other people ultimately would.

The story of Christianity is essentially the story of Jesus. The Gospels tell of the life of Jesus and the essentially Jewish nature of his career. Most of the Gospels simply relate the life of Jesus, but the Gospel of John is different. It describes Jesus as the eternal Son of God and the word of God made flesh. Jesus himself never claimed to be divine, and it was only after his death that his followers seem to have come to this conclusion. This did not happen immediately. It was not until the fourth century C.E. that the doctrine that Jesus had been God in human form (the Incarnation) was established.

For Christians Jesus became the mediator between humans and God. They believed that the reason God had become human, in the form of Jesus, was to lead people back to God. Salvation had been won for humans by the sacrifice of Jesus on the cross. Therefore, salvation was to be found through faith in Jesus. Through this faith, Christians believed that they would be cleansed of their sins, made righteous, and that they would be sanctified and glorified by God in the life to come.

The first Christians were Jews and they had an entirely Jewish conception of God, with the exception of the divinity of Jesus, a conception that developed over time, as has been mentioned. Other changes soon appeared. Ultimately, an understanding of the Christian conception of God requires an understanding of the Trinity.

The Trinity begins with God, the Father, who is the creator of heaven and earth. God became immanent in Jesus, who is God, the Son, the divine in human form. The Son is an incarnation of the Father, who returned after his physical death on earth to live with the Father, although he remains fully present in and to his believers. Jesus promised to send the Holy Spirit to his followers after his death. The Holy Spirit, or Holy Ghost, is the spirit of God, guiding and sustaining the faithful.

The concept of the Trinity caused many problems for the ostensibly monotheistic Christians. Under pressure from a hostile Roman world to explain how Christians could worship three divine beings but still consider themselves monotheistic, Christian apologists put forward several interpretations. Some used the idea of Logos, or Jesus as the word of God, to maintain that Jesus was both God's own self-expression and a separate being distinct from God. Others described God as a single being whose different names, as the Son and Holy Spirit, described different modes of his activity. In general, Christians settled on an interpretation of a single divine substance manifested in three personas. This view is expressed in the Athanasian Creed: "The Father is God, the Son is God, and the Holy Spirit is God, and yet there are not three Gods, but one God." In Western Christianity, however, the three distinct personas have generally been stressed over the unifying substance.

Christians struggled for centuries with the problems associated with reconciling monotheism and the Trinity. Some believe that ultimately, the Trinity makes sense only as a lived spiritual experience, not as a logical or intellectual formulation. The Eastern Orthodox Churches have a tradition of contemplating the nature of the Trinity as the means to an inspiring religious experience.

Islam.   The story of Islam begins with the story of Mohammad, a member of the Quraysh tribe, which in the seventh century C.E. had recently settled in Mecca after having previously lived as nomadic herdsmen on the Arabian steppes. This act of settling in one place drastically altered their lifestyle, and new values started replacing the old. Mecca was also the location of the Kabah, an ancient and massive cube-shaped shrine. Most Arabs believed that the Kabah was originally dedicated to al-Lah (Allah), the High God of the ancient Arabian pantheon.

Allah was believed to be identical to the God of the Jews and Christians. Although Judaism and Christianity are also monotheistic, both were seen as having strayed from the authentic monotheism of Abraham, which Islam would seek to restore. Abraham lived before God had sent either the Torah or the Gospel and was therefore seen as neither a Jew nor a Christian. In the story of Abraham he has a son, Ishmael, by his concubine Hagar. When Abraham's wife, Sarah, becomes pregnant with Isaac, she demands that Hagar and Ishmael leave. God consoles Abraham by telling him that both of his sons will be the fathers of great nations. Abraham and Ishmael are said to have together built the Kabah for God in Mecca.

Muslims believe that the original religion was monotheism but that it has occasionally decayed into polytheism. At these times God would send prophets, including Moses and Jesus, to renew the message of monotheism. Each prophet brought the message in a way that was appropriate to his particular time and place. The last prophet was Mohammad, and he received messages meant for all people and all times.

Mohammad was visited by an angel, who gave him the command to recite. Although Mohammad resisted, the angel insisted, and Mohammad found the first words of scripture coming from his mouth. The Word of God, spoken in Arabic, was revealed to Mohammad little by little over a period of twenty-three years. Ultimately, these words would be compiled into what is called the Qur'an. The power of the Qur'an is based partly on the extraordinary beauty of the language. Muslims believe that to hear the Qur'an recited is to experience the divine.

The early verses of the Qur'an encourage people to look for signs of God's goodness and power in the world and to realize how much they owe to God. Muslims believe that God is omniscient and has created everything for a divine purpose. The world is governed by fixed laws that ensure the harmonious working of all things. Humans can find peace by knowing and living by these laws. People must reproduce God's benevolence in their own society in order to be in touch with the true nature of things. To believe in this is to surrender totally to God. An essential act in Islam is bowing down in prayer (*salat*), a gesture of this surrender.

In practice, these ideas mean that Muslims have a duty to create a society that is just and equitable, in which the poor and vulnerable are treated well.

Alms giving and prayer are two of the five pillars, or essential practices, of Islam. Another is the Shahadah, or the profession of faith: "I bear witness that there is no God but God and that Mohammad is his Messenger." To be a Muslim is to make God your focus and sole priority. (The *hajj*, or pilgrimage, and fasting are the remaining two pillars.)

As in Judaism, God is experienced as a moral imperative. But the God of Islam is more impersonal than the God of Judaism. Muslims believe that God can only be glimpsed in the signs of nature and is so transcendent that He can be talked about only in parables. In contrast to Christianity there are no obligatory doctrines about God. Theological speculation is dismissed as self-indulgent guesses. No one could possibly know or prove the nature of God.

Atheism

Just as the statement "I believe in God" has meaning only in context, so does the concept of **atheism.** For example, early Christians and Muslims were considered atheists by the larger society in which they lived for refusing to recognize the existing pantheon of gods. In the Qur'an an unbeliever is somebody who is ungrateful to God and refuses to honor Him. Atheism has historically meant not accepting the current conception of the divine.

In Europe it was only at the end of the sixteenth century that the term *atheist* began to be widely used. It was the time of great conflicts between Protestants and Catholics and the proliferation of many Christian sects. Rumors abounded of people—atheists—who denied the existence of God. These were much like the rumors of witchcraft, which we will discuss in Chapter 9.

In reality atheism, as we conceive of it today, was highly unlikely—perhaps even impossible—for people of the time. In sixteenth century life, religion and the Church were ubiquitous. They dominated life and were part of nearly every activity. In these conditions it is hard to imagine someone gaining enough of an outsider perspective to question God and religion. Even if someone had managed to do so, this person would have found no support for this perspective in the science or philosophy of the time. The term *atheist* was used as an insult, to describe someone who did not agree with you about the nature of God. No one would actually use the term to describe himself or herself. It would not be until the end of the eighteenth century that a few Europeans would find it possible to deny the existence of God.

The scientific developments of the seventeenth and eighteenth centuries were important to the development of atheism. By the start of the seventeenth century, leading theologians argued the existence of God on entirely rational grounds. When these arguments did not hold up well under the new science, the existence of God began to be questioned. In large part it was the way in which people conceived of the nature of God that made Him vulnerable to this attack. God was seen as a fact of life that could be examined in much the same way that the natural world was.

Another issue was a new emphasis on a literal understanding of the Bible in both Catholic and Protestant traditions. Again, these literal interpretations made the texts vulnerable to questioning from the new scientific perspective. The heliocentric theory of Copernicus and Galileo was condemned by the Roman Catholic Church not because the theory endangered belief in God, but because it contradicted the scriptures. Many years later, the discoveries of Lyell and Darwin would call into question the biblical account of creation.

With the eighteenth century and the Enlightenment came new ideas of science and progress. Enlightenment was seen as achievable by people on their own, without relying on the traditions of the Church or revelation from God. However, most of the philosophers of the Enlightenment did not reject the idea of God outright, just the conceptions of a cruel God who threatens people with eternal damnation. They believed in a god, but not the God of the Bible. However, a few people truly were beginning the trend away from God, and by the end of the century there were philosophers who were proud to call themselves atheists. There was also an idea that science, which was the foundation for questioning God, would ultimately replace religion.

Science has not been the only factor in the growth of atheism. The challenge of horrific historical events such as the Holocaust have also played a role. Some people believe that growing atheism is just the natural result of living in a more secular society.

Just as there are different kinds of beliefs in god, there are different kinds of atheists. Some distinguish between weak atheism (disbelief in any god) and strong atheism (denial of the existence of any god). Many people who profess a belief in a god still live their lives as if there was none. Another approach is agnosticism, which is the idea that the question of the existence of a god is unsolvable, unprovable.

While the numbers of people with no belief in a god have grown dramatically in Europe over the years, it is interesting to note that the same phenomenon has not occurred in the United States. Although church attendance and membership in traditional religious denominations have fallen, 99 percent of Americans still say that they believe in God, whatever they mean by that.

Conclusion

The **isomorphism** between gods and people is striking. Gods resemble us in appearance, thoughts, and actions. They have human emotions and display the best and worst of human behavior. The structure of human society is a model for that of the gods in ways that are both simple and complex. Of course, the powers possessed by supernatural beings go far beyond those of humans. Gods are creators and destroyers. As such, gods are part of the explanatory system for how the world works. The existence of gods answers many of the big questions in life: How did the world begin? Why are we here? The existence of spirit beings answers many of the smaller ones: Why do we get sick? What goes bump in the night?

Summary

Gods and spirits are supernatural beings that generally do not have human origins. The distinction between gods and spirits is to some degree arbitrary. Spirits are less powerful than gods, are more localized, and are frequently collections of nonindividualized supernatural beings that are not given specific names and identity. Examples include the leprechauns of Ireland, the jinn of the Middle East, and the angels and demons of the monotheistic religions. Spirits include guardian spirits, ancestral spirits, and shamans' spirit helpers. Spirits live in the human world, interacting with humans. They exhibit complex personalities. They may provide protection, success, and luck but also are blamed for minor mishaps. Spirits often reside in natural and human-made objects. Places of special beauty or unusual character may be inhabited by spirits. Such places may be dangerous, and they may be venerated.

Gods are more powerful than spirits. They control major forces of nature, such as the wind, rain, and fertility. Gods are anthropomorphic, with names, origins, and specific attributes. They are born, marry, and sometimes die; they love and lust; they are wise and dull, loving and hateful, generous and miserly; some are sympathetic to human beings, others are hostile. A hierarchy of gods makes up a pantheon, usually with a supreme god at the top. Many types of gods can be recognized, including creator gods, otiose gods, trickster gods, and attribute gods.

Theorists have proposed that the nature of the gods in a society mirrors important cultural elements, such as that group's social structure. For example, Horton proposed that the importance of a high god in African religions was related to increased contact with the outside world and the importance of achieved status over ascribed status. Swanson tested the functionalist ideas of Durkheim and found that religious hierarchy was more likely to be found in a society that also had a decision-making hierarchy that contained at least three different levels. He also found that the number of attribute gods related to amount of specialization. Psychosocial anthropologists believe that humans project qualities of important figures such as parents onto the gods.

Some scholars believe that the earliest human religions centered on fertility, a lunar cycle as opposed to solar one, and the worship of a goddess. Examples of goddesses are Ishtar of the ancient Near East, Isis of ancient Egypt, and Kali from Hinduism. From an etic viewpoint the role of the Virgin Mary in Catholicism has some characteristics of a goddess. With the development of the monotheistic religions the goddess was suppressed, as these religions conceived of god in largely male terms.

Polytheistic religions recognize many deities. The more familiar monotheistic religions believe in a single omnipotent and omniscient God. Judaism believes that the Jews have been chosen to enter into a special relationship with God. Out of Judaism came Christianity. The story of Christianity is essentially the story of Jesus, who was God who became human to lead people back to God. In Islam, Allah was believed to be identical to the God of the Jews and Christians, religions that were seen as having strayed from the authentic monotheism of Abraham, which Islam would seek to restore.

Atheism has historically meant not accepting the conception of the divine that is found in a particular society at a particular time. It was not until the end of the eighteenth century that atheism took on its present meaning of denying the existence of God.

Suggested Readings

Michael Cuneo, *American Exorcism: Expelling Demons in the Land of Plenty* (New York: Doubleday, 2001).
   [A look at exorcism, largely Christian evangelical, in the United States.]

Felicitas D. Goodman, *How about Demons? Possession and Exorcism in the Modern World* (Bloomington: Indiana University Press, 1988).
   [A look at possession in different cultures, including a discussion of the role of altered states of consciousness.]

Michael Shermer, *How We Believe: The Search for God in the Age of Science* (New York: Freeman, 2000).
   [A look at reasons why people say they believe in God.]

Fiction:

Dan Brown, *The Da Vinci Code* (New York: Doubleday, 2003).
   [A story of murder and conspiracy that focuses on the importance of the feminine divine.]

Neil Gaiman, *American Gods* (New York: Harper Collins, 2001).
   [Old gods battle new ones for control in America.]

Sue Monk Kidd, *The Secret Life of Bees* (New York: Penguin Books, 2002).
   [Set in South Carolina in the 1960s, a young girl's life is influenced by three beekeeping sisters and a Black Madonna.]

Suggested Web Sites

http://godchecker.com
   A database of all known gods.

www.atheists.org
   The web site of the American Atheists.

www.amnh.org/exhibitions/meeting_god/index.html
   Meeting God: Elements of Hindu Devotion from the American Museum of Natural History.

www.religioustolerance.org/god_devel.htm
   Various ideas about God from Religious Tolerance.org.

www.newadvent.org/cathen/06608a.htm
   Catholic beliefs about God.

members.aol.com/bjw1106/marian.htm
   Apparitions of the Virgin Mary.

Study Questions

1. The world is full of examples of supernatural beings. We can categorize many of them as gods and spirits. What are the definitions of gods and spirits given in this chapter? Is this always an easy distinction to make? Why or why not? What does this tell us about systems of classification?

2. As we learned in Chapter 1, the functional approach to the study of religion looks at the role that religious practices play in the functioning of a society. Apply this approach to Zar possession in the northern Sudan.

3. Gods are supernatural anthropomorphic beings. What exactly does this mean?

4. In what ways does the concept of a monotheistic God appear in Judaism, Christianity, and Islam?

5. The terms *atheism* and *agnosticism* are often used in American culture. What exactly do these terms mean? Why do you think it is more common for people in Europe to say that they are atheists than people in America?

Endnotes

1. D. J. Hayward, *Vernacular Christianity among the Mulia Dani* (Lanham, MD: University Press of America, 1997).

2. J. Boddy, "Spirits and Selves in Northern Sudan: The Cultural Therapeutics of Possession and Trance," *American Ethnologist,* 15 (1988), pp. 4–27.

3. Opinion Dynamics Poll for Fox News, September 2003.

4. S. D. Gill, *Native American Religions: An Introduction* (Belmont, CA: Wadsworth, 1982), pp. 28–29.

5. R. Horton, *Patterns of Thought in Africa and the West: Essays on Magic, Religion and Science* (Cambridge: Cambridge University Press, 1994).

6. G. E. Swanson, *The Birth of the Gods: The Origin of Primitive Beliefs* (Ann Arbor: The University of Michigan Press, 1960).

7. R. F. Barton, *The Religion of the Ifugao.* American Anthropological Association *Memoirs,* No. 65, 1946.

8. The following discussion is based on the work of Karen Armstrong in *A History of God: The 4,000-Year Quest of Judaism, Christianity and Islam* (New York: Ballantine Books, 1993).

9

Witchcraft

One of the most interesting topics in the anthropology of religion is **witchcraft.** However, witchcraft is not a single, unified concept. When anthropologists speak of witchcraft, they generally refer to individuals who have an innate ability to do evil. A witch does not depend on ritual to achieve his or her evil ends but simply wills misfortune to occur. In this sense witchcraft is clearly different from sorcery. (Of course, there is nothing to prevent a witch from using magic, but this would lie outside the definition of witchcraft.) In some cultures witchcraft can be unconscious and unintentional; one can be a witch and not even know it.

Although in our culture we tend to think of witches as females, traditionally both sexes have been accused of witchcraft. Witchcraft accusations reflect underlying social tensions in a society. Individuals who exhibit antisocial behavior and people in relationships characterized by conflict are likely targets. Along these lines, cultures in which witches are considered primarily to be women will tend to exhibit tension between the sexes.

The concept of individuals with such propensities for evil is found in a wide variety of areas, including New Guinea, Southeast Asia, the Americas, and Europe. However, the best-developed discussions of witchcraft in the anthropological literature describing witchcraft in small-scale societies are those of witchcraft in African societies. In these societies witchcraft is a very common belief and refers to the ability of a person to cause harm by means of a personal power that resides within the body of the witch.

The term *witchcraft,* however, is also used to refer to other religious phenomena. Witchcraft, encompassing many of the features found in African witchcraft, was found in peasant communities in Europe from medieval to early modern times. Because the people in these communities believed that only God could heal, individuals who practiced healing arts and midwifery were often stigmatized and thought of as being witches. When witchcraft became of interest to various Christian churches, the idea of witchcraft changed to reflect an association with Satan. This led to the famous witchcraft executions in Europe and colonial America.

Finally, drawing on the healing activities of European peasant witches, Neo-Pagan and Wiccan religious systems that have developed in relatively modern times have embraced the concept of the witch, but in a positive way. We will explore all of these conceptions of witchcraft in this chapter.

The Concept of Witchcraft in Small-Scale Societies

The idea of witchcraft as an evil force bringing misfortune to members of a community is found in a great number of societies throughout the world. In these societies witchcraft is evil; there are no good witches. Unlike sorcerers, who perform magic rituals to achieve their evil ends, witches simply will death and destruction. And they will happen, for the source of this evil is a power that lies within the body of the witch.

The power of a witch is clearly a supernatural power. Some witches fly through the air. Others can change their outward physical appearance to that of an animal. Witches have personal characteristics that are the antithesis of those that characterize a good, moral person. Witches might practice cannibalism and incest; they show hatred, jealousy, and greed. Thus they become personifications of all that is evil in a society. Witchcraft beliefs become a way of objectifying antisocial behavioral traits.

Witchcraft among the Azande

The Azande are a large cultural group living in southern Sudan and northeastern Democratic Republic of Congo (formerly Zaire). The Azande of the southern Sudan were residing within the British Colony of Anglo-Egyptian Sudan in the early part of the twentieth century. Between 1926 and 1930 the British anthropologist E. E. Evans-Pritchard made three expeditions to Zandeland. These experiences led to the publication in 1937 of Evans-Pritchard's analysis of witchcraft in his important ethnography *Witchcraft, Oracles and Magic among the Azande*.[1]

One the factors that makes the study of Zande witchcraft so important is that among the Azande witchcraft is an everyday topic of conversation, and people will discuss witchcraft in great detail with an outside observer. Therefore Evans-Pritchard had access to a great deal of information.[2]

The Zande Belief in Witchcraft. As with many African peoples, the Azande believe that witchcraft, or *mangu*, is something that exists within the body of a witch. The Azande actually describe this something as a physical substance that exists within the body of witches. It is described in many ways. For example, it might be "an oval blackish swelling . . . in which various small objects are sometimes found."[3] It appears to be associated with the intestines or perhaps the liver. And how are the Azande able to describe witchcraft substances? It is because in the days before the British established control over the area, an autopsy was performed on people who had been accused of witchcraft when alive, to determine whether they were truly witches or not.

However, because witchcraft is inherited, an autopsy of an accused witch would also prove that a particular living person, related to the deceased, was or was not a witch. *Mangu* is thought to be passed down from parent to child of the same sex—from father to son and from mother to daughter. Therefore if a man were proven to possess witchcraft substance, this conclusion would extend to that man's father, sons, brothers, and so on. However, the Azande rarely have a theoretical interest in witchcraft. What is important is whether a person at a particular point in time is acting as a witch toward a specific person. A person can possess *mangu* and yet not act as a witch. (As we shall see shortly, the identification of witches is more commonly done through divination, which was discussed in Chapter 6.)

There are many consequences to the fact that *mangu* is a part of the body. For example, the *mangu* of children is relatively harmless. The witches to be feared are older individuals. Although witchcraft is contained within the physical body, its action is psychic. The psychic aspect of *mangu* is the soul of witchcraft. It usually, but not always, leaves the physical body of the witch at night, when the victim is asleep, and is directed by the witch into the body of the victim. As it moves, it shines with a bright light that can be seen by anyone during the nighttime. However, during the day it can be seen only by religious specialists.

All types of misfortune that are not clearly caused by some other factor are attributed to witchcraft. This includes accident, illness, and death but also economic misfortunes such as the loss of a crop or the failure of some technological operation. Although there are methods for dealing with witchcraft, it is only in the case of death that there is a demand for compensation from the witch, the killing of the witch, often through sorcery, or the execution of the witch by the legal authority. These latter consequences occurred only for witches who had been held responsible for many deaths.

A Case of Witchcraft.   What is important to an Azande is not the philosophy of witchcraft, but its operation in a specific individual. The following is a description of the behavior of the Azande when faced with a case of witchcraft.[4]

Witchcraft accusations are based on real social tensions that exist in Zande society. Witches are never strangers, nor are they people who stand in a superior social position. (It would be very foolish to accuse a chief or priest of witchcraft.) Accusations grow out of real antisocial, negative emotions and behavior, such as greed, envy, and hatred. Certain social relationships within Zande society are common breeding grounds for such emotions, and this is reflected in the pattern of witchcraft accusations. Witches can be either men or women, but although men may bewitch either men or women, women tend to attack only other women.

Let us take as our example a case in which a woman is accused of causing the illness of her co-wife. The Azande practice plural marriages, and the relationship between co-wives is often cordial. Co-wives spend a great deal of time in each other's company and aid and assist one another in the performance of household tasks. Yet tension may develop between them, especially if the husband favors one wife over another or one wife is jealous of the other for other reasons.

In a family consisting of a man and his two wives, the senior wife is ill, and this illness has lasted a considerable amount of time. The husband must first determine the cause of her illness. There are several causes of illness, including sorcery, and to sort things out, the husband needs to consult an oracle. Zande oracles were described in some detail in Chapter 6. The best known are *dakpa*, the termite oracle; *iwa*, the rubbing-board oracle; and *benge*, the poison oracle.

The husband might begin by consulting *dakpa* because it is a relatively simple and inexpensive form of divination that can be performed by the man himself. If *dakpa* suggests that witchcraft lies at the root of his wife's illness, he needs to go to a specialist and consult *iwa*, the rubbing-board oracle. Not only do these oracles provide the man with information and suggest courses of action (including herbal remedies and the performance of therapy rituals), but it is thought that if the witch learns that someone is trying to determine the cause of the illness, the witch might stop so as not to risk being accused.

If all of the steps thus far have failed to stem the tide of the illness, however, the husband will consult *benge*. After confirmation that witchcraft is indeed the cause of the elder wife's illness, the operator of the oracle must identify the witch. The problem is that *benge* can give only a yes or no answer (e.g., the chicken that has been fed the poison can only live or die). However, this does not prove to be a problem because a witch is always someone known to the victim, and the cause of a witchcraft attack is usually associated with greed, envy, hatred, or some other antisocial behavior.

However, let us look at this from an etic viewpoint. In placing names before the oracle, one would select those people in the community who exhibit antisocial behavior, because there is a probability that one of them is the witch. (A person who does not exhibit antisocial behavior would certainly not be a witch.) Because antisocial behavior tends to occur frequently in stressful social relationships, among people one knows, accusations tend to be associated with particular relationships, such as co-wives. Let us say for the sake of argument that the probability of an individual whose name is placed before the oracle being identified as a witch is one-half, since one-half of the chickens will live and one-half will die. Then it follows that a person who shows antisocial behavior and whose name is put to the oracle has a fifty-fifty chance of being accused of witchcraft.

Once the witch has been identified through the poison oracle, the husband can elicit the assistance of the chief, who will send a deputy to handle the affair. This neutral intermediary confronts the witch, who invariably claims innocence. However, according to Zande witchcraft belief, it is possible to possess *mangu* (witchcraft substance), which might be acting up without the accused person's conscious knowledge. This gives the accused person a way out. She can perform a simple ritual in which she takes water into her mouth and spits it out, thereby "cooling" her witchcraft. If the elder wife gets better, then *benge* is praised for identifying the witch. The witch does not suffer any stigma. The Azande focus on the situation at hand, and as long as the witchcraft ceases, everything is fine. If the woman continues to be ill, then either the accused person was not sincere in cooling down her witchcraft or she did indeed stop but some other witch started. This cycle continues until the woman recovers or dies.

One can imagine that being accused of witchcraft might cause the accused person to consider what behaviors led to this turn of events. Perhaps she will now go out of her way to be solicitous about the health of her co-wife and may assist her in her work. The result is a more harmonious household. Of course, the elder wife can become ill again, but the younger wife might not necessarily be the witch who caused the new illness.

An Analysis of Zande Witchcraft Beliefs.   Evans-Pritchard wrote that "the concept of witchcraft . . . provides [the Azande] with a natural philosophy by which the relations between men and unfortunate events are explained and a ready and stereotyped means of reacting to such events. Witchcraft beliefs also embrace a system of values, which regulate human conduct."[5]

All peoples seek explanations for things that happen in the world, especially misfortune. It is in this arena that people frequently turn to supernatural causes, such as spirits, sorcery, or witchcraft. The Azande think of all misfortune as being due to some supernatural agency.

Evans-Pritchard describes the case of a fallen granary. These structures are built on stilts to elevate them off the ground so that wild animals will not get into the granary and eat the grain. The shade of the granary is an important meeting place where people congregate during the heat of midday. After the harvest, the weight of the grain stored in the granaries is great, and Zandeland is home to a great many termites. Although the men carefully examine the pillars and replace damaged ones before each harvest, it is still possible that termites will weaken the stilts and the granary will fall. If people are sitting under the structure when it falls, they may be seriously injured.

The immediate explanation for the accident is quite simple: Termite-weakened wood stilts could not bear the weight of the grain, and the granary collapsed. Yet the Azande explain this course of events as an example of witchcraft. The key question here is not "Why did the granary collapse?" but "Why were these particular individuals sitting under this particular granary when it collapsed?" The answer is witchcraft. To most Americans the fact that these two events occurred at the same time—certain people sitting under the granary and the collapse of the granary—is simply coincidence or bad luck. However, the Azande do not accept the concept of coincidence. The fact that these specific individuals were injured was due to witchcraft.

Because of this way of thinking about cause and effect, witchcraft becomes a good explanation for misfortune. Antiwitchcraft rituals and the identification of the witch provide a plan of action, or what Evans-Pritchard called "a ready and stereotyped means of reacting to such events." However, witchcraft cannot be used as an excuse for incompetence or simply bad behavior. If a particular activity fails because the person is not skilled, then it is not witchcraft. Witchcraft also cannot be used as an excuse for adultery if the adulterers are caught.

Witchcraft among the Navaho

Whereas Zande witches are born with *mangu,* in other cultures the power of witchcraft is one that is sought. Again, immoral and antisocial behavioral traits are as-

BOX 9.1 • *Witchcraft and AIDS in Africa*

Witchcraft accusations still occur in the modern world. News articles from countries throughout Africa report cases of witchcraft accusations and often the killings that result. Old women and children are frequently the targets. Witchcraft remains a default explanation for misfortune, including soccer game losses. Illness in particular is often explained as resulting from the activity of witches, especially in cases in which the illness leads to premature death.

The AIDS epidemic has hit African countries particularly hard. For example, in 2001 more than 2.2 million adults died from AIDS in the countries of sub-Saharan Africa.[a] In many parts of Africa, AIDS is thought to be caused by witchcraft. Although people recognize that they have a disease, the ultimate causal agent is believed to be a witch. Like Evans-Pritchard's example of the collapse of a granary, the question is not what caused this to happen, but who is responsible for it. This conception answers important questions that modern medicine often cannot, such as "Why me? Why now?" AIDS itself is well suited to these explanations. Although public campaigns have stressed that there is an epidemic, relatively few people who have the disease have exhibited symptoms, and few know that they are infected. Thus it appears as though specific individuals have been singled out.

Public health education campaigns in much of Africa are difficult for a number of reasons. Large proportions of the population are illiterate or semiliterate, especially in the rural areas where AIDS is most prevalent. A poor communications infrastructure also makes it difficult to spread the prevention message. Cultural and religious traditions often inhibit any open discussion of sexual practices. Poverty and the subordinate status of women also play roles.

The attribution of AIDS to witchcraft, though, is also a major impediment to public health campaigns, the essential message of which is personal responsibility for one's own sexual behavior. If AIDS is seen as the result of witchcraft, the individual is absolved from any responsibility—the disease is seen not as the result of their own actions, but instead as resulting from the malicious activities of another. This creates large difficulties for prevention programs.

In addition, AIDS education focuses on the fact that the AIDS virus is transmitted through body fluids, such as blood and semen. As we saw in Chapter 6, such items are traditionally seen as just the materials a sorcerer would want in order to perform contagious magic.

[a]UNAIDS, "Report on the Global HIV/AIDS Epidemic, July 2002", as reported on the web site www.avert.org (an international HIV and AIDS charity).

sociated with witchcraft. They drive the individual to do whatever he or she must do to gain power that eventually will satisfy this emotional need. As our example we will examine witchcraft beliefs among the Navaho of the American Southwest. (It should be noted that although we are using the ethnographic present, it has been many decades since the last documented case of witch killing among the Navaho.)

In contrast with the Azande, the Navaho are very reluctant to discuss witchcraft. Many deny its existence, although this might be because admitting to knowledge of witchcraft is seen as suspicious. Yet witchcraft beliefs are found throughout Navaho society. In contrast with the Azande, Navaho witches are individuals who seek to be initiated into the Witchery Way.

Witchcraft is generally associated with immoral and antisocial behavior such as greed, vengeance, and envy. Greedy witches obtain wealth by robbing graves. Another method is to pair up with another witch. One witch causes the illness, and the other witch attempts to "cure" the victim; the fee is then split between the two witches. Witches are thought to meet in caves at night, where they practice incest and cannibalism, have intercourse with dead women, and perform rituals to kill victims. Witchcraft beliefs act in many ways to enforce social norms. For example, if you do not care for your parents properly, they can become witches.

Initiates often learn witchcraft from a relative—a parent, grandparent, or spouse—and a major part of the initiation is the killing of a close relative, often a sibling. Witches are both men and women, although male witches are more common. Female witches tend to be old women.

A common way for witches to kill is through the use of corpse powder, made from the bones and flesh of a corpse. A witch will pour some of the powder into the hogan (the Navaho house), infecting the inhabitants. The witch might also place some of the corpse powder into the mouth and nose of the victim while the victim is sleeping or might blow the powder over people attending a ceremonial. Most Navaho carry gall medicine, a form of antiwitchcraft medicine, made from the gallbladders of several different animals, especially when entering a crowd.

Witches are said to be able to transform themselves into animals and can move extremely fast over the land, usually at night. There are many signs of the presence of a witch, such as the restless behavior of animals and the barking of dogs. Sometimes the witch is actually seen at night fleeing a homestead, often appearing as an animal. Frequently, the witch leaves behind large animal tracks.

There are many ways in which a witch can be identified. The tracks left by the witch can be followed to someone's home. Sometimes, if the witch has been shot fleeing a homestead, a person might show up with an unexplained gunshot wound the next morning. People who show suspicious behavior might be identified as witches, or witches may be found through divination.

When a witch is captured, he or she will usually try to bribe the captors with money and jewelry. The witch is then made to confess, because confessing often effects a cure. Sometimes the witch will be tied up and not be fed or given water until he or she confesses. If a confession is not forthcoming, the witch is killed. Even if a witch is never caught, it is believed that he or she eventually will be killed by lightning.

Witchcraft beliefs among the Navaho serve the same general functions as witchcraft beliefs do among the Azande. Clyde Kluckhohn writes: "One of man's peculiarities is that he requires 'reasons' for the occurrence of events. One of the manifest 'functions' of belief in witchcraft is that such belief supplies answers to questions which would otherwise be perplexing—and because perplexing, disturbing."[6]

Navaho witchcraft beliefs also provide for the culturally sanctioned manifestation of immoral and antisocial behavior. The witch is the personification of evil and thus defines what is bad. Behavioral traits such as greed and envy, personality traits that contradict basic Navaho values, and such behaviors as cannibalism, incest, and nakedness are things that Navahos find horrifying. People who exhibit antisocial behaviors are likely to be identified as witches and eventually eliminated from society. Witchcraft beliefs also act to prevent the accumulation of wealth. Navaho values stress the sharing of wealth and the responsibility of one individual to assist another. The accumulation of material goods is often considered to be a sign of witchcraft. Periods of intense social stress are often associated with witch killings.

Witchcraft Reflects Human Culture

The study of Zande witchcraft demonstrated that witchcraft beliefs and accusation reflect interpersonal behavior between people in stressful situations and that stressful behavior is frequently a recurring situation in particular social relationships. Thus, as we saw in our example, the interpersonal relationship between co-wives has a potential of being a difficult relationship, and this stress is manifested in the form of witchcraft accusations. This point is clearly illustrated when we compare the systems of witchcraft belief in two different but related societies: the Nupe and Gwari of West Africa.

The Nupe and the Gwari are neighboring societies in the Guinea Coast culture area. They live in similar habitats and interact socially and economically with one another. Their social organizations are very similar; they even speak closely related languages. And many aspects of their religious practices are similar or identical.

These two societies accept the existence of witchcraft, and the details of this belief are similar except for the sex of the witch. Among the Gwari, witches are both men and women; among the Nupe they are always women, although the operation of a woman's witchcraft activities must be aided by a man. There are ways of countering and preventing the operation of witchcraft. Among the Gwari it is through rituals that rid the entire community of witchcraft. Witches are identified through divination, and the victims are both men and women. The pattern among the Nupe is different. Here the witchcraft of women is controlled through secret activities of the men.

According to our hypothesis that witchcraft accusations are signs of difficult social relationships, we might want to examine differences in interpersonal relationships in the two groups. Among the Nupe the general picture is one of antagonism between men and women, reflected in the fact that witches are always women and men have the ability to control the activity of female witches. Further study reveals a major difference in marriage relationships in the two groups. Among the Gwari, marriage is generally free of tension, but this is not the case with the Nupe. This is likely due to differences in the economic systems. Among the Nupe, married women can become itinerant traders and have the potential of economic success. Their husbands are often in debt to their wives, and wives take over certain economic tasks that usually fall within the sphere of activity of men. These include paying for feasts and gathering together the bridewealth for sons.

Men are angry and resentful over the situation but really cannot do anything about it. In addition, among the Nupe, itinerant traders can be married women who leave young children in the care of extended family, and even refuse to have children, to be free to ply their trade. Although men condemn this activity as immoral, once again they are helpless to do anything about it. It is this anger and hostility that are projected into the world of witchcraft, where witches—interestingly, visualized as itinerant traders—are women who can be controlled by the men. Thus men have power over women in the realm of witchcraft but not in the real world.

Euro-American Witchcraft Beliefs

Although Euro-American ideas about witchcraft show some similarities to those of small-scale societies, there are many important differences. Both cultures see witches as evildoers, but ideas of witchcraft in Europe were influenced by Christian ideas about the nature of evil. As was discussed in Chapter 8, one of the challenges facing Christianity (as well as Judaism and Islam) is how to explain the existence of evil when God has been described as unique, all-powerful, and all-good. One answer to this problem posits the existence of an evil spirit of great power. In Hebrew this spirit was called Satan, the adversary. This was translated in Greek as *diabolos* and in English as the devil. Satan is not a major figure in the Hebrew Bible; however, he did receive a great deal of attention in Judaism during the Apocalyptic period (200 B.C.E. to 150 C.E.), a time during which Jews were focused on the idea of an imminent apocalypse and the coming of the messiah. However, from that time on, the rabbis came to dominate Judaism, and Satan received very little attention.

One important event during the apocalyptic period was the origin of Christianity; the New Testament prominently features Satan. The message of the New Testament is that Jesus Christ saves us from the power of the Devil (see Chapter 8). Part of the new definition of the evil of witchcraft is that witches are individuals who have made a pact with the Devil.

The Connection with Pagan Religions

We said earlier that in small-scale societies the concepts of witchcraft and sorcery are quite distinct. This changes with European witchcraft beliefs, in which sorcery gets bound up with witchcraft—thus our common perception of witches doing spells. There were also important changes in the conception of sorcery. Previously, sorcery had been seen as largely mechanical, a manipulation of the supernatural. Now sorcery became associated with the invocation of spirits. Although sorcery had always been an antisocial behavior and seen as a hostile act, sorcery was now defined as also being hostile to God. The spirits of sorcery were defined as demons. Therefore, anyone doing sorcery, or for the most part any magic, was seen as calling upon the servants of Satan.

Some have argued that this was part of the larger persecution of pagan religious practices. Christians were arguing that Jesus was the Son of God, and a large part of their argument was based on the miracles that he performed. Skeptics of the day were likely to counter with the argument that Jesus was merely another sorcerer, performing magic. So for Christians the only legitimate magic became the magic performed by Jesus; all other magic was the work of the Devil. Magic and witchcraft became not just crimes against society, but **heresy**—crimes against God.

The Christian theology of the time argued that pagan magic and religion were all the work of the Devil, part of his plan to lure people away from the truth of Christianity. The pagan gods and goddesses were thus redefined by Christians as servants of Satan. However, at the level of popular religion many of the pagan beliefs and gods were absorbed into the Christian religion.

The nature of the Catholic Church's response to heresy underwent dramatic changes during this time. Beginning in the twelfth century, laws dealing with heresy became more severe. A factor in this state of affairs was the revival of Roman law. Under Roman law people are seen as part of the corporation that is the state and therefore must follow its principles. In the late Roman Empire several codes had declared that crimes against God were worthy of punishment by death. The revival of Roman law encouraged the imposition of harsher penalties for heresy. For example, burning became the punishment of choice for relapsed heretics and was increasing in frequency. Witches, as heretics, were burned as well. However, from the fifteenth century onward, witches were treated even more harshly than other heretics. Heretics were burned only in the case of relapse; witches were burned on a first conviction.

Before the thirteenth century the only way for a heretic to be brought to trial was if an individual made an accusation against that person. It was not long, though, before bishops began holding **inquisitions,** or formal investigations. Instead of waiting for an accusation, the authorities began to actively go looking for heretics, particularly witches. By the end of the thirteenth century, inquisitors were assigned to most areas of continental Europe. Most of the inquisitors came from the Franciscan or Dominican religious order.

At the beginning, most sentences appear to have been penances such as wearing a cross sewn to one's clothes or going on a pilgrimage. The goal of the inquisitor was primarily to identify the guilty and get them to confess and repent in order to restore them to the fold. Only a small number of the cases resulted in execution. These were generally reserved for relapsed heretics or for obstinate heretics (those who refused to repent). In time, though, the punishments, especially for witches, became more severe.

Inquisitions were a powerful means of enforcing sanctions against heretics and witches. At first the bishops were encouraged in their efforts, but between 1227 and 1235 the papal Inquisition was established. The power of the Inquisition was constantly being corroborated and expanded. For example, in 1252 Innocent IV issued the papal bull *Ad Extirpanda.* This bull authorized the imprisonment of heretics, the seizure of their possessions, and their imprisonment, torture, and execution. All of this was done on what was usually minimal evidence. The procedures of the Inquisition were such that guilt was easy to establish and innocence was difficult to defend. It should be noted that although the Inquisition was a

Catholic institution, Protestants were also involved in the conviction and execution of witches during this time.

The Witchcraze in Europe

At the end of the Middle Ages witches were believed to be individuals, both male and female, who had formally repudiated Christianity and made a pact with the Devil. Witches were believed to ride by night and to have secret nocturnal meetings. As we saw with witchcraft in small-scale societies, witches generally represent all that is evil and antisocial. In this case witches were believed to have orgies, to engage in sacrificial infanticide and cannibalism, and to desecrate Christian holy objects such as the crucifix and the **Eucharist.**

The period known as the Witchcraze began at the end of the Middle Ages (around 1450) and lasted for about 200 years. Many scholars date the start of the Witchcraze to the time at which the Inquisition began actively seeking out witches. Although people associate this with the "Dark Ages," it actually was a product of the Renaissance and Reformation. The Witchcraze was a time in which many people were accused, convicted, and executed as witches. Exact numbers are hard to come by, but estimates range from a few thousand to several million people.

One invention in the 1450s in particular helped to spread these ideas: the printing press. One of the most important books published during this time was the *Malleus Maleficarum,* or the *Hammer against Witches,* which was published by the Catholic Church in 1486 (see Figure 9.1). The *Malleus* spells out the Church's beliefs about witches at the time. Witches were people who renounced the Catholic faith and devoted themselves, body and soul, to the service of evil. Witches offered unbaptized children to the Devil and engaged in orgies that included having intercourse with the Devil himself. Witches were also typically believed to shift shapes, fly through the air, and make magical ointments. The *Malleus* also stated that witches were more likely to be women than men, something we will return to later. The *Malleus* spelled out what to do with a witch: All witches must be arrested, convicted, and executed. It is important to note that even people who spoke out against the Witchcraze did not challenge the actual existence of witches. To do so at this time would have been tantamount to declaring oneself an atheist.

People who were accused of witchcraft were interrogated to obtain a confession. The questions they were asked presumed their guilt. For example, common questions included where and when they met with the Devil. The question of whether or not they had done such a thing was never asked. Torture was a common means of gaining a confession. In 1628 a man named Johannes Junius was executed as a witch. What is unusual about this case is that he was able to smuggle a letter out of prison to his daughter before he died. What follows is a portion of that letter:[7]

> Many hundred thousand good-nights, dearly beloved daughter Veronica. Innocent have I come into prison, innocent have I been tortured, innocent must I die. For whoever comes into the witch prison must . . . be tortured until he invents some-

MALLEVS
MALEFICARVM,
MALEFICAS ET EARVM
hæresim framⅇâ conterens,
EX VARIIS AVCTORIBVS COMPILATVS,
& in quatuor Tomos iuſtè diſtributus,

*QVORVM DVO PRIORES VANAS DÆMONVM
verſutias , præſtigioſas eorum deluſiones , ſuperſtitioſas Strigimagarum
cæremonias , horrendos etiam cum illis congreſſus ; exaⅇlam denique
tam peſtifera ſeⅇla diſquiſitionem , & punitionem compleⅇluntur.
Tertius praxim Exorciſtarum ad Dæmonum , & Strigimagarum male-
ficia de Chriſti fidelibus pellenda ; Quartus verò Artem Doⅇlrinalem ,
Benediⅇlionalem , & Exorciſmalem continent.*

TOMVS PRIMVS.
Indices Auⅇlorum , capitum , rerùmque non deſunt.

Editio nouiſſima , infinitis penè mendis expurgata ; cuique acceſſit Fuga
Dæmonum & Complementum artis exorciſticæ.

*Vir ſiue mulier,in quibus Pythonicus, vel diuinationis fuerit ſpiritus, morte moriatur
Leuitici cap. 10.*

ⅬⅤⅭⅮⅤⲚⅠ,
Sumptibus CLAVDII BOVRGEAT,ſub ſigno Mercurij Galli.

M. DC. LXIX.
CVM PRIVILEGIO REGIS.

thing out of his head. . . . When I was the first time put to the torture, Dr. Braun, Dr. Kötzendörffer, and two strange doctors were there. The Dr. Braun asks me, "Kinsman, how come you here?" I answer, "Through falsehood, through misfortune." "Hear you," he retorts, "you are a witch; will you confess it voluntarily? If not, we'll bring in witnesses and the executioner for you." I said, "I am no witch, I have a pure conscience in the matter; if there are a thousand witnesses, I am not anxious." [The witnesses were brought forward.] And then came also—God in the highest heaven have mercy—the executioner, and put the thumb-screws on me, both hands bound together, so that the blood ran out at the nails and everywhere, so that for four weeks I could not use my hands, as you can see from the writing. . . . Thereafter, they first stripped me, bound my hands behind me, and drew me up in the [strappado]. Then I thought heaven and earth were at an end; eight times did they draw me up and let me fall again, so that I suffered terrible agony. . . . And so I made my confession . . . but it was all a lie.

As the sixteenth century progressed, the Witchcraze only increased in intensity. Religious conflict, popular movements, and wars during the Reformation exacerbated social tensions, which were then reflected in witchcraft accusations. The Witchcraze did not decline until the late 1600s and early 1700s.

The Witchcraze in England and the United States

The Witchcraze in England was at first somewhat different from that in continental Europe. England had no inquisition, no Roman law, and only a weak tradition of heresy—all of which had contributed to the Witchcraze elsewhere. There was no English translation of the *Malleus Maleficarum* until modern times. English witchcraft remained closer to the idea of sorcery, with an emphasis on the power of witches to place hexes and curses. In the 1500s English witches were not believed to fly, conduct orgies, or make pacts with the Devil. Instead, they harmed livestock, caused diseases, and hurt infants and children. The first statutes against witchcraft in England were not passed until the mid-1500s. Even then, witches were prosecuted under civil, not religious, law. This is why witches in England, and later the United States, were hanged and not burned. Burning is the punishment for heretics.

Ideas more like those on the European continent eventually made their way into England through Scotland and King James I, who was a major proponent of the Witchcraze. The height of the Witchcraze in England occurred during the 1640s. The English Civil War at the time was producing even greater anxieties and insecurities. America lagged even farther behind; the first hanging of a witch in New England did not occur until 1647.

By far the most famous of the witch trials in the Americas occurred in Salem in 1692. This trial is well documented and has been extensively studied. The immediate cause of the trials appears to have been two young girls (ages nine and eleven) who were experimenting with divination techniques in an attempt to discover who their future husbands would be. In the process, they managed to scare themselves and began exhibiting nervous symptoms. They thrashed around and assumed odd postures. The father of one of the girls was Samuel Parris, the local minister. He called in a physician to examine the girls, but the doctor was unable to find anything wrong. It was this physician who first suggested that the girls might be victims of a witch's spell.

The girls' behavior became worse, and soon other young girls and young women also began to suffer from fits and convulsions. The girls were questioned and named three women as witches: Sarah Goode, Sarah Osborne, and a West Indian slave named Tituba. Soon more were accused. The fits increased in intensity. The girls screeched, howled, reported visions, and suffered from mysterious tooth marks. The trials themselves were dramatic affairs at which the girls exhibited these symptoms. In all, nineteen people were executed, and more than 100 were jailed.

Most of the commentaries on the Salem trials focus on what, from an outsider's perspective, was really going on here. Early suggestions included the girls being delusional and the whole thing being a vicious prank. Perhaps they enjoyed the attention, or maybe they were overcome by the power of suggestion. More recent research has suggested a possible biological component in the form of ergot poisoning. Ergot poisoning comes from eating a particular mold found in the grain rye, and among its symptoms are hallucinations.

The events that took place in Salem, like many cases of witchcraft, resulted from the ebb and flow of everyday activities of people that characterize living in a community. Witchcraft accusations were the end result of stressful social relationships as well as situations arising from the politics, economics, and religious practices of the community.

Salem was not a single community. It was a farming society at the edge of the settled world at that time. In the not too distant past, before the period of the witchcraft trials, Salem had been attacked by Indians and needed to defend itself. By the time of trials, Salem was a rapidly growing community, one that included an extensive hinterland, and as the population grew, so did pressures on the land. In fact, many neighborhoods of the town were petitioning the colonial government for status as independent villages.

As is common in many societies throughout the world, those accused of witchcraft were primarily people living on the fringes of society. Many were marginalized and powerless women without husbands, brothers, or sons to protect their interests. Others were those who dealt with folk remedies and midwifery. "When such remedies went bad, and when face-to-face dispute resolution failed, the customers who paid for the cures or the potions might conclude that the purveyor was at fault. Thus premodern malpractice became witchcraft."[8]

Functions of Euro-American Witchcraft Beliefs

Many of the functions that we discussed for small-scale societies are applicable here. Witches define all that is wrong and immoral. People who exhibit antisocial behavior or who stand out in any way are the most likely targets of witchcraft accusations. In the European example, witches helped to define the boundaries of Christianity and the cohesion of the Christian community. Witches were people who turned their backs on Christianity and made a pact with the Devil. They were heretics—people who sinned against God.

Witches also fulfill our unconscious need to blame someone for the misfortunes that we experience in our daily lives. It is more psychologically satisfying to have an identifiable individual who can be blamed and punished than to shrug our shoulders and attribute misfortune to bad luck. In general, patterns of witchcraft accusations also reflect deeply felt conflicts and divisions in a culture. The studies have shown this to be true for Salem, for example. Deeply felt moral divisions over the governance of the church, along with neighborhood and family conflicts, were showcased in the Salem witch trials.

Witches as Women

Although both men and women were tried and executed as witches during the Witchcraze, many more women were killed than men. There are many reasons for

BOX 9.2 • *The Evil Eye*

Although not usually thought of as witchcraft, belief in the evil eye has many of the characteristics associated with witchcraft. The power of the evil eye, like that of witchcraft, lies within the body of the individual, who might or might not be aware of it. This belief is found primarily in India, the Near East, parts of Europe, and Mexico.

A person with the evil eye is able to cause illness or some other type of misfortune simply by looking at or praising someone or something. This is especially the case with babies, and in many societies it is considered bad form to praise or say something complimentary about a child, or the child could become ill and perhaps die. The concept is associated with envy, and people with the evil eye are jealous over the success or good luck of others.

One can avoid the evil eye by wearing charms that ward away the danger and by the recitation of certain formulas. When complimenting a person or praising a person, one makes sure to begin and end the compliment with a special formula. Spitting or particular hand gestures are also used to protect one against the malignant power of the evil eye. Another strategy is to conceal one's good fortune and avoid looking prosperous.

The idea of the evil eye varies from society to society. In the Mayan region of Mexico illness may be caused by *ojo* or the evil eye, by a man or animal simply looking at a child.[a] People with the evil eye are dangerous, and one must deal with them with great care. One can recognize these individuals by a mole, a prominent vein, or a mark between the eyebrows. Cures may be effected by some type of contact with the person who has the evil eye. For example, a man who has brought about sickness in a child might be asked to place the child's finger in his mouth or rub some of his saliva on the child's mouth.

[a]R. Redfield and A. Villa Rojas, *Chan Kom: A Maya Village* (Washington, DC: Carnegie Institution of Washington, 1962).

this. First, the *Malleus Maleficarum* itself says that women are more likely to be witches. This is because, according to the *Malleus*, women are weaker, stupider, more superstitious, and more sensual than men. The *Malleus* tells us:[9]

All wickedness is but little to the wickedness of a woman. . . . What else is a woman but a foe to friendship, an inescapable punishment, a necessary evil, a natural temptation, a desirable calamity, a domestic danger, a delectable detriment, an evil of nature, painted in fair colours. . . . The word woman is used to mean the lust of the flesh, as it is said: I have found a woman more bitter than death, and a good woman more subject to carnal lust. . . . There are more superstitious women found than men. And the first is, that they are more credulous; and since the chief aim of the devil is to corrupt faith, therefore he rather attacks them [than men]. . . . Women are naturally more impressionable, and more ready to receive the influence of a disembodied spirit. . . . They have slippery tongues, and are unable to conceal from their fellow-women those things by which evil arts they know. . . . they are feebler both in mind and body. . . . Women are intellectually like children. . . . She is more carnal than a man as is clear from her many carnal abominations. . . . She is an imperfect animal, she always deceives. . . . And indeed, just as through the first defect in their intelligence they are more prone to abjure the faith; so through their second defect of inordinate affections and passions they search for, brood over, and inflict various vengeances, either by witchcraft, or by some other means. Wherefore it is no wonder that so great a number of witches exist in this sex.

Beliefs about witches included intercourse with the Devil. During a witch's interrogation she was asked to name demons that had been her lovers and to describe the Devil's phallus. The fact that the Devil is almost universally perceived as male might have been a factor in labeling women as witches.

Sixteenth century Europe was unusually misogynistic. Some historians have suggested that this was due to demographic changes. More men than women died from the plague and from warfare. As a result, there was a demographic imbalance, with more women living alone than usual. The social position of a woman living alone in a patriarchal society, in which women were defined in relation to men, would have been difficult. The weaker social position of women made them easier to accuse. Another demographic change that likely had an impact was the increasing movement from the countryside to life in the city, with the accompanying increase in insecurities.

Among women, midwives appear to have been a particular target. Infant and maternal mortality rates were both high at the time and these deaths, along with any deformity or illness, were likely to be blamed on the midwife. Some researchers have also noted the connection between the persecution of midwives as witches and the rise of the profession of male doctors.

Wicca

The term *Neo-Paganism* refers to pre-Christian religious traditions that have been revived and are practiced in contemporary times. One of the best known of the Neo-Pagan religions is the Wiccan religion.

Roots of the Wiccan Movement

The beginnings of the Wiccan religion can be traced to the publication of several important books. The first was *The Witch Cult in Western Europe*, written by anthropologist Margaret Murray in 1921. In this book Murray examined the Witchcraze, which is referred to by Wiccans as "the Burning Times." She focused on what she believed to be the connection of the Witchcraze to the persecution of practitioners of pre-Christian religions. She believed that there was an unbroken line between pre-Christian goddess-based religions and women who were labeled as witches. This claim is very controversial, and most Wiccan practitioners today see their religion as a reconstruction, not a continuation, of earlier practices. The timing of the publication of the book importantly coincided with the suffragist movement in the United States, an early feminist movement that centered on gaining for women the right to vote. The idea of a pre-Christian religion that valued and worshipped women was appealing, and a return to such religious practices fit in well with ideas of female empowerment (see Chapter 8).

The Wiccan movement took off in the 1950s. This was largely due to the work of Gerald Gardner (1884–1964), who wrote *Witchcraft Today* (1954) and *The Meaning of Witchcraft* (1959). Gardner was an amateur anthropologist who, in 1908, studied the Dyaks of Borneo. Gardner continued Margaret Murray's idea that witchcraft was a pre-Christian religion in Britain. Gardner then went on to say that he had found and joined a coven of witches whom he believed to be among the last remnants of this old religion.

Wiccan Beliefs and Rituals

There is much variety in Wiccan beliefs and practices. Here we will discuss some of the most common features. Wicca is a polytheistic religion, although which of the pagan gods and goddesses are named varies. Gender equality—the god and the goddess—are stressed, as is nature as a manifestation of deity.

The religion is in many ways nature-based and includes a ritual calendar. One set of rituals is performed at full moons and is associated with the goddess. There are also eight Sabbats, or solar festivals, related to the god. The Sabbats happen seasonally and are related to such events as times of planting and harvesting. They also are seen as symbolic as events in the life of the god and goddess. The Sabbats include Samhain (the New Year festival discussed in Chapter 7, the death of the god), Yule (the Winter Solstice, rebirth of the god through the goddess), Imbolc (February 1, associated with purification and fertility), Ostara (the Spring Solstice), Beltane (April 30, when the young god becomes a man), Midsummer (when powers of nature are seen as being at their peak), Lughnasadh (beginning of the harvest), and Mabon (the second harvest, the waning of the god).

The rituals themselves are varied but often begin with the casting of a circle to create a sacred space. After the circle is cast, invocations are recited to the four cardinal directions (see Figure 9.2). As part of this, or after this, the gods and goddesses are invoked to observe the ritual. From this point, the ritual will vary according to its purpose. Common elements include singing and chanting, the manipulation of symbols, and a ritual meal.

Common Wiccan symbols include images or candles to represent the god and goddess. The **athame,** or ritual knife, and wand are commonly used to cast the circle. Cauldrons and cups are symbolic of the goddess. A broom may be used to sweep and thus purify an area. The pentacle is another Wiccan symbol (see Chapter 3).

The use of magic is also characteristic of Wiccan religion. This includes both folk magic and ritual magic. Contrary to common misperceptions, all magic in Wicca is to be used for good and never for evil. This can be seen in the Wiccan Law of Return. A karmalike idea, this law says that whatever good you do will return to you, as will any evil. There are several variations on this, such as the Three-fold Law, which says good and evil will return threefold, and the Ten-fold Law, which

FIGURE 9.2 *Wiccan Ritual.* Saluting the four cardinal points during a Wiccan ritual.

says that good and evil will return tenfold. Wiccans also have a moral rule known as the Wiccan rede. In essence, this rule says that you can do whatever you want as long as it does not harm anyone.

The Growing Popularity—and Persecution—of Wicca

Although exact numbers of adherents are difficult to come by, Wicca has expanded rapidly, primarily in North America and Europe. The religion has also recently gained important official recognition. The U.S. Armed Forces chaplain's handbook now contains a section on Wicca, and a Wiccan practitioner recently won a court case affirming the right to practice the religion in jail.

Wicca has many features that make it appealing, especially to young women. These include the lack of sexist beliefs and discrimination in general and a focus on the female aspects, or the goddess. A concern for nature and the environment also fits in well with modern ideas. Whereas for some the morality of traditional religions seems excessively restrictive, Wicca has a single moral rule (the Wiccan rede). The practice of Wicca is very flexible and allows for personal involvement. Individuals can practice the religion alone or within a group and are free to add their own symbols and rituals as they see fit.

Wicca or other forms of witchcraft and magic have also appeared in many popular media presentations in recent years. However, despite the growing numbers of Wiccan practitioners and the increasing media exposure, Wicca remains a religion that is largely misunderstood. Practitioners are often persecuted and the subjects of hate crimes. Some of this misunderstanding comes from the Wiccan use of the term *witch* and symbols such as the pentagram, which for most North Americans and Europeans have strong negative connotations; they see these as signs of devil worship. For Wiccans the idea of a devil is a Christian notion, and so they have no connection with it. (See Box 9.3 for a discussion of Satanism.)

Wiccans choose to use the term *witch* because for them it has a different but important meaning and connotations. For them *witch* was a term that was unfairly applied to pagans, healers, and people who practiced an age-old tradition of folk magic. To call themselves witches is seen as reclaiming the term and reaffirming their heritage.

Other Neo-Pagan Religions

Although certainly the most popular Neo-Pagan religion in North America, Wicca is not the only one. Among the others are Druidism and Asatru, although it should be noted that the lines between these three religions are not always clearly drawn.

Druidism is a reconstruction of the ancient religion of the Celts. Because the ancient religion was based largely on an oral tradition, there is no set of scriptures for practitioners to work with. Most of the information we have on Celtic religion comes from sources with a possible bias. This includes Greek and Roman writers (the Celts had previously been at war with both countries) and from the recording (with possible modification) of Celtic myths by Christian monks. Much blending also occurred between Druid and Christian traditions. A good example of this is the holidays, such as the origins of Halloween in the pagan holiday of Samhain (see Chapter 7).

Asatru is also known as Norse Heathenism. In contrast to Druidism, Asatru is based on a surviving historical record, and an attempt has been made to maintain the religion as closely as possible to the original religion of the Norse people. *Asatru* is an Icelandic word that means belief in the Asir, or the gods. The gods include familiar ones such as Thor, Odin, and Loki. At its peak the original religion of Asatru would have covered most of Northern Europe. This area was one of the last to convert to Christianity. For example, Iceland did not convert until 1000 C.E., and Sweden was ruled by a pagan king until 1085 C.E.

The government of Iceland officially recognized Asatru as a legitimate religion in 1972. Since this time, Asatru has rapidly grown in former Norse countries and also in Europe and North America. Several of the Wiccan holidays discussed above, including Ostara and Yule, come from Norse religious traditions. These traditions, too, were often incorporated into the incoming Christian religion. Ostara is the goddess of fertility, and her holiday is celebrated at the time of the spring equinox. She was known by the Saxons as "Eostre," which later became "Easter." Among her symbols are the egg and the hare.

BOX 9.3 • *Satanism*

Wiccans are often accused of being devil wor-shippers. As you can tell from the description of the Wiccan religion in this chapter, that is most definitely not true. They do not believe in Christianity, so why would they worship the Christian Devil? Most modern Satanists also do not conform to what most people con-ceive them to be. We must distinguish be-tween people who have been labeled Satan worshippers by others, which for some con-servative Christian groups would include any non-Christian religion, and those who label themselves as Satanists.

Very few people actually worship Satan as the personification of evil, although some do claim to worship a Lucifer or Satan whom they believe is an ancient deity mis-takenly identified as the Devil by Christians. The view these Satanists have of Satan is a pagan image that focuses on power, virility, and sexuality. To most Satanists, though, Satan is more like a force of nature than a deity. Their Satan is not the Christian Devil and has nothing to do with the Christian Hell, demons, buying people's souls, human sacrifice, or truly evil deeds. Satanists do not even believe that Heaven and Hell exist.

Although there is much variety in the beliefs of Satanists, we can describe some of the more common beliefs. Satanists generally believe that each person is fully responsible for his or her own life, and the emphasis is on the individual, not on a god or goddess. Lusts and desires are seen not as sins to be avoided, but as possibilities to be experienced. Life it-self is respected and valued; despite common misconceptions, Satanists do not advocate or practice animal or human sacrifices.

The largest of the many religious tra-ditions within Satanism is the Church of Satan, founded by Anton Szandor La Vey in 1966. In the forward to *The Satanic Bible* (1969), Burton Wolfe states, "Satanism is a blatantly selfish, brutal philosophy. It is based on the belief that human beings are in-herently selfish, violent creatures."[a] Lavey

believes that the Judeo-Christian traditions have taught us to suppress our true feelings, which has resulted in nothing but misery. The Church of Satan could be described as a form of **hedonism.** Satanists believe in the gratification of all of one's desires. Instead of abstinence, Satanists believe in indulgence. The behaviors that the Catholic Church la-bels as sin are seen as virtuous. The Church of Satan does recognize sins, but they are entirely different ones, including stupidity, pretentiousness, self-deceit, and conformity. The Church of Satan says that although it is important to be kind to those who deserve it, one should not waste love on those who do not deserve it. Do not turn the other cheek; instead, seek vengeance.

Rituals are conducted and generally are one of three types: ones that involve sex magic, ones that are focused on healing or happiness, and destruction rituals focused on a specific victim. (Satanists believe that if a person is targeted by a destruction ritual but does not deserve it, that person will not be harmed.) The use of magic in Satanism does resemble somewhat the magical practices of Wicca. However, many Satanists think that the Wiccans are hypocrites because they limit their magic to positive uses. In contrast, al-though Satanists use magic to benefit them-selves and their friends, they also use the magic and rituals to harm their enemies.

The most important symbol of the Church of Satan is the Sigil of Baphomet, which is a goat's head drawn within an in-verted pentagram, with the pentagram sur-rounded by a circle. At the time *The Satanic Bible* was written (1969), it was common for Satanists to use a naked woman as an altar, symbolizing that Satanism is a religion of the flesh, not the spirit. This is now rarely used. Although Satanists have often been blamed for kidnapping and the sacrifice of people and animals, this appears to be largely urban legend. Again, the religion of Satanism is largely misunderstood.

[a]Burton H. Wolfe, introduction to A. S. La Vey, *The Satanic Bible* (New York: Harper Collins, 1969), p. 18.

Conclusion

Fear of the existence of supernaturally evil individuals appears to be universal. And who should we fear most as potential evildoers? People who stand out, people with whom we have existing conflicts. If my neighbor is jealous of my success, might she not want to bring me down and cause me harm? Of course, she might well think the same of me. As with many religious phenomena, witchcraft accusations are closely tied to other social phenomena—in this case reflecting existing tensions and fears. In reality the most common way to become a witch is to be accused of being one.

Witchcraft is a fascinating subject within the realm of religious beliefs and behaviors. Studying this phenomenon is made more complicated by the different ways in which the term has been used in small-scale, European, and modern Neo-Pagan communities. Our continuing interest in the subjects of magic and witchcraft can be seen in popular media representations such as the television shows *Bewitched*, *Charmed*, *Sabrina the Teenage Witch*, and *Buffy the Vampire Slayer* and of course the extremely popular Harry Potter book series. However, these fantasy representations differ significantly from the real phenomena. First, these sources show magic and witchcraft as very similar phenomena, if not one and the same. Second, witches are portrayed in a very positive light, which fits only the Wiccan definition. In small-scale societies, practicing witchcraft is by definition antisocial behavior. Even Wiccans would argue with many of the representations of the powers of witches, which are shown as being far beyond those that are actually claimed.

The rise of the Neo-Pagan religions and their redefinition of witchcraft are but one example of how religions rise and fall and change over time. This topic is one that we will explore in greater detail in the next chapter.

Summary

The idea of witchcraft as an evil force bringing misfortune to members of a community is found in a great number of societies throughout the world. Unlike sorcerers, who perform magic rituals to achieve their evil ends, witches simply will death and destruction and it happens, for the source of this evil is a supernatural power that lies within the body of the witch. Witches possess personal characteristics that are the antithesis of those that characterize a good, moral person. The concept of witchcraft in small-scale societies is largely based on the work of E. E. Evans-Pritchard among the Azande of the Sudan. Evans-Pritchard concluded that a belief in witchcraft serves three functions: It provides an explanation for the unexplainable; it provides a set of cultural behaviors for dealing with misfortune; and it serves to define morality.

Ideas of witchcraft in Europe were influenced by Christian ideas about the nature of evil. Christianity accepts the existence of an evil spirit, known as Satan or the Devil. In this belief system witches are individuals whose evil power originates with a pact with the Devil. In Europe, witchcraft beliefs were merged with sorcery. Sorcery became associated with the invocation of spirits, which was defined as being hostile to God. Anyone doing any form of magic was seen as calling on the servants of Satan. Magic and witchcraft became not just crimes against society, but heresy—crimes against God. The period known as the Witchcraze began at the end of the Middle Ages (around 1450) and lasted for about 200 years. In Euro-American witchcraft beliefs, witches define all that is wrong and immoral. People who exhibit antisocial behavior are the most likely targets of witchcraft accusations. Witches also fulfill our unconscious need to blame someone for the misfortunes that we experience in our daily lives. In general, patterns of witchcraft accusations reflect deeply felt conflicts and divisions in a society.

Wicca is one of a group of religious movements known as Neo-Paganism, a term referring to pre-Christian religious traditions. Wicca is a polytheistic religion that stresses gender equality. The religion is in many ways nature-based, including the ritual calendar. Other Neo-Pagan religions are Druidism and Asatru.

Suggested Readings

Scott Cunningham, *The Truth about Witchcraft* (St. Paul, MN: Llewellyn Publications, 2002).
[A description of the basic beliefs, symbolism, and rituals of Wicca.]

Alan Dundes, editor, *The Evil Eye: A Casebook* (Madison: University of Wisconsin Press, 1992).
[Description of the evil eye in different cultures.]

Peter Charles Hoffer, *The Devil's Disciples: Makers of the Salem Witchcraft Trials* (Baltimore, MD: Johns Hopkins University Press, 1996).
[A detailed analysis of the Salem witchcraft trials.]

Loretta Orion, *Never Again the Burning Times: Paganism Revived* (Prospect Heights, IL: Waveland Press, 1995).
[An ethnography of Wiccans.]

Jeffrey Russell, *The History of Witchcraft: Sorcerers, Heretics, and Pagans* (London: Thames and Hudson, 1980).
[A look at witchcraft in tribal societies, historical Europe, and modern times.]

Fiction:

Rudolfo Anaya, *Bless Me Ultima* (New York: Warner Books, 1999).
[The story of a young boy growing up in New Mexico in the 1940s dealing with conflicts between religious traditions including the presence of witches.]

Elenore Smith Bowen, *Return to Laughter* (New York: Doubleday, 1954).
[An anthropological novel tracing the adventures of a female anthropologist working in West Africa written under a pen name by Laura Bohannan based on work among the Tiv of Nigeria.]

Suggested Web Sites

www.law.unkc.edu/faculty/projects/ftrials/salem/SALEM.HTM
The Salem Witchcraft Trials of 1692.

www.fordham.edu/halsall/source/witches1.html
Medieval Sourcebook: 15th Century Witchcraft Documents.

www.malleusmaleficarum.org/
  The text of the Malleus Maleficarum.

www.churchofsatan.org/
  The Church of Satan web site.

http://altreligion.about.com/mbody.htm?once=
  true&
  The Alternative Religions section from About.
  com.

www.religioustolerance.org/witchcra.htm
  Information about Wicca.

www.witchvox.com/xbasics.html
  Information on Neo-Pagan religions from The
  Witch's Voice.

www2.roanoke.edu/history/Leeson/Witchcraft/
  newintro.html
  Links to the history of witchcraft.

Study Questions

1. Discussion about witchcraft is made difficult by the several meanings of the term. To what different phenomena has the term *witchcraft* been applied?

2. How does the concept of witchcraft in Zande religion aid the Azande in coping with the stresses of their lives?

3. What are the major differences between witchcraft belief among the Azande and the Navaho?

4. The gender of witches differs from society to society. Among the Azande witches are male and female, but in the European and American Witchcraze, witches were most often female. Why? What does this tell us about the function of witchcraft beliefs in human societies?

5. Magic and witchcraft have become popular subjects in American culture in recent years. In what ways do these popular depictions differ from anthropological descriptions of magic and witchcraft?

Endnotes

1. E. E. Evans-Pritchard, *Witchcraft, Oracles and Magic among the Azande* (Oxford, England: Clarendon, 1937).

2. The name of the society is Azande. However, when used as an adjective, the word becomes *Zande*.

3. E. E. Evans-Pritchard, op. cit., p. 22.

4. This case study is based on a case seen in the film *Witchcraft among the Azande* (Filmedia).

5. E. E. Evans-Pritchard, op. cit., p. 63.

6. C. Kluckhohn, *Navaho Witchcraft* (Boston: Bacon, 1944), p. 82.

7. G. L. Burr (ed.), *The Witch Persecution in Translations and Reprints from the Original Sources of European History* (Philadelphia: University of Pennsylvania, 1898–1912), vol. 3, no. 4, pp. 26–27.

8. P. C. Hoffer, *The Devil's Disciples: Makers of the Salem Witchcraft Trials* (Baltimore, MD: Johns Hopkins University Press, 1996), p. 75.

9. *The Malleus Maleficarum of Heinrich Kramer and James Sprenger*, unabridged on-line reproduction of the 1928 edition, Part I, Question VI, www.malleus maleficarum.org.

10

Syncretism and Religious Movements

Small-scale societies are being drawn more and more into the larger, often more complex, world. In doing so, they are exposed to many influences that result in change—both positive and negative. We have much to learn from these societies, including the effects of culture contact, how cultures change over time, and how new religions come into being. This is a starting point from which to look at cultural and religious change in the larger-scale cultures in which we live. Our comparative study of various religious systems and our understanding of basic anthropological principles now place us in a position to analyze aspects of our own culture from an entirely new perspective. This is what we will attempt to do in this final chapter.

This chapter discusses several topics. We will begin with a study of the process of culture change, especially in the context of outside influence resulting from economic, political, and social exploitation. We will see how the processes of change can lead to the demise of a culture or adjustments for survival. In many contact situations the dominated culture reacts with the formation of new religious movements that frequently combine cultural elements from both the dominant and dominated societies. Such revitalization movements not only are found among tribal peoples, but also form the basis of today's Western religions, including many new religious movements. Such movements are always affected by existing cultural ideologies and raise many questions, including how new religions will be perceived by the society at large.

Adaptation and Change

Throughout this book we have seen examples of how religion reinforces a society's culture and worldview. Religious institutions also provide mechanisms for dealing with the inevitable stresses that are part of living. In general, religious

247

practices tend to be very conservative. This conservatism is derived from their sacred nature and the fact that a society's belief system is usually considered to be ancient—that is, it was practiced in the old time by the ancestors.

However, change does occur. In fact, change must occur if a society is to endure. The world does not exist in a steady state. Changes happen in the climate, in the availability of food and water, in the presence of hostile peoples on one's borders. If the society is to survive, it must adapt and change to meet the challenges brought about by this changing world.

However, we should not think of a society as a perfectly tuned machine meeting stress and change in stride. Sometimes changes occur too slowly or too quickly to be effective, or change does not occur at all. Sometimes changes appear that are maladaptive. Yet in the long run, if a society is to survive, it must adapt to some degree to the world as it exists.

Mechanisms of Culture Change

Generally speaking, societies that are technologically simple tend to be relatively isolated from outside influences and tend to change slowly over time. Internal change can and does occur through the processes of **discovery** and **invention.** A discovery is a new awareness of something that exists in the environment. One comes across a new type of fruit and "discovers" it as a new source of food. An invention occurs when a person, using the technology at hand, comes up with a solution to a particular problem. For example, a plentiful supply of inedible, poisonous fruits or nuts might be made available as food by the invention of a technology that processes the plant material so as to get rid of the poison. This was the case for the use of the acorn by Native American groups in California. A discovery is often simply a matter of putting two and two together to get four.

However, discovery and invention might not be valued in a society and might be infrequent occurrences. And the society's worldview may hamper the development and acceptance of new ideas. For example, we will see shortly how the Australian Dream Time acts to discourage change.

Societies do not exist in isolation; people are aware of the existence of other communities beyond their boundaries. Relationships between neighboring groups may be relatively friendly, as when they engage in trade. Frequently, however, relationships are hostile.

Nevertheless, the mere existence of other cultures with different technologies, social organizations, and religious practices exposes a society to new ideas and new technologies. Two groups living in the same general area may have many similar problems, especially problems related to exploitation of the environment for food and water. When two groups, such as those within a culture area, face similar problems, solutions that are developed in one group through discovery and invention might be adopted by the other. This apparent movement of cultural traits from one society to another is called **diffusion.** Technological traits are more likely to diffuse than are social and religious traits. Sometimes it is only the idea that moves from one culture to another, and stimulated by that idea, the receiving society invents a new trait, a process called **stimulus diffusion.**

An example of stimulus diffusion took place in 1821 when a Cherokee by the name of Sequoyah unveiled a writing system for the Cherokee language. (This was not technically an **alphabet,** but a **syllabary,** in which each symbol stands for a syllable.) Although the writing system was not based on the English alphabet, Sequoyah had observed people placing marks on pieces of paper that conveyed information. Armed with the idea, he invented a system of writing.

When a trait diffuses from one culture to another, it is often altered to a greater or lesser degree to become consistent with the rest of the receiving culture. Perhaps the use of a hallucinogenic drug is introduced into a society from a neighboring group. Yet how that drug is used in ritual might differ. Differences will occur in which rituals the drug is used, who uses it, and what it means. In Chapter 1 we studied the idea of holism, the idea that all parts of a culture are interrelated and all are a reflection of the same worldview. An introduced trait has to be altered to fit into the cultural system and to reflect the basic premises of the culture.

Acculturation

Sometimes, however, the influence of one culture on another is more intense. Rather than sporadic contact through trade and other joint activities, one society might assume political and/or economic control over another. If both societies are fairly equal politically and economically, both societies will borrow traits from one another, and over time the societies will become more and more similar. Usually, however, one society is able to dominate the other, and the dominant culture undergoes far less change than does the subordinate one. The dominant society is the one that, usually because of a more developed technology and wealth, is able to establish control over the subordinate one. In this case the subordinate culture experiences change as traits are accepted, often at a rate that is too rapid to properly integrate the traits into the culture.

This process is referred to as **acculturation.** A society that has undergone change of this type is said to be acculturated. Thus an anthropologist who enters a tribal village and sees cans of soda, metal knives, pots and pan, and a radio knows that this is an acculturated community. When the dominated society has changed so much that it has ceased to have its own distinct identity, we say that it has become **assimilated.**

Acculturation and Religion.   We have been stressing political and economic influence of one society on another, but what about religion? The ability of one group to establish control over another is usually due to technological, economic, and political factors. However, once this control has been established, it is possible for features of other parts of the culture, such as religion, to flow from one society to the other. Religion may play an especially important role because a dominated culture might look for religious explanations for what is occurring and the dominating group might use religious justifications for its actions.

Some societies are very receptive to new religious ideas and are able to graft them onto their own religion. Why not add what appears to be a powerful foreign god to the existing pantheon? It can't hurt. For example, the Christian God often becomes yet another god in the pantheon, and selected elements of Christian ritual may be incorporated into traditional rituals.

To those living in the Western world this incorporation of elements from one religion into another might seem strange. Christianity, Judaism, and Islam are exclusionary in that members of these religions are excluded from practicing rituals of other religions. When a person converts, he or she gives up all former religious beliefs. However, we saw in Chapter 8 how even these religions adopted some beliefs of the surrounding cultures during their development.

In many societies people practice rituals from different religious systems more on the basis of need that anything else. For example, in Japan someone might travel to a Shinto shrine to ask for blessings on the family, be married in a Christian ritual, and be buried in a Buddhist ritual. Small-scale societies often are able to assimilate new religious practices with a degree of ease. However, Christian missionaries, for example, demand exclusion. One of the most stressful aspects of the presence of missionary activity is the pressure to give up one's former religion.

The Case of the Yir Yoront.   The process of acculturation has been well documented among the Yir Yoront, an aboriginal tribe living on the west coast of the Cape York Peninsula in northern Australia. Western manufactured goods and outsiders began to filter into their territory beginning in the late nineteenth century. Because of the relative isolation of this area, the exposure to the outside began slowly. Of all the objects that were introduced, the one that had the greatest impact was the steel axe. Although the Yir Yoront were already using an axe, it was made of stone, not steel.

The stone axe was an important item of technology in the traditional culture of the Yir Yoront. All adults used the stone axe for a variety of economic tasks. The axe also played an important role in defining social relationships. The axes were owned by older men, and the pattern of borrowing by women and younger men reinforced the superiority and importance of age and being male. Also stone axe blades had to be obtained from peoples to the south, and hence a system of trade and intertribal activities had developed.

The introduced steel axe quickly replaced the stone axe in Yir Yoront technology. The substitution was a relatively simple one—technologically, at least. The Yir Yoront appreciated the fact that the job at hand could be accomplished more quickly and efficiently with the new axe. However, it was no longer necessary to obtain the stone axes in trade from other tribes, and trade and other intertribal social activities ground to a halt. Also, the indiscriminate distribution of axes to young men and women profoundly affected the nature of social behavior.

Perhaps the greatest disruption that the steel axe and other Western innovations caused was in the religious domain. In Chapter 3 we examined the totemism that characterizes Australian Aborigine religion. Yir Yoront society was divided into about two dozen clans, a specific type of kinship group. Each clan was associated with a number of totems. Totems included not only animals, but also celestial objects, time of day, fire, technological items, activities such as swimming, and supernatural beings such as ancestors, ghosts, and rainbow serpents. The stone axe was a totem of the Sunlit Cloud Iguana clan, and it played an important role in the clan's totemic myths.

Most important for our story, the totemic system postulates the existence of the Dream Time, the time in which the world as the Aborigine knows it today was created. Everything that exists in the present world—the physical landscape, plants and animals, people, cultural objects, human behavior—exists because it was created in the Dream Time. The world of today is a reproduction of the world of the past. Any specific trait, be it a manufactured object or a custom, exists because it existed in the Dream Time.

The concept of the Dream Time was a major brake on culture change, since any new trait, whether internally discovered or invented or externally adopted through diffusion, could not be incorporated into their culture because it did not exist in their Dream Time. (Neighboring groups had their own version of the Dream Time, and this would explain differences in their cultures.) Of course, change did take place, but very slowly. Any new trait required a justification within a myth, and myths would slowly be altered, or old myths remembered, to account for the new object or custom. A gradual myth-making process was at work.

The existence of the steel axe, as well as other foreign cultural items, caused many problems for the Yir Yoront. First, whose totem was the steel axe? Although the Sunlit Cloud Iguana Clan claimed the steel axe as their totem (was not the stone axe their totem?), other clans made claims as well.

However, the greatest impact on the Yir Yoront was that the myth-making process could not keep up with the influx of new ideas. Eventually, it became apparent that the society was experiencing new things that did not exist in the Dream Time. Something was very, very wrong. Lauriston Sharp writes:[1]

> Both intellectually and emotionally a saturation point is reached so that the myriad new traits which can neither be ignored nor any longer assimilated simply force the aboriginal to abandon his totemic system. With the collapse of this system of ideas, which is so closely related to so many other aspects of the native culture, there follows an appallingly sudden and complete cultural disintegration, and a demoralization of the individual such as has seldom been recorded elsewhere.

Syncretism

The process of acculturation does not always involve the complete replacement of one trait by another or the complete acceptance of a new trait. There often is a reworking of the trait through a process known as syncretism. Syncretism is a fusing of traits from two cultures to form something new and yet, at the same time, permit the retention of the old by subsuming the old into a new form. A classic example of syncretism is the case of the introduction of cricket by missionaries in the Trobriand Islands in 1903. The purpose was to introduce British values and to replace warfare and magic with competitive sports. Yet what occurred was something quite different. This case is discussed in Box 10.1.

BOX 10.1 • *Trobriand Cricket*

The British game of cricket was introduced to the Trobriand Islanders in 1903 by missionaries. The game was played throughout the British Empire, and the formal rules of the game were carefully followed. However, something very different happened in the Trobriands.[a]

The missionaries faced three major problems, as they saw it. First, Trobrianders engaged in violent, ritual warfare. Second, as we saw in Chapter 6, magic played a very central role in Trobriand activities. Finally, the Trobrianders had a very open attitude toward sex. The missionaries hoped to counter some of these problems, especially warfare, through the introduction of competitive sports, in which aggression could be moved to and controlled on the cricket field and other venues.

However, this was not to be, for the Trobriand Islanders took the game, which they accepted into their culture with great enthusiasm, and shaped it to fit Trobriand culture rather than the other way around. In other words, syncretism took place. Athletic competition was reinterpreted in terms of traditional competition among chiefs and ceremonial exchanges. It had many of the characteristics of warfare. Players dressed as warriors and painted their bodies with the same patterns that were used in war. They threw the ball in the same manner as they threw a spear. There was no limit to the size of the teams; sometimes as many as fifty men played on a team. War magic was used in attempts to control the outcome of the game. Games were sponsored by powerful chiefs, who used cricket as part of the complex of ceremonial exchanges that are used to define chiefly statuses. Of course, the sponsoring chief's team always won.

Perhaps the most interesting aspect of Trobriand cricket is the military-type dances performed by each team when they entered the field and when certain events occurred, such as scoring. Much to the consternation of the missionaries, many of these chants and marches were quite erotic.

[a]The case of the introduction of cricket in the Trobriand Islands is well known among anthropologists because of the film *Trobriand Cricket* made in the 1970s by Gary Kildea and Jerry Leach.

Previously in this text we have seen several examples of syncretism, such as the origins of Halloween and the Day of the Dead. Other examples include the syncretism of Shinto and Buddhism in Japan and that of Christianity and indigenous religions in Africa. In this section we will be looking at entire religious systems that were formed through the process of syncretism.

Haitian Vodou

Vodou is a religion that is found in the country of Haiti and in the Haitian **diaspora**. It is a religion that is extremely rich in symbolism, with art and dance playing central roles in ritual. Vodou grew out of several religions indigenous to West Africa, especially the religions of the Fon, Kongo, and Yoruba peoples. The term *vodou* comes from the Fon language of Dahomey (now Benin) and means "spirit" or "deity." However, the term is used largely by outsiders to describe this religion. Practitioners merely say that they "serve the spirits."

History of Vodou. The country of Haiti occupies the western third of the Caribbean island of Hispaniola, which was discovered by Christopher Columbus in 1492. In 1697 Haiti became a French colony. (The rest of Hispaniola today is the Spanish-speaking country of the Dominican Republic.)

The French colony of Haiti eventually became one of the richest colonies in the Caribbean, largely because of plantation agriculture dedicated to sugar cultivation and activities related to sugar, such as the production of molasses and rum. Efficient sugarcane production required large plantations created out of the dense forest. Because sugarcane cultivation is very labor intensive, large numbers of slaves were brought from Africa. The end result was a severe degradation of the forest and the land and the establishment of one of the most brutal forms of slavery in the New World. Because the life expectancy of slaves was low, new slaves had to be continually imported from Africa. The most intense period of importation of slaves was between 1730 and 1790.

The slaves soon outnumbered the French colonists, who lived in constant fear of slave rebellions. To thwart attempts at rebellion, slaves were housed and worked in small work gangs spread out over a plantation. These gangs included individuals from different tribes who spoke different languages; this made communication and the planning of revolts difficult. Soon Creole French evolved from French and the various African languages for the purpose of communication. (A **creole language** is one that has developed from the blending of two or more languages and that has become a first language learned by children.)

In the late seventeenth century the French government decreed that all slaves had to be baptized and instructed in the Catholic religion. Yet other than a baptism ceremony, slaves were given little or no religious instruction, since few land owners allowed priests on their land for this purpose. Over time the slaves became vaguely aware of the most basic tenets of Catholicism, but they continued to practice their African religions. Because of language difficulties, the priests who did provide instruction were limited to the telling of stories from the Bible illustrated by colored posters or **chromolithographs** of Jesus, Mary, and the Saints.

In 1790 the feared slave revolt came to pass. After a prolonged struggle Haiti, the first black republic in the New World, declared its independence in 1804. The establishment of a republic formed of ex-slaves was not popular with its neighbors, and diplomatic recognition was withheld for some time. As a result Haiti became isolated from the rest of the world. The Vatican recalled its priests in 1804 and broke off relations with Haiti; Catholic clergy did not return until 1860. It was during this period of isolation that Vodou developed.

Haiti is nominally a Catholic country, although many Protestant churches have been established. Yet Vodou remains strong, and the majority of professed Catholics—and indeed many Protestants—also practice Vodou.

Vodou Beliefs.   Vodou is in many ways a West African religion. It worships many of the same deities, and Vodou rituals closely resemble African rituals. Haitian Vodou has a pantheon of deities called *lwa*, which are similar to the *orisha* of the Yoruba (see Chapter 8). Altars are constructed containing objects that are infused with spirits, and offerings and sacrifices are made to appease the *lwa* (Figure 10.1). Dance and music play major roles in Vodou ritual.

Vodou is a religion that is made up of elements from a number of traditions that have melded to form something new and distinct, an example of syncretism. The dominant elements in Vodou are those from traditional West African religions and Catholicism, but French folk beliefs and elements from **Freemasonry** also appear. Vodou is practiced primarily by people living in poverty, and it is characterized by folk art using contemporary materials such as plastic, sequins, plaster, enamel, and mirrors.

As in most West African religions, a high or otiose god is recognized, but he plays little or no direct role in the daily lives of the people (see Chapter 8). Because he is so remote, there is no sense in dealing with him. The direct interactions between the supernatural and humans are through the *lwa*, the intermediary deities. There are a large number of *lwa*. Although there are some *lwa* that seem to be universal, many are regional. New *lwa* are constantly coming into being when they announce their existence through possession or in a dream. Others simply disappear.

The *lwa* can be divided into several pantheons. The two most important are the Rada and the Petwo *nanchon,* or nations. The Rada *nanchon* consists of deities that would be very familiar to a Yoruba. These are African deities and are thought to be very ancient. In contrast are the Petwo *lwas.* They are aggressive and assertive, born out of the slave experience. Many first appeared during the period of isolation in the early nineteenth century. Another important group of *lwas* are those associated with death.

Table 10.1 lists some of the more important *lwa.* However, the situation is much more complicated than is shown in the table, since many deities appear in different manifestations. Each deity has a particular personality, domains over which he or she rules, and particular symbols. These symbols include not only physical objects and artistic motifs, but also particular ways of speaking and music and dance movements. Each *lwa* is known to be partial to certain foods that are used as offerings. In general, the Rada *lwa* like things that are "cool," such as candies and sweet drinks; the Petwo *lwa* like things that are "hot," such as strong drinks like rum and spicy foods.

An example of syncretism is the association of particular *lwa* with Catholic saints and manifestations of the Virgin. Symbolism in the chromolithographs used by early priests who attempted to bring Christianity to the slaves was seen as symbolic of the deities. Perhaps the oldest and most venerated of the deities is Danbala, the Rada serpent deity. His domain is rain, fecundity, and wisdom. Danbala is depicted as Saint Patrick, who is pictured on the chromatographs with snakes at his feet. In Vodou art Danbala is often seen with his wife Ayida Wèdo, the rainbow serpent.

Agwe, another Rada spirit, is the god of the sea and ships and is depicted wearing a naval officer's uniform. Offerings to Agwe that are found on an altar include small boats, shells, and metal fish. Agwe is often pictured as Saint Ulrich, holding a fish. His consort is Lasirèn, the mermaid who brings luck and riches

FIGURE 10.1   *Voudou Altar.* This replica of a Vodou altar was set up as part of the exhibit "Sacred Arts of Haitian Vodou" at the American Museum of Natural History in New York. Vodou priest Sauveur St. Cyr is seen in front of a painting of the *lwa* Azaka/ St. Isador, the *lwa* of agriculture.

from the ocean's depths. Deep in the ocean Lasirèn produces music, and she is the patron saint of musicians. She is often depicted as Saint Martha with a dragon.

Ezili is the name that encompasses a group of female deities that are associated with the Virgin Mary. Ezili Freda is a Rada *lwa* who enjoys the finer things in life—fine clothes, jewels, and perfumes—and is associated with love and luxury. Her love is unrequited, her heart pierced with knives, and she is shown in art as the Mater Dolorosa weeping. On her altar she is offered sweet drinks and foods, and her images are sprayed with perfumes. Another manifestation of Ezili is the Petwo *lwa* Ezili Dantò. She is seen dressed in bright, multicolored fabrics and appreciates rum and fried and spicy foods. She is depicted holding her daughter Anaïs and is a fiercely protective mother. She is associated with the black Madonnas, such as Mater Salvatoris, with the Christ child reinterpreted as her daughter.

TABLE 10.1 *The Lwa of Haitian Vodou*

Lwa	Role	Symbols	Seen as	Colors
Legba	As the guardian of the threshold between humans and the supernatural, Legba is the first *lwa* to be greeted in ritual	Crutches, pipe, rooster	St. Peter	Orange, yellow, red
Danbala and Ayida Wèdo	*Lwa* of rainfall and fertility, Danbala is the oldest of the *lwa;* his wife is the rainbow spirit	Serpent, rainbow, lightning bolts, bishop's attire	St. Patrick	White
Agwe	Protector of ships at sea	Ritual boat, shells, admiral's attire	St. Ulrich holding a fish	Green
Ezili Dantò	*Lwa* of fertility and motherhood; protector of mothers	Heart, knife, black pig	The Black Madonna	Multicolor
Ezili Freda	*Lwa* of love and luxury	Hearts, flowers, doves	Madonna of Sorrows	Pink, white
Gede	*Lwa* of death; healer, trickster deity	Cross, skull and crossbones, top hat, sunglasses missing one lens	St. Gabriel	Black, purple
Azaka	*Lwa* of agriculture	Straw hat, straw bag, pipe	St. Isidore	Green, white, denim
Lasirèn	Female *lwa* of the sea; brings luck and money; patron deity of musicians	Mermaids, fish, mirror	St. Martha with a dragon	Blue, white
Ogou	*Lwa* of war and military might; protector of cars	Fire, iron, swords	St. James	Red and blue of Haitian flag

Santeria

Other religious movements, similar in form and function to Vodou, developed throughout the Caribbean, Brazil, and other part of the New World where slaves were imported to work the large plantations. Santeria developed in Cuba from a fusion of West African religions, primarily Yoruba, and Spanish Catholicism.

Slavery lasted longer in Cuba than in Haiti. Independence of this last Spanish colony in the New World occurred, with the aid of the United States, in 1898. By this time there were a large number of freed slaves as well as communities of freed slaves in remote mountainous areas and various mutual aid societies and social clubs in urban areas. Santeria developed out of these societies, and today it has spread to other areas in the New World, including the United States. In the United States in areas with large Hispanic populations, such as Los Angeles, the religion is most often seen in the context of Botanicas, or stores that sell charms, herbs, and other materials used by followers of the religion.

Santeria deities, called by the Yoruba name *orisha* (see Chapter 8), show the same syncretism as the Haitian *lwa.* The *orisha,* known by their Yoruba names, are associated with particular saints: Ogun is Saint Peter, Obatala is Saint Mercedes, and Shango is Saint Barbara.

Although Santeria is the name by which this religion is now most commonly known, the name was originally pejorative, used by the Spanish to note what they saw as an unusual amount of attention being paid to the Catholic saints as opposed to Jesus Christ. The proper name for the religion is *Regla de Ocha,* or Rule of the Orisha, although Santeria is used as well. The religion is also known for being secretive. Relatively little information about beliefs, rituals, and symbols is released to the general public.

One reason for the secrecy is the use of animal sacrifice in ritual, which has led to conflict between practitioners of Santeria and political authorities in the United States. The issue is whether animal sacrifice should be permitted as part of the First Amendment protection of the free exercise of religion or whether it should be banned under statutes preventing cruelty to animals. The matter has not been resolved, but most American police organizations have become more understanding and permissive about this practice, and the courts have generally upheld the right to practice animal sacrifice.

Revitalization Movements

Societies that are situated next to each other experience diffusion, the flow of culture traits that are then adjusted to fit into the receiving culture. This is especially true if the two societies are roughly equal in terms of technology and economy. However, the situation often arises, especially in today's world, in which one culture is able to establish economic and political dominance and superimpose itself on another. The situation can be a direct takeover, as when one society conquers another and maintains economic, political, and military control, or it can be indirect, as when a missionary or an economic enterprise—a shoe factory, for example—shows up in a community. A missionary or factory manager might not have the political power of a conquering state but still represents a more technologically advanced society with things that people learn to want and need.

The flow of events differs in each situation, but generally speaking, a massive introduction of items from a dominant culture can have a dramatic effect on the receiving culture. As we saw in the case of the Yir Yoront, the end result could be the destruction of a culture. The people might survive, but they end up becoming a mere reflection of the dominant culture, living on the fringes of that culture. Moreover, demoralization sets in that manifests itself in alcoholism, crime, drug use, and other maladaptive behaviors.

One society might be totally assimilated into another, it might simply disappear as an entity, or it might exert itself and become a viable subculture within the larger culture. Frequently, however, there is a reaction that often manifests itself as a religious or secular movement known as a **revitalization movement.** (This is not the only situation in which revitalization movements arise. They can also result from some environmental disaster such as a drought or epidemic.)

A revitalization movement is one that forms in an attempt to deliberately bring about change in a society. The change is perceived as more bearable and satisfactory to those under pressure. The movement may be secular, but they are very frequently religious movements, complete with mythology, ritual, and symbolism, and may result in the formation of a new religion. These are deliberate activities, frequently initiated by an individual or a small group that promises better times and solutions to the problems that besiege the community or are perceived as a threat to the community.

Revitalization movements arise from a number of perceived stressful and often traumatic situations. These situations include political and economic marginalization (loss of effective political participation), economic deprivation and poverty, and malnutrition and high levels of chronic or epidemic diseases. There may also be less tangible stresses within the social structure that arise when a culture is discriminated against by the dominant society and when there is a perception that the values of the community are being threatened.

Anthony Wallace describes several stages in the development of a revitalization movement.[2] In the early stages of contact or other stressors, change is occurring, but at an acceptable rate, with relatively normal stress. Over time, the stress levels become intolerable to some people. This phase is characterized by an increase in illness, alcoholism and drug use, and crime. For many individuals, although these behaviors are dysfunctional, they serve as a temporary adjustment to change.

Increasing exposure to the dominant society and the increasing influx of new traits, many of which cannot easily be integrated into the existing culture, increase the amount of stress on the individual. Means of livelihood may be restricted, and new economic patterns may emerge that are not consistent with the ideals of the culture. For example, individualized wage labor may replace family-based economic activities with the effect of tearing the family apart and increasing the isolation of individuals. Alcoholism, drug use, and crime may become endemic as normal social relationships within the society break down. Sometimes the dominant culture deliberately attempts to destroy the indigenous religious pattern (often by ridicule and destruction of sacred objects and sacred spaces), and attempts may be made to substitute the religious practices of the dominant culture for those of the subordinate one. However, not all such movements are religious. They can be political, such as many of the elements of the Celtic revival in Ireland described in the next subsection or the Communist movements in many countries.

At this stage the society may disintegrate and cease to exist as a separate unit, with the members of the society assimilating into the dominant social group (often at the margins of that group). However, another possibility is revitalization. Revitalization begins when an individual or a small group constructs a new, utopian image of society and establishes a model of this image. At the same time the dominant social group becomes contrasted as evil. The founder of the movement may be a charismatic leader or prophet, and the story that establishes the legitimacy of the movement is often thought of as supernatural.

People who join the movement think of themselves as being elected to a special status, and attempts are made to bring more people in the fold. Although somewhat flexible at first, over time the philosophy and rules become set, and the group sets itself off, often with great hostility, from the main society. At this point the movement, if successful, becomes firmly established and relatively stable. The movement can become part of the mainstream, having successfully brought about a change in the culture. Or the movement may remain an isolated one that either persists or eventually disappears, often in a dramatic and terrible way.

Types of Revitalization Movements

We can recognize several types of revitalization movements. **Nativistic movements** develop in tribal societies in which the cultural gap between the dominant and subordinate cultures is vast. These movements stress the elimination of the dominant culture and a return to the past, keeping the desirable elements of the dominant culture to which the society has been exposed, but with these elements now under the control of the subordinate culture.

Revivalistic movements attempt to revive what is often perceived as a past golden age in which ancient customs come to symbolize the noble features and legitimacy of the repressed culture. For example, the Celtic revival in Ireland stressed the revival of ancient Celtic customs and provided symbols of rebellion against the occupying British. Once the Irish Republic gained independence, many items from the past became symbols of a new national identity, such as the revival of the Celtic language, arts and crafts, and place names. In addition to these secular examples, some Neo-Pagan groups have also attempted to revive ancient Celtic religious practices. Many of the Neo-Pagan movements discussed in Chapter 9 would be considered revivalistic.

Millenarian movements are based on a vision of change through an apocalyptic transformation; **messianic movements** believe that a divine savior in human form will bring about the solution to the problems that exist within the society. Of course, these four types are not always clearly differentiated from one another, and elements of one may appear in another. We will examine examples of these types below.

Cargo Cults

The term **cargo cult** comes from the word *cargo*, which in the **pidgin** English spoken in New Guinea and the islands of Melanesia means "trade goods." (The culture area of Melanesia includes New Guinea and the islands to the east, including the Trobriand Islands.) These movements began along the coast in the late nineteenth century but reached their peak during and after World War II, when the U.S. military brought in large quantities of manufactured goods.

When the first outsiders entered this region, explorers, missionaries, and colonial administrators brought with them a wealth of manufactured goods that sparked the imaginations of the native peoples and became highly desirable items. The newcomers were seen as conduits for the goods, and the outsiders were perceived as being very powerful. In the context of the native culture, power comes from knowledge of the supernatural. Thus the activities of the missionaries resonated with the population, and much of the interest in the newly introduced Christianity was an interest in discovering the ritual secrets that the missionaries used to bring the *cargo* from over the sea from the Land of the Dead.

Soon it became clear to the local peoples that the key to controlling the *cargo* was not to be discovered through Christian rituals because the missionaries refused to share the magical secrets with them. Other negative factors included the Europeans' unwillingness to share many of their goods with the natives, the condescending way the Europeans treated the natives, and the appearance and behavior of the Europeans.

This disillusionment led to the emergence of a number of stories that explained what the local people were experiencing. The main puzzles were the origin and control of the *cargo* and the power of the outsiders. The Europeans did no obvious work and engaged in a number of very strange activities. The manufactured goods must have been made in the Land of the Dead by the ancestors of the Melanesians. The Europeans, through ritual, intercepted the airplanes and stole the *cargo* that was meant for the local people.

The solution to the problem was to discover and learn the Europeans' magic. Then the people could rid the land of the outsiders and permit the ancestors to land the planes and bring the *cargo* directly to their descendants. This would also usher in a period of paradise on earth and, in some cases, the return of the ancestors. To accomplish this goal, the Melanesians carefully examined the behavior of the Europeans to find a clue to their powerful magic.

Several cargo cults emerged over the years. They often appeared in response to a prophet who had dreams or who had otherwise discovered the secret used by the Europeans in controlling the *cargo*. These movements utilized activities of the Europeans as the basis of ritual, but these European behaviors were terribly misunderstood. The activities, seen as magic rituals, varied from place to place. They included making marks on paper, running flags up poles, marching with sticks over their shoulders, and dressing up in European-style clothes and sitting around a table with a vase of flowers in the center. One group cleared a long strip of land in imitation of a landing strip, complete with a control tower.

As sad as these things are, they are overshadowed by another aspect of the cargo cults. In some movements the prophet announced that the ancestors and the manufactured goods would not appear until the people destroyed their traditional sacred objects or exposed these objects to people who were not supposed to see them, such as women and uninitiated boys. In other movements success would not happen as long as the people had adequate food, so pigs and crops were destroyed. The results were tragic.

One of the best known of the early cargo cults was the Vailala Madness, which occurred between 1919 and 1923. It centered on divination trances. Old rituals were set aside, and new rituals, containing many Christian elements and military-style activities, appeared. For example, messages from the dead could be received through flagpoles. In 1932 and 1933 a cargo cult emerged among the Buka people. They believed that steamships would arrive with *cargo,* and a large warehouse was built to store these manufactured goods. However, the steamship would not arrive as long as the people had food, so they destroyed their farms.

The Naked Cult of 1944 through 1948 featured the cult members going around naked and fornicating in public. Other elements included the destruction of villages, the construction of communal houses, and destruction of things received from the Europeans. People stopped working for the Europeans and waited for the arrival of the Americans, which would mark the beginning of the period when the followers of the prophet would receive the *cargo.*

The Ghost Dance of 1890

The policies of the U.S. government toward Native Americans in the late nineteenth century were those of forced assimilation. This was facilitated by the destruction of traditional food resources, restriction of communities to small tracts of land and reservations, and forced education at boarding schools for children, where they were forbidden to speak their language or practice their culture. Many communities were moved great distances onto land that was insufficient in amount and fertility to feed the community. The results were poverty, starvation, crime, alcoholism, and the breakup of the family and other traditional social patterns. It is not surprising that one of the ways in which the people reacted to these activities was through the development of nativistic movements.

Early in 1889 a Paiute named Wovoka (?1858–1932), who lived in Nevada, had a vision. Wovoka was illiterate and never kept a journal or wrote letters and, after December 1890, never gave interviews. What follows is the essence of what occurred.

Wovoka received a "Great Revelation" on New Year's Day in 1889. He moved into an altered state of consciousness for a period of time, awakening during an eclipse of the sun. (This was interpreted by some as death followed by rebirth.) Wovoka then told the people that he had been to Heaven and talked with God. He had visited with his dead ancestors, who were once again young and healthy. God had told Wovoka that the Indians were no longer to lie, steal, fight, or drink alcohol. Wovoka had then been given a traditional dance that lasted three (or five) nights. If people followed the rules and faithfully performed the dance, they would go to Heaven, where they would once again be young.

Although this aspect of the vision appears to be a positive adaptation to the changes that had occurred, there was a great deal more to the vision. Wovoka told of an apocalypse during which new earth would cover the world, burying the Whites, followed by a return of the land and animals, including the buffalo, to their original condition. The Indians would inherit this land, and the dead would return to the earth—hence the name the Ghost Dance.

Although the new religion incorporated many Native American traditions, such as meditation, prayer, and ritual cleansing, it also incorporated many Christian elements. The vision itself took place in a Christian Heaven. Wovoka had spent time as a young man on the Wilson ranch. The Wilsons were devout Christians—specifically, Presbyterians—and they undoubtedly exposed the young Wovoka, or Jack Wilson, as he was also known, to Christianity. The Ghost Dance religion included many examples of syncretism.

In the fall of 1890 news of Wovoka's vision had spread eastward and had reached the reservations of the Sioux living on the northern Plains. A delegation traveled to Nevada, where they joined hundreds of native people who had traveled from many different tribes to see Wovoka. Wovoka met with the delegations and told them of his visions and taught them the dance.

The Sioux delegation returned to their reservations and told the people what they had seen and what they had been told. On receiving the news, the Sioux began to congregate in large numbers to dance the Ghost Dance. These gatherings alarmed the local government agents. Finally, the militia was called out to break up the dancing, and the Sioux fled into the countryside, where they were rounded up and returned to the reservations.

As part of these operations the militia found and surrounded a large group camped by a creek in South Dakota called Wounded Knee. On December 29, 1890, while tensions were high, the shaman Yellow Bird urged the people to resist the soldiers. He reminded the warriors that the Ghost Dance religion preached that the bullets from the enemy would not penetrate the "ghost shirts" that they wore. A young warrior then drew his rifle from under a blanket and fired on the soldiers. Immediately, the militia opened fire on the group, using bullets and two-pound shells; within a few minutes more than 200 men, women, and children lay dead. Even today, over 110 years later, this event colors much of the relationship between Native American groups and the U.S. government.

The Church of Jesus Christ of Latter-Day Saints (Mormonism)

Many new religious movements emerged in the United States in the early nineteenth century. It was a time of great stress and crisis for a country that was heading into a Civil War. The Industrial Revolution was bringing with it many changes in traditional lifestyles, including the movement of many people to cities and the subsequent breakdown of old ideas of community. The proliferation of many different Christian **sects,** or new branches of a mainstream religion, led to **choice fatigue,** as a single dominant church was replaced by numerous options. Out of this stress grew many revitalization movements, including the Shakers, the Seventh Day Adventists, and the Church of Jesus Christ of Latter-Day Saints (LDS). Today, LDS is the fastest-growing faith group in American history, with over eleven million members worldwide.

The LDS Church was founded by Joseph Smith (1805–1844). He grew up in New York, where his family were "seekers"—what we might call nondenominational Christians. Smith was very troubled by the number of Christian sects that existed at the time and wanted to know which was the true Christianity. Smith received his first vision at the age of fourteen. In this vision God and Jesus came to him and told him that all of the various sects were in error and that he should not join any of them.

A few years later, when Smith was seventeen, he had three visitations from the angel Moroni to prepare Smith, as a prophet, to restore the true Christian Church. Moroni revealed to him the location of golden tablets on which was written additional biblical history. Smith was able to use special stones buried with the tablets to translate them into what is now known as the *Book of Mormon: Another Testament of Jesus Christ*. This book did not replace the Christian Bible but rather supplemented it. The book is named after Mormon, an ancient prophet who compiled the sacred record, and is the source of the name *Mormons* for members of the LDS church.

The early LDS Church was heavily persecuted. In 1844 Smith was jailed for his destruction of an opposition printing press in Illinois. While he was in jail, a mob attacked the jail and killed Smith and his brother. His death provoked a crisis in the group. However, God sent a revelation that Brigham Young would be the next leader of the group. It was Young who led them to what became Salt Lake City, Utah. There, the LDS Church encountered difficulties with both the Native Americans who were already living in the area and the U.S. government, which refused Utah recognition as a state because of the LDS practice of polygamy. Utah finally received statehood after an 1890 church revelation from God that disallowed plural marriages.

In some ways LDS beliefs are similar to those of evangelical Christianity, including the literal truthfulness of the Bible, atonement, resurrection, and tithing. However, there are also significant differences. For example, while most conservative Christians believe that salvation is based on faith alone, Mormons believe that salvation also requires good works. In Chapter 8 we discussed the difficulties of the concept of the Trinity for monotheistic Christianity. Here, too, the LDS Church differs. The deity is seen as being Trinitarian; God, Jesus, and the Holy Spirit are seen as three separate entities, God and Jesus being separate deities of flesh and bone. Smith described God as self-made, as finite, and as having a material body. The Holy Spirit is seen as a Spirit Personage.

Another obvious difference is the additional biblical texts in the *Book of Mormon*. The history related there says that a group of Israelites departed from the Middle East around 600 B.C.E., before the time of the Babylonian captivity, and came to North America. This included a patriarch, Lehi, and his two sons, Nephi and Laman. Two tribes, the Nephites and Lamanites, are descended from the sons. The two groups lived in a state of continual feuding, and eventually, the Lamanites killed off the Nephites (around 385 C.E.). The Book also says that after his resurrection, Jesus came to North America, where he performed miracles and delivered sermons. He also selected twelve disciples from among the Nephite tribe.

The Mormons believe that these are the same doctrines that were held by the very early Christian Church. They believe that they are restoring the original church of the apostles to how it was in the first century of the Common Era.

New Religious Movements

New religious movements have generally branched off of older, more established religions and thus have many features in common with the older, mainstream religion. If the new group is still considered mainstream and differs on just a few points from the mainstream religion, it is referred to as a **denomination.** Examples of Christian denominations are Baptist and Lutheran; Islamic denominations would include Sunni and Shi'a. A sect is even more different from the older religion than a denomination is. Although still connected to the mainstream religion, sects are generally associated with a founder or leader and new revelations. Examples of Christian sects include the Church of Jesus Christ of Latter-Day Saints, discussed earlier. There are real challenges with the term **cult.** This word has several different meanings, and it is used in different ways by different people.

The "Cult" Question

Historically, a cult is a particular form or system of religious worship. This includes specific devotion to a particular person or thing. Thus the Catholic Church speaks of the cult of Mary. However, very few people use the term *cult* with this meaning. Although there are some neutral definitions—such as considering a cult to be a small, recently created, and spiritually innovative group—most definitions are associated with more negative imagery.

Even those who use the term *cult* with negative meanings do not agree on what a cult is. For example, evangelical Christian groups, such as the Counter-Cult Movement, label as a cult any religious group that accepts some, but not all, of what evangelicals accept as Christian doctrines. Thus, the LDS church, Jehovah's Witnesses, and the Unification Church (discussed later) are all considered to be cults. However, a group such as the Wiccans does not get attention from this group because they are not a Christian-derived religion. This highlights the gate-keeping issue that often presents itself when a new group splinters off. Who gets to decide who can call themselves Christian? Some fundamentalist Christian groups carry this even farther and define any religion that deviates from their beliefs—be it Judaism, Buddhism, or a UFO religion—to be a cult.

On the other side is the Anti-Cult Movement. Largely composed of mental health professionals, this group targets what they consider to be dangerous and authoritarian mind control ("brainwashing") and doomsday cults. They are most concerned with what they see as deceptive recruitment techniques and psychological techniques used to control members. The media also play a large part in how religious groups are perceived. When the term *cult* is employed by the media, it is most often used to refer to a small religious group with a charismatic leader who is brainwashing his followers and is in total control of them. The group is seen as evil and usually as believing that the end of the world is imminent.

Because of this confusion and the often negative connotations of the term, many researchers avoid the term *cult* altogether and instead prefer the term *new religious movement.* However, this debate points to another area of disagreement about how some of the more extreme new religious movements are perceived. In one point of view there is a continuum from mainstream religions to denominations and sects. **High demand religions** are at the far end of this continuum but otherwise are no different from other religious groups and should be regarded as such. Others argue that these high demand groups cross the line and perhaps should not be considered religions at all, but rather something that masquerades as religion. Some believe that these groups are so far removed from the mainstream culture that they become dangerous—the normal controls no longer are operating. Of course, the problem with this latter point of view is who gets to decide. As it involves judging the beliefs and practices of a religious group, it is one that we will avoid in this book. Instead, we will focus on the perspective that high demand religious groups are just one end of the continuum of religious expression while acknowledging the challenges and dilemmas these groups present for the larger society.

Characteristics of High Demand Religions

All religious groups require their members to believe certain things and to behave in certain ways. All groups require some degree of conformity from their members. However, groups do vary in the level of this demand and the degree of control they attempt to exert over members. Here we will examine groups that are at the high end of this continuum.

An example of a higher-end demand situation that very few would label a cult is a Roman Catholic monastery. Monks must follow a strict schedule of sleep, work, and prayer. Their diet is limited, and they often take oaths of celibacy and even silence. They must accept without question the decisions of those in authority. These are traits that are commonly associated with high demand groups.

In high demand groups the beliefs and behaviors of group members are strictly controlled. Common methods used to control beliefs include long hours of work with little or no free time, a restricted sleep schedule, strict control of access to outside information, and creation of a view of the outside world as unsafe and threatening. Behavior also may be controlled by public shaming and humiliation and isolation from outside contacts. Communal living is common, and members may be given new names and identities to signify their break with their past lives and their affiliation with, and devotion to, the new group.

Some researchers claim that the endless repetition of prayers and other techniques are in actuality autohypnotic techniques. For example, a person might be taught that when faced with criticism of the group, he or she should repeat a certain phrase over and over. Another area of concern for some observers is the deceptive recruitment techniques that some groups use. Of course, some of these techniques are found in groups that are not considered to be high demand, and quite a few of them are used by organizations that are generally not questioned, such as Army boot camps.

Mind Control?   One of the major issues surrounding high demand religious groups is whether or not mind control or brainwashing could or does take place.

A proposition of the anticult movement is that the pressures exerted by these groups move beyond normal social pressure and constitute a unique form of influence that can be all-controlling. However, many social scientists question this assertion. How is "brainwashing" different from other forms of social influence and normal socialization? Why do we not say that people converting to mainstream groups are being brainwashed? Were we all brainwashed by our parents to accept the beliefs of our cultures and our religions? Are advertising, military training, and schooling all examples of brainwashing?

An interesting study by Jeffrey Pfeifer looks at how we label these different areas of social influence differently. In this study, people were presented with a fictional paragraph describing a student named Bill. They were told that Bill left college either to join a Catholic seminary, to join the Marines, or to join the Moonies. Several high demand techniques were described:[3]

> While at the facility, Bill is not allowed very much contact with his friends or family and he notices that he is seldom left alone. He also notices that he never seems to be able to talk to the other four people who signed up for the program and that he is continually surrounded by [Moonies, Marines, Priests] who make him feel guilty if he questions any of their actions of beliefs.

When asked to describe Bill's experience, those who thought Bill joined a Catholic seminary labeled it as "resocialization"; those who thought he joined the Marines frequently labeled it as "conversion." Only those subjects who thought that Bill joined the Moonies used the term "brainwashing."

Many studies have failed to support the idea of brainwashing. Several of these have focused on the issue of recruitment, with the idea that if these groups did have some way to override free will and control a person's mind, then everyone, or at least almost everyone, who attends a recruitment meeting for one of these groups should in fact convert. This turns out not to be the case.

Sociologist Eileen Barker studied the Unification Church in her book *The Making of a Moonie.* She found that only a small percentage of people who attended Unification Church recruitment seminars actually joined the church. Another study by psychiatrist Saul Levine looked at over 800 people who had joined controversial religious movements. He found that more than 80 percent dropped out within two years. These are hardly the statistics one would expect if the groups had mind control over their members.[4]

Genuinely Dangerous Religious Groups.   This is not to say that there are no religious groups that should not be considered dangerous, either to their individual members or to the society at large. The question is how to identify these groups. Once we get past obvious features such as torture and murder, the criteria are not all clear. And not all of these groups will even be of the high demand variety.

However, there are a few characteristics that have been suggested as early warning signs of a dangerous group. One of these is the authority claimed by the leader of the group and what that person does with this authority. An example is when the leader sets up ethical rules that everyone must follow—except for the leader himself or herself. This can also extend to the leadership dictating important personal details in the lives of followers, such as whom a person can marry.

Another feature of a dangerous group is when the group sees itself as being above the law or as not having a social contract with the secular state. Although some people place apocalyptic ideology on the list, this is in and of itself not necessarily a danger sign. However, when the group believes they will be soldiers in God's army during this apocalypse and begin to stockpile weapons for this battle, the issues change.

Religion and the Law

The First Amendment to the U.S. Constitution addresses the right to the free exercise of religion. However, the Supreme Court has recognized that religious conduct can be regulated for the protection of society. A distinction has also been made between beliefs and practices. Laws cannot be made against what a person believes, but legislation can be passed against actions that are seen as harmful to society.

The commonly used criteria for deciding cases on the free exercise of religion came out of the 1963 Supreme Court's decision in *Sherbert* v. *Verner*. These criteria have become known as the Sherbert-Yoder Test and have been summarized as follows:[5]

1. Are the religious beliefs in question sincerely held?
2. Are the religious practices under review germane to the religious belief system?
3. Would carrying out the state's wishes constitute a substantial infringement on the religious practice?
4. Is the interest of the state compelling? Does the religious practice perpetuate some grave abuse of a statutory provision or obligation?
5. Are there alternative means of regulation by which the state's interest is served but the free exercise of religion is less burdened?

Deprogramming.   One of the legal issues associated with new religious movements revolves around the practice of "deprogramming" members of these groups. Although deprogramming is no longer as common as it was in the 1960s and 1970s, a discussion of the practice illustrates many of the legal issues of the free practice of religion.

Deprogramming generally consists of physically removing the person from the group in question. The person is usually taken to an isolated location, where he or she is presented with the inconsistencies in the beliefs of the group and presented with an alternative belief system (usually a conventional religion or a more secular emphasis on the American way of life). The individual is told that he or she has been brainwashed into joining the group and believing its doctrines. Family members usually initiate these deprogrammings, and the pull of family ties is also an element.

Many controversies spring from deprogramming efforts. First is the simple fact that these often involve illegal activities such as kidnapping, assault, battery, and illegal restraint. It also brings up the larger civil liberties issue: Does every adult have the right to belong to and believe in any religion that he or she chooses?

Many have argued that the deprogrammers use many of the same techniques that they accuse the cults of using. They argue that deprogramming is an intensive indoctrination process in which the person's belief system is systematically destroyed, to be replaced by anticult ideology. Studies comparing the attitudes of people who have left new religious groups voluntarily with those who were involuntarily deprogrammed have shown that while voluntary former members are often ambivalent or even positive about the former group, individuals who have been deprogrammed often describe the former group using common negative cult stereotypes.

Studies have also shown that success of the deprogramming is not guaranteed: As many as half of the subjects of deprogramming eventually return to the group from which they were taken. In many cases deprogramming efforts seem to be the result of parent-child conflict in which the children, usually adults, are making choices that the parents do not understand. This is often exacerbated by negative media coverage of new religious movements, which seems to confirm the parents' worst fears.

Medical Issues.   Another issue arises with religious groups that for one reason or another refuse modern medical treatment either in specific circumstances (e.g., Jehovah's Witnesses refuse blood transfusions) or altogether (e.g., many Christian Scientists). The problem revolves around two issues: the right to refuse medical treatment for yourself (which the courts have generally upheld) and the right to refuse medical treatment for a minor child (in which case the courts almost always intervene). In general, the belief in prayer treatment is accommodated only as long as there is no serious risk to the child's life. However, this remains controversial.

Examples of New Religious Movements

Recent decades in the United States have seen the development of many new religious movements, including several that could be labeled as high demand. Many of these movements remain under the radar of cultural awareness, but some have come to our attention in dramatic, and often tragic, ways. This includes the Branch Davidians and Heaven's Gate groups.

As was discussed previously, new religions do not come out of nowhere. They are derived from older religious traditions. In the United States these are often Christian based. Many of the new religions, for example, derive important elements of their ideology from the Book of Revelation, which describes an apocalyptic world transformation.

Branch Davidians (Students of the Seven Seals).   The Students of the Seven Seals can be traced back to a group that broke off from the Seventh Day Adventists in the 1940s. Led by Victor Houteff, the new sect shared a number of the same beliefs as the Seventh Day Adventists, such as a belief in the imminent return of Jesus Christ. However, Houteff taught that Christ would return only when at least a small number of Christians had sufficiently purified themselves and that he himself was a messenger sent from God to conduct this necessary cleansing. The key to all of this was secret information contained in a scroll that is described in the Book of Revelation in the Christian New Testament, which is said to contain a description of the events that will occur when Christ returns and the world as we know it ends. The scroll is protected by seven seals, hence the name of the group. They are also known by the nickname *Branch Davidians.*

After Houteff's death, control of the group passed to his wife, who prophesied that the world would end in April 1959. When this did not come to pass, some people did leave the group, but the religion persisted, with several new leaders. A man named Vernon Howell joined the group as a handyman in 1981 and soon married the daughter of a prominent member of the community. There was a struggle for power, and Howell took control of the group in 1987. He later changed his name to David Koresh, after the biblical King David and the Babylonian King Cyrus. By the early 1990s the group had over 100 members.

Under David Koresh the group came to believe that the death of Christ had provided salvation only for those who died before Christ did, that is, before 32 C.E. People who had died since that time could be saved only by the actions of the current prophet. The Book of Revelation says that the Lamb of God will open the seven seals and trigger the sequence that ends the world as we know it. Traditionally, Christians have made the interpretation that the Lamb of God is Jesus Christ. The Branch Davidians believed that the Lamb of God was David Koresh himself. After the breaking of the seals, a battle would occur in which the Branch Davidians believed they would play a major role, hence the need for weapons. After the battle they alone would ascend to heaven to be with God.

The group's practices included many that are typical of high demand religious groups. The group lived communally and led a highly regulated, disciplined life. Koresh exerted control over such areas as sex and marriage. Couples were separated and marriages were dissolved, and Koresh persuaded women in the group to join him as his "spiritual wives," which included sexual access. Everyone else was expected to remain celibate. Members were not allowed to go to the movies or engage in competitive activities. The length of women's dresses and their hairstyles were regulated. Koresh himself had veto power over all decisions. The practice that brought them to the attention of the U.S. government, however, was the gathering of a large supply of weapons.

In 1993, in Waco, Texas, the Bureau of Alcohol, Tobacco and Firearms (ATF) decided to arrest Koresh on firearms violations. When ATF agents attempted to arrest Koresh, a firefight erupted in which six Branch Davidians and four agents died. A fifty-one-day siege followed. Finally, federal agents fired tear gas grenades and used tanks to try to penetrate the building. Several fires had started in the compound, and Koresh and at least seventy-five of his followers, including twenty-one children, died.

Much has been written about the events of Waco, and much remains unclear. However, one factor is that the federal officials failed to take the Branch Davidians' religious beliefs seriously and to consider this as a factor in their strategy. Koresh apparently believed that the raid was the start of the war of Armageddon, which he believed was to begin with an attack on the Branch Davidians. This case points out the problems associated with the freedom of religion, especially when the group is armed and awaiting a millenarian battle. How do we balance religious freedom against the need for order and security?

Unification Church (Moonies).   The members of the Holy Spirit Association for the Unification of World Christianity are also known by the derogatory term *Moonies* after the founder of the movement, Reverend Sun Myung Moon. When Moon was fifteen years old, Jesus Christ appeared to him in a vision and gave him the responsibility of completing the work that Jesus had begun. The Unification Church was founded in Seoul, Korea, in 1954 with the goal of uniting Christian denominations around the world and bringing unity among all major religions. Moon believed that this was necessary in preparation for the second coming of Christ. Missionaries were sent to Japan and the United States beginning in the 1950s, but the religion did not see significant development in the United States until Reverend Moon came to the country in the early 1970s.

The main beliefs of the church are contained in the text *Divine Principle*, which was published in 1973. The text tells of new truths or the new Principle that has been revealed through Reverend Moon. This text explicitly says that the time for the second coming of Christ is the present and focuses on the family as the purpose of creation.

The practice for which the Unification Church is best known is the large joint weddings presided over by Reverend and Mrs. Moon (Figure 10.2). Some have included thousands of people, and the couples are often matched up by Reverend Moon a month or less in advance.

The Unification Church teaches that before Adam and Eve were married in Eden, Eve had an affair with the Archangel Lucifer, which caused the spiritual fall of mankind. Eve later had premarital sex with Adam, which caused the physical fall of mankind. Taken together, these two illicit sexual acts caused Adam and Eve to form an imperfect family. It was this sin that let Satan take control of the world. God's plan, by which Jesus would redeem humanity and undo the harm caused by Adam and Eve, was for Jesus to form a perfect marriage. However, Jesus was killed before he could do this. Through his subsequent spiritual resurrection Jesus would make spiritual salvation possible for those who believe in him. Unfortunately, physical salvation is not possible because Jesus did not complete his task.

Complete salvation, both spiritual and physical, will be possible only after the arrival of the "third Adam" (Jesus is seen as the second Adam) and his subsequent perfect marriage. The third Adam is seen as the second coming of Christ and the perfect man, who will marry the perfect woman. Together they will become the "true parents" or the spiritual parents of humankind. Although the Unifica-

FIGURE 10.2 *Mass Wedding of the Unification Church.* Reverend Moon performs a mass wedding ceremony.

tion Church has never made this official claim, many members believe that Reverend Moon and his wife, Hak Ja Han, are the True Parents.

UFO Religions

Some new religious movements have imported elements of modern technology, such as space travel and cloning, as a basis for a philosophy that, while not always seen as a religion to outsiders, clearly serves as such. Most scholars consider UFOs to be within the realm of the paranormal or supernatural, thus fitting in with our definition of religion (see Chapter 1). The UFO groups describe extraterrestrial beings, or "ufonauts," in the same way that supernatural beings are described in more traditional religions. These beings are often seen as spiritual beings who have come to earth to help humans in some way. They are described as wise and as having powers beyond those of ordinary humans.

Another common religious theme is the idea of an imminent apocalypse. The world is seen as being on the verge of destruction. The "ufonauts" will somehow rescue the human race, usually preventing a nuclear war or selectively removing people from the planet to preserve the species. "Ufonauts" are often seen as having been involved in the original creation of humans or the planet.

As we saw in the previous section, many of the new religious movements in the United States are based in some part on the Christian religion. Even many of the UFO religions exhibit syncretism and contain significant Judeo-Christian elements.

Heaven's Gate.   The Heaven's Gate movement was the last of three organizations founded by Marshall Applewhite, also known as "Do," and Bonnie Trusdale Nettles, also known as "Ti." Passages from the Christians Gospels and from the Book of Revelation were reinterpreted as referring to UFO visitations. They saw the earth as in being in the control of evil forces. However, they saw themselves as being among the elite who would be saved from the evil on earth and taken to the next level.

Members of the group lived communally in a house in San Diego. They dressed in unisex clothing and were all celibate. Eight of them, including Applewhite, had been voluntarily castrated. This was seen as preparation for the next life, in which there would be no sexual activity and no gender identity. Members were required to separate themselves from family and friends and to completely detach themselves from human emotion and material possessions. Their lives focused on following a disciplined regimen referred to as the *overcoming process,* through which they could overcome human weaknesses and prepare themselves for a physical transition to the next kingdom.

The group saw humans in a dualistic way: that the human soul was a superior entity that was only temporarily housed in a physical body. Much of the metaphor was that of gardening. The soul was seen as a plant in a container, but this container could be left behind, and the soul could be replanted in another container. The Heaven's Gate members believed that extraterrestrials had planted the seeds of current human beings millions of years ago and were coming to reap the harvest of this work by taking spiritually evolved individuals to join the ranks of spaceship crews. The members believed that by committing suicide together at the right time, they would leave their containers (or bodies) behind and be replanted into another container at a level above that of human existence.

The correct time was seen as March 1997, near Easter. They believed that a spaceship was hiding in the tail of the Hale-Bopp comet. Twenty-one women and eighteen men voluntarily committed suicide in three groups on three successive days.

Raelians.   The Raelian Movement was founded in 1973 by French race car driver and journalist Claude Vorilhon, known as Rael to his followers. Vorilhon says that while walking in the mountains around France, he had an encounter with space aliens, during which he was given a message for humans about our true identity. He was told that a team of extraterrestrial scientists, the Elohim, created humans in laboratories and then implanted them on earth. *Elohim* is a term found in the Hebrew Bible, where it is translated as "God." Rael says that the word means "those who came from the sky."

Over the next five days, Vorilhon continued to meet with the extraterrestrials, who gave him new interpretations of parts of the Bible. For example, the Elohim chose the earth as a place to conduct DNA experiments, and they built laboratories for this purpose in what is now known as the Holy Land. They first created plants, then animals, and finally humans "in their own image." The humans were at first housed in these laboratories, referred to in the Bible as the Garden of Eden, but they proved to be too aggressive and were forced out.

Vorilhon was also told that prophets, who are the offspring of the Elohim and human women, have been sent in the past. These prophets included Buddha, Moses, Jesus, Mohammad, and Joseph Smith. Rael, as the extraterrestrials named Vorilhon, is the last of forty prophets, sent to warn humans that since the end of World War II we have entered the Age of Apocalypse. Instead of destroying themselves with nuclear weapons, humans can choose instead to change their consciousness. This change will enable humans to inherit the scientific knowledge of Elohim. Through science, four percent of humans will be able to clone themselves. After doing this, they will be able to travel through space and create life on other planets.

Rael focuses on cloning as the only hope for immortality. Four annual rituals are held so that the Elohim can fly overhead and record the DNA code of the Raelians. Most members are loosely affiliated with the group and acknowledge the Elohim as their fathers. The more committed members join the Structure. The Structure works to further the two main goals of the movement: to spread Rael's message and to build an intergalactic space embassy in Jerusalem to receive the Elohim when they arrive in the year 2025.

The Raelians have received the most attention from journalists through their organization CLONAID and their claims to have successfully achieved human cloning. However, they have been unwilling to offer any scientific proof that they have in fact cloned a human being, and most observers believe this to be highly unlikely.

Fundamentalism

The last several decades have seen a declining membership in traditional religions in the United States. They have largely been replaced by a growth of membership in new religious traditions, primarily Neo-Pagan and New Age groups (see Chapter 9) and Christian fundamentalist groups. Although fundamentalist groups in the United States are based in Christianity, other religious traditions—namely, Judaism and Islam—also have important fundamentalist movements.

The term *fundamentalism* originated in the nineteenth century. At that time it was used to refer to the opponents of liberal Protestantism who were urging a return to the "fundamentals" of Christianity. Because of this, many non-Christian groups question the broader usage that the term has acquired today. Again, this is an issue of insider and outsider perspectives. Although some groups object to having the term *fundamentalism* applied to them, from an analytic perspective we can see that these groups do have many features in common and can be referred to by the same term.

In many ways fundamentalists groups are easier to define by what they are against than what they are for. These groups protest against, and fear, modernization in general and the secularization of society in specific. The world has changed dramatically in recent times. The Enlightenment, new scientific discoveries, political revolutions such as the American and French Revolutions, and a general increase in commercialization and industrialization have had a large impact on cultures and their worldviews. Society is no longer focused on the big questions of morality and salvation. Change is now prized over continuity. An emphasis on production and commercial efficiency has replaced more traditional values. Loyalty to and identification with the state have replaced loyalty to and identification with one's religious group. Fundamentalists express outrage at these trends.

Although there are many different fundamentalist groups, they have reacted to modernization in some similar ways. Richard Antoun describes fundamentalism "as an orientation to the modern world, both cognitive and emotional, that focuses on protest and change and on certain consuming themes: the quest for purity, the search for authenticity, totalism and activism, the necessity for certainty

BOX 10.2 • *Religious Violence and Terrorism*

Although religious violence is nothing new, the last few decades of the twentieth century saw an increase of religious violence and terrorism around the world. Some of this is linked to new fundamentalist movements. Examples of religious violence can be found in all of the world religions and in smaller religious groups as well. Christianity is associated with attacks on abortion clinics in the United States and with the Oklahoma City bombing in 1995, not to mention the ongoing religious conflicts in Northern Ireland. The Middle East has seen much violence perpetrated by both Jews and Muslims, including the assassination of Yitzhak Rabin, Baruch Goldstein's attack at the Tomb of the Patriarchs, and Hamas suicide bombers. Sikhism is associated with the assassination of Indira Gandhi, and a sect of Japanese Buddhism with the Tokyo subway gas attack. The September 11, 2001, attack on the World Trade Center towers in New York and the Pentagon near Washington, D.C., is only one of many recent examples of religiously motivated violence.

Much of this violence has been referred to by the term *terrorism*. Terrorism can be defined as, "public acts of destruction, committed without a clear military objective, that arouse a widespread sense of fear."[a] Such acts are generally committed with a deliberately exaggerated level of violence. The violence is justified by reference to religious beliefs, including the idea that the act is part of an ongoing cosmic war, a battle between good and evil. Thus those who commit the acts are seen as martyrs to the cause; those who are attacked are defined as demons and agents of Satan.

Mark Juergensmeyer argues that such acts are highly symbolic and, as such, can be analyzed in much the same way that religious ritual is. For example, the timing and location of attacks are usually highly symbolic. The violence is meant to send a message, although the intended message is not always the one that the general public perceives.

[a]M. Juergensmeyer, *Terror in the Mind of God: The Global Rise of Religious Violence* (Berkeley: University of California Press, 2000), p. 5.

(scripturalism), selective modernization, and the centering of the mythic past in the present."[6]

Totalism is a reaction to the increasing separation of religion from other domains of life. Fundamentalists believe that religion is relevant to, and should be a part of, all parts of a society. Religious texts play an important role in fundamentalist beliefs. **Scripturalism** refers to the practice of justifying beliefs and actions by reference to the religious text. These texts are generally held to be inerrant and represent certainty and stability in a rapidly changing world. Another aspect of the importance of religious texts is the idea that these texts are relevant to life today, what Antoun calls **traditioning.**

Other important themes of fundamentalist groups include millenarianism and a focus on the perceived struggle between good and evil. These groups also are characterized by activism. Antoun points out that "Fundamentalism is inherently oppositional and minoritarian. It is the protest of those *not* in power."[7] It is important to note that he means political and cultural power, not necessarily economic power.

Although the themes of fundamentalist groups are very similar cross-culturally, individual movements obviously have arisen in response to very different cultural and historical circumstances. The growth of Christian fundamentalism in the United States was a reaction to the secular Protestant ideology that was very important in the early days of the country. A belief in secular progress and ideas such as manifest destiny served to elevate nationalism to the level of religion. In contrast, Islamic fundamentalism is largely a reaction to Western colonialism and the general outrage at the extent of Western cultural and economic infiltration into Islamic countries. And Jewish fundamentalism has its roots in reactions to the strong anti-Semitism of the late nineteenth and twentieth centuries in eastern and central Europe.

Conclusion

Religions exist to answer questions, to show us a culturally defined correct path, to make us feel safe and secure in the world we live in. Any specific religion is strongly connected to the culture and circumstances in which is it found. But what happens when those conditions change? The religion no longer meets these needs, needs that we require to be fulfilled. A new religion, more suited to the new situation, is needed, and thus a revitalization movement is born. In the case of fundamentalism, what might be most comforting is to attempt to return to the old ways with which we were once so comfortable. But both revitalization movements and fundamentalism are likely to be popular in periods of rapid social change, when the current ways of doing and thinking about things are no longer satisfying. Both spell out a clear path, a new path (or the return to a former one) that they say will lead people out of despair and into a better future, which will answer questions and provide meaning to life. And in the end, isn't that the point of religion?

Summary

Culture change occurs through the processes of discovery, invention, and diffusion. One discovers something that already exists. An invention occurs when a person, using the technology at hand, comes up with a solution to a particular problem. Diffusion occurs when cultural traits move from one society to another. When a trait diffuses from one culture to another, it is often altered to become more consistent with the rest of the receiving culture. Acculturation refers to the situation whereby a culture is significantly changed because of exposure to the influence of a politically and technologically dominant culture. When a culture changes so much that it loses its identity, it is said to have become assimilated into the dominant culture. Sometimes there is a reworking of the trait through a process known as syncretism, in which traits from two cultures fuse to form something new and yet, at the same time, permit the retention of the old by subsuming the old into a new form. Many New World religious systems, such as Vodou in Haiti and Santeria in Cuba, have formed from a fusion of traditional Africa beliefs and European religious beliefs and cultures.

A revitalization movement is a movement that forms in an attempt to deliberately bring about change in a society. The change is perceived as more bearable and satisfactory to people under pressure from a dominant culture. These are deliberate activities, frequently initiated by an individual or a small group that promises better times. We can recognize several types of revitalization movements. Nativistic movements develop in tribal societies and stress the elimination of the dominant culture and a return to the past but with desirable elements of the dominant culture brought under the control of the subordinate culture. Examples are the cargo cults of New Guinea and the Ghost Dance in the United States. Revivalistic movements attempt to revive what is perceived as a past golden age, and ancient customs come to symbolize the features and legitimacy of the repressed culture. Millenarian movements are based on a vision of change through an apocalyptic transformation. Messianic movements believe that a divine savior in human form will bring about the solution to the problems that exist within the society. Many mainstream religions developed as revitalization movements.

A new religious movement that has branched off of a more established religion and yet is still considered mainstream is referred to as a denomination. A sect is still connected to the mainstream religion but is generally associated with a founder or leader and new revelations. The term *cult* is used in many ways but usually in a negative sense. Many researchers today avoid the term *cult* and use the term *new religious movement.*

All religious groups require some degree of conformity from their members. However, groups do vary in the level of this demand and the degree of control the group attempts to exert over members. At one end of the spectrum are high demand groups, in which the beliefs and behaviors of group members are strictly controlled. Sometimes the activities of such groups become dangerous to its members and to society.

Suggested Readings

Nancy Tatom Ammerman, *The Bible Believers: Fundamentalists in the Modern World* (New Brunswick, NJ: Rutgers University Press, 1987).
[An ethnography of modern fundamentalists.]

Richard T. Antoun, *Understanding Fundamentalism: Christian, Islamic and Jewish Movements* (Walnut Creek, CA: AltaMira Press, 2001).
[Looks at the common characteristics of fundamentalist movements.]

Karen Armstrong, *The Battle for God* (New York: Alfred A. Knopf, 2000).
[A discussion of fundamentalism, focusing on Protestant fundamentalism in the United States, Jewish fundamentalism in Israel, and Muslim fundamentalism in Egypt and Iran.]

Karen McCarthy Brown, *Mama Lola: A Vodou Priestess in Brooklyn* (Berkeley: University of California Press, 2001.
[A person-centered ethnography of an immigrant woman practicing Vodou in New York City.]

Michael F. Brown, *The Channeling Zone: American Spirituality in an Anxious Age* (Cambridge, MA: Harvard University Press, 1997).
[An anthropological look at channeling in America, focusing on issues of identity and how channeling reflects American culture.]

Susan Friend Harding, *The Book of Jerry Falwell: Fundamentalist Language and Politics* (Princeton, NJ: Princeton University Press, 2000.)
[A look at Christian fundamentalism as seen through the life of Jerry Falwell.]

Michael Hittman, *Wovoka and the Ghost Dance* (Lincoln: University of Nebraska Press, 1990).
[A detailed description of the Ghost Dance religion with many original documents.]

Mark Jurgensmeyer, *Terror in the Mind of God: The Global Rise of Religious Violence* (Berkeley: University of California Press, 2000).
[A comparative look at religious violence and terrorism.]

Fiction:

Kurt Vonnegut, *Cat's Cradle* (New York: Dell Publishing, 1988).
[An apocalyptic story that includes a small Caribbean nation in which a religion called Bokononism is practiced.]

Robert Heinlein, *Stranger in a Strange Land* (New York: Berkeley, 1961).
[Valentine Michael Smith, raised by Martians, returns to earth and founds his own church.]

Suggested Web Sites

www.unification.net
The web site of the Unification Church.

http://religiousmovements.lib.virginia.edu/welcome/welcome.htm
Religious Movements home page at the University of Virginia.

www.religioustolerance.org/newage.htm
Discussions of New Age spirituality.

www.psywww.com/psyrelig/hg/index.html
Heaven's Gate web site.

Study Questions

1. Cultures are constantly changing and adapting to external change through discovery, invention, and diffusion. Define each of these terms, and provide an example of each from American culture.

2. While the intentions of missionaries might be good, the effects of their activities are often harmful to small-scale societies. Why? If you were a missionary trained in anthropology, how would you approach your mission?

3. Vodou and Santeria are practiced by immigrants from Haiti and Cuba in most large urban centers in the United States. Yet the members of these religions prefer to perform their rituals in secret, out of sight of their neighbors. Why? What particular religious practices do you think would especially offend a typical American urban resident?

4. Although we tend to think of revitalization movements as occurring primarily in small-scale societies, can you make the argument that Christianity and Islam began as revitalization movements?

5. Why do high demand religions develop? Why do people join these religions?

6. Some anthropologists have argued that it would have been better if the government had dealt with the Branch Davidians at Waco, Texas, as a religious cult rather than as a political movement. How could this have been accomplished? Do you think that the destruction at Waco could have been avoided? Why or why not?

Endnotes

1. L. Sharp, "Steel Axes for Stone-Age Australians," *Human Organization,* 11 (1952), p. 464.

2. A. F. C. Wallace, *Culture and Personality* (New York: Random House, 1970).

3. J. R. Lewis, "Overview," in J. R. Lewis (ed.), *Odd Gods: New Religions and the Cult Controversy* (Amherst, MA: Prometheus Books, 2001), p. 41.

4. Ibid., pp. 32–33.

5. W. C. Shepherd, *To Serve the Blessings of Liberty* (Chico, CA: Scholars Press, 1985), quoted in J. R. Lewis (ed.), op. cit., p. 63.

6. R. T. Antoun, *Understanding Fundamentalism: Christian, Islamic and Jewish Movements* (Walnut Creek, CA: AltaMira Press, 2001), p. 2.

7. Ibid., p. 13, italics in original.

Glossary

acculturation   The process whereby a culture accepts traits from a dominant society.

achieved status   A status that one has because of a factor other than automatic membership due to gender, age, kinship affiliation, and so forth.

acrostic   A word that is derived from the first letter of a series of words.

aerophone   A musical instrument in which air is blown across or into some type of passageway, such as a pipe; includes whistles and flutes.

age grade   A series of consecutive statuses defined by age.

age set   A social group that contains members of one sex within a specific age span.

agnosticism   The idea that the nature of the supernatural is unknowable, that it is as impossible to prove the nonexistence of the supernatural as it is to prove its existence.

aleuromancy   Divination by use of flour, as in fortune cookies.

alphabet   A system of writing whereby each symbol stands for a speech sound.

altered states of consciousness   Any mental state that differs from a normal mental state.

analytic definition   A definition that focuses on the way religion manifests itself or is expressed in a culture.

ancestor worship   The veneration of ancestors, who may bring aid to their descendants or, if neglected, may bring misfortune.

angel   In Judaism, Christianity, and Islam, spirit beings who act as mediators between God and human beings.

animatism   The belief in an impersonal supernatural power.

animism   A belief in spirit beings.

anthropocentrism   Belief that humans are set off from the animal world.

anthropology   The study of humanity.

anthropomorphic   Nonhuman entities that have human characteristics.

anti-therapy ritual   A ritual that is performed to bring about illness, accident, or death.

apantomancy   Divination by a chance meeting with an animal.

apocalypse   Ultimate devastation or the end of the world.

archaeology   The study of prehistoric people from the analysis of their physical and cultural remains.

archetype   A main character of the collective unconscious.

artificial divination   Refers to noninspirational divination.

ascribed status   A status that one automatically has because of gender, age, kinship affiliation, and so forth.

assimilation   A condition whereby a dominated culture has changed so much because of outside influences that it ceases to have its own distinct identity.

astrology   The belief that all of the stars and planets, as well as the sun and moon, influence the destiny of people and that reading the sky can be used as a divination technique.

athame   The ritual knife used in Wiccan rituals.

atheism   Disbelief in or denial of the existence of God or gods.

attribute god   A god that rules over a narrowly defined domain.

avatar   The incarnation or embodiment of a god in human form.

calendrical ritual   A ritual that is performed on a regular basis as part of a religious calendar.

cargo cult   Religious movement occurring among small-scale societies of Melanesia in response to culture contact; the movement focuses on the attainment of trade goods.

choice fatigue   A situation in which individuals in a culture are faced with too many options, such as when a single dominant church is replaced by numerous denominations and sects.

chromolithograph   A type of colored printed poster.

cicatrization   Scar formation at the site of a cut or wound.

circumcision   A surgical procedure during which the foreskin is removed from the penis.

clitoridectomy   A surgical procedure characterized by removal of the clitoris as well as parts or all of the labia minora.

cognition   The processes of the human brain, including perception, attention, learning, memory, concept formation, and problem solving.

collective conscious   A set of beliefs shared by members of a social group that functions to limit the natural selfishness of individuals and promote social cooperation.

collective unconscious   Inborn elements of the unconscious that are manifested in dreams and myths.

communitas   A state characterized by a sense of equality, community, and camaraderie.

contagious magic   Magic that is based on the Law of Contagion, utilizing things that once were in physical contact with an individual.

cordophone   A musical instrument with taut strings that can be plucked or strummed, hit, or sawed, such as a harp and violin.

creator god   A god that is responsible for the creation of the physical earth and the plants and animals that live upon it.

creole language   A language that develops from the blending of two or more languages and that becomes a first language learned by children.

crisis ritual   A ritual that arises spontaneously, frequently in times of crisis.

cross   An upright pole with a transverse piece in the middle or near the top. Used for execution by the Romans; now a symbol for the Christian religion.

cult   Historical meaning is a particular form or system of religious worship. Most commonly used to describe a small, recently created, and spiritually innovative group, often with a single charismatic leader. Connotations of the term include that the leader is evil, is in total control of his followers, and believes that the end of the world is imminent.

cultural anthropology   The study of contemporary human societies and their cultures.

cultural relativism   Attempting to analyze and understanding cultures other than one's own without judging them in terms of one's own culture.

culture   Human beliefs and behaviors of a society that are learned, transmitted from one generation to the next, and shared by a group of people.

culture area   A geographical area in which societies share many cultural traits.

cursing ritual   An anti-therapy ritual that involves reciting a curse to bring about illness and death.

deliberate divination   Divination that someone sets out to do.

demon   A spirit being, usually evil.

denomination   A religious group that differs on just a few points from the mainstream religion.

diaspora   Movement of a population out of their homeland.

diffusion   The apparent movement of cultural traits from one society to another.

discovery   New awareness of something that exists in the environment.

displacement   The ability to use symbols to refer to things and activities that are remote from the user.

divination   Supernatural techniques for obtaining information about things unknown, including events that will occur in the future.

divination ritual   A ritual that is used for the purpose of divination.

diviner   A religious specialist who specializes in divination.

doctrine of signatures   Belief that physical structures found in nature, such as the shape of a plant, are indicative (or signatures) of their potential use in healing.

dowsing   Method of divination whereby water and other underground resources are located by use of a forked stick.

emic analysis   The study of a society through the eyes of the people being studied.

emotive divination   Inspirational divination.

empirical   Perceived through our senses.

endocannibalistic anthropophagers   The term *endocannibalism* refers to the eating of one's own people, and the term *anthropophagers* refers to the eating of human bodies.

essentialist definition   A definition that looks at the essential nature of religion.

ethnobotany   The anthropological study of the use of plant material, especially in healing.

ethnocentrism   Using one's own culture as the basis for interpreting and judging other cultures.

ethnographer   A person who produces an ethnography.

ethnographic present   Speaking or writing about cultures in the present tense although what is described might no longer exist.

ethnography   The descriptive study of human societies.

etic analysis   The study of a society using concepts that were developed outside of the culture.

Eucharist   A Christian sacrament that commemorates Jesus Christ's last supper by consecrating bread and wine.

evolutionary approach   An approach that focuses on the questions of when and how religion began and how it developed through time.

folklore The knowledge of a people that is transmitted through jokes, riddles, songs, proverbs, folktales, legends, and myths.

foraging band Small communities that subsist by hunting, fishing, and gathering wild plant foods.

forensic anthropologist A specialist in the analysis of the human skeleton in a legal context.

fortuitous divination Divination that simply occurs without any conscious effort.

Freemasonry A fraternal order whose origins are thought to date back to the 14th century in Europe. Many elements of their beliefs and practices are known only to those who have been initiated. Freemasons are also known for their use of symbolism.

functional approach An approach that is based on the function or role that religion plays in a society.

functional definition A definition that is based on the role that religion plays in a society.

fundamentalism A religious movement characterized by a return to fundamental principles, usually including a resistance to modernization and an emphasis on certainty through a literal interpretation of scriptures.

ghost A soul of an individual after death that remains in the vicinity of the community.

god An individual supernatural being, with a distinctive name, personality, and control or influence of a major aspect of nature (such as rain or fertility), that encompasses the life of an entire community or a major segment of the community.

God module A part of the temporal lobe of the brain that is associated with religious experiences.

graphology Divination through handwriting analysis.

haruspication Divination by the examination of entrails of sacrificed animals.

healer A religious specialist who concentrates on healing.

hedonism Pursuit of or devotion to pleasure as a matter of principle.

herbalist A specialist in the use of plant and other material in curing.

heresy Crimes against God.

high demand religion A religious group in which much is demanded of members in terms of strict adherence to rules for thought and behavior.

holism The study of human societies as systematic sums of their parts, as integrated wholes.

homeopathic magic Magic that is based on the Law of Similarity.

horticulture The use of cultivated domesticated plants without the use of fertilizers, plows, irrigation, and other agricultural technologies.

human universals Characteristics that are found in all human societies.

hunting and gathering rite of intensification A ritual whose purpose is to influence nature in the quest for food.

hypothesis In science, a tentative statement based upon experimental and observational data that is subject to further study.

ideological ritual A ritual that delineates codes of proper behavior, promotes community solidarity, articulates the community's worldview, and assists the community in managing crises.

idiophone A musical instrument that is struck, shaken, or rubbed, such as a rattle or bell.

image magic A form of homeopathic magic in which an image represents a living person or animal, which can be killed or injured through doing things to the image.

imitative magic Magic that is based on the Law of Similarity.

incorporation The final stage of a rite of passage in which the individual is reintroduced to the community in his or her new status.

increase rite A type of ritual whose purpose is to aid the survival and reproduction of a totemic plant or animal.

incubi Male demons who have sex with human women while they sleep, resulting in the birth of demons, witches, and deformed children.

infibulation The piercing of a body part.

Inquisition A unit of the Roman Catholic Church that convened to judge cases of heresy.

inspirational A type of divination that involves a spiritual experience, such as a direct contact with a supernatural being through an altered state of consciousness

invention Coming up with a solution to a problem using the technology at hand.

isomorphism A similarity in form and structure.

jinn In the Islamic religion, a spirit being created of fire.

karma The effect of a person's behavior during the series of phases of the person's existence. Karma is seen as determining the person's destiny.

kiva A ceremonial chamber, often built underground, that is found among Native American societies in the American Southwest.

Law of Contagion Things that were once in contact continue to be in contact after the physical connection is severed.

Law of Similarity   Things that are alike are the same.

Law of Sympathy   Magic that depends on the apparent association or agreement between things.

liminality   The state of ambiguous marginality that characterizes the transition phase of a rite of passage.

linguistics   The study of language.

liturgy   A prescribed form for public religious worship.

magic   Ways in which a person can compel the supernatural to behave in certain ways.

magician   A practitioner who specializes in controlling the supernatural through magic.

mana   An impersonal supernatural force.

medium   A practitioner who intentionally communicates with the supernatural to find information.

membranophone   A musical instrument that incorporates a taut membrane or skin such as a drum.

menarche   A young woman's first menstruation.

messianic movement   A type of revitalization movement that is based on the appearance of a divine savior in human form who will bring about the solution to the problems that exist within the society.

millenarian movements   A type of revitalization movement that envisions a change through an apocalyptic transformation.

misogynistic   Characterized by a hatred of women.

modernity   A philosophical movement based on ideas of rationality, objectivity, reason, and science as the means of gaining knowledge, truth, and progress.

monomyth   A theme common to many myths that tells of the adventures of a culture hero.

monotheism   A belief in one god.

mummification   A technique of preserving a dead body involving drying and preservatives.

mystery religion   A religion whose beliefs, practices, and true nature are known only to those who have been initiated into the religion.

myth   A sacred story that provides the basis for religious beliefs and practices.

nativistic movement   A type of revitalization movement that develops in traditional societies that are threatened by the activities of more technologically advanced societies.

natural divination   Inspirational divination.

necromancy   Divination through contact with ancestors or the dead.

Neo-Paganism   A revival of pre-Christian religious practice.

new religious movement   A historically recent religious movement, often involving new leaders and new scriptures or new interpretations of older religious traditions.

noninspirational   Forms of divination that are performed without the direct involvement of supernatural beings.

occasional ritual   A ritual that is performed when a particular need arises.

omen   A fortuitous happening or condition that provides information.

omnipotent   Being all-powerful.

omniscient   Being all-knowing.

oneiromancy   Divination by the interpretation of dreams.

operant definition   A definition in which we define our terms so that they are observable and measurable and therefore can be studied.

oracle   A specific device that is used for divination.

ordeal   A trial by divination that is performed on the body of the accused person to determine guilt or innocence.

orientation association structure   The part of the brain that enables us to distinguish ourselves from the world around us and to orient ourselves in space.

ornithomancy   Divination from reading the path and form of a flight of birds.

otiose god   A god who is too remote and too uninterested in human activities to participate in the activities and fate of humans.

palmistry   Divination through the reading of the lines of the palm of the hand.

pan-Indian   Refers to activities that draw from many different Native American traditions.

pantheon   All gods and goddesses in a polytheistic system.

participant observation   A research method whereby the anthropologist lives in a community and participates in the lives of the people under study while at the same time making objective observations.

pastoral nomads   Societies that subsist primarily by herding domesticated animals.

pentacle   A five-pointed star.

pentagram   A five-sided figure.

periodic ritual   A ritual that is performed on a regular basis as part of a religious calendar.

peyotism   The ritual use of peyote, a hallucinogenic cactus.

Pharaonic circumcision   A surgical procedure performed on women that involves the complete removal of the clitoris and the labia minora and majora, the two sides of the wound then being stitched together, leaving a small opening.

phrenology Divination through the study of the shape and structure of the head.

physical anthropology The study of human biology and evolution.

pidgin language A simplified language that forms from the fusion of two languages.

pilgrimage A journey to a sacred place or a sequence of sacred spaces at which rituals are performed.

polytheism A belief in many gods.

positivism A philosophy that emphasizes empiricism, or observing and measuring, saying that the only real knowledge is scientific knowledge and any knowledge beyond that is impossible.

possession An altered state of consciousness that is interpreted as a deity taking control of a person's body.

postmodernism An emphasis on subjectivity over objectivity and a tendency toward reflexivity, or self-consciousness; all knowledge is seen as being a human construction that scholars must seek to deconstruct.

presentiment A feelings that a person may have that something is about to occur.

prescriptive ritual A ritual that a deity or religious authority requires to be performed.

priest A full-time religious specialist who is associated with formalized religious institutions.

prophecy Divination through the communication of a prophet.

prophet Someone who communicates the words and will of the gods to his or her community, acting as an intermediary between the people and the gods.

protective ritual A ritual that is performed at the start of, or during, a dangerous activity to protect the participants or to protect the community against disaster.

psychoduct A pipe or tube that connects a tomb to a temple through which the spirit of the deceased may travel into the temple.

psychosocial approach An approach to the study of religion that is concerned with the relationship between culture and personality and between society and individual.

Purgatory A place for souls who die with lesser faults for which there has been no repentance or for which the penalty is not wholly paid during the lifetime.

rank The relative placement of a status in the society.

reincarnation A belief in an immortal, eternal soul that is born again and again in different bodies.

relic An object of religious veneration, especially a piece of the body or a personal item of a religiously important person, such as an ancestor or saint.

religion The realm of culture that concerns the sacred supernatural.

religious ritual A ritual that involves the manipulation of religious symbols.

revitalization movement A movement that forms in an attempt to deliberately bring about change in a society.

revitalization ritual A ritual that is associated with a revitalization movement.

revivalistic movements A type of revitalization movement that attempts to revive what is often perceived as a past golden age.

rite of passage A ritual that occurs when an individual changes status, serving to legitimize the new status and to imprint it on the community's collective memory.

ritual A patterned, recurring sequence of behaviors.

sacred An attitude wherein the subject or object is set apart from the normal, everyday world and is entitled to reverence and respect.

scapulamancy A divination technique in which a dried scapula, or shoulder blade, is placed in a fire and the pattern of cracks and burns are interpreted.

scripturalism The practice of justifying beliefs and actions by reference to the religious text.

sect A new branch of a mainstream religion, usually involving new revelations, new scriptures, and a new leader.

separation The first phase of a rite of passage in which an individual is removed from his or her former status.

shaman A part-time religious specialist who receives his or her power directly from the spirit world and acquires status and the ability to do things through personal communication with the supernatural.

shrine An object or building that contains sacred objects or is associated with a venerated person or deity.

situational ritual A ritual that arises spontaneously, frequently in times of crisis.

small-scale Describes relatively small communities that practice foraging, herding, or technologically simple horticulture.

social charter A story that establishes the proper organization and rules of behavior of a society.

social rite of intensification A type of ideological ritual that functions to reinforce the belief system and the values of the society, performed as a periodic ritual or an occasional ritual in times of stress.

sorcerer A magician who specializes in antisocial, evil magic.

sorcery Compelling the supernatural to behave in certain ways, usually with evil intent.

soul The noncorporeal, spiritual component of an individual.

spell The words that are spoken in a magic ritual.

spirit A supernatural being that is less powerful than a god and is usually more localized; often one of a collection of nonindividualized supernatural beings that are not given specific names and identities.

spirit possession An altered state of consciousness that is interpreted as a spirit taking over control of a human body and is either deliberately induced by a ritual performance or the consequence of an illness caused by a spirit taking control.

status A social position that is defined in terms of appropriate behavior, rights and obligations, and its relationship to other statuses.

stigmata Bodily wounds or pain considered by Christians to be visible signs of participation in the sufferings of Christ.

stimulus diffusion What occurs when an idea moves from one culture to another and stimulates the invention of a new trait.

succubae Female demons who have sex with human men while they sleep, resulting in damnation of the men's souls.

supernatural Entities and actions that transcend the natural world of cause and effect.

supreme god A god who resides at the top of a pantheon.

swastika A symbol formed by two lines crossing at right angles with their ends bent at right angles in a clockwise or counterclockwise position.

syllabary A system of writing in which each symbol stands for a syllable.

symbol A shared understanding about the meaning of certain words, attributes, or objects; something that stands for something else.

sympathetic system The arousal system of the brain.

syncretism A fusing of traits from two cultures to form something new and yet permitting the retention of the old by subsuming the old into a new form.

tabu Objects and persons that are supernaturally prohibited. May also refer to certain behaviors that would bring about negative consequences through supernatural means.

tasseography Divination through the reading of tea leaves.

technological ritual A ritual that attempts to influence or control nature, especially in those situations that affect human activities and well being.

testable The ability to develop new experiments and observations that will test the validity of a conclusion.

theory In science, a framework for understanding that is supported by a large amount of consistent scientific data.

therapy ritual A ritual whose function is to cure.

totalism The belief that religion is relevant to, and should be a part of, all parts of a society.

totem A symbol or emblem that stands for a social unit.

totemism A religious system that assigns different plant and animal species to specific social groups and postulates a relationship between the group and the species formed during the period of creation.

traditioning The idea that religious texts are relevant to life today.

transition The second phase of a rite of passage during which a person is in a liminal state and is moved from one status to another.

transmigration A situation in which a soul passes from one body to another—human, animal, or even an inanimate object.

trickster god A god who gave humans important things or skills, often by accident or through trickery.

trickster story A story involving a trickster deity.

unitary state An altered state of consciousness in which an individual experiences a feeling of becoming one with the supernatural.

vampire A person who has died before his or her time and who brings about the death of friends and relatives until his or her corpse is "killed."

witchcraft The ability of a person to cause harm by means of a personal power that resides within the body of the witch.

worldview The way in which a society perceives and interprets its reality.

zombie A corpse that has been raised from the grave and animated.

Index

Photo Credits: p. 62, © Douglas Bryant, DDB Stock Photography; p. 78, © Prentice Hall, Inc.; p. 90, New Mexico Department of Tourism; p. 99, left: © Bettmann/Corbis, center: © Otto Lang/Corbis, right: © Catherine Karnow/Corbis; p. 101, The Granger Collection, New York; p. 114, © The British Museum; p. 120 © Peter Johnson/Corbis; p. 140, © Peter Essick/Aurora Photos; p. 156, © Earl & Nazima Kowall/Corbis; p. 170, © David Paterson/ Getty Images/Stone Allstock; p. 182, AP/Wide World Photos; p. 190, © Danny Lehman/ Corbis; p. 210, © Archivo Iconografico, S. A./Corbis; p. 213, © Earl & Nazima Kowall/ Corbis; p. 235, The Granger Collection, New York; p. 241, © Rebecca McEntee/Corbis Sygma; p. 256, AP/Wide World Photos; p. 271, © Bettmann/Corbis.